the Scorpion
and
the Tarantula

The Struggle to Control Atomic Weapons
1945–1949

BY JOSEPH I. LIEBERMAN

The Power Broker: A Biography of
John M. Bailey, Modern Political Boss

The Scorpion and the Tarantula:
The Struggle to Control Atomic Weapons   1945–1949

JOSEPH I. LIEBERMAN

the Scorpion
and
the Tarantula

The Struggle to Control Atomic Weapons
1945–1949

Houghton Mifflin Company Boston
1970

FIRST PRINTING   C

The author is grateful to the following for permission to quote.

Atlantic-Little, Brown and Co. *Memoirs 1925–1950* by George
Kennan, copyright © 1967 by George F. Kennan.
Aage Bohr. Memoranda of Niels Bohr regarding his correspond-
ence with Peter Kapitza in 1944.
Vannevar Bush. The Papers of Vannevar Bush from Manuscript
Division of the Library of Congress.
Harper & Row. *Now It Can Be Told* by Leslie Groves and
Journals of David Lilienthal: The Atomic Energy Years by
David E. Lilienthal.
Houghton Mifflin Company. *Mr. Baruch: The Man, the Myth,
the Eighty Years* by Margaret L. Coit and *The Private Papers of
Senator Vandenberg,* Arthur H. Vandenberg, Jr. (editor).
Rear Admiral William H. Leahy, U.S.N. (Ret.). The Papers of
Admiral William Leahy from Manuscript Division of the
Library of Congress.
William H. Makepeace (Executor of Estate of Bernard M.
Baruch). The Bernard M. Baruch Papers, Princeton University
Library.
Pennsylvania State University Press, 1969, University Park and
London. *The New World, 1939–1946* by Richard G. Hewlett
and Oscar E. Anderson.
Princeton University. *The Forrestal Diaries,* Walter Millis
(editor).
Simon & Schuster, Inc. *From Hiroshima to the Moon* by Daniel
Lang, copyright © 1945, 1946, 1947, 1948, 1951, 1955, 1956,
1957, 1958, 1959 by Daniel Lang.
Stanford University Press. *Atomic Energy in the Soviet Union*
by Arnold Kramish.
University of Chicago Press. *A Peril and a Hope* by Alice Kim-
ball Smith, copyright © 1965 by The University of Chicago.
University of North Carolina Press. *Hiroshima Diary* by
Michihiko Hachiya, translated by Werner Wells.
John Wiley & Sons, Inc. *Niels Bohr,* S. Z. Rosenthal (editor).
Yale University Library. Henry L. Stimson Diary.

For Betty

Acknowledgments

THANKS ARE DUE to Professor Leon Lipson of the Yale Law School, who directed my writing of the original manuscript; to Professor Richard Hewlett, the Historian of the United States Atomic Energy Commission, for his assistance and good counsel; to the very helpful staff members of the Yale University Library, the Princeton University Library, and the Library of Congress where much of my research was done; to my friend Richard Sugarman and his friend David Scott for their critical reading of the manuscript; to my former colleagues at the New Haven law firm of Wiggin and Dana for granting me a leave of absence to complete the writing of this book; to the steadfast women who have given me secretarial help, Mrs. Sophie Powell, Mrs. Gertraud Wood, and Miss Sherry Streeter; and to Mr. and Mrs. Alexander Sharp and Mr. and Mrs. Jon Stein for their kind hospitality during my working visits to Princeton and Washington.

I can never sufficiently thank my unsung coworkers in this and other labors: my children, Matthew and Rebecca, who came into my life during the four years of work on this book and made every day more worth living, and their mother, to whom this book is dedicated, for keeping them out of the attic while I was writing, and, even more, for her devotion, patience, caring, and sharing.

Preface

THIS IS the story of a disastrous failure of statecraft.

It is the history of the futile efforts to control atomic weapons during the first years of the atomic age while America was still the world's only nuclear power. It begins during 1943, much before the first atomic explosion at Los Alamos, in the efforts of a few anxious men to force the Allied countries to consider not only how to build the bomb but also how the bomb might be controlled once it was built. It ends in September of 1949 when the Soviet Union formally entered the nuclear arms race by detonating an atomic device of its own.

On August 16, 1945, ten days after Hiroshima, Winston Churchill predicted in the House of Commons that there would be "perhaps three or four years before the great progress in the United States can be overtaken." In those years, he said, "we must remold the relationships of all men, of all nations in such a way that these men do not wish, or dare, to fall upon each other for the sake of vulgar, outdated ambition or for passionate differences in ideologies, and that international bodies by supreme authority may give peace on earth and justice among men." [1]

In the three or four years that followed, the nations of the world and their statesmen showed themselves unequal to the appeal expressed in Churchill's lofty rhetoric. Their opportunity was unprecedented and would never be repeated. Today, men speak of marginal questions — of stopping the testing of atomic weapons or prohibiting their spread. In 1945, they spoke with reasonable hope of fundamentals — of prohibiting the manufacture of all atomic bombs and placing the development of all atomic energy under international control. But statesmen of the East and the West, including Churchill, were unable to follow his admonitions, and so these epic strivings ended in complete failure.

Although the period of the American atomic monopoly stretches up to 1949, I am primarily concerned in this study with events before the attacks on Hiroshima and Nagasaki and in the first year and a half after them. This span of time encompasses the period of initial policy formulation and genuine international negotiations. When Bernard Baruch resigned as America's representative to the United Nations Atomic Energy Commission in January of 1947 and the Soviet representative, Andrei Gromyko, set off on a new tack, it was clear that a nuclear arms race was inevitable. The negotiations continued because public opinion would not let them stop, but they became no more than the exchange of propaganda blasts.

The decision to drop the atomic bomb on Japan and the later establishment by the United States of a system of domestic atomic control are both topics that have been well covered elsewhere. I consider them here only indirectly and as they relate to the primary question of how atomic weapons could be controlled throughout the world after the war was over.

The failure to achieve international control of atomic weapons coincided with the outbreak of the cold war and, of course, was a major cause of that unique and sustained conflict. The title of this study is taken from Louis Halle's description of the cold war:

> If you put a scorpion and a tarantula together in a bottle the objective of their own self-preservation will impel them to fight each

other to the death. For the moment, at least, no understanding between them is possible . . . From the point of view of each, the
basic situation is that the other is trying to kill him . . .

This [the cold war] is not fundamentally a case of the wicked
against the virtuous. Fundamentally, it is like the case of the scorpion and the tarantula in the bottle, and we may properly feel
sorry for both parties, caught as they are, in a situation of irreducible dilemma.[2]

That is the spirit in which I have recorded what my research
has revealed. I have also tried to answer the primary question of
whether this truly was "a situation of irreducible dilemma."

J. I. L.

New Haven, Connecticut
1970

Contents

I

Before Hiroshima

I

A Quiet Beginning

THE ATOMIC AGE began quietly, far from the monstrous pillar of flames that evaporated a steel tower and petrified the desert at Los Alamos, far from the massive dust clouds and wildfires that choked and scorched Hiroshima and its people.

The atomic age began in Chicago in a hushed squash court under the west stands of the Amos Alonzo Stagg Field. At the north end of the court on a balcony ten feet above the floor stood Enrico Fermi, the gentle, dark-skinned, Italian physicist who had traveled from his native country in 1938 to receive the Nobel Prize in Sweden, only to be criticized severely by Mussolini's press for failing to wear a Fascist uniform and give the Fascist salute when receiving that award. He never returned home. Now, Fermi stood before an instrument panel that controlled the experimental machinery on the floor below. At 3:25 P.M. on that afternoon of December 2, 1942, Fermi guided the electrically controlled rods out of the pile. "This is going to do it," he said confidently. "Now it will be self-sustaining." His face was expressionless; his eyes darted quickly from dial to dial. Soon he broke into a broad smile. "The reaction is self-sustaining. The curve is exponential." For twenty-eight minutes the nuclear reactor operated on its own. Under Fermi's mastery, mankind had managed its first controlled liberation of the power within the atom. At 3:53 P.M., the click of the galvanometers became a menacing rattle and Fermi said quietly, "Okay, zip in." The historic experiment was over. Eugene Wigner, a Hungarian physicist, produced a bottle of Chianti and gave it to Fermi. A small cheer went up from the twenty people who jammed that historic court. Together, they drank an unspoken toast to a new age. Fermi, however, would not allow himself the luxury of wandering elation. "We'll call it a day," he announced to his crew. "Lock the control rods in the safety position and come back tomorrow morning. Then, we'll start the new series of experiments." [1]

From this quiet moment of scientific accomplishment, a direct line may be drawn to the explosion at Los Alamos, the devastation at Hiroshima and Nagasaki, and the nuclear arms race that followed. In the years after the Second World War, atomic scientists were in the vanguard of public efforts to achieve international control of atomic weapons and an end to the arms race. One absolute means of controlling the atomic bomb, however, would have been achieved if the scientists themselves had simply refused to employ their genius for its construction. But before and during the war, the scientists not only built the bomb; they also argued their governments into wanting to build it in the first place. Their actions grew out of a mixture of motives — fear, patriotism, curiosity, and adventure.

In the 1930s, two dramatic currents came together in the minds of the best scientific men — the one pure science, the other pure politics. The first, of course, was the burgeoning of knowledge and control of the atomic nucleus which reached fruition in Fermi's experiment in Chicago. The second was the spreading of political tyranny and military aggression throughout the world, particularly by Hitler's Germany. Together, these two very dissimilar forces combined to make the development of atomic weapons an irresistible alternative to the scientific community.

Leo Szilard is an example of the kind of man upon whom

these forces worked. A lonely, often arrogant and cynical person, Szilard was nonetheless a humanitarian in the most comprehensive sense. He was heavyset with a leonine head and a smile that softened the caustic remarks he was apt to make. Born in Hungary, he studied for several years in Germany under Albert Einstein and Max Planck. With Hitler's ascendancy, he moved to London and there not only pursued his science but also persuaded the British scientific community to begin a rescue operation for German Jewish scientists who were rapidly losing their jobs. One of the Englishmen who worked with Szilard during this period recalls: "We thought that Szilard was a rich Hungarian aristocrat but he needed a job as much as the others but never mentioned it." [2] In 1938, Szilard was at Princeton during the extended visit there of Niels Bohr, the great Danish physicist. Recent developments in nuclear science by the Europeans, Hahn, Strassman, and Meitner, which Bohr reported, and the postulation by Bohr himself of the theory that new neutrons were produced when fission occurred in the uranium atom, had made the physics department at Princeton seem to Szilard "like a stirred up ant heap." On January 21, 1939, Szilard wrote to Lewis L. Strauss, a New York financier who was his friend and patron: "I see however in connection with this new discovery potential possibilities in another direction. These might lead to a large scale production of energy and radioactive elements, unfortunately also perhaps to atom bombs." [3] Almost immediately, Szilard went to work with Fermi at Columbia University on a series of experiments which confirmed Bohr's theory. Two or three neutrons were indeed released when fission occurred in the uranium nucleus.

Acutely aware of the military implications of this discovery and distressed by the consequences of further German breakthroughs, Szilard was able to convince his scientific colleagues in America to prohibit publication of their own experimental conclusions. But, Frédéric Joliot-Curie, working in Paris with Hans von Halban and Lew Kowarski, soon made the same experimental confirmations and refused Szilard's plea to maintain secrecy.

Szilard's respect for the German scientific community as well as his uneasiness over Hitler's frequent public references to secret German weapons now convinced him that inactivity on his part could spell no less than disaster for the Western world. He drafted a letter to President Roosevelt in which he documented recent discoveries in nuclear science and their implications for warfare. The letter urged Roosevelt to initiate a governmental review of the matter and then to take appropriate and rapid action. Szilard's highly refined tactical sense moved him to bring this letter to the ultimate scientific eminence, Albert Einstein, from whom he received a very sympathetic response. A colleague has said of Einstein: "Freedom, his Jewish people, mankind — these and his science were what he cared for. As the Nazis expanded their power in Europe, Einstein saw destruction threatening all that he held of value." [4] Einstein gladly signed Szilard's letter on August 2, 1939. Szilard then took it to another New York financier friend, Alexander Sachs, who was a confidant of President Roosevelt. On October 11, 1939, Sachs delivered this letter personally to Roosevelt at the White House. "Alex," Roosevelt declared after discussing the letter with Sachs, "what you are after is to see that the Nazis don't blow us up. This requires action." [5]

Roosevelt's "action" was minimal, but it put America on the path to the Manhattan Project, Los Alamos, Hiroshima, and beyond. All this at the instigation of Szilard and Einstein, scientists whose spirits had been terrified by the menace of German nazism and whose instincts would not allow them to turn away from one line of scientific discovery, even though they knew it might produce weapons of unprecedented destructiveness.

Similar circumstances moved Great Britain, America's partner in atomic development, to its earliest governmental concern with atomic energy. Otto Frisch and Rudolph Pierls, two Jewish refugees from nazism, produced a memo on the possibilities of thermal diffusion which led the British government to create a committee to plan Britain's role in atomic development. Both Frisch and Pierls were kept off this committee because one had just been naturalized and the other was technically an enemy alien. When Pierls learned of this, he wrote a blunt letter to the responsible officials saying that the exclusion of Frisch and himself would do no more than slow down the work of the committee, and besides, "What point was there in trying to keep their own secret from them?" [6] The argument was compelling, and both of them were immediately appointed to the committee.

A British scientist who was a member of this so-called Maud Committee which carried on these earliest investigations into atomic weaponry for Great Britain has said:

> Perhaps we should have studied the moral and political implications of the bomb and thought about its use. Perhaps too we should have considered whether radioactivity was a poison outlawed in spirit by the Geneva Convention. But we didn't. The truth was that all the energies of the Maud Committee were bent on answering two questions. Was a uranium bomb scientifically possible? If so, could the British and their allies make one before the Germans? . . . In this stage, there was no dilemma for British scientists. All except the convinced pacifists were deeply committed to the war and to the defeat of Nazi Germany. The refugees from Europe who played such an important part in the development of the bomb were the most deeply committed of all. [7]

Plans for the development of an atomic bomb by the United States were not limited to the minds of the refugees who had run from fascism to America's shores. The coincidence of atomic discoveries with the spread of tyranny in Europe during the thirties impressed several native American scientists as well. During 1938 and 1939, as political and military events in Europe became more menacing, three scientific men met regularly in Cambridge, Massachusetts, and talked of the inevitability of American involvement in the European war.

One of these was Vannevar Bush, a tall, gaunt New Englander who wore rimless glasses and fought a constant losing battle against an unruly shock of hair that refused to stay off his forehead. Born in 1890 in Everett, Massachusetts, the son of a Universalist minister, Bush was educated at Tufts and Harvard, from which he graduated in 1916 with a doctorate in electrical engineering. Well known for his crisp mind and exceptional administrative capacities, Bush had become vice president of the Massachusetts Institute of Technology. A colleague once described him as a man who was "not apologetic about his patriotism." [8] That personal quality was energized during the 1930s, particularly in response to the strident isolationism of fellow Americans like Charles Lindbergh who, in a well-publicized venture, had been allowed by Goering to witness the building of the Luftwaffe.[9]

Also in Cambridge was James Conant, a man who looked and acted very much like Bush. Perhaps that is why they would function together so smoothly and productively as co-czars of American science throughout the war. Conant's appearance was thoroughly scholarly, and he had less of a taste for dry Yankee humor than did Bush. A professor of chemistry at Harvard, he had become president of that esteemed university in 1933 at the age of forty.

The third member of this important Cambridge group was Karl Compton, a physicist who had been born in Ohio and studied advanced nuclear science in Göttingen, Germany. The son of an ordained Presbyterian minister and the brother of a Nobel Prize winner in science, Karl Compton occupied the president's chair at the Massachusetts Institute of Technology in 1938.

Together, Bush, Conant, and Compton agreed that they could make no greater contribution to their country than to prepare its scientific community to be of maximum service in the war that they knew was coming. It was crucial, these three concluded, that there be someone in Washington who could give counsel to the government on scientific matters and yet be outside of the governmental bureaucracy. In 1938, with this in mind, Vannevar Bush accepted an invitation to become president of the Carnegie Institute in Washington.

As Hitler's armies swept into France during June of 1940, Bush convinced President Roosevelt to strengthen the National Defense Research Committee and make him its chairman. This committee would guide all the scientific efforts directed toward the war and particularly the development of the atomic bomb. More than a year later, at the prodding of E. O. Lawrence, the man who had built the first cyclotron at the University of California, Bush and Conant became alarmed at the slow pace of American work on atomic energy and persuaded Roosevelt to make the final, larger commitment which developed into the Manhattan Project, whose sole aim was the construction of an atomic bomb for use in the war.

The two most important installations of the Manhattan Project were in Los Alamos, New Mexico, and Chicago, Illinois. In the minds of the two men who directed these laboratories there is further reflection of the motives that moved scientists into this deadly project and away from any thought of controlling atomic weapons by not working on them.

At the Metallurgical Laboratory in Chicago where most of the critical early work was done, the director was Arthur Holly Compton, younger brother of Karl Compton and a scientific giant in his own right. In 1927, Arthur Compton had won the Nobel Prize for his work with x rays. A large, handsome man with dark, compelling eyes and a full black mustache, Compton was deeply religious, abstained from drinking, and had the kind of easy, steady personality that could harmonize a laboratory full of brilliant scientists. In looking back at the unanimous decision of scientists to join the Manhattan Project, Compton has said:

> Human destruction has the same repulsiveness to the soul of the searcher after nature's truth as it does to the artist engaged in the search for beauty. But these men recognized that they were part of their national community and must use their knowledge for the nation's defense. Not to do so would at the very least mean great peril. Perhaps, in the very destructiveness of this great new force would appear the possibility of bringing a disastrous war to a quicker end.[10]

The director at Los Alamos was Julius Robert Oppenheimer, a tall and extremely thin man whose frame made him appear perpetually ill. Oppenheimer had large blue eyes which conveyed a troubling sense of melancholy. Born in New York, the son of a German Jew who had come to this country at the age of seventeen and become a successful businessman, Robert Oppenheimer was educated at Harvard and, like so many scientists of his generation, in Germany. Oppenheimer lived the first three decades of his life in exclusive communion with his science. He learned of the stock market crash of 1929 long after it happened and first voted in the election of 1936 at the age of thirty-two. It was the economic suffering of his students during the depression and, ultimately, his "continuing, smoldering fury about the treatment of Jews in Germany," where he had relatives, that finally awakened Oppenheimer to the need to participate in the life of the community around him. An extremely refined and gentle spirit, Oppenheimer nonetheless participated in the early speculation about the feasibility of an atomic bomb and then directed its development. Long afterward he said of this work:

Almost everyone realized that this was a great undertaking. Almost everyone knew that if it were completed successfully and rapidly enough, it might determine the outcome of the war. Almost everyone knew that it was an unparalleled opportunity to bring to bear the basic knowledge and art of science for the benefit of the community. Almost everyone knew that this job, if it were achieved, would be a part of history. This sense of excitement, of devotion, and of patriotism in the end prevailed.[11]

The fact that Germany failed to build an atomic bomb does not reflect any sharper moral sense on the part of the German scientific community. The Germans had simply miscalculated. They had concluded that the development of an atomic bomb would take more money, men, and material than any nation could afford to allocate while waging a world war.

Nor were Soviet scientists immune to the emotions which moved their Western counterparts. After Germany attacked Russia in 1941, twenty of the foremost Russian scientists issued this appeal to their colleagues throughout the world:

On us scientists rests the duty of finding means to resist Fascists. We Soviet scientists are employing all our endeavor to secure the early defeat of Hitler's hordes. But we know that this can be secured only by the concerted struggle of all the peace-loving nations, all the progressive people of the world. The scientists of the world must devote all their energies and all their knowledge to the fight against the most horrible tyranny history has ever known, against Hitlerism.[12]

Driven by their own insatiable curiosity and the force of external political events, the scientists themselves sowed the seeds of their later guilt. When the war was over, Einstein said in melancholy afterthought: "Had I known that the Germans would not succeed in developing an atomic bomb, I would have done nothing for the bomb." [13]

The history of attempts during the war to force the Anglo-

American governments to plan for postwar control of atomic energy is very much the story of atomic scientists doing penance for the original sin they had committed in conceiving and building the bomb. First compelled by their superior knowledge to involve themselves in an endeavor whose products could devastate mankind, the brilliant laborers of the Manhattan Project then came to feel that fate had placed upon them the burden of protecting an unknowing world from the uncontrolled use of these weapons after the war was over. In large measure, they were right to feel themselves obliged. They had been placed in a small, select company of men who knew of a development which would radically affect not only the course of international relations but the security of every individual anywhere on the globe. The entire Manhattan Project was, in that sense, a very undemocratic venture; the scientists sought to democratize it by assuming the role of advocate for the ignorant masses of humanity.

Their initial efforts were indirect and perhaps somewhat defensive. During the autumn of 1942, E. I. du Pont de Nemours and Company was selected to operate the important uranium separation plant which was then being built at Oak Ridge, Tennessee. Until construction on that installation was completed, the Du Pont personnel were assigned to the Metallurgical Laboratory in Chicago. The mix of scientists from academia and scientists from industry was not an easy one. Although the differences can be caricatured beyond reality, it is true that the life-style of the scientists who had come from the universities was less orderly than that of the scientists who had come from the research laboratories of American industry. But the more important anxieties which were aroused by the presence of the Du Pont personnel in the Metallurgical Laboratory were based on the academicians' sudden fear that their extraordinary wartime efforts in the field of nuclear science were going to fall under a postwar Du Pont monopoly. Such thoughts particularly activated the younger scientists who had formed their political philosophies on American campuses during the depression years and were thus generally liberal, prolabor, and antibusiness. The foreign-born scientists who were then working in Chicago were likely to be uneasy about any concentration of power including, quite naturally, the one which Du Pont represented. And so the academic scientists decided during the summer of 1943 that it was time to organize.

Like everything else in the Manhattan Project, this organization required the permission of the project's supervisors. The permission was reluctantly granted, and the group met four or five times during that summer, but always with a military guard present. To a man like James Franck, this armed presence in a scientific laboratory brought back bitter memories of the Germany from which he had fled. He articulated these recollections in one moving address to the group which brought the younger members to the edge of revolution. The military guard soon interrupted and said that the organization had better disband "unless they wanted to be shipped off to Guadalcanal." [14] The infuriated scientists went immediately to the director of the laboratory, Arthur Compton, who assured them that Guadalcanal was not in their future. These meetings soon ceased, however, when the associate director of the Metallurgical Laboratory, Samuel Allison, complained to his friends that he was spending too much of his time explaining their actions to the powers above. The scientists agreed. They submitted a memorandum of their complaints and concerns and promised themselves they would come together again when the pace of work at the laboratory allowed them to do so.

2

The Futile, But Visionary, Efforts of Niels Bohr

ONE OF THE FEW authentic heroes of the earliest period of striving for international control of atomic weapons is Niels Bohr. His heroism sadly is more tragic than triumphant. He deserves tribute for prescience and determination, but not for success.

A large, fair-complexioned man, with fleshy features that gave him the look of some friendly fowl, Niels Bohr was born in Copenhagen in 1885. His father, Christian, was an internationally recognized physiologist. His mother, Ellen, a graceful and warm woman, was the daughter of D. B. Adler, a Danish Jewish banker and liberal member of the national legislature. The Bohr home in Copenhagen was a center for the intellectual community of that city. Niels Bohr was educated in Denmark and then at Cambridge. From 1913 to 1927, he led the world's development of quantum physics. During the 1930s, his theoretical work was fundamental to the expansion of man's knowledge of the atom and ultimate ability to unleash the power within it. He also wrote amply in philosophy. Beloved for his gentle, modest spirit, he was tenderly devoted to his family and his colleagues. In the words of his friend, Justice Felix Frankfurter, "Bohr was a man weighed down with a conscience and with an almost overwhelming solicitude for the dangers to our people." [1] Although his later life was touched with melancholy over the course of human events, Bohr was, at his roots, an optimist and loved to tell the story of three Chinese philosophers who had come together to taste vinegar, the

Chinese symbol for the spirit of life. The first drank of it and said, "It is sour." The second said it was bitter. Then Laotze tasted it and exclaimed, "It is fresh." [2]

Widely acknowledged as the greatest living physicist of his time, Bohr enjoyed the easy access to the salons of European royalty. Field Marshal Smuts of Great Britain once described Bohr as "a man at the mention of whose name one should stand bareheaded — greater than Newton, greater than Faraday." An invitation to a luncheon with Bohr during the war moved Smuts to exclaim: "This is tremendous as though one was meeting Shakespeare or Napoleon — someone who is changing the history of the world." [3]

When Copenhagen fell to the Nazis in 1940, Bohr was warned that he might be incarcerated because of his immense knowledge of atomic science. But he stayed on, out of devotion to his homeland, and also particularly so that he might aid the many Jewish scientists who had sought refuge from nazism at Bohr's institute in Copenhagen. He became an intimate of the Danish underground and, through those circles, in early 1943 received a message from James Chadwick, a foremost English physicist with whom Bohr had worked. Sir John Anderson, the overseer of the British atomic energy program, had just discovered that Bohr was in Copenhagen and immediately directed Chadwick to do anything necessary to bring him to Britain. Chadwick's message came to Bohr via the British intelligence service, which turned it over to the intelligence office of the Danish general staff. The message was handed to Bohr in a bunch of door keys, one of which had a tiny hole drilled in its side. Out of this hole came a piece of microfilm, no more than ½ mm on either side, which, when placed under a microscope, revealed Chadwick's message written on the stationery of Liverpool University.

It was quite plainly an invitation to Britain:

I have heard in a roundabout way that you have considered coming to this country if the opportunity should offer . . . There is no scientist in the world who would be more acceptable both to our university people and to the general public. I have in mind a particular problem in which your assistance would be of the greatest help . . . All I want to do is to assure you that if you decide to come you will have a very warm welcome and an opportunity for service in the common cause.[4]

Bohr replied on microfilm which was inserted into the same hollow door key and returned via many hands to Chadwick. He was grateful, as he told Chadwick, that his English friends had not forgotten him, but he did not yet feel able to leave his country or his friends in Denmark: "I feel it to be my duty in our desperate situation to help resist the threat against the freedom of our institutions and to assist in the protection of the exiled scientists." He had appreciated Chadwick's reference to atomic weapons and added that "neither such duties nor even the dangers of retaliation to my collaborators and relatives might carry sufficient weight to detain me here if I felt that I could be of real help in other ways, but I do not think that is probable. Above all I have to the best of my judgment convinced myself that in spite of all future prospects any immediate use of the latest marvelous discoveries of atomic physics is impracticable." Bohr did not, of course, know of the immense American effort which had made his judgment fallible. Then, in his final sentence, Bohr revealed that the idea which he would argue persistently in the coming years to scientists and statesmen throughout the world had already formed in his mind during the occupation in Denmark:

However, there may, and perhaps in a near future, come a moment where things look different and where I, if not in other ways, might be able modestly to assist in the restoration of international collaboration in human progress. At that moment, I shall make an effort to join my friends.[5]

By the end of September 1943, things did indeed look different. Bohr and his brother Harold, a renowned mathematician, learned from unimpeachable sources that the Jewish population of Denmark was about to be deported and that in connection with that German action, they were both to be arrested. Bohr went quickly to his contacts in the resistance movement. In the month that had passed since August 29, 1943, when the Danish government had resigned after having refused a German ultimatum, Bohr had been in almost daily communication with the resistance. Now, it was Bohr himself who was forced to flee. On the evening of September 30, 1943, the day he had learned that his arrest was imminent, Bohr, his wife, and his brother boarded a crowded fishing boat and, evading German patrols, landed safely on the southern coast of Sweden. It is a measure of the quality of this man that, while his wife waited there for the arrival of their four sons, he rushed to Stockholm and on the following evening, September 30, was in conference with the Swedish Undersecretary for Foreign Affairs, arguing that proper and immediate advances by the Swedish government to the Nazis could save the entire Jewish population of Denmark. Then, in a frantic series of conferences that took him to the Swedish Foreign Minister and finally to the King, Bohr successfully facilitated the entrance of the escaping Jewish population of Denmark into Sweden.

A few days after his arrival in Stockholm, Bohr received a telegram from Lord Cherwell, Churchill's personal scientific adviser, urging him to come to England at once. He accepted and, on October 2, 1943, was placed in the empty bomb bay of an unarmed Mosquito plane which traveled with sufficient speed to make the trip safely. The trip was not without incident, however. Bohr's head was too large to accommodate the required helmet and earphones. When the pilot announced to Bohr that the plane had reached an altitude which required use of the oxygen mask, the scientist did not hear and rapidly fainted, in which state he was found by the pilot who thought he was dead. By the time the plane landed in Scotland, however, he had regained consciousness.

In London, Bohr was told of the great advances which the Americans and British had made in their development of atomic energy by Sir John Anderson, later to become Lord Waverly, Chancellor of the Exchequer. Anderson was a dour Scottish civil servant who had been trained in physical chemistry and done work with uranium. His biographer has described him as "the apotheosis of the Civil Service." [6] Anderson had followed the work on atomic energy closely and, in August 1941, recommended to Churchill that a Cabinet Minister be appointed to coordinate atomic energy activities. Churchill agreed and appointed Anderson.

From their first meeting, Bohr and Anderson, two very dissimilar men, established a strong personal friendship which was based, no doubt, on their common concern with the dread products of atomic energy. In the following years, Anderson was to be a foremost advocate of Bohr's strategy for achieving international control of atomic weapons.

Now, in early October 1943, Bohr sat with Anderson for hours and heard the fascinating and sometimes tempestuous story of the Anglo-American development of atomic weapons.

Two months before his first meeting with Niels Bohr, Anderson had participated actively in a successful conference at Quebec which produced the primary written agreement that formally bound the United States and Great Britain together in atomic endeavors. Arriving at that formal pact had not been a simple process. Churchill and Roosevelt first discussed atomic energy at Hyde Park during a hot afternoon in mid-June 1942. In the presence of Harry Hopkins, Roosevelt's preeminent counselor, they

agreed to proceed jointly with the critical work of atomic development, pooling their information and sharing the results of their
labors. They also agreed that the major installations of this project should be located in America, far from the striking range of
the Luftwaffe. Although none of this was put on paper, its impact
on the course of atomic development and particularly on the success of attempts to achieve international control of atomic weapons would be critical, not only because of the exclusive partnership agreement it established between the two allied nations, but
also because of the tenor of the relationship between Churchill
and Roosevelt which it revealed. In matters of atomic energy,
Churchill's effect on Roosevelt was predominant.

During the months that followed, suspicions arose between
the English and Americans working on the atomic bomb project.
These were primarily the reflection of a change in the tempo of
America's atomic effort. In the interim, the Manhattan Project
was formally established and Vannevar Bush appointed chairman
of a military policy committee that oversaw its activities. Then in
September of 1942, Leslie Groves, a career military man, was
chosen as director of the Manhattan Project itself. Groves was a
burly, hard-driving man with lively blue eyes and a neat brown
mustache. His father had been an Army chaplain of stern bearing, who taught his sons to observe the Sabbath without frivolity
and scolded them whenever they spent too much time reading
the sports pages of the daily newspaper. Educated at MIT and
then West Point, from which he graduated with honors in 1918,
Leslie Groves had spent almost all of his service time as a military
engineer. He had overseen the construction of millions of Army
barracks, the Pentagon, and the detention camps which America
had ungraciously built for its Japanese residents. From the moment of his appointment, Groves believed that the Manhattan
Project would determine the outcome of the war. He therefore

imposed an extraordinary system of security on all aspects of the project, keeping to a minimum the number of men who knew more than the workings of one section of the vast project. The General believed that nothing would be gained by sharing atomic information with the British. Vannevar Bush and James Conant, who had become chairman of the National Defense Research Committee, agreed.[7]

During December 1942, Groves, Bush, and Conant carried their arguments to the Secretary of War, Henry L. Stimson, and finally to the President. At the same time, Stimson and Roosevelt had been shaken by the news of an agreement between Great Britain and Russia for the exchange of information on new weapons discovered by either nation. This pact had been signed on September 27. To the President and his Secretary of War, it suddenly seemed that if atomic information was shared with the English, then that information might find its way into Russian hands. On the day after Roosevelt learned of the Anglo-Russian pact, he wrote to Bush approving of the policy which Bush had recommended for severely limited atomic interchange with the British.[8]

This was the first of many occasions on which Western anxiety over the Soviet Union determined a most important question of atomic energy control. To most of the men with power in the governments of America and England, the wartime alliance with Russia was no more than an uneasy union with an enemy nation, an alliance built upon the unique necessities of war. They were unable to liberate the unparalleled problem of atomic energy from this view. General Groves has said that "there was never from about two weeks from the time I took charge of this project any illlusion on my part but that Russia was our enemy and that the project was conducted on that basis. I didn't go along with the attitude of the country as a whole that Russia was a gallant ally. I always had suspicions and the project was conducted on that basis."[9]

Early in January 1943, James Conant prepared a memorandum detailing the terms of exchange with Britain which Roosevelt had approved. The English could receive information of scientific value but they would not be given access to any of the manufacturing and engineering work that related directly to construction of the atomic bomb. Conant and Bush soon revealed their stance in a Washington conference with Wallace Akers, an engineer and executive of Imperial Chemical Industries, the British analogue of Du Pont. Akers had become director of Tube Alloys, the British code name for atomic work. His position in the British project was roughly equal to Groves's in America. The message which his American colleagues now conveyed jolted Akers's gentlemanly equilibrium. Six months before Akers had sent his deputy, M. W. Perrin, to the United States to have a look at the American atomic work. Perrin reported back to Akers that the Americans would soon "completely outstrip us in ideas, research, and application of nuclear energy and that then, quite rightly, they will see no reason for our butting in . . . The time available for making any plans for coordinated work between the Americans and ourselves is extremely short." Akers agreed with this estimate.[10] Therefore, on hearing Conant and Bush in January 1943, he became politely irate and suggested that if that was the American position then the British would have to hold up transmission of technical information which America had requested in nonatomic military areas. Conant was unmoved and agreed that perhaps such action would be necessary.[11]

Sir John Anderson was similarly unsettled when he learned in England of this new laconic American posture. He cabled Churchill who had just left for the Casablanca Conference: "One cannot help suspecting that the United States Military Authorities . . . wish to gain an advance upon us and feel that having benefited from the fruits of our early endeavors they will not suffer unduly by casting us aside." [12] Receiving this message in Casablanca, Churchill contained his instinctive fury but, nonetheless, in a minor huff queried Roosevelt and Hopkins about the departure in American policy. With an air of finality, Churchill declared that the atomic work was of great importance. Unless there was full cooperation and complete pooling of information, Great Britain would be compelled to go ahead on its own and that would be "a sombre decision." It would mean diversion of resources from the war in Europe. Roosevelt and Hopkins, preoccupied with other matters on which they desired Churchill's aid, quieted the Prime Minister and assured him that everything would be set in order as soon as they returned to Washington.[13]

Over the next several weeks and into the spring of 1943, Churchill regularly wrote to Hopkins about atomic energy, refining his argument and inquiring after the state of American thinking on the subject. Hopkins continued to respond in vague phrases which indicated that the matter was being attended to but not settled. For his part, Hopkins had raised the question with Bush, who then reviewed the American position with Stimson, Conant, and Groves. They saw no reason to alter their previous decision. Bush conveyed this result to Hopkins and attached a significant addendum. He and his colleagues had concluded that the manufacturing and engineering information which the British were demanding had no substantial relation to the war effort. If the United States was able to build the bomb, then the Allied position in the war would be immeasurably assisted. Nothing would be added by the British also possessing this manufacturing knowledge. The only possible value such information would have to Britain, Bush continued, was for postwar use. Bush, Conant, and Groves had concluded in their conversations with several of the Englishmen, particularly Akers, that the real British aim was to possess atomic energy information for postwar commercial applications. Like the young scientists at the Chicago Metallurgical

Laboratory, Bush was angered by the thought that this great American enterprise might be turned into a postwar business bonanza. Bush, however, was more worried about Imperial Chemical Industries, Ltd., than about Du Pont. He told Hopkins that the entire problem of postwar control and application deserved separate and comprehensive consideration at a later stage of the war.[14]

At the end of April, Churchill, still having received no specific response from Hopkins, decided it was time to visit Washington personally. It is true that there were important nonatomic military decisions to make, but Churchill's travel plans were activated largely by his desire to settle the atomic problem. On May 25, the final day of the conference, Churchill raised the question of atomic interchange. Hopkins soon summoned Bush to the White House for a conference not with the principals, Churchill and Roosevelt, but with himself and the British scientist Frederick Lindemann, then Lord Cherwell. An Oxford don and old friend of Churchill's, Cherwell served the Prime Minister during wartime as personal adviser, particularly in scientific matters. Cherwell was a large man with exotic tastes and pronounced biases. Openly hostile to Negroes and Jews, he viewed Hitler's banishing of Jewish scientists not so much as an act of unspeakable inhumanity but as an exercise in "indescribable stupidity." [15]

Cherwell went combatively to the point. Why were the Americans intent on excluding their English allies from atomic development? Bush responded with a vigorous explanation of the American attitude, especially as it related to Britain's postwar interests. Cherwell acknowledged that Britain desired comprehensive atomic knowledge primarily for postwar application. However, the application Britain had in mind, he contended, was not commercial but military. The bomb would be necessary after the war for the defense of the English position in Europe, primarily as a counterbalance to Russian power. This declaration brought

Hopkins quickly to Bush's side of the argument. The two Americans suggested that it was improper for them to decide a question of such long-term significance to the course of international relations. Roosevelt simply could not commit a future American Administration to this path. The discussion ended finally in stalemate, with a directive from Hopkins to Bush that he do nothing further until directed.[16]

Although Bush waited for almost a month, until June 24 when he was summoned to lunch with the President, Roosevelt himself had apparently made an unadvised decision of his own. For on May 26, 1943, a day after Bush's confrontation with Cherwell, Prime Minister Churchill had cabled Sir John Anderson from Washington concerning his meeting with Roosevelt:

> The President agreed that the exchange of information on tube alloys should be resumed and the enterprise should be considered a joint one, to which both countries would contribute their best endeavors. I understood that his ruling would be based upon the fact that this weapon may well be developed in time for the present war and that it thus falls within the general agreement covering the interchange of research and invention secrets.[17]

The luncheon discussion between Bush and Roosevelt on June 24 was intended as a briefing for the President on the state of the Manhattan Project and, perhaps more important, as an opportunity for the President to convey to Bush his decision on interchange with the British. But when the President asked Bush what he thought of the British problem, Bush surprised him with the report of Lord Cherwell's statements on Britain's postwar military need for the atomic bomb. Bush left the meeting feeling that he was to continue to sit tight.[18] Roosevelt, one suspects, was slightly uncomfortable with the decision he had already made. Churchill, however, was relentless. Early in June, he had written

Hopkins to make arrangements for a staff meeting that could express the oral agreement he had made with Roosevelt in Washington. Having heard nothing by the end of the first week in July, the Prime Minister wrote Hopkins once more demanding action. Roosevelt, now more than a little perplexed, sought counsel from Hopkins, who advised simply: "I think you made a firm commitment to Churchill in regard do this when he was here and there is nothing to do but go through with it." Roosevelt agreed. On July 20, he wrote to Bush:

> While I am mindful of the vital necessity for security in regard to this, I feel that our understanding with the British encompasses the complete exchange of all information.

He directed Bush to "renew, in an inclusive manner, the full exchange of information with the British Government regarding tube alloys." At the same time, Roosevelt wrote to Churchill confirming their earlier agreement and suggesting that he send Sir John Anderson to America to detail the compact.[19]

When James Conant read Roosevelt's letter to Bush, he immediately called Groves and said that the President had made a "mistake" which was not in the best interests of "the war effort, the United States, and the eventual peace of the world." Groves "completely shared" this opinion.[20] Vannevar Bush was then in London with Stimson on another scientific mission, unrelated to atomic energy. On July 15, Bush had been taken to see Churchill who promptly exploded over his difficulty in getting the Americans to adhere to the atomic agreement he claimed he had achieved with Roosevelt. Bush did not falter in Churchill's presence. Once more he presented his argument, particularly his unwillingness to consider at that time matters which were essentially of postwar significance. Churchill said he was unconcerned with the period after the war. His only interest was winning the war.

Then perhaps an agreement could be reached, Bush said. He promised to discuss the matter with Stimson.[21]

On July 22, 1943, Bush and Stimson went with Stimson's assistant, Harvey Bundy, to No. 10 Downing Street for a conference with Churchill, Cherwell, and Anderson. At that moment, none of the participants had yet seen Roosevelt's letters of July 20. The Prime Minister began the discussion, complaining bitterly of America's reluctance to treat Britain as an equal partner in atomic development, even though Roosevelt had agreed to that course. He disclaimed any interest in the postwar commercial applications of atomic energy but spoke, with characteristic eloquence, of Britain's more critical need in the postwar period to be able "to maintain her future independence in the face of international blackmail that the Russians might eventually be able to employ." [22] In a memorandum to Churchill before this conference, Anderson had written: "We cannot afford after the war to face the future without this weapon and rely entirely on America, should Russia or some other power develop it." [23] Now Anderson suggested to the Americans that they had been misled by Wallace Akers into fearing private commercial exploitation of atomic energy by British businesses after the war. Churchill seized the moment and proposed a five-point plan which he hoped Roosevelt and he might sign:

1. The wartime development of atomic energy would be completely joint with open interchange of all information.

2. Neither America nor Great Britain would use atomic weapons against the other.

3. Neither of the nations would pass information concerning the project to third parties without the consent of the other.

4. Each government would agree not to use atomic energy against other parties without the consent of the other.

5. The President of the United States could limit the flow of information to Great Britain for commercial and industrial applications of atomic energy, as he deemed equitable in light of the great American expenditures on the project.

Henry Stimson listened attentively and then agreed that the proposal had merit. He would put it to Roosevelt as soon as he returned to Washington. Roosevelt had, of course, already obliged himself to a far more generous relationship and would have no difficulty in accepting Churchill's five-point plan. Early in August, Anderson came to Washington to work out the details of the agreement with Bush. On August 19, 1943, Roosevelt and Churchill signed the agreement at their conference in Quebec.

The worst apprehensions of Bush and Conant about postwar commercial atomic exploitation by the British had seemingly been overcome. Their dismay at Britain's postwar military plans for using the atomic weapon as a force in international relations, particularly against Russia, remained altogether undiminished. If anything, the future use of atomic weapons was silently assented to in the Quebec Agreement of August 1943. The State Department, which was supposed to have primary responsibility for international relations, did not even know of the existence of atomic weapons at this point in time and would not know of them for more than a year to come. Bush, Conant, and Stimson would take up the international implications of the matter many times in the months that followed, but at Quebec, under Churchill's stimulus and control, the die had been cast. The most troubling aspect of the Quebec Agreement as it related to the later attempts to achieve international control of atomic energy was that it involved not a conscious decision by the United States but a passive acquiescence to Churchill's view of the postwar world and of the role that atomic weapons should play in it.

This was the state of atomic relations when Niels Bohr first spoke with Sir John Anderson in London during October 1943. At Quebec, the British and Americans had agreed that, pursuant to their new atomic understanding, almost the entire English atomic energy team would be transferred to the various installations of the Manhattan Project within the United States. Now Bohr — the preeminent scientist of his generation — became a trump card in Britain's implementation of the Quebec Agreement. At the end of November 1943, Bohr and his son Aage, who was also a physicist, traveled by ship across the Atlantic to America as part of the British team.

Unlike the rest of the British Tube Alloys crew, Bohr was going to America not primarily to help build the bomb but to stimulate thoughts about how to control it. Not that he believed the bomb should not be built or that he argued against its use in the war. He did neither. At Los Alamos his presence was a great morale booster for the scientists who toiled there, as if a patron saint had appeared in the flesh to urge on the faithful. Bohr himself was amazed by what he saw. He wrote:

> What until a few years ago might have been considered a fantastic dream is at the moment being realized in great laboratories erected in secrecy in some of the most solitary regions of the States.[24]

General Groves gave Bohr access to all parts of the laboratory, with a general assignment to share with the others anything that came into his gifted mind about the operations there. Groves appreciated Bohr's greatness but was slightly apprehensive about what he took to be the scatterbrained, loose-tongued quality of the Dane. He therefore assigned an armed detective to travel with Bohr and his son wherever they went and compelled them to use the pseudonyms Nicholas Baker and James Baker.

But Bohr's most important activity in America was not in the laboratories so much as in the embassies and offices of the highest government officials. His thoughts were not so much on the present as on the future. He foresaw that the postwar world would be dominated by the Allied powers, particularly America and Russia. The ideological differences between these two great nations and the increasing isolation of the Soviet Union perplexed Bohr. Building cooperation between America and Russia would not be easy, but he knew how necessary it was for the tranquillity of the world. These thoughts were not the thoughts of a seer, for his vision had a quality of predictability about it. But Bohr went beyond the predictable to consider the productive role which the atom bomb, in all its startling uniqueness, might play. Properly handled by the diplomats, it might well be the catalyst that would impel the United States and the Soviet Union to disenthrall themselves from their mutual suspicions. Bohr came to believe deeply in this vision and to argue it with all the zealous conviction of a true believer. Accustomed to gaining access to European royalty on the shortest notice and usually having his way with them, Bohr would soon be frustrated to find that the leaders of the great Western democracies were far more difficult to see and ultimately impossible to convince.

After his first visit to Los Alamos, Bohr wrote to Sir John Anderson: "The more I have learned and thought about this new field of science and technique, the more I am convinced that no kind of customary measures [of control] will suffice for this purpose and that no real safety can be achieved without a universal agreement based on mutual confidence." [25] Anderson had arranged for Bohr to have direct access to the British ambassador in Washington, Lord Halifax. When Bohr reached Washington early in 1944, he went immediately to the British embassy and was warmly greeted by Halifax and the British Minister, Sir Ronald Campbell. On this and several occasions to follow, Bohr spoke with them of his vision of the postwar world. Fundamental to his thoughts was the need for an early approach to the Russians for the specific purpose of bringing them in on atomic development. Both Halifax and Campbell were taken with Bohr's reasoning and gave him every encouragement. They agreed, however, that in view of America's predominant role in atomic development, the initiative must come from the United States. It would be necessary for Bohr to make contact with Roosevelt.

For this, Bohr turned to Justice Felix Frankfurter, whom he had come to know in London before the war when they were both involved, along with the Archbishop of Canterbury, in a committee to aid scholars in exile from Hitler's Germany.[26] Now the difficult problem was how to raise the question with Frankfurter without committing a breach of security. Having lived during the weeks in America in constant companionship with General Groves's security guards, Bohr appreciated the importance of not appearing to spread the news of atomic development to anyone who might not otherwise already know of it. Bohr used the Danish Minister in Washington as an intermediary and renewed his acquaintance with Frankfurter at a tea at the Danish legation. Then, in February 1944, Bohr visited Frankfurter in his chambers at the Supreme Court for a private conversation. Very early in the discussion the Justice referred to a secret scientific project known to him as "X." Bohr was relieved to realize that Frankfurter was speaking of the atomic bomb work which he had apparently learned of from a nervous young member of the Manhattan Project. Now, Bohr could proceed with his discussion of the political implications of this dread endeavor. Frankfurter was moved by Bohr's arguments and promised to take them up with the President at the earliest convenient moment.

After a few months in Los Alamos, Bohr returned to Washington in April 1944 and learned from Frankfurter that the matter had been discussed with Roosevelt. The Persident had apparently been very responsive to these new ideas. Bohr's thoughts coincided with his own, Roosevelt told Frankfurter, although he had not yet discussed any of these with his scientific advisers. "A solution to this problem might be more important than all the schemes for a world organization," the President had said. Finally, Frankfurter reported that the President had instructed him to inform Bohr that he was eager to discuss with Churchill the question of postwar control of atomic weapons. Bohr and apparently Frankfurter interpreted this to mean that Roosevelt was asking Bohr to serve as his emissary to Churchill to raise these questions with the Prime Minister. Lord Halifax, who had regularly reported back to Anderson on the state of Bohr's thinking, agreed that it would be most important for Bohr to talk with the Prime Minister personally.[27]

Thrilled with this turn of events, Bohr quickly left for London, full of hope and expectation. There he met several times with Sir John Anderson to report on his discussions in Washington and to consider the next steps. The reports from Halifax had led Anderson to believe in Bohr's message. In fact, he had already brought these arguments before Churchill in a long memorandum prepared at the end of March 1944, in consultation with Lord Cherwell. Anderson had written that he could see only two alternative courses, the one being a nuclear armaments race in which the United States enjoyed a "precarious and uneasy advantage" for a time, the other being international control. "No plans for world organization which ignore the potential of Tube Alloys can be worth the paper on which they are written," Anderson told

Churchill. If a decision was made to seek international control, Anderson argued, then it was important to convey to the Russians "the bare fact that the Americans expected by a given date to have this devastating weapon and for inviting them to collaborate in preparing a scheme for international control." If the Russians were told nothing, he continued, then when they learned of the development, as they certainly would, their attitude would be much less cooperative. Anderson's specific suggestions for action were that Churchill inform the other members of the War Cabinet of the atomic development and that "the Foreign Secretary should be asked to set on foot an immediate study of the practical and political problems of international control." When Churchill returned this memorandum to Anderson, it was marked throughout with the Prime Minister's acerbic comments. At the end, Churchill had written flatly: "I do not agree."

Anderson did not want to depress Bohr with this story, but it convinced him that he was not the one to attempt to arrange a meeting between Bohr and Churchill. To Bohr, Anderson said only that he had tried several times to draw the Prime Minister's attention to the problem of postwar atomic control, but it had been impossible to take him away from the immediate demands of the war.

This discouraged Bohr, but he refused to return to the United States without accomplishing what he believed to be his mission for Roosevelt. He set out to find other intermediaries to Churchill and ultimately arrived at two who were successful. One was Sir Henry Dale, a scientific friend of Bohr's who was president of the Royal Society. Bohr had talked with Sir Henry of atomic weapons and the future in the most secret place the two could find, an iron park bench in the middle of Hyde Park. Now Dale wrote eloquently to Churchill, imploring him to see Bohr, whom he described as "first among all the men of all countries who are now active in any department of science." He added that Bohr might bring the latest news from America of the atomic project. Bohr's other advocate was Churchill's confidant, Field Marshal Smuts, Prime Minister of South Africa, an erudite man who was in absolute awe of Bohr. Though Smuts had not yet been informed of the atomic work, he wrote to Churchill asking for an audience for Bohr who, he said, was extremely desirous of meeting the Prime Minister. There was no specific mention of atomic weapons.

While Bohr waited to hear from Churchill, his presence stirred Sir John Anderson to try once more to turn the Prime Minister's attention toward the problems of postwar control. Anderson's medium on this second occasion was a War Cabinet paper concerning future world organization. "I cannot help feeling," he wrote, "that plans for world security which do not take account of Tube Alloys must be quite unreal. When the work on Tube Alloys comes to fruition the future of the world will in fact depend on whether it is used for the benefit or destruction of mankind." Admitting once again that it was somewhat strange for Britain to be taking the initiative in this matter, Anderson reported to Churchill that he now had reason to believe that Roosevelt was quite concerned with the topic. He pleaded for Churchill to send Roosevelt a message which might begin the necessary dialogues. In fact, he attached a draft of such a telegram. Churchill was unmoved. At the bottom of the memorandum he wrote: "I do not think any such telegram is necessary nor do I wish to widen the circle who are involved." [28]

Then, during May 1944, Lord Cherwell, at Anderson's urging, began to prod Churchill. He reported a conversation with Prime Minister Mackenzie King of Canada, who had urged that the problem of international atomic control be considered. "I must confess," Cherwell said to Churchill, "that I think plans and preparations for the postwar world or even the peace conference are

utterly illusory so long as this crucial factor is left out of account."
Recognizing the impossible demands on the Prime Minister's
time, Cherwell suggested that Field Marshal Smuts might be
brought in on the matter and asked to advise Churchill on
problems associated with postwar atomic control. Churchill acquiesced to this request, saying that Smuts should be involved
but that the tightest secrecy must still be maintained. He also told
Cherwell: ". . . our associations with the United States must be
permanent and I have no fear that they will maltreat us or cheat
us." Churchill's unwillingness to upset the delicate balance that
had been achieved in the Quebec Agreement of 1943 was apparently part of the cause of his reluctance to consider international control. But there was something more to it. As had become clear in the negotiations leading up to that agreement,
Churchill had formed a preconception of the postwar world. He
envisioned Russia's emerging from the war as the foremost European power, a definite threat to Great Britain. In these circumstances, Britain's possession of atomic weapons would be its sole
counterbalance to Soviet strength. The proposals for postwar control which Anderson and Cherwell were urging on him were based
on early involvement of the Soviet Union in atomic development,
a step which would remove from Britain what Churchill took to
be the equalizer in postwar international politics. He was therefore predictably uninterested.

The pleadings of Smuts, Cherwell, and Dale finally induced
Churchill to grant Bohr an interview. After more than a month
of waiting, on May 16, 1944, Bohr and Churchill, two most remarkable men of their times, met at No. 10 Downing Street. In
Bohr's view, the meeting could not have gone worse. Perhaps
Churchill was not feeling happy that day. Perhaps Bohr's low-
toned, slightly garbled English annoyed him. Perhaps he was preoccupied with the imminent invasion of Europe. Perhaps he was

simply acting with the churlishness of a person forced to do something he did not want to do. In any case, the meeting was a fiasco.
Throughout the session Churchill engaged Lord Cherwell, who
was also present, in contentious argument over unrelated matters.
Bohr was never able to turn Churchill's attention to the problem
of control, nor to convey adequately the message he felt he had
brought from Roosevelt. As the meeting ended, Bohr, searching
for some hope, asked Churchill if he might send him a memorandum on the matter that was foremost in his mind. "It will be an
honour for me to receive a letter from you," Churchill responded,
"but not about politics."

This final act of unkindness left Bohr heartbroken, but not
for long. Later in the day, he began a letter to Churchill which
contained a dramatic description of the atomic energy project
and the message from Roosevelt. Bohr also began a series of
conversations with Smuts, who was now deeply immersed in
thoughts of atomic energy. Like Anderson, Halifax, and Cherwell, Smuts had been impressed with Bohr's reasoning, and
particularly his vision of the role that might be played in the
postwar world by the international community of scientists.
During June 1944, Smuts sent a memorandum on the subject
to Churchill, which contained many of Bohr's ideas. He cautioned against the belief that the secret of atomic weapons might
be kept for very long and suggested that a failure to disclose it
until after the war would cause the most destructive competition
in the history of the world. The Prime Minister must consider
the topic with President Roosevelt, Smuts argued, and particularly the question of whether Stalin should be informed. Churchill's response to this latest plea was slightly more encouraging.
He agreed to discuss it with Roosevelt when next they met,
probably during the autumn.[29]

Bohr's visit to London was therefore not without effect. He

had even received encouragement from one thoroughly unexpected source.[30] Immediately prior to his departure from Washington for London during April, Bohr had received a note at
the Danish legation from Zinchenko, the counselor of the Soviet
embassy in London, informing him that there was a letter waiting
there for him from his scientific colleague Peter Kapitza, the
foremost Russian physicist. On arrival in London, Bohr discussed
this note with British security officers, who suggested that he
attempt to have it forwarded to his hotel in London, but that
he agree to pick it up personally at the Soviet embassy if it was
requested that he do so. Zinchenko did, in fact, make such a
request, and so Bohr went to the embassy at five o'clock on the
afternoon of April 20, 1944. When Bohr arrived, Zinchenko
handed him Kapitza's letter and asked him to read it. It had
been written long before on October 28, 1943, when the Russians
first learned of Bohr's escape from Denmark. The letter was very
much like the one Chadwick had written to Bohr on microfilm
while he was still in Denmark:

> All we Russian scientists feel very anxious about your fate. Of
> course you are the best judge of what path you must take through
> all this tempest, but I want to let you know that you will be wel-
> come in the Soviet Union where everything will be done to give you
> and your family a shelter and where we now have all the necessary
> conditions for carrying on scientific work . . . If you come to
> Moscow, you will find yourself joined with us in our scientific
> work. Even the vague hope that you might possibly come to live
> with us is most heartily applauded by all our physicists: Joffe,
> Mendelshtom, Landau, Vavilov Tam, Alhanov, Semenov, and
> others . . . We have very little information about English physi-
> cists. Occasional exchange of telegrams is all that we know. They,
> like us, are hard at work fighting for our common cause against
> Nazism.

Bohr looked up from the letter and thanked Zinchenko for
transmitting it to him, saying that the letter was indeed very

kind. He talked of his long friendship with Kapitza and of his visit to the institute in Moscow during June 1937. Zinchenko remarked that Kapitza was a very prominent man in the Soviet Union. Bohr readily agreed, acknowledging Kapitza's great contributions to science and technology in the years before the war and adding that he had no doubt that his Russian colleague had achieved further important accomplishments since then. That was very much the case, Zinchenko said. After some further reminiscences by Bohr of his friendships with other Russian scientists, Zinchenko declared that "the great hopes for the future lie not least in the mutual respect which the fight for the common cause had created in countries like England and Russia." He contrasted this to the difficult times before the war "when Russia had so few friends in other countries." Bohr interrupted to say that this was never the case within scientific circles and went on to speak of the importance of international scientific cooperation in promoting mutual understanding.

Then Zinchenko changed the subject. He said he knew that Bohr had recently been to the United States. That was so, Bohr said. In America he had received many encouraging impressions of the wish for international cooperation and hoped soon to visit Russia also. Zinchenko then asked what information Bohr had received concerning the work of the American scientists during the war. Bohr's answer was oblique. The American scientists, like their counterparts in Russia and England, had surely made very large contributions to the war effort which would no doubt be of great importance for the appreciation of science everywhere after the war. At the end of this very friendly talk, Bohr offered to send a reply to Kapitza in due time. Zinchenko said that would be wonderful and added that he would send a telegram to Kapitza, telling him that Bohr had received the letter.

Bohr immediately sat down to record this meeting for the British security forces. He also prepared a reply to Kapitza, in which he offered thanks for the kind letter and said that it would be a "pleasure to me for a time to participate with you and my other Russian friends in the work on our common scientific interests." At the moment, however, his plans were "quite unsettled." He promised to write again as soon as he knew more. "For many reasons indeed," Bohr concluded, "I am hoping that I shall soon be able to accept your most kind invitation and come to Russia for a longer or a shorter visit."

For Bohr, this had been an extremely fortunate, unexpected interchange. It raised, in his mind, the dream of carrying his argument for atomic control not only to the scientists and statesmen of the West, but to those in the Soviet Union as well. But that was a later step. First he must see Roosevelt. He returned to Washington in June 1944, after the invasion of northern France and reported directly to Frankfurter on his unsuccessful meeting with Churchill. The Justice was soon able to discuss this with Roosevelt, who asked to have a memorandum from Bohr on the subject and expressed a desire to meet the great scientist. Encouraged by this favorable response, Bohr devoted all his energies to the memorandum for Roosevelt, working incessantly in the withering heat of June in Washington. Since there was no secretary to whom he could entrust such thoughts, Bohr dictated his visionary words to his son and companion, Aage. While Aage typed, Bohr darned socks or sewed on buttons for the two of them. Like all of Bohr's writing, this memorandum went through many stages of preparation before he was ready to date it on July 3, 1944, and turn it over to Frankfurter for presentation to the President.

From his earliest days in grammar school in Copenhagen, Bohr's worst subject had been composition. The memorandum to Roosevelt was no different. It was heavy with words, but its message was unmistakable:

The fact of immediate preponderance is . . . that a weapon of an unparalleled power is being created which will completely change all future conditions of warfare . . . Quite apart from the question of how soon the weapon will be ready for use and what role it may play in the present war, this situation raises a number of problems which call for most urgent attention. Unless, indeed, some agreement about the control of the use of the new active materials can be obtained in due time, any temporary advantage, however great, may be outweighed by a perpetual menace to human security . . . The terrifying prospect of a future competition between nations about a weapon of such formidable character can only be avoided through a universal agreement in true confidence . . .

The prevention of a competition prepared in secrecy will therefore demand such concessions regarding exchange of information and openness about industrial efforts including military preparations as would hardly be conceivable unless at the same time all partners were assured of a compensating guarantee of common security against dangers of unprecedented acuteness . . . The main point of the argument is that the accomplishment of the project would not only seem to necessitate but should also, due to the urgency of mutual confidence, facilitate a new approach to the problems of international relationship.

The present moment where almost all nations are entangled in a deadly struggle for freedom and humanity might seem most unsuited for any committing arrangement concerning the project . . . The aggressive powers . . . must ultimately surrender, but even when this happens, the nations united against aggression may face grave causes of disagreement due to conflicting attitudes towards social and economic problems. By a closer consideration, however, it would appear that the potentialities of the project as a means of inspiring confidence just under these circumstances acquire most actual importance. Moreover, the momentary situation would in various respects seem to afford quite unique possibilities which might be forfeited by a postponement awaiting the further development of the war situation and the final completion of the new weapon.

In view of these eventualities, the present situation would seem to offer a most favourable opportunity for an early initiative from the side which by good fortune has achieved a lead in the effort of mastering mighty forces of nature hitherto beyond human approach.[31]

Roosevelt read these words with great interest and looked forward to his meeting with their author. Bohr came to the White House at four o'clock on the afternoon of August 26, 1944,[32] and spoke in private with the President for an hour and a half. This meeting with Roosevelt was Bohr's happiest moment as a statesman. It filled him with hope and satisfaction. The President began by saying that he had read the professor's memorandum very carefully and shared the hopes expressed therein. He asked Bohr to enlarge on those thoughts. Repeating the central themes of the memorandum, Bohr proceeded to speak at length about the importance of an early approach to the Soviet Union. This was the heart of his proposal and he knew that many would argue that the Western powers would have much to lose by such an initiative. It must be assumed, he told Roosevelt, that the Russians knew of the Anglo-American attempts to build an atomic bomb. Russian scientists were surely working on the matter themselves, and they had the skill and industrial capacity to manufacture a bomb when the war with Germany was over. If the United States and Great Britain said nothing about the bomb to the Russians before it was used, great suspicions would be aroused among Soviet leaders. An unprecedented opportunity would be lost to break through the ideological differences separating the two countries to establish a climate of confidence. The initial approach need not be very specific, but if the Russians responded favorably, then the entire matter might be opened up for discussion.

Roosevelt thrilled Bohr by agreeing entirely with his analysis. An approach to Russia must be tried. Stalin, he said, was sufficiently perceptive and realistic to appreciate the revolutionary qualities of this new weapon. The President then went on to tell Bohr of the problem he had at Teheran in preventing clashes between Stalin and Churchill, as if to imply that their uneasy relationship might somehow affect an approach to Russia on atomic matters. He was to meet once more with Churchill in the near future and would discuss with him then an early meeting with Stalin on the matter. As the interview ended, Roosevelt urged Bohr to communicate with him at any time and said that he would particularly like to talk with him again after the meeting with Churchill. Bohr took advantage of this opening by writing to Roosevelt in September with the suggestion that one possible approach to the Russians might be through the Russian scientists themselves. He discussed his relationship with Kapitza and many of the other Soviet scientists and stated his confidence that they were sincere believers in the value of international cooperation. So high were his hopes now that Bohr went so far as to draft a letter to Kapitza and to prepare himself for a visit to Russia after Roosevelt's meeting with Churchill.

But when Churchill and Roosevelt met later in September the worst that Bohr could imagine occurred. Roosevelt did a complete about-face which can only be explained as the result of Churchill's dominance in their discussions of atomic energy. The second Anglo-American conference at Quebec in little more than a year began on September 13, 1944, in what Churchill described to his War Cabinet as "a blaze of friendship." [33] Atomic energy was not discussed until some days later when Churchill and his family went to Hyde Park for a farewell visit with Roosevelt before returning to England. There, on September 19, in the quiet of the evening hours in the Hudson River countryside, they discussed a host of atomic questions which would literally determine the future course of human history. There is no indication that Roosevelt had talked with any of his primary scientific

or diplomatic advisers before these critical words were ex-
changed with Churchill. The resulting aide-mémoire which both
heads of state initialed that day make this clear:

1. The suggestion that the world should be informed regarding tube alloys with a view to an international agreement
   regarding its control and use is not accepted. The matter
   should be regarded as of the utmost secrecy; but when a
   "bomb" is finally available, it might perhaps, after mature
   consideration, be used against the Japanese, who should be
   warned that this bombardment will be repeated until they
   surrender.

2. Full collaboration between the United States and the British
   Government in developing tube alloys for military and
   commercial purposes should continue after the defeat of
   Japan unless and until terminated by joint agreement.

3. Enquiries should be made regarding the activities of Professor Bohr and steps taken to ensure that he is responsible
   for no leakage of information particularly to the Russians.[34]

In the sweep of a single evening's discussion, Churchill had
not only nullified Bohr's heroic attempts to move the world toward postwar cooperation, but he had also totally negated the
worried efforts of Bush, Conant, Stimson, and the others to prohibit postwar British commercial exploitation of atomic energy.
The second paragraph of the Hyde Park aide-mémoire effectively
repealed the fifth section of the Quebec Agreement of 1943
which had left the question of postwar commercial applications
totally up to the President of the United States. The later heated
debates over whether the bomb should be dropped on Japan
seem smothered in pathos when one considers that this decision
had already been made at Hyde Park in 1944. The third para-

graph of the mémoire is pure Churchill and reveals better than anything the tenor of the discussion that day. Not only were Bohr's suggestions rejected, but his honor and integrity were discredited.

After the conference, Churchill wrote to Cherwell in a further attempt to eliminate Bohr:

> The President and I are much worried about Professor Bohr. How did he come into the business? He is a great advocate of publicity. He said he is in close correspondence with a Russian professor, an old friend of his in Russia to whom he has written about the matter and may be writing still. The Russian professor has urged him to go to Russia in order to discuss matters. What is all this about? It seems to me Bohr ought to be confined or at any rate made to see that he is very near the edge of mortal crimes.[35]

Cherwell immediately came to Bohr's defense, telling his Prime Minister that he was being slightly ridiculous. "I have always found Bohr most discreet and conscious of his obligations," Cherwell said, adding that most of the scientific facts concerning atomic weapons "have been publicly discussed for at least six or seven years" and are "published every silly season in most newspapers." [36]

In Washington, Bohr waited anxiously for several weeks for the call to the White House which never came. Slowly he learned what had happened at Hyde Park. Then, later in the autumn of 1944, he returned to Los Alamos, disappointed with his failure but prepared to do battle again before the war was over.

3

Bush, Conant, and Stimson
Begin to Lobby for Atomic Control

DURING THE ANXIOUS WEEKS of the fall of 1944 Niels Bohr found himself forced to make gentle inquiries as to why the President had not summoned him. On one such occasion he was deflected to the quarters of Vannevar Bush at the Office of Scientific Research and Development. The clever Yankee scientist listened sympathetically to his Danish colleague and assured him that he would do all he could to promote his ideas within the Roosevelt Administration. In fact, Bush had been thinking along very much the same lines, as his efforts before the Quebec Agreement of 1943 had shown. More than a half year before his meeting with Bohr, on April 17, 1944, Bush had sent his colleague and thinking partner, James Conant, the copy of a memorandum on postwar atomic control which he had received from an English diplomat. In an accompanying note, Bush recalled their plans to prepare some formal papers on the problems of international and domestic control of atomic energy in the postwar period. Conant agreed and, in a handwritten note on the back of Bush's memo, wrote: "I'm inclined to think the only hope for humanity is an international commission on atomic energy with free access to all information and rights of inspection." [1]

A few months later the restive scientists of the Manhattan Project stirred Bush to accelerate his timetable. With most of the critical work at Chicago now finished or transferred to the other installations of the Manhattan Project at Los Alamos, Oak

Ridge, or Hanford, the scientists at the Met Lab in Chicago had time to worry about the future. They were perplexed at this stage not only over what would come of their work and how the bomb would be used, but also with their own personal futures. In the spring of 1944 a rumor raced through the Chicago laboratory that 90 percent of the personnel there were going to be dismissed and the laboratory ultimately disbanded. Arthur Compton, who was the director of the laboratory, put these rumors to rest. But still the anxiety continued. During the summer of 1944, pressure mounted again for some comprehensive look into the future of atomic energy development. On July 13, 1944, Zay Jeffries, a distinguished metallurgist from General Electric, who was on loan to the Manhattan Project, proposed to Compton that a prospectus be prepared on "nucleonics" — his term for the new industry that would be based on atomic energy. Compton quickly agreed and asked Jeffries to head such a committee whose other members were all Manhattan Project scientists.

Word of this tumult in Chicago reached Bush through Compton and James Franck. Bush wrote to Franck that he shared his concern over postwar problems, but that the time for making proposals had not yet come. It was, however, proper to begin planning, and he and Conant had every intention of doing so in the very near future. In August, Bush informed Compton and Franck that the Military Policy Committee, of which he was chairman, had appointed Richard Tolman, a Cal Tech scientist, to head a committee on postwar needs.

Jeffries and his committee labored diligently over the summer months and into the fall of 1944. They canvassed the Metallurgical Laboratory for ideas and so their report is, in one sense, a reflection of the thoughts of the men who had done the earliest work on atomic weaponry. Early in its existence, the Jeffries Committee decided that it would not limit itself merely to technology but go on to the problem of politics. The report they presented to Arthur Compton on November 18, 1944, not only outlined future applications of atomic energy and power but also contained a section titled: "The Impact of Nucleonics on International Relations and the Social Order." [2] In that section, the Jeffries Committee declared that there should be no doubt that other nations, including the Russians, were diligently involved in the building of atomic bombs. Postwar security could therefore not be based on the dream of sole possession of the atomic weapon by the United States. In fact, the United States would be at a disadvantage because in any atomic war the aggressor enjoys the advantage, even if that aggressor is much smaller than its victim. "The existing gap between continued technologic progress and our relatively static political institutions tends to widen," the committee wrote. Their conclusion was similar to Bohr's:

> We believe that the inevitability of the development of nucleonics by some if not all nations shows compellingly, because of its potential military consequences, the necessity for all nations to make every effort to cooperate now in setting up an international administration with police powers which can effectively control at least the means of nucleonic warfare.

The report of Professor Tolman's committee was thoroughly technical and did not touch on questions of international control. Bush and Conant, however, now saw that it was time to take up those cudgels themselves and to argue their government into some form of action. On September 19, 1944, they addressed a five-page memorandum to Secretary of War Stimson, in which they advocated "the fullest disclosure of the essential scientific facts but not the blue prints of the manufacturing process or the construction of the bombs, either at the time the atomic bomb is used, or if this has not occurred before the close of the Japanese war, at the time of the surrender of Japan." [3] It was mandatory that America be prepared immediately after use of the bomb to enact domestic control legislation and to enter into a treaty with Great Britain and Canada to determine the future nature of their atomic partnership, they argued. At this time and for many months to come Bush and Conant had no knowledge of the sweeping agreement at Hyde Park. As one might expect from their earlier arguments, this memo of September 19 was not terribly generous to the British. They did not choose on this occasion to detail their thoughts on the matter of international control of atomic energy but simply stated once more that the secret of the atomic bomb was no secret at all, and that other nations would possess these devastating new weapons in due time.

Three days after this first memo to Stimson, Bush and Conant began to appreciate how tardy their timing had been. On Friday, September 22, 1944, Bush was called to the President's office at the White House where he found Lord Cherwell, who had come down from the Quebec Conference. Also there was the President's special military adviser, Admiral William Leahy, who had apparently just learned of the atomic bomb project. Bush was startled to find that the topic of discussion would be atomic weapons and particularly their place in the postwar world. Fresh from his Hyde Park meeting with Churchill, the President had certain ideas set firmly in his mind. "I was very much embarrassed," Bush told Conant later that day, "to find myself discussing this subject in the presence of a British representative before having had any opportunity to advise with the President on it privately." [4] Roosevelt expressed his support of the closest possible atomic relations between Britain and the United States after the war, including joint development of atomic energy for military and commercial purposes. "On this," Bush said to

Conant, "I was of course in no position whatever to state what was actually in my mind, namely that too close collaboration with the British, without considering simultaneously the entire world situation, might lead to a very undesirable relationship indeed on the subject with Russia." Bush did find the opportunity, however, to say that after the war there should and would be the widest discussion of atomic science and that he "hoped that this scientific discussion would be participated in also by the Russians." Alluding somewhat defensively to the fact that he and Conant had recently given the Secretary of War a memorandum on postwar questions, Bush offered to tell Stimson that the President was interested in discussing this matter with him. Roosevelt said that would be fine. The President then raised one other question. Should the atomic bomb be used against Japan or should it merely be employed as a threat with full-scale experimentation occurring within America? Bush answered that there were "many sides to this question," but that fortunately it did not have to be approached for some time until the bomb had become a proven fact. "It would be inadvisable to make a threat unless we were distinctly in a position to follow it up if necessary," Bush added. As the conference ended, Roosevelt spoke once more of the importance of the Anglo-American atomic partnership, saying that the only thing which he could see that would interrupt the partnership would be if he and the Prime Minister, Cherwell and Bush were all killed in one railway accident, since they "all saw eye to eye." Cherwell recalled later that in response to this declaration, "Bush said nothing." [5]

Bush left this session deeply shaken by the manner in which the President was pushing ahead without consulting his advisers. He and Conant agreed later that day that they must say to Stimson particularly that he should insist upon giving his advice on this question, even if it was not requested. On the following morning, Bush carried his anxieties to Stimson's personal assistant, Harvey Bundy, a sturdy, faithful Boston lawyer and father of two sons who would later become leading American statesmen in their own right. Bundy was equally troubled by Bush's report and promised to put him in conference with Stimson as soon as possible.

This was arranged for Monday afternoon, September 25, 1944.[6] Stimson was also, not surprisingly, upset to hear from Bush of the conference with Roosevelt and Cherwell. This, however, was not a unique experience for him. He recited to Bush several instances where Roosevelt had recently gone ahead in negotiation without consulting his advisers. Stimson was also pessimistic about the possibility of turning the President's attention to the subject of atomic energy for "a sufficient length of time to give him the reasoned thinking of people who have been studying the subject." But why, Stimson asked, was Bush upset with the trend of the President's own thinking on the matter? Bush's answer was directly to the point:

> I stated that it seemed to me that the President had evidently thought he could join with Churchill in bringing about a US-UK postwar agreement on this subject by which it would be held closely and presumably to control the peace of the world, and I felt that this extreme attitude might well lead to extraordinary efforts on the part of Russia to establish its own position in the field secretly, and might lead to a clash, say 20 years from now.

On the other hand, Bush continued, if there were complete scientific interchange between all nations, then the risk of a secret race would be lessened and the possibility of achieving an international agreement for the control of atomic weapons would be increased. Stimson agreed that this course must be explored. Bush then suggested that he and Conant might prepare a comprehensive position paper on the subject. Stimson, who was thoroughly harassed and fatigued himself by the demands of the war, "grasped at this and said that he would be much indebted" to them if they could prepare such a paper.

Over the next five days, Bush and Conant summoned the ideas they had been discussing for several years and put them into an extremely comprehensive seven-page memorandum which they sent to the Secretary of War on Saturday, September 30, 1944. They also enclosed a three-page condensation of their thoughts. Beginning with a predication that the United States would possess a functional atomic bomb by August 1, 1945, they went on to discuss the future military potential of the weapon, including the development of a hydrogen bomb and the likelihood of using "a robot plane or guided missile" to deliver these devastating weapons. Once more, they emphasized the temporary quality of the Anglo-American advantage which, they said, "lies entirely in the construction of plants for the manufacture of materials." The fundamental basis for construction of the bomb, they continued, "presents no great difficulty and the way that anyone would naturally try to accomplish this will succeed." The Soviet Union could probably develop atomic weapons within three or four years, Bush and Conant wrote. A policy of atomic secrecy was not only illusory but might also have very negative effects on the course of international relations because of the suspicion it would cause within the Soviet Union and other countries. Their proposal, therefore, was to create an "international office responsible to an association of nations" which would guarantee full interchange of information and have access to atomic facilities throughout the world. "It appears to us that Russia would be the one most reluctant to enter into this combination, but since we hold the advantage, if only temporary, in this art it would seem that the *quid pro quo* was evident," Bush and Conant declared. Reluctance would not be limited to the Russians, as they saw it, particularly when it came to inspection of technical installations:

> This . . . would presumably be violently opposed in this country as well as Russia since it would mean in the last analysis the opening of all industrial plans to officials of an international organization. We believe, however, that if people in this country and in other countries are convinced of the terrific potentialities of the new weapons which now lie just over the horizon they will be willing to provide for such an arrangement with due safeguards to commercial secrets.

Three weeks passed before Stimson mentioned to Bush that he had read the memorandum of September 30 and found it very helpful. He had, however, "not yet decided what he ought to do about the subject." [7]

November 1944 was a quiet month in the pursuit of atomic control. Bush traveled to Europe on war business, and Stimson was preoccupied with other matters. Roosevelt, however, was not without advice on the atomic question. Without the knowledge of Bush, Conant, or Stimson, the President was visited early in November by Alexander Sachs, the New York economist and financier who had carried Einstein's famous atomic energy letter to him in 1939.[8] Sachs had stayed abreast of the atomic bomb project. Now, as part of a memorandum to the President on the final phase of the European war and emerging aspects of the Far Eastern war, he submitted a very detailed proposal for use of the atomic bomb:

> Following a successful test, there should be arranged
>
> a) a rehearsal demonstration before a body including internationally recognized scientists from all Allied countries, supplemented by representatives of the major faiths;

b) that a report on the nature and portent of the atomic weapon be prepared by the scientists and other representative figures;

c) that thereafter a warning be issued by the United States and its Allies in the Project to our major enemies in the War, Germany and Japan, that atomic bombing would be applied to a selected area within a designated time limit for the evacuation of human and animal life, and finally;

d) in the wake of such realization of the efficacy of atomic bombing, an ultimatum demand for immediate surrender by the enemies be issued in the certainty that failure to comply would subject their countries and peoples to atomic annihilation.

Sachs contended that this proposal would greatly enhance the political and moral position of the United States in the postwar world. He later added that "while it would have reduced the surprise impact and destruction of life, it would not, save for a minor delay, have diminished the military effectiveness of the threat of total annihilation." Roosevelt engaged Sachs in a lengthy discussion of the proposal and in the end, as Sachs remembers, the President agreed that this was indeed the way the bomb should first be used. Roosevelt, himself, left no record of the conversation.

When Bush came home from Europe, he immediately returned to his personal crusade for postwar atomic control. On December 8, he met with Bundy, Conant, and John M. McCloy, a Wall Street lawyer and long-time friend of Stimson's who now served as Assistant Secretary of War. At this meeting Conant and Bush tried to stimulate the proper thoughts in the heads of their two colleagues from the War Department. They proposed the appointment of an advisory committee to work under the Secretary of War on the necessary legislation to secure postwar domestic control of atomic weapons. On the question of international control, they suggested that it was time for the State Department to be informed. Bundy and McCloy agreed. Four days later, on

December 13, 1944, Bush was able to discuss these matters again with Stimson, who also agreed to the appointment of a committee and to the involvement of the State Department. On the question of international control, the Secretary of War made it quite clear to Bush that he had "very evidently and quite appropriately not yet made up his mind as to what our position should be." [9]

For the administrators of America's atomic program, the last two weeks of December 1944 were taken up with a minor tempest over the flow of Manhattan Project information to French scientists who were involved in the work of the project and who were now returning to liberated France. There was concern about an attempt by France to shoulder its way into the exclusive Anglo-American partnership, and also about the political dispositions of some of the leading French nuclear scientists who happened to be members of the French Communist party. Meanwhile Bush continued to prod Bundy on the question of international control. Together, these two forces moved Stimson to request a meeting with Roosevelt at the end of December.

For Stimson, this marked the beginning of the last and most critical stage of a magnificent career in public service. Born to a New York family whose American roots went as far back as seventeenth-century Massachusetts, Stimson had been educated at Yale College and trained in the law at Harvard. A strong supporter of Theodore Roosevelt, Stimson was chosen as Secretary of War by President Taft. When that term of duty was over, he returned to the practice of law in New York City as a partner of Elihu Root. In 1929 he was called to Washington once more as Secretary of State in Herbert Hoover's Cabinet. Throughout the 1930s he argued against the growing spirit of isolationism in America and finally in June 1940 told a Yale commencement audience that the United States must immediately enact a system of universal, compulsory military training because only the British fleet stood between Hitler and the Western Hemisphere. A day later, Roosevelt asked Stimson to become his Secretary of War. In his personal character and political idealism, Stimson attained a quality of nobility. In the coming struggle over atomic weapons and their control, his decency and trust would be constantly tested.

At eleven o'clock on Saturday morning, December 30, 1944, General Watson called Stimson from the White House to say that the President would see him at noon.[10] Stimson hurriedly summoned General Groves and together they spent fifteen minutes with Roosevelt. The matter of leakage to the French dominated the conversation. Roosevelt was intrigued with the motives of the various parties, and particularly with the possibility that atomic information was finding its way through France to the Soviet Union. Groves reported that the Russians were definitely spying on the American project, particularly at the University of California at Berkeley. Stimson interrupted this discussion of international intrigue to hand the President a copy of a report Groves had prepared for General Marshall. In it he predicted, as Bush before him had done, that the bomb would be ready by August 1, 1945, and that in light of the progress of the war in Europe the target was Japan. Groves also revealed that he had already begun to train a special unit for the atomic attack on Japan. It was carrying out simulated bombing exercises at a base in Utah. The President approved of Groves's report and then indicated that he had to proceed with other business. When Stimson said there was much more to discuss, the President, now more intrigued with the project, invited him to return the following day at noon.

Stimson arrived at the White House at noon on that Sunday and found the President still in bed. There he was able to turn

Roosevelt's attention at last to the primary question of international control. Roosevelt said that he had followed Stimson's advice and yesterday informed Secretary of State Stettinius of the Manhattan Project. Their attention turned then to the coming conference with Churchill and Stalin at Yalta. Troubled by Roosevelt's failing health, Stimson asked why the conference had been scheduled so far from America. The President said that Stalin had set the place and given as his reason his doctor's orders that he not travel far. Both the President and his Secretary of War were troubled by Russia's intentions. Stimson talked of a stern memorandum he had received from General Deane in Moscow in which the General warned America against being too generous toward the Russians and suggested that American negotiators should always insist on a *quid pro quo* relationship. Stimson then turned the conversation to the atomic project as it related to the Soviet Union. He said that he knew the Russians were spying on the American work, but that they had not yet obtained any real knowledge of it. While he "was troubled about the possible effect of keeping from them even now that work," he "believed that it was essential not to take them into our confidence until we were sure to get a real *quid pro quo* from our frankness." Stimson added that he had no illusions about the possibility of keeping such a secret permanently, but he "did not think it was yet time to share it with Russia." Roosevelt said he thought that he agreed with that estimate. There, the discussion and the notable events of the year ended.[11]

Bush learned of this meeting of Roosevelt and Stimson a few days later and was disappointed that nothing had been done to further the appointment of an advisory comittee. He was also led to believe that there had been little discussion of the international aspect of the problem. Throughout January he continued to nudge Harvey Bundy to produce action.

Meanwhile, Secretary of State Stettinius, having been recently allowed into the new world, began pondering atomic questions in a very primitive way. He appointed his Assistant Secretary, James Dunn, to be the department's specialist on atomic energy matters, but Dunn never would find himself near the center of active thought on the problems of postwar control. The War Department, through Bush, Conant, Groves, and Stimson, continued to dominate this vital field of American policy until well after the war was over. On his way to the conference at Yalta during January 1945, Stettinius began to worry in a defensive way about the Soviet Union and the bomb. Roosevelt had told Stettinius of the atomic bomb in rather dramatic fashion, summoning his Secretary upstairs to one of the private rooms at the White House and saying that a bomb was being developed which was so great that "it might be possible to drop this bomb in New York City at Forty-second Street and the resulting explosion would lay New York low." To Stettinius, Roosevelt's description had "seemed like a fantastic dream." [12] On his way to Yalta, Stettinius stopped over in the Azores for a night and sat there the following morning with General Marshall after both of them had enjoyed a "hearty American breakfast" on a terrace looking out across an airfield at the sun rising over the hills across the valley. Their thoughts turned to the unreal question of what to do if the Russians asked about atomic energy at the conference. It is hard to understand how these two eminent statesmen could have imagined that the Russians would embarrass themselves by asking about a project whose contents were supposed to be secret from them. At any rate, Stettinius and Marshall agreed that they "could not plan ahead for such an eventuality and that the matter therefore would have to be handled, depending upon the circumstances and the conditions, as and if it arose." [13] This obtuse conclusion was discussed by Stettinius with Roosevelt in the President's room at Yalta after breakfast on February 5, 1945, and Stettinius reports the President "agreed with the General's position that we should handle any Russian questions if and as they arose." [14] This, of course, was no policy at all.

As February began in Washington, Bush continued the pressure on Bundy, particularly for the appointment of an advisory committee on domestic control problems. He went so far as to begin suggesting the names of possible members, including George L. Harrison, president of the New York Life Insurance Company, and a special consultant to Stimson, as chairman of this advisory committee. Finally, on February 13, Bundy told Bush that Stimson had approved the idea of a committee, but still there was no movement on the question of international control. [15]

Two days later, Bush took the initiative again in a conference with Stimson. [16] The Yalta Conference had just ended on a very friendly note, with the announcement of a meeting in San Francisco during April to draft a United Nations charter. This encouraged Bush in his hopeful view that the Russians could be dealt with productively on the question of atomic energy. He put before Stimson a draft letter to Roosevelt, suggesting the inclusion of a section on scientific interchange in the United Nations Charter, with special emphasis on scientific developments that had military applications. But Stimson was not yet prepared to be so generous toward the Russians. His libertarian spirit had been troubled by the recent Russian claims that Soviet security depended on firm relations with the buffer countries including Poland, Bulgaria, and Rumania. As Stimson saw it, "such firm relations would be quite different from complete independence on the part of these countries." Stimson therefore told Bush that although he agreed that a plan for complete scientific interchange was "along the right lines, it would be inadvisable to put it into full force yet until we had gotten all we could in Russia in the way of liberalization in exchange for S–1 [the American code name for the atomic bomb project]." Bush suggested that perhaps Soviet intentions might be tested by proposing an interchange of information on the question of bacteriological warfare. Stimson agreed that this was one way to go at the problem. "He is a very wise man," Bush wrote of Stimson after this conference, "and I only wish that he had more of the vigor of youth when he is so badly needed."

During the first week in March 1945, Bush and Conant complained to Bundy once more that although the idea of an advisory committee had been approved, nothing had been done to make it a fact. On Monday afternoon, March 5, Bundy finally had a two-hour discussion with Stimson on the future of atomic energy, and brought the matter to the top of the secretary's mind where it would stay for the remaining six months of his service. Stimson wrote of this conference in his diary:

> We are up against some very big decisions. The time is approaching when we can no longer avoid them and when events may force us into the public on the subject. Our thoughts went right down to the bottom facts of human nature, morals, and governments, and it is by far the most searching and important thing that I have had to do since I have been here in the Office of the Secretary of War because it touches matters which are deeper even than the principles of present government.[17]

When Roosevelt returned from Yalta, Stimson felt that the time had come to speak with him more forcefully of atomic energy in the postwar world. He requested an interview at the White House and began to prepare for it on Thursday morning, March 15, 1945, expecting the appointment to be granted for Friday or Saturday. Instead, the White House called that morning with an invitation to have lunch with the President. This made Stimson "hustle like fury," as he put it, in order to get ready for the meeting. Roosevelt began by referring to a memorandum he had received from James Byrnes, the Director of War Mobilization, who revealed that the word was out that Bush and Conant "had sold the President a lemon" in the Manhattan Project. Byrnes suggested the appointment of a committee of outside experts to evaluate the project and to protect the President from future criticism. Stimson quickly assured Roosevelt that there was very little doubt that the bomb would work, adding that "practically every physicist of standing was engaged with us in the project." Outlining the future of the atomic weapon, Stimson went easily into a discussion of what he called, "the two schools of thought that exist in respect to the future control after the war of this project." One of these was "the secret, close-in attempted control of the project by those who control it now." The other was "international control based upon freedom both of science and of access." [18] Stimson added that these questions must be settled before the first bomb was used and that the President must be ready with a statement to be released on the subject as soon as the world knew about it. Roosevelt agreed that this was the course to follow. Nothing more definitive was said about which school of postwar policy the President favored. Stimson left, hoping that he had stirred within his war-weary colleague's spirit the same anxious concern that Bush, Conant, and Bundy had stirred within him. At their next meeting, he would develop the central themes further and try to move the President toward a decision. But sadly there was no next meeting.

4

Scientific Agitation

FAR AWAY from this quiet meeting of Roosevelt and Stimson, the scientists in Chicago, surrounded by the wall of silence General Groves had built around them, were increasingly perplexed. Their professional worries over the future course of atomic energy research and development continued. To these were added more comprehensive concerns about international control of atomic weapons and, as 1945 began, about what use would be made of the bomb in the war. A consensus on these questions emerged, at least among the most vocal members of the Met Lab. One of them wrote later:

> We were troubled by the fact that except for the scientists and the Army there was no foreknowledge of the tremendous implications of the atom bomb, and we felt someone should attempt to represent the public conscience and that at least we scientists should discuss among ourselves the tremendous social and political implications of atomic warfare.[1]

This feeling of isolation was understandable but unnecessary. The consensus among the scientists about questions of international control was entirely along the lines that Bush and Conant had been arguing to the nation's leaders since the previous autumn. It is unfortunate that the Chicago Met Lab workers did not know this, for it would have saved them many months of anxiety.

Two political developments stirred the scientists to action

during the early months of 1945. One was the course of the war in Europe. After the Battle of the Bulge, the early defeat of the Germans was becoming more likely. Information from liberated France made it clear that the German atomic bomb project had fallen flat. The American bomb would therefore not be used against Germany, but against Japan. For many of the atomic scientists, building the bomb for use against Japan simply to end the war sooner was a far less appealing goal than building the bomb to destroy Nazi Germany. Their feelings against Japan had not risen to the level of their fury against the Nazis. The desire for revenge against the Germans among the European refugee scientists was never matched by a similar desire, so widespread among Americans, for revenge against the Japanese for their attack on Pearl Harbor. Nor did the scientists ever feel that they were in a competition with the Japanese to build the bomb first. They knew that the Japanese did not have the capacity to build a nuclear weapon during the war.

The other development which moved the scientists during the early months of 1945 was the Yalta communiqué and the emerging plans for a United Nations organization. They were deeply troubled by the universal ignorance of atomic weaponry — a factor which would entirely change the nature of the postwar world that the United Nations was supposed to harmonize and make orderly.

These two forces moved two leading scientist-statesmen to action once more: Leo Szilard and Niels Bohr.

Szilard, the restless, innovative Hungarian who had moved America into atomic development during the late thirties, now resolved to move it toward sensible use and control of the fruits of that development. In March 1945, he wrote a memorandum which he hoped to take to Roosevelt. In this paper Szilard did not argue against use of the bomb over Japan but merely stated his understanding that Japan would be the target. His emphasis was on the postwar picture. He portrayed the uncontrolled atom as a menace to the United States because when this country's atomic head start was overcome, as it certainly would be, the densely populated urban centers of America would be entirely susceptible to atomic destruction. Szilard also discussed the temptation that would exist for aggressor nations to take the advantage by striking first with nuclear weapons. He went on to consider methods of international control, including the possibility of denaturing atomic material. Perhaps, he concluded, all use of atomic energy would have to be prohibited because it would be impossible to allow for peaceful development and still prevent military use of this new power source. At least, Szilard wrote to the President, these problems should be considered.[2]

Once again Szilard decided to ask Albert Einstein to be his messenger to the White House. Einstein was agreeable and wrote to Roosevelt on March 25, 1925, expressing Szilard's concerns and requesting a Presidential interview for him:

> I understand that he [Szilard] now is greatly concerned about the lack of adequate contact between scientists who are doing this work and those members of your Cabinet who are responsible for formulating policy. In the circumstances, I consider it my duty to give Dr. Szilard this introduction and I wish to express the hope that you will be able to give his presentation of the case your personal attention.[3]

The President did not see this letter before leaving the White House on March 29 for a period of rest in Warm Springs, Georgia.

Bohr meanwhile had become anxious over the loss of precious time during which the Russians might be brought in on atomic development. He knew that work on the bomb was close to a successful completion. If the weapon were used without prior consultation with the Russians, Bohr concluded, there would be very little hope of avoiding a nuclear arms race. Time was running out. In March 1945, he sat down once more to prepare a memorandum. In it he proposed early contact with the Russians and added:

> In preliminary consultations between the governments with the primary purpose of inspiring confidence and relieving disquietude, it should be necessary only to bring up the problem of what the attitude of each partner would be if the prospects opened up by the progress of physical science, which in outline are common knowledge, should be realized to an extent which would necessitate exceptional action . . . All such opportunities may, however, be forfeited if an initiative is not taken while the matter can be raised in a spirit of friendly advice. In fact, a postponement to await further developments might, especially if preparations for competitive efforts in the meantime have reached an advanced stage, give the approach the appearance of an attempt at coercion in which no great nation can be expected to acquiesce.[4]

Bohr discussed these ideas again with the British ambassador, Lord Halifax, and requested that he be called to London to confer once more with Sir John Anderson. This visit was made during March 1945. Although Anderson was as positively inclined toward Bohr's ideas as he had been on every earlier occasion, he told Bohr that Churchill's unswerving opposition made any further attempts in England futile. Bohr's emphatic concern over the tardiness of an approach to the Russians had not altered his prospects with Churchill in the slightest. The only course was to return once more to America and try to see Roosevelt again.

Bohr arrived in Washington on April 4, 1945, and immediately went to see Halifax, who decided to consult Justice Frankfurter about tactics. On April 12, Halifax and Frankfurter walked together through Rock Creek Park in Washington, agreeing on the need to put Bohr's ideas once more before Roosevelt. As their walk ended, the springtime air of Washington was suddenly filled with the sound of bells tolling. Roosevelt had died in Warm Springs. Later Frankfurter wrote to Halifax: "Odd wasn't it that our dear friend should have died the very time you and I were pooling our forebodings." [5]

And so the visionary thoughts of Stimson, Bohr, and Szilard never reached Roosevelt. Before his death the President was so preoccupied with the war and so weary from the long years of service that he never really focused on the problems of postwar control of atomic energy. It is impossible to say whether the course of events would have been different if he had lived. His advantage would have been in the experience of office. He would not have had to go through the process of learning his way as Truman after him did. But Roosevelt's tendency to defer to Churchill in these matters makes it ultimately unlikely that the atomic future would have been different from what it was.

During the late afternoon of April 12, 1945, Vice President Harry S. Truman was fulfilling the major responsibility of his office, presiding over the United States Senate. Uninterested in the debate going on then regarding river rights under a treaty with Mexico, he took up a pen and paper and began a letter to his mother and sister back home in Missouri. The journey for Truman from his home in Missouri to that chair in the Senate had not been a speedy one. His first job, which he stayed at for eleven years from 1906 to 1917, was working on his father's farm. After service in World War I, he opened a haberdashery store in Kansas City with his soldier friend Eddie Jacobson. That failed three years later, and only then, at the age of thirty-eight, did Truman enter politics. By 1934 he was running successfully for the United States Senate as a New Dealer. Then ten years later, Roosevelt, in search of stability and anonymity, asked Truman to run for Vice President. Truman had never lost his very common touch. On that late afternoon in April 1945, Truman wrote to his mother and sister about his new job: "I have to sit up here and make parliamentary rulings — some of which are common sense and some of which are not." At the end of the letter he advised: "Turn on your radio tomorrow night at 9:30 your time and you'll hear Harry make a Jefferson Day address to the nation." Little more than two hours later Roosevelt was dead and at 7:09 P.M., "Harry" was being sworn in as President of the United States.[6]

After the first brief Truman Cabinet meeting that evening, Stimson stayed on when all the others had solemnly filed out of the room. He asked to speak with the new President about an important matter. Stimson wanted Truman to know about an immense project then under way — "a project looking to the development of a new explosive of almost unbelievable destructive power." That was all he would say at that time, and this left the new President "puzzled." The next day, James Byrnes filled in the story. Truman now recalled the one previous contact he had with the Manhattan Project. During the war his famed Truman Committee, which specialized in watching the expenditure of federal moneys, had been about to investigate the Manhattan Project. They were stopped by Stimson in a phone call to Truman who simply took the Secretary of War's word for it that this was off limits. No further questions were asked. Otherwise, Roosevelt, Stimson, and all the others had either forgotten to tell Truman about the atomic bomb or chosen not to. The previous Vice President, Henry Wallace, had been a member of an overseer committee from the beginning of the Manhattan Project, probably because of his scientific background. When it came to Truman, however, no one had considered the prospect of Roosevelt's mortality.

Roosevelt's death deepened the anxieties of the scientists in

Chicago. They did not view Truman as the kind of man who would be sympathetic to their concerns. James Franck, the German Nobel Prize winner who was chief of the chemistry section of the Chicago laboratory, chose this occasion to recollect a promise Arthur Compton had made to him. Like so many of the others, Franck was a Jew who had run from his homeland to America to escape nazism. Born in 1882, Franck had distinguished himself among his scientific colleagues during World War I by seeing active duty in the German Army and rising to the rank of captain, an exceptional position for a Jew in the German military caste system. From 1920 he had been the head of the Second Physics Institute at the University of Göttingen where young physicists from throughout the world, including Oppenheimer and Karl Compton, had come to study. When he won the Nobel Prize in 1925 for experimentation in atomic research which confirmed some of Bohr's earlier theories, Franck's students carried him through the streets on their shoulders in a torchlight parade. Eight years later, with the onset of Hitlerism, he resigned his chair at the university and was rapidly attacked by thirty-three of his colleagues in a public letter for sabotaging the new Germany. At first he had hoped to remain in Germany, but then in 1934 he realized that the situation was intolerable and fled to Copenhagen to join his friend Bohr. From there he went on to America.

Franck's voice was soft and his manners gentle. He had dark skin and black hair, which was no doubt a legacy from his Sephardic ancestors who had traveled from Spain to Hamburg. His thin face was dominated by narrow brown eyes that were capable of radiating their great sadness or great joy and reminded his colleagues of Einstein's.[7]

When Arthur Compton had asked James Franck to become the chief of the chemistry section of the Met Lab, he had agreed on the sole condition that if no other nation had built an atomic bomb by the time the United States was prepared to use its weapon, Compton would enable him to argue about its use at the highest level of the American government. In April 1945, Franck decided to collect on Compton's promise. With the assistance of his friend and former student at Göttingen, Eugene Rabinowitch, Franck wrote a memorandum which expressed the ideas then current at the Met Lab. Franck's statement was very much like the ones Bohr and Bush had been arguing for several months. He spoke of the impossibility of maintaining the atomic secret and the American advantage and concluded that pursuit of international control was the only rational course. Franck's deepest concern was the oath of secrecy which the scientists had taken. He described the Army's regulations as "intolerable" because they had brought about a conflict "between our conscience as citizens and human beings and our loyalty to the oath of secrecy." He explained:

> We read and hear about all the efforts which the best statesmen devote to peace planning in Dunbarton Oaks, San Francisco, etc., and we hear about plans to control industries, etc., in the aggressor states, but we know in our hearts that all these plans are obsolete because the future war has an entirely different and a thousand times more sinister aspect than the war which is fought now. How is it possible that the statesmen are not informed that the aspect of the world and its future is entirely changed by the knowledge that atomic energy can be tapped, and how is it possible that the men who know these facts are prevented from informing the statesmen about the situation? [8]

Compton was faithful to his promise to Franck. Arising from the cloud of desperation that fell over the Met Lab after Roosevelt's death, Franck's memorandum and plea to be heard struck Compton as an opportunity. By arranging for Franck to be heard, he might overcome some of the other scientists' anxiety and fatalism. On April 21, 1945, Compton traveled with Franck to Washington. There, over breakfast at the Wardman Park Hotel, the two scientists met with Henry Wallace, Secretary of Commerce and former Vice President. Wallace had been one of the original members of the five-man committee appointed by Roosevelt in 1941 to oversee atomic development, but he had hardly been at the center of atomic activity in recent months. The breakfast discussion was friendly but hurried. Wallace took a copy of the Franck memorandum and passed it along to Vannevar Bush. Franck returned to Chicago, hardly reassured.

Once again, however, Franck and his concerned colleagues in Chicago had somewhat more cause for hope than they knew. Henry L. Stimson had begun to move in the direction of their concerns. On April 24, 1945, twelve days after Truman had ascended to the Presidency, Stimson decided he had given the nation's new leader enough time to catch his breath. He wrote to Truman, suggesting that they talk about atomic energy in the immediate future. The President's interest in the subject had been heightened by his talk with Byrnes, who had said that the new weapon "might be so powerful as to be potentially capable of wiping out entire cities and killing people on an unprecedented scale." In fact, Byrnes had told Truman, "the bomb might well put us in a position to dictate our own terms at the end of the war." [9] Truman summoned Stimson for discussion at noon on April 25, the day following his request. The Secretary of War brought General Groves with him, although Groves entered the White House through a separate underground passage to avoid a joint arrival with Stimson that might set the press to wondering. Stimson had a memo with him on the impact of the atomic bomb on the postwar world. In this, Truman noted, Stimson was unlike Byrnes because he "seemed at least as much concerned with the role of the atomic bomb in shaping of history as in its capacity to shorten this war." [10] The President, Stimson, and Groves sat together in the sunlit office reading over Stimson's memo and then one prepared by Groves. These recited the history of the bomb project and predicted its success within four months. By August, a bomb would be ready for use against Japan which, according to Groves, "had always been the target." [11] Stimson spoke out against the notion of keeping the atomic secret or advantage very long and added that "probably the only nation which could enter into production within the next few years is Russia." He argued for a system of international control which would be unique in its demands on the nations of the world. A select committee of advisers should be designated by the President, Stimson said, to recommend "action to the Executive and Legislative branches of our government when secrecy is no longer in full effect." According to the secretary, "The committee would also recommend the actions to be taken by the War Department prior to that time in anticipation of the postwar problems." It is not clear whether Stimson had in mind the question of how the bomb should be used or the matter of planning for postwar control. [12]

Stimson's conclusion, however, was clear and moving:

> Our leadership in the war and in the development of this weapon has placed a certain moral responsibility upon us which we cannot shirk without very serious responsibility for any disaster to civilization which it would further . . . If the problem of the proper use of this weapon can be solved, we would have the opportunity to bring the world into a pattern in which the peace of the world and our civilization can be saved.

When the interview was over, Stimson thought the discussion "had very much interested" Truman. For his part, the President found it "enlightening," and thought, as he saw Stimson to the door, "how fortunate the country was to have so able and so wise a man in its service."

Niels Bohr chose that same day to visit Vannevar Bush with a copy of the memorandum he had prepared for Roosevelt but never given him. By this time Bohr had lowered his sights. If the sharing of atomic development with other nations was impossible, then at least some announcement of the existence of the atomic bomb and some consideration of its control should begin immediately while the wartime alliance was still in effect. Bohr never mentioned Russia by name, but no one could mistake his intent. Bush reassured his troubled colleague that he was in complete agreement with this view and was using much of his energy to argue it to Stimson and the President. He sent a copy of Bohr's memorandum to Harvey Bundy at the War Department with a strong accompanying letter of support. Reminding Bundy of his earlier attempts to have an advisory committee appointed, Bush said, "the sudden death of the President probably resulted in complete lack of any definite action." [13] Time was now very short, Bush said, and "there are certain steps which should be taken at once, because they will be timely at the present moment and will not be nearly as timely later on."

Bush's letter had the desired effect. It moved Bundy once more into action. On May 1, 1945, he and George Harrison met with Secretary Stimson to talk about the formation of the advisory committee because, as they put it, "we are getting close to the time when something is likely to happen which will require publicity." [14] Stimson agreed. He also liked the list of members Bundy had suggested. It included Stimson himself as chairman, with Harrison as his alternate and administrative chief on the project. The other members were to be Undersecretary of the Navy Ralph Bard, Bush, Assistant Secretary of State William L. Clayton, Karl Compton, Conant, and a special personal representative appointed by the President.

Stimson took this list with him to Truman's office at 11:30 on the following morning and had a "very pleasant and satisfactory conference" there on the creation of the advisory committee. The President accepted the names which Stimson proposed, adding his belief that those would be sufficient without a personal emissary of his own. Stimson, however, wanted Truman to be represented and suggested that they try to think of a man "with whom the President had close personal relations and . . . who was able to keep his mouth shut." [15] A day later, after conferences with Bundy and Harrison, Stimson telephoned Truman to suggest James Byrnes as the Presidential representative on the committee. Truman said he would think about it. Later in the afternoon, he called Stimson to say he had talked with Byrnes in South Carolina and Byrnes had accepted the appointment.

On May 4, 1945, Stimson mailed letters of appointment to the members of the advisory committee, telling them that their job would be "to study and report on the whole problem of temporary war controls and later publicity, and to survey and make recommendations on postwar research, development and controls, as well as legislation necessary to effectuate them." [16] All of the members quickly accepted, except Conant who wrote a thoughtful letter to Stimson on May 5 expressing doubt as to whether he and Bush "were proper representatives of the scientific group, for we have been primarily distant administrators rather than active participants." That was exactly what many of the scientists themselves had been muttering, and it is a mark of Conant's acumen that he appreciated it. He also told Stimson of the "growing restlessness" among the Manhattan Project scientists about the international implications of the bomb. "Many of the scientists have a feeling of reluctance about the whole endeavor," Conant wrote, "and wish, as I certainly do, that there had been some physical reason why the undertaking proved to be impossible." America's relations with Russia were of particular concern to the scientists, who feared that a failure to communicate with the Russians before employing the bomb would lead to a secret armaments race. To allay the anxieties of the scientists, Conant asked for permission to distribute his and Bush's memorandum of the preceding September 30 and to tell the Chicago people that Stimson had conveyed some of these ideas to Truman. Conant also urged that a panel of leading scientists be appointed to advise this new committee which Stimson had appointed.[17]

Stimson insisted that Conant be on the committee, but agreed that a few of the leading scientists could be shown the Bush-Conant memorandum and that an advisory scientific panel should be appointed from among the active participants in the Manhattan Project. This eventually included Arthur Compton, Enrico Fermi, Ernest O. Lawrence, and J. Robert Oppenheimer — an imperfect group for the purposes Conant had in mind because they too were administrators and not among those most agitated over the postwar atomic future. They were certainly concerned, but they were not legitimate representatives of the young scientists who were most anxious or the older men, like Szilard and Franck, who were most restless.

Wasting no time at this late hour, Stimson summoned the committee into session on Wednesday, May 9, 1945. He had called it an "interim committee" out of deference to Congress which might later want to create a permanent body with similar functions. Most of those men who came to the War Department that day did not even know the basic scientific facts behind atomic weaponry. Stimson therefore introduced the subject and Groves followed with a more comprehensive scientific lesson. They met again on May 14 to consider what publicity should be released after the weapon was used and what should be the nature of government support for atomic research. The records of this meeting do not indicate that there was any consideration given to the question of *whether* the bomb should be used or to how its use might affect the prospects of international atomic control after the war. Bush, however, distributed a copy of his and Conant's memorandum of September 30, 1944, together with a copy of the report of the Jeffries Committee. He also urged George Harrison, as leader of the committee, to talk with Niels Bohr.[18]

On that same day, however, Stimson was discussing use of the bomb and its relation to the postwar world with the British Foreign Secretary, Anthony Eden, who was visiting Washington. In the preceding weeks Stimson's attitude toward Russia had hardened as a result of a series of petty conflicts with the Russians and broader discussions with American statesmen. He had been especially angered by the Russians' refusal to allow American planes and officers behind Soviet lines in Poland and eastern Germany to collect and bring home American prisoners who were being uncovered by the Russian advance through Germany. The Soviets had also turned down an American request for permission to visit Gdynia, Poland, to have a look at some captured German submarines which might be of help to the American Navy in its activities in the North Sea.[19] Stalin himself had continued to make claims on the countries of Eastern Europe based on his vision of the security which the Soviet Union had won in war. The Americans viewed these claims very dimly. Stimson had recently had a "rather gloomy" luncheon with Averell Harriman, the American ambassador to Moscow. Harriman told the Secretary of War, in response to his inquiries on the subject, that "he didn't think there was any chance of getting the seeds of liberalism into Russia in the shape of liberalizing and implementing the new constitutions for the sixteen Soviet provinces or zones which

Stalin has put forth but never implemented." Stimson then "talked over very confidentially" the role of the atomic bomb as it related to Soviet-American relations.[20]

This was the state of Stimson's thinking when he sat down to confer with Eden on May 14. They spoke at great length about the bomb and its possible effect on the Soviet Union. When the discussion with Eden was over, Stimson had come to some conclusions. He reported to John McCloy that "the time now and the method now to deal with Russia was to keep our mouths shut and let our actions speak for words. The Russians will understand them better than anything else." The Russians had taken the lead, Stimson had told Eden, "because we have talked too much and have been too lavish with our beneficences . . . This [the atomic bomb] was a place where we really held all the cards. I called it a royal straight flush and we mustn't be a fool about the way we play it. They can't get along without our help and industries and we have coming into action a weapon which will be unique. Now the thing is not to get into unnecessary quarrels by talking too much and not to indicate any weaknesses by talking too much." [21]

These preeminent diplomatic matters finally received some attention — albeit casual — from the Interim Committee at its third meeting on May 18, 1945. The major business of that session was a review of draft statements which had been prepared for release after the bomb was dropped on Japan. When that work was over, James Byrnes, knowing that he would soon be appointed Secretary of State, said that he wanted to talk about some of the relevant, international questions. He had read the Bush-Conant memorandum of September 30, 1944, and wondered particularly about their estimate that it would take the Russians only three or four years after the war to build an atomic bomb. If this were so, then it would have considerable bearing on whether the President should tell the Russians about the bomb before it was used. General Groves, who was again in attendance though he was not a member of the Interim Committee, took issue with the Bush-Conant estimate, claiming it would more likely take the Russians twenty years to build a nuclear weapon. Conant explained his disagreement and there the discussion how to relate to Russia ended.[22] The next meeting of the committee was scheduled for May 31, at which time the scientific panel would be heard.

One scientist, however, did not wait his turn. The change in Presidents had not altered Leo Szilard's desire to bring his plea to the White House.[23] In fact, his concern with atomic use and control had intensified after the German Armies surrendered to General Eisenhower on May 7. With a talent at tactical maneuvering that would elicit awe from the most seasoned statesman, soldier, or politician, Szilard began an intricate series of moves that he hoped would bring him finally to a conference with Truman at the White House. His most exciting discovery was that Albert Cahn, a young mathematician working at the Chicago laboratory, had once labored in the political vineyards for the Pendergast machine in Kansas City — the habitat from which Harry S Truman had emerged. Szilard persuaded Cahn to travel with him to Kansas City to offer an introduction there. In a bizarre confrontation this great scientist was able to convince the minor potentates of Kansas City politics to try to arrange an interview for him with the President. Truman was no doubt shocked to receive a request for a meeting with a Chicago scientist from his former political cronies. Nevertheless, he was sufficiently moved either by the source of the request or its apparent topic to turn the matter over to his personal secretary, Matthew Connelly, with the suggestion that the concerned scientist be sent to visit James Byrnes, who was then at home in Spartanburg,

South Carolina. Szilard did not know why he was being sent
to Byrnes but was delighted on May 25 to make this trip anyway.
He brought Walter Bartky, associate dean of the physical sciences
at Chicago, and Harold Urey of the Columbia University Laboratory of the Manhattan Project.

It would be difficult to find two more different people than
Szilard and Byrnes. The one, an arrogant, idealistic, and opinion-
ated physicist who was very much the European and seemed to
enjoy goading people in authority; the other a complete southern
gentleman, moderate in philosophy and practical in instinct, who
had served as United States Senator and Supreme Court Justice
and in little more than a month would become Secretary of State.
Their meeting in May 1945 on the subject of atomic weapons
followed a predictable course. It was a fiasco. After reading
Szilard's memorandum, Byrnes announced that General Groves
had told him that Russia had no uranium and therefore could
not participate in an atomic arms race. Controlling himself,
Szilard described this as "an exceedingly unlikely assumption."
Byrnes next dismissed Szilard's appeal "that scientists including
himself should discuss the matter with the Cabinet." Of the
Hungarian physicist personally, the South Carolina statesman
thought even less: "His general demeanor and his desire to
participate in policy-making made an unfavorable impression
on me." For their part, Szilard, Bartky, and Urey were heartbroken over what they took to be Byrnes's primitive view of
atomic energy as a card up his sleeve to be employed with
bravado in international relations, particularly against the Soviet
Union. They concluded that Byrnes did not even know about
the nonmilitary uses of atomic energy. Much of their time on
that afternoon in South Carolina was therefore spent in a frantic
effort to educate Byrnes. There was only the slightest opportunity
for Szilard to present an argument he had recently entertained

that perhaps the wisest way to avert an atomic arms race would be for the United States not to bring the bomb into the war against Japan, but, in fact, to lead the Soviet Union to believe that the Manhattan Project had failed. Byrnes was less concerned with use of the bomb in the war than he was with the way in which the weapon might be used to make the Russians "more manageable" in Eastern Europe after the war. When Szilard returned to Chicago and learned that Byrnes would soon become Secretary of State, he was horrified and concluded that his ideas would receive no consideration.

When General Groves learned of the Szilard-Byrnes meeting from the security guard he had assigned to follow Szilard, he immediately summoned Bartky to Washington for a reprimand. Bartky, however, used the occasion to educate Groves on how deeply ran the currents of concern among the Manhattan Project scientists. If Bartky's arguments had any effect on Groves, that was undoubtedly the only positive result of the Szilard-Byrnes confrontation.

At this same time, another member of the Manhattan Project, far from the center of scientific lobbying in Chicago, somehow managed to get through to the top of the American government with ideas that were in some ways more radical than the ones Szilard had argued. During the third week in May 1945, Stimson's doctors ordered him to take a week's rest or face a physical collapse. For once he obeyed and traveled north to Highhold, his rambling shingled home in Huntington, Long Island, which sat on the summit of the central ridge of Long Island and looked out at the Sound to the north and the distant ocean to the south. From there he called the President on Sunday, May 27, 1945, to report that he was feeling better and planned to return to Washington. Stimson told Truman that he was going to spend the entire coming week and most of the rest of the time after that solely on the atomic bomb and its ramifications. On Wednesday, May 30, George Harrison, knowing that his chief was immersed in thoughts of atomic energy, brought in a letter from Owen Brewster, an engineer for the Kellex Corporation in New York who was one of a small team toiling there for the Manhattan Project on the gaseous diffusion process of separating uranium isotopes. Brewster was a Quaker who, when originally asked to go to work on the atomic bomb project, had written to General Groves requesting that he be relieved of his duties. Groves, however, convinced him to stay on for the good of his country. But the general had been so taken by Brewster's thoughts that he showed his letter to Stimson who read it and said: "This man is a man of integrity." Now, in May 1945, Brewster had taken up his pen once more to write to no less a personage than the President, with copies to Stimson and General Marshall. It was the copy of this letter that Harrison brought in to Stimson on that last Wednesday in May 1945. Like the others who had written before him, Brewster predicted the impossibility of America's remaining an atomic monopolist for very long. One day great chunks of the world would be consumed by nuclear flames, Brewster warned, unless some system of international control was achieved. Brewster stopped short of suggesting that the United States not use any atomic weapons against Japan if that seemed militarily necessary. He did, however, urge that the country announce its possession of the bomb and its willingness to demonstrate its power, but that it also renounce any plans for world domination founded on this unique new force. He also advocated cessation of atomic production as a show of good faith. Stimson considered this to be a "very important" letter. He sent a copy to Marshall, asking him to read it before the meeting of the Interim Committee on the following day, and resolved to bring another copy to the President.

5

The Interim Committee's
Perfunctory Response

STIMSON WAS therefore not without policy alternatives when he convened the important two-day meeting of the Interim Committee in the Pentagon on the morning of May 31, 1945. Although he was not feeling hopeful about the Russians, he had not yet made up his mind about an approach to them about the bomb. The thoughts of Bush, Conant, Bohr, and Brewster concerning postwar international control were familiar to him. On the question of whether to use the bomb, however, and how its use might affect the prospects for international control, it is not clear that he had been exposed to any thoughts which would have moved him to try to stop the momentum of the Manhattan Project. It was now moving, largely on its own with perhaps a slight assist from General Groves, toward an atomic attack on Japan. General Groves had already activated his forces for bombing against Japan. Special plane crews had been in training for almost a year at the Wendover Air Force Base in Utah. Several possible targets had been selected. A detailed procedure for transport and final assembly of the bomb had been established. It would have taken a very compelling policy argument and a strong man to turn this powerful juggernaut from its course — especially in light of the two billion dollars that had been spent on the Manhattan Project with little specific knowledge by Congress. To base an argument against use of the bomb on speculative and somewhat vague notions of the way its use might affect the prospects for postwar control would have been wise but hardly likely to succeed. General Groves has spoken rather poignantly of the role of the President of the United States in the decision to use the bomb: "As far as I am concerned, his decision was one of noninterference — basically a decision not to upset the existing plans." [1] To Groves, Truman was "like a little boy on a toboggan. He never had an opportunity to say 'we will drop the bomb.' All he could do was say no." [2] And Churchill, who had reason to know, wrote: "The historic fact remains and must be judged in the aftertime that the decision whether or not to use the atomic bomb to compel the surrender of Japan was never even an issue." [3]

At the May 31 meeting of the Interim Committee, the question of whether or how to use the bomb was given its only formal consideration, and this was not lengthy or deep. The matter was not even on the agenda. During the morning session in Stimson's office it came up only indirectly as part of a broader presentation on the state of the weapon by the four members of the scientific panel — Arthur Compton, Fermi, Lawrence, and Oppenheimer. Stimson's primary concern during this discussion seemed to be to impress the scientists that there were thinking men at the top deciding how the product of so much scientific labor was going to be used. He told them that he did not regard the atomic bomb "as a new weapon merely but as a revolutionary change in the relations of man to the universe and that we wanted to take advantage of this, that the project might even mean the doom of civilization or it might mean the perfection of civilization, that it might be a Frankenstein which would eat us up or it might be a project by which the peace of the world would be helped in becoming secure." [4]

When the scientists dwelled too long on the destructive potentialities of atomic energy, Stimson nudged them to reflect on some of the nonmilitary possibilities. Oppenheimer took this opening and responded very generally. The nonmilitary goals of atomic energy development were most general — the advancement of human welfare. The proper atmosphere for such progress could be created only if the United States offered free interchange of atomic information with emphasis on peacetime uses. It would be especially beneficial if this offer came before the bomb was used. These ideas were, of course, not new to Stimson, but now he asked what kind of inspection would be effective against abuse of an international exchange and control agreement and how democracies would fare against totalitarian states. The scientists immediately rallied to the flag, claiming that the advantage would lie with the democracies. Their reasons for saying this were not clear, although they did cite the Anglo-American success in atomic development as compared to the Nazi failure. As always, Vannevar Bush kept his balance. He doubted that the United States could stay perpetually ahead of the Soviet Union in atomic development.

At 11:30 Stimson had to leave the meeting for a White House ceremony. While he was gone the discussion turned toward a question he had raised. Should the United States tell the Soviet Union about the bomb? The scientists answered yes, stressing the traditional Russian friendliness toward international science. Oppenheimer suggested that the Russian attitude not be prejudged but tested in a step-by-step inquiry and plan of exchange. General Marshall was less sanguine. During the war he had found the Russians to be distinctly uncooperative in sharing military information, a fact which he attributed to their notion of what was necessary for their own security. He tended toward a strong postwar non-Soviet alliance which could keep the Russians in line, but he was not against telling them about the bomb. He even wondered out loud whether it might not be desirable to invite two prominent Russians to the first atomic test at Los Alamos in July.

Then James Byrnes stepped in and the matter was decided. If any initiative was made to the Russians, Stalin would undoubtedly ask to be made a full partner, the future Secretary of State said. Byrnes's inexperience at international relations makes one wonder at the certainty with which he made such proclamations about the Soviet character. The United States simply could not afford to have Russia as a partner in atomic development, he continued. Therefore the best course was to push full speed ahead with nuclear development while trying to improve relations with the Soviet Union in the broader area of international relations. Byrnes clearly did not agree with those who suggested that America's covertness in matters of atomic energy would itself seriously limit the possibilities of harmonious international relations with the Soviet Union. When Byrnes was finished, "all present indicated their concurrence."

This turn of the discussion made a great deal of what followed anticlimactic or, perhaps even worse, deceitful. "Throughout the morning's discussions," Arthur Compton later recalled, "it seemed to be a foregone conclusion that the bomb would be used." E. O. Lawrence had briefly mentioned the possibility of giving the Japanese "some striking but harmless demonstration of the bomb's power" before going ahead and using it against a populated area of Japan. At lunch, when Stimson had rejoined the group, Byrnes took Lawrence up on this suggestion and asked one or two of the others what they thought about it. Arthur Compton began a similar discussion with Stimson during the meal. Then, Stimson opened up the question for consideration by the full group. It received about ten minutes of attention. Oppenheimer wondered whether there was any show of atomic weapons that would be sufficiently compelling to induce the

Japanese to surrender. Others, like Conant, asked what would happen if the demonstration were a dud or if the plane carrying the bomb were shot down. Still others spoke of the value of the shock effect of the atomic bomb. There the discussion ended meekly without any resolution that might deter General Groves's vast machine.

That afternoon's program involved several decisions which would also have a major impact on the course of postwar attempts to achieve international control, but again that particular dimension was not considered. After general discussion the committee agreed, at Stimson's suggestion, on two conclusions: first, that the United States should choose a target in Japan which was not a civilian area but which would nevertheless inflict a profound psychological shock on the Japanese; and, second, that the Japanese should be given no warning before the attack. At the afternoon session on the following day, Byrnes turned these conclusions into a resolution which would be forwarded as the committee's recommendation to the Secretary of War and the President. His recommendation was adopted unanimously.

Thus, the Interim Committee had achieved the purpose one suspects that Byrnes at least had come to attribute to it, and that was the ratification of decisions that had already been made. Stimson was thrilled with this meeting, not so much for its resulting recommendations as for the manner in which the scientists seemed to get on so well with the statesmen. "I think we made an impression upon the scientists that we were looking at this like statesmen and not like merely soldiers," he wrote in his diary that night.

On that same day, June 1, 1945, when he started America on a path which would end in nuclear attack on Japan, Stimson began a quiet campaign that resulted in the only humane aspect to the otherwise thoroughly inhumane bombing of Hiroshima.

It was an act of either contradiction or absolution or perhaps both. It was not a major deed of heroism, and it did not save any lives. It was, however, a touching exercise, which turned the American atomic war machine from the course it desired.

During the spring of 1945, the son of an old friend of the Stimsons had come to dinner with them. This young soldier was a devoted student of Oriental history. He talked with great compassion of the past glories of the city of Kyoto, Japan, the ancient capital of that country which was noted for its lovely imperial residences and religious shrines. Stimson was touched by this young man's story and went to a history book to read more of this city. He recalled having visited Kyoto many years before during his term as governor of the Philippine Islands. The intent of the young man's reflections was clear and Stimson agreed with him. Kyoto must be saved from the Air Force fire bombing raids which were destroying many of the cities of Japan. Stimson based this conclusion on a remarkable desire to maintain the reputation of the United States for fair play and humanitarianism because he believed that reputation was "the world's biggest asset for peace in the coming decades." In hindsight it is difficult to understand why that same consideration did not play a larger role in the decision to attack Hiroshima and Nagasaki. On that day of the Interim Committee meeting, Stimson summoned General "Hap" Arnold of the Army Air Force to his office. He first complained that the Air Force had not been adhering to its promise to carry out precision bombing on Japan. General Arnold said that the stories from Tokyo were exaggerated and that more civilians would be killed in Japan than in Europe because the Japanese industries were more scattered. Then Stimson came to the point. There was one city that the American Air Force must not touch unless it had his permission, and that was Kyoto. Arnold accepted the order.[5]

A few days later, on Wednesday, June 6, Stimson solemnly reported the recommendations of the Interim Committee to President Truman. The President said that Byrnes, "who seemed to be highly pleased with what had been done," had already told him of the committee's work. Stimson went on to outline the suggestions as he understood them. In the first place, "there should be no revelation to Russia or anyone else of our work in S–1 until the first bomb had been successfully laid on Japan." The greatest complication in this regard, Stimson said, was "what might happen at the meeting of the Big Three." Truman revealed that he had postponed that meeting until July 15 "on purpose to give us more time." This did not put the Secretary of War at ease. He felt that the first successful detonation might not occur until later than that and was concerned that the President should be prepared if the Russians brought up the subject at Potsdam and asked to be taken in as partners. He advised Truman that if this happened he should do "just what the Russians had done to us, namely to make the simple statement that as yet we were not quite ready to do it."

On the question of postwar international atomic control, Stimson could report very little because the Interim Committee had given the subject scant attention. There was really no committee to perform that task. The only suggestion the committee had was "that each country should promise to make public all work that was being done on this subject and that an international committee of control should be constituted with full power of inspection of all countries to see whether this promise was being carried out." Stimson agreed that this scheme was "imperfect and might not be assented to by Russia, but that in that case we were far enough ahead of the game to be able to accumulate enough material to serve as insurance against being caught helpless." No disclosure of the atomic work should be made to anyone until all such promises of control were established and guaranteed, Stimson declared. He also raised the question of what *quid pro quo*s might be expected from the Russians for taking them in on the atomic partnership. The President said he had been thinking about that, along the same lines as Stimson, "namely the settlement of the Polish, Rumanian, Yugoslavian and Manchurian problems." In conclusion, Stimson said, there were two reasons why the atomic problem still made him anxious: first, because he "did not want to have the United States get the reputation of outdoing Hitler in atrocities" and second, because he was "a little fearful that before we could get ready, the Air Force might have Japan so thoroughly bombed out that the new weapon would not have a fair background to show its strength." This was a rather convoluted moral perspective and Truman laughed when he heard it, saying that he understood what Stimson meant.[6]

Before leaving the Interim Committee meeting on June 1, 1945, Arthur H. Compton had asked what he could report to his perplexed colleagues back in Chicago. He was told that he could inform them of the existence of the committee, but not of its members or its work, and that he might assure them that the committee had given and would continue to give the fullest hearing to the views of the scientists. The members of the scientific panel were encouraged to put their four great minds to work on any of the problems that had been discussed at the Pentagon and especially on the form of a postwar control organization. Fermi, Lawrence, Compton, and Oppenheimer agreed to meet in a few weeks at Los Alamos to discuss these questions.

Compton reported what he could to the Met Lab workers on Saturday, June 2, in Chicago and told them that he would bring to the next meeting of the scientific panel any proposals they might care to prepare. The scientists immediately appointed six committees to consider education, controls, research, organization, production, and social and political implications. The last committee, the most important in the short run, was chaired by James Franck and had as members Szilard, Donald Hughes, Glenn Seaborg, Joyce Stearns, J. J. Nickson, and Eugene Rabinowitch. The scientists, now troubled that the bomb might be dropped before their views were considered, worked at a zealous pace. The Franck committee was most anxious because its work concerned the immediate question of how and whether to drop the bomb. Franck and his colleagues finished their report and submitted it to Compton by June 11. There is more than a little bit of pathos in this great display of energy, since the Interim Committee had already come to a decision regarding the use of the weapon, which Stimson had subsequently relayed to the President. But Compton was prohibited by the Interim Committee from revealing any of its conclusions to the other scientists.

The men at the Met Lab were so anxious and by this time paranoiac that they prevailed upon Franck to sidestep the scientific panel and take their report directly to Washington. Arthur Compton met Franck in Washington and accompanied him to Stimson's office. The Secretary, however, was not in town and so they were forced to leave the Franck Report with his assistant, George Harrison.

In its statement, the Franck committee argued, like so many before, that it was foolish for the United States to believe that an atomic arms race could be avoided by simply keeping the work of the Manhattan Project secret. Borrowing an idea from Szilard, the committee contended that the United States would be in an especially vulnerable position in a nuclear war because of its concentrated population centers. The only sure way to avoid a nuclear arms race and war was through international cooperation. Such cooperation would depend upon the kind of trust among nations that they feared the United States could not soon enjoy after dropping a deadly bomb on Japan. America would be feared but never respected or trusted, and trust and respect were the only possible foundations for postwar international cooperation. The committee's suggestion: an announcement of the bomb's existence and a demonstration of its force on some uninhabited island. Then, if the Japanese refused to bow, America would at least have secured a moral foundation for an atomic attack on Japan and not absolutely jeopardized the chances of postwar control.[7] This proposal was similar to the one Alexander Sachs had made to President Roosevelt during November 1944. Lewis Strauss had suggested the same idea to the Secretary of the Navy, James Forrestal, with no effect.

The members of the Franck committee were moved by one other consideration which they did not articulate in their report. To drop the bomb on Japan would be an international crime, which was simply wrong regardless of its military or diplomatic justification. Men like Leo Szilard "had been willing to approve and even to urge the use of the bomb against the Germans, for in this case it would be an evil less than that of the human destruction he felt sure would result if the Nazis should gain victory. He could not persuade himself that the case was the same with regard to the Japanese."[8] General Groves attributed the scientists' dilemma to their own "racial problems in Germany." They "apparently found themselves unable to generate the same degree of enthusiasm for destroying Japan's military power," he said.[9]

Although the decision to use the bomb against Japan already had been made, the Franck Report was not without some impact. It stimulated a review and perhaps a little more. On June 16, 1945, George Harrison called Arthur Compton at Los Alamos where he was meeting with the other three members of the scientific panel. Harrison had read the Franck Report and wanted the panel's views on the question of using the bomb. He was not opposed to bringing the Franck Report before the Interim Committee but wanted it to follow a statement on the subject from the scientific panel. Harrison had been at the earlier meetings of the Interim Committee and heard the abbreviated discussion of whether to use the bombs directly against Japan, so he had reason to know what the thoughts of the members of the panel would be.

Compton had seen the Franck Report when he deposited it with Harrison four days earlier in Washington. In fact, he had left a covering letter, summarizing its contents and undercutting its recommendation. He had written to Stimson: "The report did not mention two possible consequences of failing to make a military demonstration: prolongation of the war and loss of the opportunity to impress the world with the national sacrifices that enduring security demanded." [10] Fermi, Lawrence, and Oppenheimer had not seen the Franck Report itself, but they were surely familiar with its contents, having worked with its authors at various times over the preceding years.

The burden placed upon the four members of the scientific panel was an uncomfortable one. "We were determined to find, if we could," Compton wrote ten years later, "some effective way of demonstrating the power of an atomic bomb without loss of life that would impress Japan's warlords. If only this could be done." [11] Ernest Lawrence was the last to believe it could be done, but he too finally signed the panel's report:

> The opinions of our scientific colleagues on the initial use of these weapons are not unanimous . . . Those who advocate a purely technical demonstration would wish to outlaw the use of atomic weapons, and have feared that if we use the weapons now our position in future negotiations will be prejudiced. Others emphasize the

opportunity of saving American lives by immediate military use, and believe that such use will improve the international prospects, in that they are more concerned with the prevention of war than with the elimination of this special weapon. We find ourselves closer to these latter views; we can propose no technical demonstration likely to bring an end to the war; we see no acceptable alternative to direct military use.[12]

The Franck Report, however, had stimulated the four members of the scientific panel to reconsider one of the earlier recommendations of the Interim Committee. In its report to the committee the panel now declared:

> . . . we recommend that before the weapons are used not only Britain, but also Russia, France and China be advised that we would welcome suggestions as to how we can cooperate in making this development contribute to improved international relations.

This idea was seized upon by Bush and Conant when the full Interim Committee met again in Washington on Thursday morning, June 21. First, however, the committee formally considered the Franck Report. Harrison simply described the document. After a very brief discussion, it was decided that in view of the inability of the scientific panel to find an acceptable alternative to military use, the earlier decision to bomb Japan must be reaffirmed. Then Bush and Conant picked up the panel's suggestion of informing all of America's wartime allies of the existence of the bomb before its use. This was, of course, a policy they had been promoting for almost a year. They argued that notification could be the crucial factor in conditioning postwar relations with the Soviet Union. The committee agreed and recommended that the President be advised that they had concluded it would be wise for him to inform the Russians at the upcoming Big Three conference at Potsdam of the existence of the bomb and of his plan to use it against Japan. He should also stress America's commitment to work with its allies to insure the peaceful use of the new weapon after the war.

A number of other decisions relating to atomic control were reached at that June 21 meeting. Much effort was expended in preparing to inform the world of what lay behind the atomic bomb. The draft of a statement for President Truman to issue after the nuclear attack was discussed, with the committee's deciding to eliminate a sentence in which the President committed himself to seeking an international agreement on control on the theory that Truman himself had to make that decision separately. General Groves also reported to the committee that during the spring of 1944, at the urging of Bush, he had asked Henry D. Smyth, a Princeton physicist, to prepare a technical history of the Manhattan Project which could be issued shortly after the first atomic explosion and might avoid much unfounded or speculative public discussion.[18]

The Franck Report helped elicit one other response which did not affect the course of American policy but is nonetheless proof that there was at least one man who stood up and said no. In the days following the June 21 meeting of the Interim Committee, one of its members, Ralph Bard, the Undersecretary of the Navy, spoke several times with George Harrison about his uneasiness over the decision to bomb Japan. He wondered particularly about the decision not to give any warning to Japan before the atomic attack. Such a course would do great damage, he thought, to "the position of the United States as a great humanitarian nation and the fair play attitude of our people generally." On June 27, Bard, who had been an industrial financier and consultant in Chicago before assuming his position in the Navy Department, put his displeasure into a letter to Stimson. "The Japanese government may be searching for some opportunity which they could use as a medium for surrender," he wrote. Why not arrange a meeting with Japanese emissaries somewhere on the China coast after the three-power conference at Potsdam? There the Japanese could be informed not only of the atomic weapon but of the imminent Russian invasion of Japan. Together with assurances about the future of the Emperor, Bard thought, this might present "the opportunity which the Japanese are looking for." No one could know how such a maneuver would fare but, Bard argued, nothing whatsoever would be lost by trying. Harrison had Bard's memorandum taken immediately to Stimson who read it without response. On July 1, 1945, Ralph Bard resigned as Undersecretary of the Navy. The Interim Committee therefore was no longer unanimous.[14]

Stimson had not been present at the June 21 meeting of the committee. His doctor had ordered him once more to return to Highhold for a few days of rest. On Friday, June 22, he spoke with Harrison by phone and learned that the Interim Committee "had some strong recommendations to make in respect to the relations with Russia." Stimson thought these over and then called Harrison back, asking him to have Bush and Conant prepare a memorandum on that particular subject. This was quickly done and forwarded to Highhold where it much impressed Stimson. The argument was no different from the one Bush and Conant had been making for months. Together with the Franck Report, Bard's protest, and perhaps a momentary easing of Stimson's coolness toward Russia, this memorandum changed the Secretary's mind. He decided that Russia must be informed at Potsdam about the atomic bomb.[15]

Back in Washington on July 3, 1945, Stimson went to the White House to talk with Truman about the new opinion of the Interim Committee. Ironically, when Truman sat down with Stimson that afternoon, he had just finished attending the swearing in ceremonies for his new Secretary of State, James Byrnes. The message which Stimson brought from the Interim Committee was no less than a reversal of the position Byrnes had argued decisively at the earlier meeting of the committee. The new Secretary, however, would yet have the last word.

Truman greeted Stimson in the anteroom to his office that day and invited him in to talk "as long as you like." He appreciated the time, Stimson told the President, for this was a subject that "couldn't be talked over in the machine-gun style but it was more the kind of thing that ought to be talked over a fire, at the fireside in the evening or when we had plenty of time." Then, Stimson went to the purpose of his visit. On second look, the Interim Committee had changed its mind about notifying the Russians. Speaking without notes, Stimson "summed it up informally" by telling the President that at Potsdam "he should look sharp and if he found that he thought that Stalin was on good enough terms with him, he should shoot off at him what we had arranged . . . in other words, simply telling him that we were busy with this thing and working like the dickens and we knew he was busy with this thing and working like the dickens and that we were pretty nearly ready and we intended to use it against the enemy, Japan; that if it was satisfactory we proposed to then talk it over with Stalin afterwards with the purpose of having it make the world peaceful and safe rather than to destroy civilization." What if Stalin pressed for details? Then, Stimson suggested, the President should simply tell him "we were not yet prepared to give them." Truman listened attentively and said he understood the position which Stimson had described. He agreed that that was the best way to do it.[16] Stimson's proposal to Truman was not quite what Bush and Conant had advocated and was far short of the early Soviet involvement Niels Bohr had sought, but it was more than many, including the British, desired and might well provide a foundation for Soviet-American cooperation in postwar atomic energy development.

Stimson's next duty was to receive formal British consent to the proposed atomic attack on Japan, as required by the Quebec Agreement of 1943. On July 4, 1945, he met at the Pentagon with the Anglo-American Combined Policy Committee which had been established in the aftermath of that agreement. Stimson himself served as chairman. Along with the Secretary at the meeting were Bush, Groves, Harrison, and Bundy. Representing the British were Lord Halifax, Sir James Chadwick, Field Marshal Henry Wilson, and C. D. Howe. Wilson gave the immediate consent of the British government to the planned bombing of Japan. When it came to the disclosure of information both to the Russians before the attack and to the public at large afterward, there was less agreement. After listening to the American plan to issue a scientific history of the project as a way of limiting public anxiety and creating an international atmosphere of openness, Halifax said simply that "the greater the amount of information which was disclosed to other countries, the less inducement there might be for them to agree to measures of international control, should we ever decide to suggest them." But, Stimson said, most of the scientific thinking on the subject was already known and, besides, he was thinking more of the question of informing Stalin at Potsdam. "If nothing was said at this meeting about the . . . weapon," Stimson continued, adopting the arguments of Bush, Conant, and Bohr, "its subsequent early use might have a serious effect on the relations of frankness between the three great Allies." He had advised the President to watch the atmosphere at Potsdam and if it seemed to be one of "mutual frankness," then he should inform Stalin of the atomic bomb. Halifax would say only that he would inform Sir John Anderson of Stimson's plan.[17]

During this period, Stimson also fought one more round in his struggle to save the city of Kyoto. On one occasion when General Groves was in Stimson's office to discuss the progress of the Manhattan Project, the Secretary asked him whether any targets for the atomic attack had been chosen.[18] In fact, General Groves had created a Target Committee composed of three members of the Air Force staff and four members of the Manhattan Project, which had been meeting since early in May. The committee had chosen and Groves had approved four target cities: Kokura, Hiroshima, Niigata, and Kyoto. Groves had decided to bring this decision to General Marshall for ratification, no doubt because he knew that was the easiest road to approval. He had made the rather startling decision to avoid formal consideration of the atomic attack by the Joint Chiefs of Staff, first because of "the need to maintain complete security," and second because he knew that Admiral Leahy was opposed to use of the bomb and this "would have made action by the Joint Chiefs quite difficult." This was a very brazen decision for a lesser officer to make regarding the authority of the American military establishment and demonstrates the enormous power General Groves had gained for himself in a short period of time. He was altogether correct in his perception of Admiral Leahy, however. Like other members of the Joint Chiefs of Staff, Leahy believed that the Japanese were already defeated by the Naval blockade and successful fire bombings of their islands. Equally important to Leahy was his conclusion that the atomic bomb was a "barbarous" weapon. "I was not taught to make war in that fashion," Leahy said, "and wars cannot be won by destroying women and children." He later wrote:

> These new concepts of "total war" are basically distasteful to the soldier and sailor of my generation. Employment of the atomic bomb in war will take us back in cruelty toward non-combatants to the days of Genghis Khan . . . These new and terrible instruments of uncivilized warfare represent a modern type of barbarism not worthy of Christian man.[19]

Groves was therefore wise to avoid Leahy and the Joint Chiefs. Although the general was more confident of Stimson's opinion, he was not sufficiently confident to want to discuss targets with him. Therefore, when Stimson asked about the choice of targets,

Groves said that decisions had been made but he preferred to discuss these first with General Marshall, since it was a military matter. Stimson objected. "This is a question I am settling myself. Marshall is not making that decision." He told Groves to have the report of the Target Committee brought over immediately. But again Groves demurred on the grounds that it would take some time. Stimson, now angered, said that he had all morning and that the general should use his phone to have the report brought to his office right away. Groves consented. While they were waitting, Stimson asked him what the chosen targets were. When he heard Kyoto, Stimson objected vigorously. The Secretary might change his mind after he had read the description of Kyoto, Groves said, and had heard their reasons for selecting it. He was sure he would not, Stimson replied. Now Groves took the offensive. Kyoto was a city of more than a million people and therefore must be involved in much war work even if there were but few large factories. The city was also "large enough to insure that the damage from the bomb would run out within the city, which would give us a firm understanding of its destructive power." This argument left Stimson thoroughly unconvinced. He rose from his chair and walked over to the door to General Marshall's office which adjoined his own. He called Marshall in and explained that he was opposed to bombing Kyoto because it was the ancient capital and a religious shrine, and its destruction would ruin the reputation of the United States for being a humanitarian nation. This could not help but diminish the prospects of international harmony in the postwar world. Marshall listened, read the report when it arrived, and expressed an unclear opinion which, however, did not amount to disagreement with Stimson. Groves believed that Marshall felt "it did not make too much difference either way." [20]

6

Potsdam and the Attack

THE BIG THREE CONFERENCE was scheduled to begin at Potsdam on Monday, July 16, 1945. Stimson had decided to travel there by boat to give himself a period of calm in which to prepare unhurriedly for the meeting. He was not an official member of the conference and therefore could not attend the formal sessions, but President Truman had asked him to be present. Stimson readily agreed, wanting to be close to Truman at the time when he knew that a series of critical atomic decisions would be made. As the U.S.S. *Brazil* carried him across the ocean to Marseilles, Stimson settled his thoughts on two major decisions associated with the atomic weapon. The first was the question of a warning to Japan. Influenced by Undersecretary of State Joseph Grew, who had been America's ambassador to Japan for ten years, Stimson had recently deviated from the decision which he had originally helped the Interim Committee make. He now believed that a proper warning to the Japanese about an atomic attack and a promise to retain the Emperor might induce a surrender. His second major concern was the notification to Stalin. On this he would try to discern the atmosphere at Potsdam and advise the President accordingly.

Stimson went through the Straits of Gibraltar to land at Marseilles on Saturday, July 14, and flew from there to Berlin on the following morning in time to meet President Truman's party as it arrived by plane that afternoon. Together they drove to Babels-

berg, a former German movie colony twelve miles southeast of
Berlin in the Soviet zone, where the Russians had assigned them
to luxurious villas. Potsdam was just a short ride down the road
from there. It was a lovely town, where Albert Einstein had lived
for many years before his exile. The conference sessions were to
take place at the Cecilienhof Palace, built by Crown Prince Wil-
helm and used during the war as a hospital. Now it was brilliantly
refurbished by the Soviet government for the conference.

From his earliest moments at Babelsberg, Stimson's contacts
with the Russians displeased him. They would ultimately cause
him to alter his assessment of the prospects for postwar
atomic cooperation with the Soviet Union. Of the villa where
he was quartered, he wrote in his diary on that first evening in
Germany:

> We were a small sub-zone in the middle of the Russian Berlin zone
> and the Russians let us know very well that it was their zone be-
> cause they were picketing our little zone on every side and we
> could not walk out of it without being stopped.[1]

"Except for the heat and mosquitoes," however, Stimson found
his quarters "fairly comfortable."

A few hours after Stimson settled down in his villa in Germany, Vannevar Bush, James Conant, and General Leslie Groves
were settling into a dirt trench in the desert at Los Alamos, New
Mexico. They were due south of "zero" — the hundred-foot-tall
steel tower from which the first atomic bomb would soon explode.
It was before dawn under a sky so dark with clouds that not a
single star was visible. An occasional bolt of lightning broke
through the night illuminating the bleak desert below. A huge
searchlight probed the sky for unwanted intruders. At about
5:30 A.M., the countdown began. Forty-five seconds before zero
a mechanical robot was activated and took full control. "Now,"

Samuel Allison shouted, and a great green pillar shot up, eight thousand feet into the sky, touching the clouds, broadening as it rose higher, and turning deep purple and then orange. A huge cloud rose from the ground and followed the fire skyward, forming a bizarre and monstrous mushroom 41,000 feet high, 12,000 feet higher than the earth's tallest mountain. And then the astounding sights repeated themselves in sound; an immense roar of thunder followed by the trembling of the ground and an awesome rumbling which seemed subterranean and continued to play among the somber New Mexican hills five minutes after the detonation.

The witnesses had all felt a wave of hot wind and experienced momentary blindness. Still on their bellies in the trench, Conant and Bush extended congratulatory hands to Groves. At the base camp Oppenheimer raised his six-foot-tall body, reduced to 115 pounds by the labors of the last two years. His face loosened into an expression of relief and then melancholy as he recalled the Hindu scripture: "I am become death, the shatterer of worlds." George Kistiakowsky, Oppenheimer's assistant, excitedly embraced his boss and, remembering a hopeful wager they had made a few days before, shouted, "Oppie, you owe me ten dollars." Fermi, with characteristic singlemindedness, jumped to his feet and began dropping bits of paper to determine the force of the blast wave. The reaction of most others was more predictable. "My God," they murmured, "it worked."

The atomic bomb was a reality — one of far greater potency than its makers had anticipated. Its yield was the equivalent of 20,000 tons of TNT. Not a trace was left of the hundred-foot structural steel tower; it had been vaporized. For a thousand feet around zero, the sand was changed into petrified green glasslike material. It was "a scene of devastation that made the surrounding semi-desert appear as a fertile oasis." [2]

A cable from George Harrison reporting the wonderful, terrible news that the bomb had worked reached Stimson in Germany at 7:30 P.M. Monday evening, July 16. He took it immediately to Truman's quarters and showed it to the President and Byrnes. They were "greatly interested," although the information was still in the most general terms.[3]

Stimson had lunch with Churchill, Attlee, and several other members of the British delegation at their villa on Tuesday. He stayed there in lively discussion until 4:30 P.M. As they walked together down to the gate, Stimson told Churchill of Harrison's message. This was the Prime Minister's first notification. He was "intensely interested and greatly cheered up." Stimson turned the conversation immediately to the question of informing Stalin. He found Churchill to be "strongly inclined against any disclosure" and argued at some length against this inclination.[4]

On Wednesday morning, July 18, two more reports arrived from George Harrison. Stimson took these at once to Truman, who was "highly delighted." The President brought the cables with him to lunch with Churchill. The Potsdam Conference was the first time Churchill and Truman had met each other. For his part, Truman took "an instant liking" to Churchill. "I liked to listen to him talk," Truman has said.[5] The President handed Harrison's telegrams to Churchill and then asked him what he thought should be done about informing the Russians. Truman spoke as if he was determined to give some notification to Stalin but wondered about the timing. The President thought that the end of the conference would be best. Churchill replied that if the President was resolved to tell Stalin, then it might well be better "to hang it on the experiment which was a new fact on which he and we only just had knowledge." This was a ready-made answer to any question Stalin might raise about why he was not informed earlier, Churchill suggested. This strategy seemed to impress Truman, and he said he would consider it. The Prime Minister said that he wanted to make it clear that on behalf of His Majesty's government he would not resist the proposed disclosure to Stalin so long as it was limited to the simple fact that Great Britain and America possessed a new weapon. Those were hardly the terms in which Bush, Conant, and Bohr had envisioned the disclosure to the Russians, but Truman heartily assured Churchill that he would "at all costs" refuse to divulge any more than the fact of the weapon's existence.[6]

As the formal conferences of the Big Three began in earnest, Stimson awaited further word from America. At noon on Thursday, July 19, Lord Cherwell, who had accompanied Churchill to Potsdam, came to visit Stimson. Together with Harvey Bundy, they sat out under the trees on the grounds of Stimson's villa and talked over the atomic bomb and relations with Russia. Stimson found Cherwell to be "very reasonable on the subject of notification to the Russians, feeling about as doubtful as we." Later in the afternoon after Cherwell had left, Stimson, Bundy, and John McCloy continued the discussion. They were particularly concerned with the broader question of relations with the Russians. What, they asked each other, was the cause of the constant differences between the two countries and how might they be avoided. Their conclusions amounted to a startling form of interventionism. Their goal was no less than total reorganization of Soviet society in return for partnership in atomic development. As Stimson saw it the only road that held any hope was "getting the Russians to see that the real basis of the evil was the absence of freedom of speech in their regime, and the ironbound rule of the OGPU." He sat down to put some of these ideas in a memo and later that evening wrote in his diary:

> I have been much impressed on this visit with the atmosphere of repression that exists everywhere and which is felt by all who come in contact with the Russian rule in Germany. While the Russian soldiers and American soldiers seem to like each other individually when they meet, the people who have to deal with the Russian of-

ficials feel very differently and it greatly impairs the cooperation between our two countries. Churchill is very rampant about it, and most of our people who have seen the Russians most intimately think we have been too easy and that they have taken advantage of it.

It is a very difficult problem because they are crusaders for their own system and suspicious of everybody outside trying to interfere with it. At the same time, it is becoming more and more evident to me that a nation whose system rests upon free speech and all the elements of freedom as does ours cannot be sure of getting on permanently with a nation where speech is strictly controlled and where the government uses the ironbound hand of the secret police. The question is very important just now and the development of S–1 is bringing it to a focus. I am beginning to feel that our committee which met in Washington on this subject and was so set upon opening communications with the Russians on this subject may have been thinking in a vacuum.[7]

In the memorandum which he wrote that day Stimson expressed a remarkable optimism that something could be accomplished. He based this attitude on a conclusion that "Stalin has shown an indication of his appreciation of our system of freedom by his proposal of a free constitution to be established among the Soviets." Stimson's concern over the Soviet system was related directly to his vision of a postwar international atomic control agency. He believed that no such organization could function effectively as long as one of its "dominant members" was "a nation whose people are not possessed of free speech but whose governmental action is controlled by the autocratic machinery of a secret political police." His summation was not hopeful:

I therefore believe that before we share our new discovery with Russia we should consider carefully whether we can do so safely under any system of control until Russia puts into effective action the proposed constitution which I have mentioned. If this is a necessary condition we must go slowly in any disclosures of agreeing to any Russian participation whatsoever and constantly explore the question how our head start in X and the Russian desire to participate can be used to bring us nearer to the removal of the basic difficulties which I have emphasized.[8]

This was a fascinating assemblage of thoughts. Stimson's civilized and libertarian soul was offended by the Soviet system. His idealism was moving. Yet his conclusions were worlds away from the realm of the possible. Perhaps the problem was that the world had changed. The Russians were not the Philippinos to whom Stimson had brought the blessings of liberty during his term as American governor of those islands years before. His thoughts showed little appreciation of either the tenacity with which the Soviet leaders believed in their system or the effect that centuries of foreign invasions had had on the Russian national spirit. He also had apparently forgotten what his experts had told him about the ease with which the Russians could build an atom bomb. Three or four years of hard work to attain nuclear capability would surely be more appealing to the Russians than the externally imposed revolution in their system which Stimson contemplated.

Deeply troubled by the trend of his thinking, Stimson asked Averell Harriman, who was present at Potsdam, to visit him on Friday afternoon, July 20. He showed Harriman the memo he had prepared and asked the ambassador's opinion. Harriman agreed on the differences between the two countries but said that his years in Moscow as American ambassador had made him very pessimistic about the chances of coercing the Russians to change their system in any way. Because Stimson had great respect for Harriman's intelligence and capacity, this opinion troubled him greatly.[9]

A comprehensive report on the explosion at Los Alamos prepared by General Groves was delivered to Stimson by special courier on Saturday morning, July 21. This report made clear the tremendous destructive power which had been unleashed. That afternoon, at three o'clock, Stimson took the Groves report to the Little White House and read it to Truman and Byrnes. They were both "immensely pleased." The President particularly seemed "tremendously pepped up by it." He told Stimson that it gave him "an entirely new feeling of confidence" and he thanked the Secretary "for having come to the Conference and being present to help [me] in this way." [10] At the same time Stimson left Truman a copy of his memorandum on Russia.

Stimson returned to Truman's quarters early the following morning to talk for the first time with the President about Kyoto. Harrison had cabled from Washington that Groves had continued to insist on Kyoto's being a target for the atomic attack. Stimson now explained his position on the bombing of Kyoto to Truman, who "strongly confirmed" the view that America's image would be gravely damaged by an attack on the ancient capital and religious shrine. The President apparently was moved by Stimson's notion of doing an inhumane act in the most humane way. As Stimson was leaving, the President said that he had read the memorandum on Russia and wanted the Secretary to know that he agreed with it fully. Firsthand experiences with the Russians at Potsdam had also had a negative effect on Truman. On their second day in Germany, Truman, Byrnes, and Leahy had traveled to Berlin to view the destruction there. Much more distressing to them was what they saw along the way. As Admiral Leahy described it,

> . . . a long procession of old men, women and children presumably evicted from their homes by the Russian invaders, marching in great numbers along the country roads carrying their remaining belongings and their small babies, probably to an unknown destination and probably without hope.[11]

Potsdam was also Truman's first meeting with Stalin, and although there was an air of cordiality between them, Truman found Stalin and the other Russian representatives to be "relentless bargainers forever pressing for every advantage for themselves." At Potsdam Stalin laid claims not only to effective control of the buffer countries of Eastern Europe but also to bases in Turkey and the Italian colonies of the Mediterranean. Truman was especially upset by Stalin's rejection of his proposal for internationalization of the world's principal waterways. "Stalin did not want this," Truman said afterward. "What Stalin wanted was control of the Black Sea straits and the Danube. The Russians were planning world conquest." [12] The President was therefore entirely receptive to the theme of Stimson's memorandum.

When Stimson visited Churchill later that Sunday morning to read Groves's report to him, the Prime Minister listened excitedly and then said that this new weapon explained to him why Truman had appeared to be a different man at Saturday's session with the Russians. "He told the Russians just where they got on and off," Churchill exclaimed, "and generally bossed the whole meeting." [13]

By Tuesday morning, July 24, Stimson had received word from Harrison that the atomic bomb could be ready for use against Japan on the first clear day after August 1. When Truman heard this message he told Stimson it was "just what he wanted, that he was highly delighted, and that it gave him his cue for his warning." Once more they discussed Kyoto and Truman confirmed his earlier decision, agreeing with Stimson not only that it would be inhumane to attack Kyoto but that "the bitterness which would be caused by such a wanton act might make it impossible during the long postwar period to reconcile the Japanese to us in that area rather than to the Russians." [14]

After the conference session that afternoon, Truman rose from his chair and, leaving his interpreter and everyone else behind, went around the large table to speak with Stalin. "I casually mentioned to Stalin," Truman reported later, "that we had a new weapon of unusual destructive force. The Russian premier showed no special interest. All he said was that he was glad to hear it and hoped we would make good use of it against the Japanese." [15]

This devastatingly nonchalant announcement was, of course, altogether short of what Bush, Conant, and Bohr had desired, but it was consistent with what Truman had concluded about Russia at Potsdam and with what Churchill, Stimson, and certainly Byrnes had counseled him there. The arguments of Bush, Conant, and Bohr that a thorough disclosure to the Soviet Union of atomic weapons might diminish the mistrust and suspicion which led the Russians to act as they did at Potsdam and elsewhere were simply forgotten.

When Truman told Byrnes of his exchange with Stalin as they drove back to the Little White House that afternoon, Byrnes was surprised. He did not expect such a lack of interest. Byrnes had watched the interchange between Truman and Stalin, noting that Stalin had smiled when he heard the President's message. Byrnes guessed that when Stalin got back to his headquarters it would dawn on him that he had missed a great opportunity, and so he would return the following day with a list of questions for the President to answer. Truman agreed that this was probable. That evening these two American statesmen spoke at length about how to answer the aggressive inquiries from Stalin which, of course, never came.

Stalin's smile was no doubt full of disdain since his espionage network had already gathered and transmitted to him a great deal of information about the Manhattan Project.

Meanwhile, a series of decisions had been made at Potsdam with regard to Japan. Peace feelers from the Japanese through Moscow were rejected by agreement of the Soviet, English, and

American leaders. Stimson's argument for an early and comprehensive warning to the Japanese about the imminent atomic attack was rejected by Truman, who listened to Byrnes on that matter. On July 24, formal orders were given to General Carl Spaatz, Commanding General of the United States Army Air Forces, to carry out an atomic attack as soon as weather permitted visual bombing on one of the following Japanese cities: Hiroshima, Kokura, Niigata, and Nagasaki. On July 26, the long-awaited warning to Japan was issued by the United States, Britain, and China without prior notice to the Soviet Union. It called upon the Japanese to surrender unconditionally or face "prompt and utter destruction." There was no mention of preservation of the monarchy or of the awesome new weapon that would soon cause the "prompt and utter destruction." After furious debate within the Japanese Cabinet, this ultimatum was rejected on July 28 as nothing "of any great value."

Now Stimson rushed back to the United States by plane to coordinate activities leading up to the atomic attack. The military machine had long been directed toward this time, but Stimson was concerned that the announcements of the bombing after it had occurred be handled correctly. He worked on these and handled other administrative details Monday and Tuesday, July 30 and 31. On Wednesday, August 1, General Groves, always the good soldier, came to him with the most recent expressions of anxiety and opinion by the Manhattan District scientists. First was a petition Leo Szilard had circulated in Chicago during the first days of July because of his concern that the Franck Report was not receiving an adequate hearing, unaware that it had already been dismissed by the Interim Committee on June 21. Szilard's petition urged that the President not use atomic weapons "in the war unless the terms which will be imposed upon Japan have been made public in detail and Japan, knowing these terms, has refused to surrender." Unless this could be done, the President was urged to forbid the use of atomic bombs against Japan. The petition had been dated July 17, 1945. Sixty-nine of Szilard's fellow Manhattan District workers joined him in signing it.[16]

But the petition also brought forth opposition in the form of counterpetitions and individual protestations. A. H. Compton recalled:

> One of the young men who had been with us at Chicago and had transferred to Los Alamos came into my Chicago office in a state of emotional stress. He said he had heard of an effort to prevent the use of the bomb. Two years earlier I had persuaded this young man, as he was graduating with a major in physics, to cast his lot with our project. The chances are, I had told him, that you will be able to contribute more toward winning the war in this position than if you should accept the call to the Navy that you are considering. He had heeded my advice. Now he was sorely troubled: "I have buddies who have fought through the battle of Iwo Jima. Some of them have been killed, others wounded . . ." Tears came to his eyes. "If one of these men should be killed because we didn't let them use the bombs, I would have failed them. I just could not make myself feel that I had done my part." [17]

One petition signed by eighteen Chicago scientists asked the President to use atomic bombs, but only if the Japanese had received an opportunity to surrender and been given warnings that a new weapon would be used against them if they did not.

Compton forwarded these papers to Groves, who in turn asked Compton to take a poll of the Chicago laboratory on the question of how the bomb should be used. Since Groves knew that all the decisions had already been made, it seems that he was merely building a historical record while giving the scientists the illusion of participation. Compton gave the job to Farrington Daniels, the new director of the Met Lab. One hundred and fifty of the workers participated. Two percent of them thought that the

United States should keep the bomb a secret and not use it until it was absolutely forced to; 11 percent asked for a public demonstration; 26 percent wanted a demonstration in the United States in the presence of Japanese representatives; 46 percent thought a military demonstration in Japan and another opportunity to surrender before direct use was best; and 15 percent were for whatever use of the bomb would bring Japan to surrender most quickly and save most American lives.[18]

All this information Groves gave to Stimson on August 1, but nothing could have been less valuable to the Secretary of War then or less relevant to his concerns. The decision had been made long ago. Without consideration, Stimson had Harrison place the papers into the Manhattan District files.

Samuel Goudsmit, whose father and blind mother had been cremated by the Nazis in Holland, was a member of the intelligence division of the Manhattan Project. His job was to uncover and help destroy any German attempts at atomic development during the war. As Goudsmit followed the advancing Allied armies into Germany in 1945, it became clear to him that the Germans had failed absolutely in their efforts to build an atomic bomb. "Isn't it wonderful," Goudsmit remarked to one of his associates in the Manhattan Project, "that the Germans have no atom bomb? Now we won't have to use ours." His colleague, a career military man, replied instinctively: "Of course you understand, Sam, that if we have such a weapon we are going to use it." [19]

Shortly before 8:15 A.M. on August 6, 1945, the city of Hiroshima, Japan, was centered at zero in the bombsight of an American B–29, the *Enola Gay*. Hiroshima, a city of 318,000 people thickly settled around a quartermaster's depot, was an embarkation port that housed an armaments and airplane parts plant. The

Enola Gay's bomb bay doors clattered open and down to the earth plunged a 9000 pound package of destruction 2⅓ feet in diameter, 10⅔ feet long, known in Manhattan District parlance as "Little Boy." A parachute burst open, slowing the bomb's drop so that the *Enola Gay* and its two observation escorts could be out of the danger area at the moment of explosion. On the ground below the all-clear signal had sounded forty-five minutes before, after a previous alert. Now a few silver airplanes aroused little interest in the Japanese watchtowers; it was probably a flight of weather planes such as often overflew the area. There was little to fear from three lonely planes. Workmen had gone to their factories; some were still in the streets on their way. School children and others were out helping to remove buildings and transport valuables to the countryside in preparation for the feared fire bombing which Tokyo had already endured. Only 400 people happened to be in the city's tunnel shelters, which were capable of holding 30 percent of the population. At 8:15 A.M., the quiet of morning ended. Approximately 100 feet above the ground the atomic bomb exploded in a blinding white flash. Hot air enveloped the people on the ground. A loud rumbling noise followed, and then the city began to collapse. The ground shook, buildings fell all over, a great smothering cloud of dust closed in on everyone, and the fires began. The sky filled with a huge ball of purple fire, a half mile in diameter, that exploded into a wild maze of flames and purple clouds. An immense white smoke pillar appeared suddenly and shot ten thousand feet into the air, its top blossoming out into a great mushroom cap that kept going up until it had reached almost 50,000 feet.

Four and a half square miles of Hiroshima were completely burned out. Almost one third of the city's population was killed or missing, and almost an equal number were injured. Two days later, after no word from a confused and torn Japanese government, another atomic bomb, greater than the first and named "Fat Man" after Churchill, fell on the industrial city of Nagasaki. Because of the topography there the bomb's area of absolute destruction was limited to 1.8 square miles, but 40,000 people were killed or missing, and an equal number were injured. On August 10, the American government learned of Japan's decision to surrender.

Later Dr. Robert Serber reported from Hiroshima:

One walks for miles through a completely abandoned forgotten and deserted desert of broken tile and rusty sheet iron — once the residential area. In the center of the city all that remains are the shells of concrete buildings with completely gutted interiors.

Nagasaki was an industrial city with huge factories . . . From a distance the parts of these factories still standing have a peculiarly drunken aspect — steel frames of buildings leaning far from the vertical, bent away from the point at which the bomb struck. Standing inside the remains you are in the midst of a mass of twisted steel wreckage, tied in knots.

Japanese residential houses in both cities were almost completely wiped out to a distance of two miles from where the bomb struck. Minor damage extended to five miles. The destruction of life was so great that it will never be possible to know accurately how many people were killed.[20]

II

After Hiroshima

7

The Force from Which
the Sun Draws Its Power

ON THE MORNING *of August 6, 1945, Dr. Michihiko Hachiya
sat in his home in Hiroshima looking absently out into the garden
at shimmering leaves that reflected the sunlight of a cloudless sky.
He had just awakened and was still dressed in underclothes, tired
from his nighttime hours of duty as air raid warden at the hospital
he directed. Suddenly a brilliant light filled his room; he thought
that the lantern in the garden had exploded or that a passing
trolley had ignited extraordinary sparks. Then there was darkness
and swirling dust and his house began to fall. He struggled somehow into the garden and realized in a terrifying instant that he
was cut and bleeding from a large splinter in his thigh and a piece
of glass that had lodged in his neck. His lip was also ripped wide
open. Moving out toward the street, he stumbled and fell. When
he looked back he saw that he had tripped over a man's head. Re-
flexively he muttered, "Excuse me, excuse me, please." All around
him houses were falling. A gate crashed down onto a man. Still
clothed only in his underwear he ran through the streets holding
his arms out from his body to avoid the painful friction of the extraordinary heat that surrounded him. Fireballs twice caught Dr.
Hachiya's clothes and each time he quickly covered himself with
water, which made him shiver terribly.*[1]

In Washington, D.C., it was still Sunday, August 5, but General Leslie Groves was in his office waiting for the news. When it

did not come by seven o'clock that evening as he had expected it would, he left to play a game of tennis and then went to the Army-Navy Club for dinner with George Harrison and his wife and daughter. Back at the office the phone rang at 11:30 P.M., with the news that an atomic bomb had been successfully exploded on Hiroshima, Japan. Groves immediately informed General Marshall and prepared a brief written report for the Chief of Staff. Having done his job, Leslie Groves stretched out on a cot in his office and took a nap.[2]

President Truman learned of the atomic attack while on board the *Augusta* coming home from Potsdam. He was having lunch with members of the ship's crew when a White House watch officer brought him a cable from Stimson:

> Big bomb dropped on Hiroshima August 5 at 7:15 P.M. Washington time. First reports indicate complete success which was even more conspicuous than earlier test.

Truman quickly called Byrnes who was also on the ship and told him the news. Turning to the sailors seated around him, the President exclaimed, "This is the greatest thing in history. It's time for us to get home." A second message arrived with more details of the successful attack on Hiroshima. Greatly moved, Truman signaled to the crew in the mess hall. He had something to say. The United States had dropped an extremely powerful new bomb on Japan and it had detonated successfully. Now the President found Byrnes, and together they went to the wardroom where the officers were at lunch. "Keep your seats, gentlemen," Truman declared. "I have an announcement to make to you. We have just dropped a bomb on Japan which had more power than twenty thousand tons of TNT. It was an overwhelming success." The officers burst into cheers and Truman left to repeat his announcement personally to others at lunch in different parts of the ship. The typical reaction of the *Augusta*'s crew was probably expressed by the seaman who said: "I guess I'll get home sooner now." [3]

On Monday morning, August 6, at 10:45 A.M. Washington time, Henry L. Stimson released the statements by President Truman and himself announcing the successful attack on Japan and portraying the dimensions of the new American weapon. These pronouncements had been labored over for months. When he returned from Potsdam, Stimson had made final changes in them "which were induced by the difference of psychology" then existing as a result of the successful atomic test at Los Alamos. "I did not realize until I went over these papers now," Stimson said, "what a great change that [Los Alamos] had produced in my own psychology." Working with Bundy, Harrison, and Groves, Stimson had "put some more pep into the paper and made it a little more dramatic." [4]

Truman's statement began in epic and partisan tones: "The force from which the sun draws its power has been loosed against those who brought war to the Far East." Applauding American science and industry, the President declared that intelligence reports from Germany early in the war had compelled Roosevelt and Churchill to proceed with the secret atomic project, lest the Nazis perfect the dread weapon first. He promised that he would soon make known recommendations to Congress which would clarify "how atomic power can become a powerful and forceful influence toward the maintenance of world peace." In this first declaration on the subject, however, Truman gave no other nation, particularly not Russia, any cause to hope that America's possession of atomic weapons would be marked by generosity and openness:

It has never been the habit of the scientists of this country or the policy of this Government to withhold from the world scientific knowledge. Normally, therefore, everything about the work with atomic energy would be made public. But under present circumstances it is not intended to divulge the germinal processes of production or all the military applications, pending further examination of possible methods of protecting us and the rest of the world from the danger of sudden destruction.[5]

In his own statement, Stimson was only slightly more openhanded. Explaining that "the requirements of security do not permit of any revelation at this time of the exact methods by which the bombs are produced or of the nature of their action," Stimson added, however, that "in accord with its policy of keeping the people of the nation as completely informed as is consistent with national security, the War Department wishes to make known . . . at least in broad dimension the story behind this tremendous weapon." Stimson went on to portray the United States as a reluctant power that had not decided to build atomic bombs of its own volition but had been forced to do so by the pressure of external events. When the war began, he said, it was obvious that the use of atomic energy for military purposes was imminent and the only question was "which nations would control the discovery." Stimson traced the early agreements between Roosevelt and Churchill, unveiled the mystery of the plants at Oak Ridge, Tennessee, and Hanford, Washington, and announced the existence of the laboratory at Los Alamos. He paid special tribute to General Groves and J. Robert Oppenheimer.

Stimson had little encouragement to offer the nonatomic nations of the world on that second day of the new age. Americans could be assured, he said, that steps had been taken to control patents in the field and to protect the sources of uranium ore which were essential in atomic production, "in order to make certain that this tremendous weapon would not fall into the hands of the enemy." With Germany, Japan, and Italy lying in ruined defeat, it was logical to presume that this reference to the "enemy" was directed at the Soviet Union. Certainly the Russians must have read it that way. Thoughtless statements like this one no doubt helped cause the later American paranoia over the sanctity of atomic secrets, even though Stimson himself went on to caution that "there is no possibility of avoiding the risks inherent in this knowledge by any long-term policy of secrecy." Perhaps the only hopeful note in the message was Stimson's announcement that he had appointed an Interim Committee to submit recommendations to the President "for the postwar organization that should be established to direct and control the future course of the United States in this field, regarding both national and international control." Even this hopeful note was illusory, however, for the Interim Committee had done almost no work on the problems of international control and would do even less in the coming months, when its efforts would be concentrated on the creation of a system of domestic atomic energy control. In fact, the only advice the Interim Committee had given Truman regarding international matters was the suggestion that he notify Stalin at Potsdam of the new weapon. The President's adherence to that suggestion was, of course, thoroughly unsubstantial.

Dr. Hachiya made his way through the devastated city of Hiroshima on August 7 toward the Communications Hospital where he was the director. A hot sun beat down on the hundreds of dead bodies he passed along the way, and on the hundreds of live bodies lying in the streets, begging for water and waiting to die. The river running through Hiroshima was clogged with the corpses of people who had run there to escape and had drowned. Dr. Hachiya passed a man frozen in death on a bike leaning against a bridge rail. The fire reservoirs were like kettles bubbling over with the dead who looked as though they had been boiled alive. Streetcars stood still with dozens of lifeless bodies in them, blackened beyond recognition. Dr. Hachiya passed the swimming

*pool at the First Middle School which was also filled with the
corpses of people who must have suffocated because they did
not appear to be burned. A steady line of wounded men and
women and children walked toward the suburbs of Hiroshima to
ask for help. When he finally arrived at his hospital, Dr. Hachiya
found it loaded with people, "packed like the rice in sushi, into
every nook and cranny of the hospital."* [6]

*The next day, August 8, was again hot and clear in Hiroshima.
Throughout Dr. Hachiya's hospital people were dying from
wounds suffered in the atomic explosion. Several of the patients
began to show bloody diarrhea and were immediately isolated
because of the doctors' fear of a dysentery epidemic. During the
evening the hospital was permeated by a smell that seemed like
burning sardines. Dr. Hachiya looked outside and saw that the
odor was caused by sanitation teams who were cremating the
remains of the dead. Hundreds of bodies were burning in huge
fires that lit the sky.* [7]

In Washington that day Henry L. Stimson woke up at 5 A.M.
with a sharp pain in his chest. His doctors were called and di-
agnosed it as a minor heart attack. They reassured the Secretary
that he was all right but again ordered him to rest. A few hours
later, at 10:45 A.M., Stimson was in the White House waiting
to see the President. When he was shown in thirty minutes later,
he gave the President the latest teletype reports from Guam
regarding the damage done to Hiroshima; he also had brought
with him an Air Corps photograph of the victimized city. Truman
looked at these and remarked that such destruction had placed
a "terrible responsibility" on them. Stimson agreed and then
went on to speak of his own weariness and poor health, as if to
imply that he was unequal to the responsibility. Telling the
President of the mild heart attack he had suffered that morning,

Stimson asked for permission to resign. But Truman refused the request, imploring his Secretary of War to stay on "to be at his side and to be present when the war was over as he hoped it would be very soon." He told Stimson to take a month's rest. The Secretary said nothing but moved on to his business. He wanted to talk about whether to release the scientific report of the Manhattan Project, prepared at General Groves's direction by Henry Smyth of Princeton.

One week earlier, on August 1, 1945, Stimson had discussed the Smyth Report, a two-hundred-page document, with his top atomic advisers. The purpose of the report, as Stimson saw it, was "to backfire reckless statements by independent scientists after the demonstration of the bomb." If he could be sure that these errant pronouncements would be controlled in some other way, he would much prefer not to issue the detailed history contained in the Smyth Report. General Groves had said at the conference on August 1 that "under the circumstances of the entire independence of action of scientists and the certainty that there would be a tremendous amount of excitement and reckless statement," he believed that "the lesser evil would be for us to make a statement carefully prepared so as not to give away anything vital and thus try to take the stage away from the others." The fact that Groves, who Stimson viewed as "a very conservative man," held this opinion greatly influenced the Secretary of War. Pursuant to the Quebec Agreement of 1943, the combined Anglo-American Policy Committee had then met on August 2 to consider the Smyth Report. The British representatives were opposed to its publication, feeling that much valuable scientific data would thereby be given away. James Conant was also at the meeting and argued very strongly in favor of issuing the Smyth Report. Extreme care had been taken in the formation of the report, Conant said, assuring Stimson that "there was nothing given out which would play into the hands of our national competitors." After Groves again spoke in favor of publication, Stimson said he would so advise Truman.

Stimson reported these discussions to the President during their conference on August 8. He added that since the bomb had been used in Hiroshima and "we had experienced and sensed the attitude of the public towards it, people had changed a little and they no longer felt that it was important to put out the scientists' papers so quickly." It was a decision the President would have to make after hearing both sides because only he would have to bear the brunt of Congressional disapproval "for giving away such a valuable secret." Truman asked Stimson to bring representatives of both points of view to his office on the following morning so that he could make a decision.[8]

The floor belonged to Bush, Conant, Groves, and Harrison during the discussion of the Smyth Report at the White House on August 9. Truman, Stimson, and Byrnes sat and listened. When the protagonists were finished, Stimson spoke briefly. A great deal of care had been taken in the drafting of the statement "so as not to give away any secret which would really help a rival to build on our foundations," he said. The subject was, however, so vast and the Smyth Report so voluminous that it was impossible for laymen like himself or the President or Byrnes to determine the question. They would simply have to rely on the opinions of their scientific advisers. The President said he had listened with interest to the discussion and had made up his mind. The Smyth Report should be issued as soon as possible.[9]

The British were so distressed by this decision that they gave serious consideration to the possibility of asserting their rights under the Quebec Agreement to prohibit publication of the Smyth Report. Sir John Anderson felt that the withholding of this information would allow America and England to use the data as an inducement toward international control. In the end, however, the British realized that whatever their rights under the Quebec Agreement, the decision must be primarily an American one, and so they reluctantly acquiesced.[10] The newspapers of the following Sunday morning, August 12, therefore carried the Smyth Report.

During the Potsdam Conference, the English people had passed control of their government from Churchill to Clement Attlee, leader of the Labour Party. The son of a London solicitor, Attlee was a sixty-two-year-old, thoroughly unimposing man whom Churchill once described as "a sheep in sheep's clothing." [11] On the day he came to power, Attlee knew as little about the atom bomb as Truman had before Roosevelt's death. The chauvinistic tone of the first American statements on atomic energy after Hiroshima led the new Prime Minister to write to Truman on August 8. Referring to the existence within England and throughout the world of "widespread anxiety as to whether the new power will be used to serve or destroy civilisation," Attlee suggested that he and Truman, "as Heads of the Governments which have control of this great force, should without delay make a joint declaration of our intentions to utilise the existence of this great power not for our own ends, but as trustees for humanity in the interest of all peoples in order to promote peace and justice in the world." [12]

Truman adopted this trusteeship concept in a radio address to the American people on the evening of August 9, 1945, the day Nagasaki was attacked with history's third atomic bomb. His terms of adoption were, however, restrictive and not at all conducive to the establishment of international atomic control. After describing the work and concern of the Interim Committee, which had not really considered international atomic control, the President assured the public that the committee would not be allowed to run too far afield:

The atom bomb is too dangerous to be loose in a lawless world. That is why Great Britain and the United States, who have the secret of its production, do not intend to reveal the secret until means have been found to control the bomb so as to protect ourselves and the rest of the world from the danger of total destruction. We must constitute ourselves trustees of this new force — to prevent its misuse, and to turn it into channels of service to mankind . . .

Truman's continued emphasis on the notion of an atomic secret ran counter to the consistent advice he had received from his own scientific experts that there was no secret, but only a time gap in construction of the installations necessary for atomic capability. His reference to "a lawless world" could not have fallen very gently on the other nations, since it implied the existence of a certain barbarism everywhere on the planet except in England and America. That implication came to be increasingly questionable as horrifying reports of death and destruction began to come out of the Japanese cities on which Americans had dropped atom bombs.

Truman made one disturbingly false statement regarding Hiroshima in his radio address of August 9. "The world will note," he said, "that the first atom bomb was dropped on Hiroshima, a military base. That was because we wished in the first attack to avoid, insofar as possible, the killing of citizens." [13] While it is true that there were soldiers stationed in Hiroshima and that the city had been used as a quartermaster's depot, it is also true that the bomb was not dropped on a "military base" but in the center of a fully populated city.

On the day of the President's radio address, Dr. Hachiya continued to toil in his badly damaged hospital, trying to make it serve the wounded and the sick who had come there. The condition of many of the patients had taken a frightening turn. People who had received no open wounds from the atomic

*explosion now began to experience nausea and gaseous indiges-
tion. Blood appeared in their stools and dropped from other
parts of their bodies. On that day Dr. Okura, a dentist at the
hospital, went out to look for his wife, whom he had not seen
since the bombing. He returned with some bones that he had
picked up where she had last been noticed. Miss Hinada, a
nurse at the hospital, who had seemed normal after the explosion,
began to experience diarrhea and was soon clearly dying. At
night, there was darkness everywhere because the power system
of the city had been destroyed. Once again the only light in
Hiroshima came from the huge fires in which the dead were
continually being cremated. The air was filled with the smell
of burning flesh. In the isolation ward of Dr. Hachiya's hospital,
the stillness of night was broken by a small girl crying for her
mother who was not there, "Mother, it hurts, I can't stand it.
Eraiyo!"* [14]

Clement Attlee found Truman's radio broadcast of August 9
to be a "declaration of intentions of the kind I had in mind." In
a wire to the President, Attlee called the address an "admirable
statement" and declared:

> In these circumstances, I think that any joint declaration should
> wait until the means of control and the implications in the field of
> international relations have been more fully considered between
> those concerned.[15]

Discussion of international control of atomic weapons ceased
at this point and did not begin again until more than a month
had passed. The only action that was taken in this area by the
United States government during the period was self-protective.
On August 15, 1945, Truman ordered the appropriate departments of the government "to take such steps as are necessary
to prevent the release of any information in regard to the

development, design, or production of the atomic bomb, or in regard to its employment in military or naval warfare except with the specific approval of the President in each instance." Not until more than three months after Hiroshima would there be anything resembling the formation of an American policy on the subject of international control. During this period there was no man or group of men assigned the task of thinking out the difficult questions that constituted the atomic problem. There was little communication with America's atomic allies on the matter and none with its most important nonatomic ally, the Soviet Union. The government of America, like its people, was in a state of exhaustion and inertia, preoccupied with the return to peacetime life. In the passage of time from Hiroshima to the first tardy American governmental initiative on international atomic control, irreplaceable opportunities were lost.

On Tuesday evening, August 14, 1945, President Truman announced to the world that Japan had unconditionally surrendered. When the patients at Dr. Hachiya's hospital heard this same news from the voice of the Emperor himself they were heartbroken and angry. Two days before, their spirits had been raised by a rumor that Japan possessed the weapon which the Americans had dropped on Hiroshima but had not used it because it was too horrible. Now, however, in the aftermath of Hiroshima and Nagasaki, the Japanese Air Force had dropped these new bombs on American cities. "At last," Dr. Hachiya said, "Japan was retaliating." The whole atmosphere in the hospital changed. "For the first time since Hiroshima was bombed," Dr. Hachiya recalled, "everyone became cheerful and bright. Those who had been hurt the most were the happiest. Jokes were made, and some began singing the victory song." The formal news of surrender therefore shocked the people at

Dr. Hachiya's hospital. They were furious and cried: "How can we lose the war? What have we been suffering for? Only a coward would back out now. Those who died can't go to heaven in peace now." The doctor himself was distraught. He wrote in his diary:

> The one word — surrender — had produced a greater shock than the bombing of our city. The more I thought, the more wretched and miserable I became.[16]

The medical condition of Dr. Hachiya's patients exhibited no such rise and fall. It continued steadily downward. People were dying in increasing numbers. Many who had received no obvious wounds would suddenly begin to experience vaginal bleeding, nosebleeds, bloody sputum, bloody vomiting, bleeding ulcers, and hemorrhages beneath the skin and in the tissues. All this was ultimately followed by death. Rumors spread through the city uncontrollably. One doctor reported that he had heard that no one would be able to live in Hiroshima for seventy-five years. Someone else said that poison gas had been liberated and was still rising from the ruins of the city.[17]

As the thousands of jubilant bodies surged into Times Square in New York on August 15, 1945, to celebrate at last the surrender of Japan and the end of the war, Henry L. Stimson, the seventy-seven-year-old Secretary of War, rested at a mountain retreat in New York State's Adirondacks Range. Exhausted in body and spirit, Stimson had come away to the Ausable Club, there at St. Hubert's in the Adirondacks on August 13. In this hour of national triumph the Secretary of War's emotions were strangely mixed. It was not simply physical fatigue that prevented Stimson from enjoying the satisfying respite that might come to one who has emerged from war victoriously. Stimson knew more than the dancing crowds in Times Square and could not forget it. The conference at Potsdam had thoroughly depressed him. There he formed a discomforting opinion of Russia, America's only equal as a postwar power, an opinion which left little room for hope that the war just ended had brought the world to a time of peace. Then there was the atomic bomb whose development and use Stimson had overseen. For the mobs in Times Square, the bomb was a liberator, the means of returning their sons and husbands home, the way to remove the economic and emotional shackles with which they had lived over the preceding four years. For Stimson, however, the bomb had made his occupational pursuit of an orderly and peaceful world an even more anxious exercise, with awesome consequences in the balance. When he came out of his meeting with Truman at the White House on August 10, the day after Nagasaki, Stimson spoke to reporters in words that showed none of the excitement or relief that so many of his countrymen were feeling at that time:

> The world has changed and it is time for sober thought. It is natural that we should take satisfaction in the achievements of our science, but any satisfaction we may feel must be overshadowed by deeper emotion . . . The result of the bomb is so terrific that the responsibility of its possession and its use must weigh heavier on our minds and our hearts.[18]

Stimson was not alone in his concerns. "It has been cool in Washington this week," James Reston wrote. "One night it was down below 70, which is good sleeping weather for this town in early August. But thoughtful men have not been sleeping very well this week . . . In that terrible flash, 10,000 miles away men here have seen not only the fate of Japan but have glimpsed the future of America." [19]

When the *Queen Elizabeth* docked in New York, carrying sailors of the Eighth Fleet who had been en route to Tokyo, one news reporter found that "the men on board were as divided in opinion on the use of the atomic bomb as civilians at home have been since it was announced." [20]

In England church bells rang hosannas to victory all over the island but the bells of St. Alban's Abbey in Herfordshire were still at the direction of the dean of St. Albans, the Very Reverend C. C. Thicknesse who explained, "I cannot honestly give thanks to God for an event brought about by an act of wholesale indiscriminate massacre." [21]

Some of the Met Lab workers "walked the streets of Chicago vividly imagining the sky suddenly lit by a giant fireball, the steel skeletons of skyscrapers bending into grotesque shapes and their masonry raining into the streets below, until a great cloud of dust rose and settled over the crumbling city." [22]

In Rome, the Vatican newspaper, *Osservatore Romano* was troubled:

> The use of atomic bombs has created an unfavorable impression on the Vatican. Our thoughts turn to what is told of Leonardo. He planned a submarine, but he feared that man would not apply it to progress, namely to the constructive uses of civilization, but to its ruin. He destroyed that possible instrument of destruction. Mankind did not think as did Leonardo. [23]

British newspapers were filled with repugnance over the bomb. "My God," one Englishman told a reporter, "has the world gone crazy?" Another admitted, "Japan has never aroused my sympathy until today and now my heart goes out to her." [24]

Bishop C. Bromley Oxnam, president of the Federated Council of Churches of Christ in America, and John Foster Dulles, then chairman of the council's Commission on a Just and Durable Peace, warned that "the scientific miracle of the atom bomb might make the planet uninhabitable." [25]

On the day after the Hiroshima attack, Hanson Baldwin, the

usually restrained military affairs editor of the *New York Times,*
wrote:

> Yesterday, another chapter in human history opened, a chapter in
> which the weird, the strange, the horrible becomes the trite and the
> obvious. Yesterday, we clinched the victory in the Pacific but we
> sowed the whirlwind . . . Nor can the bomb's effects be stated.
> But it is possible that in addition to the direct destructive effects of
> the blast . . . there may be secondary and perhaps later effects.
> Those within a certain radius who escape death may be maimed,
> blinded, deafened, diseased . . . Americans have become a syno-
> nym for destruction . . . Certainly with such God-like power un-
> der man's imperfect control we face a frightful responsibility.
> Atomic energy may well lead to a bright new world in which man
> shares a common brotherhood or we shall become — beneath the
> bombs and the rockets — a nation of troglodytes.[26]

As the days passed at St. Hubert's, Henry L. Stimson regained
his strength and cleared his head. Far from the wartime pressures
of his Washington office he thought much about the atomic bomb
and listened attentively to the conflicting cries of his countrymen.
It is no doubt true that for most Americans during the weeks
after Hiroshima the initial policy statements of Truman and Stimson, together with Smyth's factual report, were enough said about
atomic energy. The masses of people were busy adjusting to
peacetime and obtaining for themselves whatever part of the
good life they believed victory in war had earned them. But
many others, whose occupation or simple instinct it was to trouble
over the state of the world beyond their own existence, had grown
anxious.

Their anxiety was deepened by the report of what had actually
happened to Hiroshima. The Japanese news service, Domei, was
the first to portray the horror of that city's fate. "The cruel sight
resulting from the attack is so impressive," Domei said, "that one
cannot distinguish between men and women killed by the fire.

The corpses are too numerous to count." [27] Such statements were initially dismissed as the final efforts of a wartime propaganda machine. But then more respected sources made Domei's report seem rather restrained. During the first days of September 1945 William H. Lawrence reported from Hiroshima to the *New York Times*:

> The atom bomb still is killing Japanese at a rate of 100 daily in flattened, rubble-strewn Hiroshima . . . I was among the first few foreigners to reach the site of this historic bombing and walked for nearly two hours today through streets where the stench of death still pervades and survivors or relatives of the dead, wearing gauze patches over their mouths, still probe among the ruins for bodies or possessions . . . A visit to Hiroshima is an experience to leave one shaken by the terrible incredible sights. It should be the last evidence needed to convince any doubter of the need to retain and perfect our air offense and defense lest the fate of Hiroshima be repeated in Indianapolis or Washington or Detroit or New York.[28]

The tactical conclusions Lawrence drew from the awful sights he had seen in Hiroshima were reinforced by many military strategists who, during that period, pondered a future dominated by atomic weapons that could be carried long distances in the air by rockets such as the German V–2s. These military men wondered out loud what this would do to the reassuring theory that the Atlantic and Pacific Oceans made America immune from attack. In late August 1945, General H. H. Arnold, the retiring Commander of the Army Air Forces, released the text of a final report he had submitted to the Secretary of War in which he foresaw a future war launched against the United States by thousands of enemy robot planes, each carrying an atom bomb.

The imminence of this strange new form of warfare, combined with the factual reports from Hiroshima and Nagasaki, seemed to lead outspoken men down two paths which were very much like the alternatives Stimson had described in his pre-Hiroshima discussions with Roosevelt and Truman. One group wanted to hold the secret of the atomic bomb close to America's chest and thereby stay ahead of the rest of the world. The other believed that the bomb had made traditional relationships among nations archaic and that an international system of atomic control must be established in which the United States would eventually turn control of the bomb over to a world authority.

One of the most intelligent articulations of the first approach came in a letter to the *New York Times* from a prominent group of private citizens including Stringfellow Barr and John Dewey:

> To trust any league, alliance, association, or treaty among sovereign nations to outlaw the production or use of atomic weapons is to trust swamps to cease producing mosquitoes. Such agreements really give the advantage to governments most likely to violate them. The probability of a nation concealing such a violation is in direct ratio to its lack of individual liberty.[29]

These keep-the-secret spokesmen hoped for the day when international relations would look to the individual and not to the nation as the basic unit. Until such time, they believed, America could not be indiscriminate in sharing its secrets, and especially could not give the secret to any antilibertarian nation, such as the Soviet Union.

Senator Allen Ellender of Louisiana saw the problem in more simplistic terms. "I fear," he said, "that if we should divulge the secret, it . . . may fall into the hands of unscrupulous leaders who might use it against us." [30] Senator Edwin Johnson, a Democrat from Colorado, added that the secret of the atom bomb must be kept by the United States "as the club behind the door to be used only when a bandit goes berserk." [31] Congressman Bender, a Republican from Ohio, introduced a bill making it a felony punishable by death for anyone "in the know" to reveal the secret of the atom bomb.[32] The North American Newspaper Alliance asked the members of Congress what they thought should be done with the secret of the bomb. Thirty-nine of thirty-nine Republicans and thirty-seven of forty-seven Democrats who answered said they would keep it. Five of the other Democrats would give it to the United Nations.[33] Polls among the public showed much the same results. In one, 73 percent believed that the United States should keep control of the atom bomb; 14 percent suggested putting it under United Nations control; and 13 percent had no opinion. When asked how long they felt America could keep the big secret, 24 percent said a year or less, 32 percent said around five years, 12 percent said around ten years, 5 percent said longer than ten years, 13 percent thought permanently, and 14 percent did not know.[34]

Adherents of the other major postwar response to nuclear weapons believed that the atomic bomb was so terrible that its sheer existence would cause men finally to join together in a single world government which would guarantee peace on earth. These people believed not only that the United States could not keep the secret of atomic weapons very long, but also that it should not. Norman Cousins, the editor of the *Saturday Review,* was one of the first to reflect this point of view in his editorial columns. Cousins shook the Sixth Conference on Science, Philosophy, and Religion held in New York City three weeks after Hiroshima by interrupting its demure academic presentations, only one of which considered the atomic bomb, with what one observer described as "a note of hysteria." Urging his colleagues to become missionaries for the abolition of war, Cousins exclaimed: "We are building soap-bubbles if we expect this problem to be automatically solved by having America, Britain and Canada keep the atomic bomb a secret to themselves. We must not forget that we were not the only horse in the derby; we just happened to finish first. The others will be along in due time." It was no longer possible, he said, to plan for world co-operation in a leisurely way. People must adjust immediately from "national man to world man." The most obsolete factor of all in the atomic age is national sovereignty, Cousins warned.[35]

And James Reston reported from Washington: "Men here are becoming convinced that in spite of these political realities, the scientific and military realities, since the atomic bomb, have necessitated our creating . . . a rule of law in the world." [36] On the Sunday after Hiroshima, Robert M. Hutchins spoke on the "University of Chicago Roundtable" radio program and predicted that the atom bomb "may frighten the peoples of the earth into taking the positive steps necessary to the creation of one world government." He continued:

> Up to last Monday, I was opposed to the idea of a world state because I believed no moral basis for it existed . . . no world conscience or conviction of the world community sufficient to keep it from disintegrating . . . I do not think we shall be any better off because of the bomb. But the alternatives seem clear. Only through the monopoly of atomic force by a world organiza-tion can we hope to abolish war.[37]

The apocalyptic writings of the period are typified by a magazine article written by Raymond Fosdic and called "The Challenge: One World or None." [38] It was a passionate piece that mixed oppressive pessimism with defiant pride and optimism that man was no common animal and would manage to control the atom and thereby assure his future:

> We were not prepared for the possibility of complete annihilation . . . which the two bombs dropped on Nagasaki and Hiroshima now portend . . . This is the point of human destiny to which all the glories and toils of the past have at last led us . . . Men of all races and faiths will rise to the challenge . . . Had we

known at San Francisco that atom bombs were only a few weeks away, it is possible that the institution would have been greatly strengthened. It must be strengthened now . . . There is a real sense in which the things that divide the peoples of the world are trivial as compared with the things that unite them . . . The human race is not a spineless brainless species to be pushed around and finally exterminated by forces which it has itself created. In spite of the atom bomb, we are still the captains of our own destiny, and we can make that destiny anything we desire.

At St. Hubert's Stimson heard this debate and began to formulate some opinions of his own. His energy returned and so did his instinctive idealism and trust. The ideas that Bush and Conant had been advocating for more than a year about the impossibility of winning a nuclear arms race and the desirability of establishing international control returned vividly to Stimson's mind. Oppenheimer, now a national celebrity because of his role in the Manhattan Project, had written Stimson during August 1945 urging immediate steps toward international control and particularly an approach to the Soviet Union. This, of course, was the policy Stimson himself had counseled before his depressing confrontation with the Russians at Potsdam. But now he could recall also a private meeting he had with Stalin on the day before their departure from Potsdam. It had been a thoroughly amicable session and, if taken on its face, gave cause for optimism. The American aristocrat and the Russian peasant agreed that day on the prospects for cooperation between their nations. Stalin had spoken of their great fortune that previously there had been no differences between the United States and the Soviet Union. Stimson suggested that this was largely because the two nations "had no reasons for dispute" and because their "natural objectives were the same." The Americans and the Russians easily understood each other, Stalin agreed, "more so than in the case of the Russians and the British or the

Russians and the French." Stimson said he hoped this was so.
Now at St. Hubert's, as he weighed his suspicions of Russia
against the fearful prospects of an atomic arms race, Stimson
concluded that the central problem of the postwar world was not
Russia but the bomb, and that his uneasiness about Russia must
be subordinated to his concern about the bomb. He recalled a
maxim he had cherished since his days at Yale, that the best way
to make a man trustworthy was to trust him. And so, with no illusions whatsoever about the Soviet Union, Stimson nonetheless
changed his mind and decided that it was imperative to take the
road Bush and Conant had long urged upon him. It might not succeed, but would America be true to its traditions and would he be
true to his own conscience if it was not tried? [39]

Stimson immediately summoned John McCloy to St. Hubert's
to work with him on a new memorandum about the atomic
bomb and America's relations with the Soviet Union. The
Secretary planned to return to Washington during the first week
in September and would deliver this paper to the President as
soon thereafter as possible. Even before he left St. Hubert's,
however, Stimson heard news which would seriously affect the
new atomic policy he had decided to advocate. McCloy, who had
returned to Washington, reported back to Stimson a conversation he had with Byrnes in which the Secretary of State made
it absolutely clear that he "was quite radically opposed to any
approach to Stalin whatever." Byrnes was about to depart for a
meeting of the Foreign Ministers in London and as McCloy told
Stimson, "wished to have the implied threat of the bomb in his
pocket during the conference." [40]

*During the weeks of Stimson's stay at St. Hubert's, conditions
had worsened for Dr. Hachiya and the people at his hospital
in Hiroshima. After the Emperor's surrender, there were several*

days of drunkenness, rioting, and looting throughout the city. Full of remorse over the greed and indecency that had overcome his people, Dr. Hachiya consoled himself by recalling the Chinese proverb: "A large fish would not grow in clean water." His patients meanwhile continued to die in alarming numbers. Hemorrhages under the skin became an almost certain preliminary to death, and the hospital wards were overcome with "spot-phobia," a frantic search for the signs that meant rapid death. Dr. Hachiya and his associates could only struggle vainly to alleviate the pain of suffering. They were unable to conceive remedies for this bizarre new plague. This feeling of helplessness demoralized them. There was no electricity in the hospital, little food, no clothes, and hardly any medical supplies. The building was covered with millions of flies that were hatching in the foul ruins of the city. Common symptoms of the atomic bomb sickness were the sudden and almost complete loss of hair, shortness of breath which sometimes lead to suffocation, profuse bleeding from the nose, anus, vagina, and all other bodily orifices.

8

Stimson Departs and Is Forgotten

STIMSON RETURNED to Washington on Tuesday morning, September 4. Although his health was much improved he was still compelled to take nitroglycerin tablets for his heart. In the Adirondacks, he had decided finally that the time had come for him to step down from public service. His crusade for a new atomic control policy would therefore be not the beginning of a sustained struggle but simply a final parting effort. For America and indeed for the rest of mankind, this was a tragic turn. Stimson was needed now more than ever before.

On his first day back in the capital, the Secretary attended a luncheon meeting of Truman's Cabinet. When he arrived at the White House, Stimson was pleased to find that Byrnes had not yet left for London. After lunch he cornered the Secretary of State in a White House corridor and spoke with him about "how to handle Russia with the big bomb." Stimson found Byrnes, as McCloy had predicted, "very much against any attempt at cooperation with Russia." He wrote of the Secretary of State in his diary that day: "His mind is full of his problems with the coming meeting of the foreign ministers and he looks to having the presence of the bomb in his pocket, so to speak, as a great weapon to get through the thing he has." Byrnes told Stimson of a number of acts of "perfidy," as he called them, committed by Stalin at Potsdam and said that in light of these he felt that "we could not rely on anything in the way of promises from them." Stimson explained his change of mind on the question but Byrnes remained amiably unconvinced.[1] Antagonism toward the Russian Communists was not the only factor affecting Byrnes's attitude on the question of atomic control. During August he had received a report from the scientific panel of the Interim Committee in the form of a letter from Robert Oppenheimer which described the prospects for atomic development. These, Byrnes learned, included the possibility of a far more powerful bomb based on hydrogen. Oppenheimer's conclusion was that the United States should immediately take whatever steps were necessary to achieve an international atomic control system. But when Byrnes read the letter, he came to a different conclusion. If Oppenheimer thought that hydrogen bombs could be made, then the United States had better be the country to make them. Byrnes asked that the word be passed along to Oppenheimer that "for the time being his proposal about an international agreement was not practical and that he and the rest of the gang should pursue their work [on the hydrogen bomb] full force." [2]

That afternoon Stimson wrote out a formal longhand letter of resignation. He delivered it personally to the President on the following morning. This time Truman said that he understood the Secretary's request and would reluctantly accept his resignation. But the President hoped that there would be an opportunity to discuss Stimson's views on the postwar world before his departure. The Secretary quickly accepted this invitation and added that he was most anxious to speak with the President about Russia and the atomic bomb. Describing his talk with Byrnes and the differences it had revealed, Stimson said that both his plan and Byrnes's "contained chances." In his, however, Stimson believed "there was less danger . . . and also we would be on the right path towards . . . establishment of an international world," while in Byrnes's plan "we would be on the wrong path in that respect and would be tending to revert to power politics." His allotted time now over, Stimson rose to leave. When Truman said he would like to hear more of all this in the near future, Stimson promised to send the President a copy of his memorandum as soon as it was complete.[3]

Stimson now returned to the Pentagon to begin the closing of his office and the opening of a last round of advocacy on the subject of atomic energy. The letter from Oppenheimer, written on behalf of the scientific panel, reached him during this period, pleasing him greatly, for it coincided with his own generous thoughts. After a week of work, on September 11, 1945, Stimson's memorandum was finished and he looked forward to a visit with Truman on the following afternoon.

On that same day, September 11, 1945, the deadly plague continued to move inexorably through Dr. Hachiya's hospital. In the terrifying circumstances that prevailed even the smallest personal improvements became cause for satisfaction. Dr. Hachiya visited that day with a pretty young girl who had been in his hospital since the day of the attack. She was lying in pus; her body was severely burned all over but somehow her lovely face had been untouched. Today she took pride in telling the doctor that she had been able to go to the toilet for the first time. A few days later the Allied occupation of Hiroshima began and all but the very sick left Dr. Hachiya's hospital.[4]

Stimson's appointment with Truman began at three o'clock on the afternoon of September 12, 1945. As was his custom, the Secretary handed the President a covering letter with the memorandum itself. The President read from the original and Stimson followed a carbon copy as they went over the documents paragraph by paragraph. In the letter Stimson referred to his earlier discussions at Potsdam "about the question whether we could be safe in sharing the atomic bomb with Russia while she was still a police state." He told the President that although he was no less mindful of this problem, he had concluded that "any demand by us for an internal change in Russia as a condition of sharing in the atomic weapon would be so resented that it would make the objective we have in view less probable." Liberation would come slowly within the Soviet Union, Stimson said, but he now believed that "this long process of change in Russia is more likely to be expedited by the closer relationship in the matter of the atomic bomb which I suggest and the trust and confidence that I believe would be inspired by the method of approach which I have outlined." [5] Niels Bohr, at home in Copenhagen and despondent over his failure to effect control of the weapons he helped make, would have been gratified to know that the ideas which he had advocated since 1943 were finally being pursued at the highest level of the American government.

In his memorandum to Truman, Stimson spoke in very frank and practical terms of the effect of the atom bomb on international politics. [6] In many quarters, including no doubt the Soviet Union, the bomb had been interpreted "as a substantial offset to the growth of Russian influence on the continent." Unless the Soviets were voluntarily invited into an atomic partnership with the United States and Great Britain, the result would be "to maintain the Anglo-Saxon bloc over against the Soviet in possession of this weapon." Such a course, Stimson declared, "will almost certainly stimulate feverish activity on the part of the Soviet toward the development of this bomb in what will in effect be a secret armament race of a rather desperate character." According to the Secretary, there was evidence that "such activity may have already commenced." America's primary concern therefore should be not when the Russians would develop nuclear capability but whether "when they get it they are willing and cooperative partners among the peace loving nations of the world."

Stimson argued that the problem of satisfactory relations with the Russians was "not merely connected with but . . . virtually dominated by the problem of the atomic bomb." These relations, he suggested, "may be perhaps irretrievably embittered by the way in which we approach the solution of the bomb with Russia." If the United States failed to take the initiative "and merely continued to negotiate with them, having this weapon rather ostentatiously on our hip, their suspicions and their distrust of our purposes and motives will increase." If the Russians were left to achieve nuclear capability as the result of an atomic armaments race, Stimson believed that "it would be much less likely that we will ever get the kind of covenant we may desperately need in the future." That risk, he concluded, was greater than any incurred in the policy he was suggesting. No one could know how Russia would respond, but Stimson recalled once again "the chief lesson I have learned in a long life," and that is "that the only way you can make a man trustworthy is to trust him; and the surest way to make him untrustworthy is to distrust him and show your distrust."

Not content to rest with this general exhortation, the Secretary had a particular proposal for Truman. Since the crux of the entire problem of international atomic control was Russia, any action aimed at achieving such control must be directed toward Russia. The approach must not be made as part of a general international scheme or "after a succession of express or implied threats or near threats in our peace negotiations." It must be made instead by the United States directly and forthrightly to the Russians. Stimson proposed that, after private discussion with the British, the United States inform the Soviet Union of its willingness to enter a general agreement leading toward control of the use of the atomic bomb and joint development of atomic power for peaceful and humanitarian purposes. This proposal would include two pledges by the United States: first, to stop manufacturing atomic bombs, provided that the Russians and British would do likewise; and second, to impound the existing stock of American atomic weapons, again providing that the Russians and British would agree "with us that in no event will they or we use a bomb as an instrument of war unless all three Governments agree to that use."

Stimson concluded his statement by emphasizing the importance of making the proposed initiative directly to the Soviet Union and not through an international organ "including many small nations who have not demonstrated their potential power in the war." The "loose debates" which would surround such a proposal in a multination forum, Stimson said, "would provoke scant favor from the Soviets." The approach should be made "just as soon as our immediate political considerations make it appropriate."

Truman had followed Stimson along each step of his presentation, and after each step had indicated his "full accord." When the Secretary finished, Truman said that "his view on the whole thing was in accord" with Stimson's. "We must take Russia into our confidence," the President declared.[7]

On the following day Stimson decided to talk once more with the State Department about control of atomic weapons. With Byrnes in London, the man in charge was Dean Goderham Acheson, an urbane and eloquent Washington lawyer who had recently become Assistant Secretary of State. Stimson was delighted to find Acheson "evidently strongly on our side in the treatment of Russia." With the permission of the President, he sent Acheson a copy of his memorandum on atomic control.[8]

A few days later Stimson called in Robert Patterson, a federal court judge from New York who had become Assistant Secretary of War and would soon be his successor as Secretary of War. Stimson had heard that Patterson was taking a contrary view to his own on the question of the atomic bomb and relations with Russia. Now he explained to Patterson the history of his own thinking on the subject from his disillusionment at Potsdam to his renewed present spirit. Patterson listened, asked a few questions and then said:

> Well, you have convinced me. I find I was wrong and I think you are right. The safest way is not to try to keep the secret. It evidently cannot be kept. I did not realize that beforehand and that being so it is better to recognize it promptly and try to get on terms of confidence with the Russians.[9]

At the President's Cabinet luncheon on Tuesday, September 18, the subject of atomic energy was discussed briefly. Truman announced that he wanted to make "control of the big bomb" the sole topic on the agenda of the regular Cabinet meeting on Friday. He asked Stimson if he was willing to attend and help out. "Of course," Stimson answered. "I would be there if I could walk on my two legs." [10]

Friday, September 21, 1945, was Stimson's last day of government service and also his seventy-eighth birthday. Although the Cabinet meeting was scheduled for later in the afternoon, the President summoned Stimson to the White House at 1:45 for the discussion of urgent business. Once there, the Secretary was ushered to the rose garden immediately behind the President's office. He was surprised to find the members of the Cabinet, other governmental dignitaries, friends, and his wife Mabel there to watch as the President awarded him the Distinguished Service Medal. Truman called the Secretary's career in public service one of the most distinguished in the history of the nation. He compared Stimson to Enoch, "of whom it was said, he was a just man." Praising Stimson for his ability to express his views in plain language, Truman said that he was very sorry to see him go.

When the brief ceremony was concluded, the Cabinet members moved into the White House for the discussion Truman had promised on the question of atomic control. Ironically, the only member of the Cabinet who was not there was James Byrnes, Stimson's major antagonist in this matter. Dean Acheson sat in for Byrnes, although he could hardly represent the Secretary of State in a discussion of atomic control, since their views were opposite. Also at the meeting were Vannevar Bush; Judge Robert Patterson; John Snyder, the head of the Office of War Mobilization and Reconversion; Senator Kenneth McKellar of Tennessee, the President Pro Tempore of the Senate; and Leo Crowley, the Foreign Economic Administrator. The President began with a direct question. What should be "the policy of this government in making available information in our possession to other nations?" He called on the "former Secretary of War, Mr. Stimson" to answer first. With the determined sturdiness of an aging warrior going to battle for the last time, Stimson now presented the argument he had made to Truman a week before. There was no way to avoid an atomic arms race except by internationalization of the weapon, and therefore the United States had better get to it right away by involving the Russians in atomic development. Each of the members of the Cabinet responded to Stimson in turn, and while they all gave deference to the departing statesman, the consensus of their expressions did not favor his point of view. Acheson and Patterson came down haltingly on Stimson's side, with the Acting Secretary of State emphasizing the need for safeguards and an assurance that the generosity of sharing atomic energy development would be reciprocated by the Russians. Fred M. Vinson, the Secretary of the Treasury, was the first to express strong opposition to Stimson. He did not understand how America could share any part of its atomic knowledge without also giving away military secrets. Attorney General Tom Clark agreed, adding that an exchange of information was likely to be a one-sided affair. Truman interrupted at this point to say that the discussion was not over whether to give the secret of the bomb away but on the question of what were "the best methods of controlling bomb warfare and the exchange only of scientific information."

Robert Hannegan, the Postmaster General and chairman of the Democratic National Committee, avoided the complexities of the issue. Expressing his respect for Stimson, he said he would support the former Secretary's position.

The Secretary of the Navy, James Forrestal, gave the opposition to Stimson its most aggressive articulation that day. He argued that the bomb was "genuinely the property of the American people" and that the Administration must be certain that it knew what the people wanted to be done with the bomb and its secrets before any action was taken. Forrestal drew a parallel between the Japanese who had been America's allies during World War I and then violated Naval agreements with the United States and the Russians who, he said, "like the Japanese, are essentially Oriental in their thinking, and until we have a longer record of experience with them on the validity of engagements . . . it seems doubtful that we should endeavor to buy their understanding and sympathy. We tried that once with Hitler. There are no returns on appeasement." Forrestal proposed that the United States exercise a trusteeship over the atomic bomb on behalf of the United Nations, just as other major powers would exercise trusteeships over geographical areas. In one sense, Forrestal was merely expanding on the concept which Truman himself had introduced in his earliest pronouncements on the atomic bomb.

Rising immediately to oppose the Navy Secretary was Henry Agard Wallace, former Vice President and then Secretary of Commerce. He had been one of the five men originally appointed by Roosevelt in 1941 to oversee the development of the American atomic bomb project. As Wallace listened to the discussion in the Cabinet Room that day, he became troubled at how "utterly green" the Cabinet was on the subject. In his view, only Truman, Stimson, and he had any background of scientific information which would allow them to discuss the matter intelligently. Wallace therefore began by asking the President exactly what was the subject under discussion. Once again, Truman said the question was whether the United States should share the scientific information with other nations, not whether factory technique or know-how should be disclosed. That was what he thought, Wallace said, adding his opinion that to a very great degree, atomic energy information had come from abroad anyway. If the United States "put the screws on our scientists, other nations could go beyond us in our discoveries," Wallace predicted. There was the gravest danger of developing a "Maginot Line type of mind about atomic secrets which competent scientists knew had not been, and were not then, our exclusive property." The question was whether we were going to follow "the line of bitterness . . . or the line of peace." Turning now to Forrestal's argument, Wallace took issue with the claim of the Secretary of the Navy that the Russians were Oriental in outlook. He pointed especially to Mongolia where, he said, the Russians' view was decidedly Western in contrast to the Chinese. Expressing his complete agreement with Stimson's position, Wallace concluded that a failure to share scientific information with the Russians would make them "a sour and embittered people." To

Forrestal, this sounded like Wallace was "completely, everlastingly and wholeheartedly in favor of giving it [the bomb] to the
Russians."

Troubled that the discussion was polarizing, Vannevar Bush
now pointed out once more that Stimson was not asking that the
full secret of the bomb, which involved manufacturing techniques, be revealed. Might it not be possible, he asked, to put
the Soviet Union to an initial test by offering to exchange basic
scientific information? Hopefully, the Russians would respond
in kind by revealing some of their own atomic development, or
perhaps even by agreeing to preliminary regulatory procedures
No one disagreed with this suggestion directly, but John Snyder
and Senator McKellar both suggested that what was needed most
was a cooling off period of perhaps six months. At that inconclusive point the discussion ended. Such a delay, as Stimson well
knew, could spell the difference between life and death for future
generations of mankind.

Stimson could not have left this meeting and public life with
very much hope in his heart. He had argued for speed and direct
initiatives, and the sentiment of the meeting favored caution and
action through the United Nations. He had pleaded for reasonable selflessness to show the Russians that they could trust
America, and the strongest voices at the meeting seemed to want
the United States to wait until the Soviets showed Americans that
they could be trusted. But at least Truman had been awakened
by the lively exchange of views. At the end of the discussion the
President invited "a memorandum from all hands summarizing
the views they had expressed; he said he did not propose to act
without the concurrence of Congress; that he had taken an
obligation, however, to send a message with his recommendations." [11]

It took no more than a few hours for a distorted version of

this Cabinet meeting to reach the *New York Times*. On the very next day the newspaper reported that Henry Wallace had argued that the secrets of the bomb should be given immediately to the Soviet Union as a guarantee of continued Big Three cooperation. Stimson's substantive suggestions were lost in the mild delirium that erupted when this *Times* story was given headline treatment in newspapers across the country. According to the story, the Navy and War Departments were vehemently against Wallace's alleged suggestion, and it was generally believed that Truman himself "would be the last to give his approval to the Wallace proposal until a working world order had been attained." Congress lost little time in expressing its angry opposition to Wallace's apparent suggestion. Senator Tom Connally of Texas, the senior Democratic member of the Senate Foreign Relations Committee, said flatly, "Complete secrecy should be maintained regarding the atomic bomb." Congressman Hatton Summers of Texas, the chairman of the House Judiciary Committee, rushed to the White House to discuss a bill he had introduced imposing the death penalty on anyone who divulged secrets concerning the atomic bomb. He emerged, evidently reassured, with the statement that he had enjoyed "a very satisfactory conference with the President." [12] Returning on Sunday from a weekend holiday at Jefferson Island in the Chesapeake Bay, the President held an impromptu news conference at the rear entrance to the White House. He denied that Wallace had ever made the reported proposal and said that he himself would be the only one responsible for the atomic bomb.

During the following week, Dr. Hachiya made his final entry into the diary he had kept of the atomic attack on Hiroshima. A group of American soldiers of occupation came to visit Dr. Hachiya's hospital. One of them stood at the window, looking

*out over the ruins and, at length, said through an interpreter:
"There must be dead still in the ruins, and I have the feeling
that if the ruins aren't removed and the bodies disposed of, ill will
between both countries will be prolonged. What is your opinion?"*

*"I agree with you," Dr. Hachiya answered. "I hear you are
using a useful machine in Kure to clean up the ruins, a 'bull-
dozer,' I think it is called. Couldn't you have one sent to help us
clean up the city? Otherwise, I am sure those who were injured
and those who lost relatives and friends will be continually reminded of the day they were bombed and hate you when they
come back to Hiroshima."*

*"It's out of the question," the American officer replied. "Amer-
ica can't afford to send such equipment in here now. What are
your thoughts regarding the bombing?"*

*"I am a Buddhist," Dr. Hachiya replied, "and since childhood
have been taught to be resigned in the face of adversity. I have
lost my home and my wealth and I was wounded but disregarding
this, I consider it fortunate my wife and I are alive. I am grateful
for this even though there was someone to die in every home in
my neighborhood."*

*"I can't share your feelings," the officer replied, sternly. "If I
were you, I'd sue the country."*

*The officer stood a while longer and gazed out the window.
Finally, he and his party departed. After he had gone, Dr. Hachiya told his friends what the officer had said.*

*"Sue the country! Sue the country!" Dr. Hachiya repeated,
over and over, to himself. But no matter how many times he repeated it, and however hard he thought, the statement was altogether incomprehensible.*

The Interim Committee met in Washington on Tuesday, September 25. Its primary work continued to be the preparation of

legislation establishing a system for domestic control of atomic energy which the President would present to Congress. That day, however, the Interim Committee also discussed Stimson's proposals for international control and resolved to support them in whatever way they could. Two of the committee members, Oppenheimer and George Harrison, went to work with Acheson and Patterson respectively on the memorandums which the President had requested at the Cabinet meeting of September 21. Patterson's statement was a fuzzy, uninspired confirmation of Stimson's position. Acheson, however, argued at great length and with typical eloquence for a direct approach to the Russians. The United Nations should be brought into the picture only after the wartime allies had come to an agreement, he said. Contending that the current state of atomic affairs must appear to the Soviet Union "to be unanswerable evidence of an Anglo-American combination against them," Acheson declared that for the United States to continue to claim itself trustee of atomic energy for the benefit of the world "will mean nothing more to the Russian mind than an outright policy of exclusion." [13]

At the same time, Acheson directed Herbert Marks, a young Washington lawyer who served him as personal assistant, to draft a Presidential message to Congress on atomic energy. The focus of the message would be domestic control legislation, but Acheson told Marks that he might gingerly incorporate some of Stimson's ideas about international control. By the end of September, Marks had completed a draft which was then placed on the assembly line of the federal bureaucracy to be inspected by the several interested agencies. At the War Department, it ran into trouble when worries were expressed about whether Marks's few statements on international control would so upset Congress that the chances of passing domestic legislation would be jeopardized. But when the draft reached Democratic Congressional leaders Alben Barkley and Sam Rayburn, they argued that the question of international atomic control was already so much on the mind of the members of Congress that it would do no harm to have some official Administration pronouncement on the matter. Truman's counsel and foremost speechwriter, Judge Samuel I. Rosenman, agreed, and so the Presidential message which was sent to Congress on October 3 contained a word about international atomic control, although its emphasis remained on domestic control.[14]

If Stimson's partisans saw this message as a victory, it was a rather tepid triumph. The President had chosen to give a little bit to both sides of the atomic control debate and thereby admitted that American policy on this most significant subject was still in flux. The so-called secrets of atomic energy would not remain so for long, Truman declared, and therefore, "the hope of civilization lies in international arrangements looking, if possible, to the renunciation of the use and development of the atomic bomb." Admitting that "the difficulties in working out such arrangements are great," he suggested that the alternative "may be a desperate armament race which might well end in disaster." The position of Stimson and his followers was partially served in the President's proclamation that "discussion of the international problem cannot be safely delayed until the United Nations Organization is functioning and in a position adequately to deal with it," but Stimson was forgotten in Truman's statement of intention to talk with Great Britain and Canada first about the problem. Timing was critical and Truman was losing time, while there was no mention at all of Russia. The President was careful to state that even the Anglo-American-Canadian "discussions will not be concerned with disclosures relating to the manufacturing processes leading to the production of the atomic bomb itself." [15]

Although Congress was relieved that the President had thrown the question of atomic control to it for decision, there was still considerable worry on Capitol Hill about the secrets. Congressman Andrew May, a powerful Democrat from Kentucky who was chairman of the House Military Affairs Committee, said he was concerned that the great grant of power to the executive branch of government in the proposed domestic control bill might still allow the President to give the secrets away. "We will put some kind of handle on that," May assured the nation.[16]

A few days later, on October 7, in a speech to the Pemiscot County Fair at Caruthersville, Missouri, Truman made a very oblique reference to his hope for international cooperation in the development of atomic energy. Commentators and Congressmen across the country were quickly triggered into paroxysms of anguish over the fate of the secrets.

On the following evening, Truman hastily summoned reporters for a late-night "old-fashioned bull session" on the front porch of the lodge at Reelfoot Lake near Tiptonville, Tennessee, which he was visiting for a brief fishing trip. But it was more than "bull" that Truman had in mind, and his purpose was not very old-fashioned at all. He wanted to talk atomic energy and specifically to make clear that he had no plans whatsoever to give away any of the crucial engineering secrets that made possible the production of atomic bombs. These would be useless anyway, he said, because "only the United States has the combination of industrial capacity and resources necessary to produce the bomb." Could Russia build a bomb eventually? one of the reporters asked. "Your guess is as good as mine," the President answered, going on to declare that the problems between Russia and the United States were not due to the fact that the United States possessed the atomic bomb and Russia did not. In fact, the President continued somewhat mysteriously, the greatest problem in relating to Russia was probably linguistic.[17]

Secretary of State Byrnes returned from the Foreign Ministers conference in London a few days after Truman had sent his atomic energy message to Congress. Exasperated by the weeks of unproductive wrangling in London, Byrnes was thoroughly unappreciative of even Truman's limited call for international negotiations on atomic energy. At London the disintegration of the wartime alliance with Russia had become a fact. A world divided into two hostile blocs seemed imminent, causing most of the diplomats in London to experience what one described as "really acute tension and worry." [18] The United States had not placed the subject of atomic energy on the agenda of the conference, and the Russians had predictably not embarrassed themselves by asking about it, leading C. L. Sulzberger to remark that "the five foreign ministers were probably the only people in the civilized world who avoided it as a topic." [19] Sources close to the Soviet delegation reported that the Russians were irked over the failure of the Western powers to offer them an equal share in atomic development.[20] There was much feeling in the British Parliament and among diplomatic observers in London that this failure had been one of the major underlying causes of the endless disagreements that characterized the London conference.

Byrnes, however, had a different view. At a meeting with the Secretaries of War and Navy, Robert Patterson and James Forrestal, he complained that before his departure for London he had "begged" Stimson not to recommend to the President that he include the subject of international consultation on atomic energy in his message to Congress. Byrnes was therefore angry that Stimson had apparently done so and that the President had agreed. This, Byrnes said, would undoubtedly "create difficulties for him." He could foresee "that at future meetings Molotov would refer to the President's statement and ask to discuss the whole question of the control of the atomic bomb." Forrestal fully agreed, adding his fear that the pressures for international negotiations would increase within the United States. This also worried Byrnes, who said that he planned to talk with the President about it. His own position was that "before any international discussion of the future of the bomb could take place, we must first see whether we can work out a decent peace." He obviously did not believe that the failure to talk about international atomic control might be a significant obstacle to that desired peace.[21]

Byrnes, Forrestal, and Patterson held another of their regular conferences a week later on the morning of October 16. Atomic energy was once again a major topic of discussion. Byrnes had been carrying his view throughout the Truman Administration and had enjoyed some success. He had asked General Marshall whether his experience with the Russians "justified him in relying on the United Nations Organization to inspect Russian plants and in telling the American people he could rely on such inspection." The General had apparently said no. To Byrnes this was the crux of the problem. He had read the report of the scientific panel of the Interim Committee and did not like it. "While it was very well for the scientists to say as they did that science has no boundaries, that certainly did not apply to either Mr. Molotov or Mr. Stalin," Byrnes declared. "It is idle to expect that we would be allowed access for purposes of inspection to Russian factories producing atomic bombs when we cannot even gain access to Hungary or Poland," he concluded.[22]

9

The Scientists and the British
Force America to Act

As THE DAYS PASSED in October 1945, Truman continued to procrastinate on questions of atomic control. The controversial domestic control bill had been sent to Congress, but the White House was not using its influence to move the bill very far very quickly. On the international front, Byrnes's arguments for delay and the pressure of nonatomic domestic matters combined to produce Presidential inaction. The pledge Truman had made to Congress on October 3 that he would seek limited international discussions on atomic control remained unfulfilled, and it probably would have stayed that way for much longer were it not for the atomic scientists and, particularly, the British government.

The most surprising factor in the public discussions of atomic weapons during the first several weeks after Hiroshima was the silence of the scientists who had built them. This was especially strange when set against their active participation in the secret deliberations on atomic energy control which had occurred before the world learned that the atom bomb existed. After Hiroshima, the public actively entered the discussions of atomic energy, but the scientists were still silenced by General Groves's security orders. Some of the more vociferous members of the Manhattan Project, like Leo Szilard, were able to tolerate this injunction only because they had been mistakenly led to believe that immediately after Hiroshima the United States entered into secret control deliberations with Britain and Russia, "as indeed it should have . . . and we did not want to embarrass the President or the Secretary of State." [1]

In the aftermath of Hiroshima and Nagasaki, James Franck's Committee on Social and Political Implications continued to meet privately in Chicago. Their restlessness grew as the public discussion of atomic energy became louder with the return of Congress to Washington in early September; the men who dominated that discussion knew little or nothing of atomic energy and, to the scientists, their statements showed it.

The atomic scientists' yearning to inform the rest of mankind of what they believed to be the full truth about atomic weapons and atomic control was given a tragic stimulus on August 21, when Harry Dagnian, a twenty-six-year-old Manhattan Project scientist at Los Alamos, accidentally set off a nuclear chain reaction. It lasted for only a fraction of a second, but in that time, Dagnian's right hand received a fatal exposure to radiation. He was immediately rushed to a hospital, where over the next three weeks he experienced all the horrible symptoms which thousands of people in Hiroshima were then enduring: loss of hair, internal pain, hemorrhaging, swelling, and finally, twenty-four days after the accident, death. [2]

On September 1, the atomic scientists' anxiety finally burst into public view during a luncheon at the Shoreland Hotel in Chicago, held to announce the formation of a new Institute of Nuclear Studies at the University of Chicago. Sam Allison, the tall, chunky, forty-four-year-old scientist who had shouted "Now" at zero hour in Los Alamos was to be the institute's director. In his remarks at that luncheon, Allison surprised everyone by complaining about government control of both scientific research and the scientists' tongues. Then he shattered the placidity of the meeting with a verbal explosion of his own. Unless the military restrictions on science ceased, Allison warned, he and his colleagues might choose to forget atomic energy and devote themselves to studying the color of butterfly wings. A reporter asked Allison whether he thought scientists would work on the bomb if they had the decision to make over again, and he said they would only if they were as mad at the dictators as they were in 1942.

In Washington, General Groves was astounded and immediately dispatched his deputy, Colonel Kenneth Nichols, from Oak Ridge to Chicago to talk with the scientists. Nichols told them that an atomic energy control bill had been prepared and would be presented to Congress. Its chances of passage might be hurt if they continued their talk about butterfly wings. They agreed to subside temporarily.[3]

The wide media coverage of this butterfly incident gave the atomic scientists some sense of their own influence and power. James Franck maintained the momentum when he released a petition signed by sixty-four of his colleagues urging the President to realize that there was no real secret to the bomb. They implored Truman to invite other nations to link up with America in joint atomic development to avoid a nuclear arms race. The press gave this statement very wide coverage.

Now, at Los Alamos and Oak Ridge, as well as at Chicago, the atomic scientists began to organize themselves to present their knowledge and opinions to the public and to the government. Formal approval of their activities did not come until more than a month later when on October 20, in response to continuing pressure, the War Department issued an order proclaiming that public discussion on atomic energy by all citizens was essential now and consistent with the best democratic principles. "American scientists in particular, because of their knowledge of the technical matters involved and because of their comprehension of the full social significance of the achievement, can contribute to it . . . Our scientists should feel that it is proper for them as citizens to join actively in public consideration of this question." In the wake of this statement, the nuclear scientists from the different Manhattan Project installations came together and formed the Federation of Atomic Scientists, a potent lobby in the Congressional debate over the May-Johnson bill for domestic control of atomic energy, and a vital but less successful source of opinion and pressure in regard to the international control of atomic energy.

The public attention which the scientists' view received did not go unnoticed at the White House. A more potent force there, however, was the British government, which had listened with dismay to the pronouncements of its foremost ally on the subject of international control of atomic energy. Truman's repeated statements that he did not intend to share the manufacturing techniques of atomic development were intended primarily for the Russians, but the British could not help but feel that they were also being excluded from the postwar exploitation of atomic power which Churchill had so arduously fought to secure. The English public and Parliament also seemed more preoccupied than their American counterparts with the need to internationalize the bomb as the only way to avoid an atomic armaments race and ultimately an atomic war. On September 25, after a flurry within England over Henry Wallace's statements at the Cabinet meeting a few days before, Clement Attlee wrote to Truman expressing a sense of urgency over atomic control and requesting a meeting with the President to discuss the matter as soon as possible. The responsible statesmen of the world, Attlee said, were faced with decisions that would affect the very survival of civilization. As he and his associates in the British government planned for the future, Attlee told Truman, he continually asked himself: "Am I to plan for a peaceful or a warlike world?" [4]

Truman's message to Congress on October 3 was an indirect answer to Attlee's plea, but when he responded directly in a letter to the Prime Minister on October 5, the President made no mention of a date for the talks which Attlee so deeply desired. The British, however, persisted. Lord Halifax repeatedly raised the question with Secretary of War Patterson throughout October. On the sixteenth day of the month, Attlee wrote once more to Truman referring to his earlier letter and explaining that he was "being subject to heavy Parliamentary pressure from both Parties to make a statement on the Government's policy." Attlee said he still hoped to exchange views with Truman before making any pronouncements but added: "It will not be possible for me to postpone discussion for long." The Prime Minister also informed Truman of his view that the Foreign Ministers conference in London had been "overshadowed by the problem" and that "the prospective conference of the United Nations will be jeopardized unless we have some clearness on our own attitude." [5]

This urgent request, together with the public clamoring of the scientists and others within the United States, simply could not be ignored by Truman. Once again, however, he delayed his response.

The President gave a first strong hint of impending talks with England and Canada in the Navy Day Address which he delivered on a windy Saturday, October 27, at Central Park in New York, before a crowd estimated at one million, while "history's greatest fleet rode at anchor in the North River." [6] Repeating his belief that efforts to control atomic energy could not await the formation of the United Nations, Truman announced that "these discussions . . . will be begun in the near future." There was nothing else new said about atomic energy, although the earlier idea of an American trusteeship over atomic energy received more explicit expression:

In our possession, as in our possession of other new weapons, there is no threat to any nation. The world, which has seen the United States in two recent wars, knows that full well. The possession in our hands of this new power of destruction we regard as a sacred trust. Because of our love of peace, the thoughtful people of the world know that that trust will not be violated, that it will be faithfully executed.

Standing hatless in a gray topcoat, Truman held out the hopeful notion that "differences of the kind that exist today among the nations that fought together so long and so valiantly for victory are not hopeless or irreconcilable." Once more, he assured Americans that the international negotiations which he contemplated would never be concerned with "the processes of manufacturing the atomic bomb."

In London and Paris, the press hailed Truman's gestures toward international cooperation but expressed dismay at his apparent intention to hold back the secrets. This policy, they said, was causing the Russians to be intransigent.

Three days later, Attlee was more explicit. He told Parliament that he and W. L. Mackenzie King, the Canadian Prime Minister, would visit the United States on November 11 for a conference with Truman devoted entirely to atomic energy. The White House soon confirmed Attlee's announcement. When President Truman was asked by a reporter whether the conference was the first step toward another meeting of the United States, Britain, and Russia, he gave a circumspect answer which could, in no way, be interpreted as affirmative.

At the beginning of November 1945, with the arrival of Attlee and King ten days away, the government of the United States was still without a policy for the international control of atomic energy. This extraordinary state of unpreparedness was only partially the result of Truman's preoccupation with the demanding web of postwar domestic problems. It was largely the result of Secretary of State Byrnes's wintry attitude toward international atomic control negotiations. Vannevar Bush, who had stayed on in Washington as head of the Office of Scientific Research and Development, appreciated the vacuum and stepped into it.

First, however, the Secretary of War, Robert Patterson, attempted to move Byrnes. On November 1, he wrote to Byrnes urging him to undertake a thorough study of the international aspects of atomic energy control in preparation for the conference with Attlee and King. Patterson had this letter hand delivered and then personally visited Byrnes later in the afternoon. After an hour of advocacy by Patterson of the need for planning and of the wisdom of Stimson's views, Byrnes was still "noncommittal." [7]

Late the next afternoon, Patterson discussed the coming conference and Byrnes's attitude toward it with Bush. They both agreed on the urgent need for preparation. Patterson then summoned his assistant, Gordon Arneson, and asked him to prepare a study of the existing relationship between England, Canada, and the United States on atomic matters and to add to that a set of policy proposals based on Stimson's memo to Truman of September 11, Patterson's memo to Truman of September 25, and Bush's memo to Truman of the same day. The last two papers had been submitted to the President in response to his request after the Cabinet-level discussion of atomic weapons on September 21. Patterson outlined for Arneson the "several stages of negotiations" as follows: "revision of agreements with the British and the Canadians, approach to Russia, and finally an approach to the UNO." For his part, Bush said that he would go directly to Byrnes and try to stimulate some thinking and action along the necessary lines. [8]

On the afternoon of the following day, Saturday, November

3, Bush visited Byrnes. Finding quite early in the conversation, as he had expected, that there was no Administration plan on atomic energy control "that goes beyond great generalities," Bush methodically outlined such a proposal for Byrnes. The Secretary was still not prepared to commit himself but advised Bush to prepare a memorandum of policy along the lines he had discussed. Any affirmative steps, however, would have to await the outcome of a conference he was going to have with the President on Tuesday, Byrnes said. Once informed of "the President's opinions and objectives," he could proceed to organize the conference.[9]

Fully appreciative of the opportunity which Byrnes's inaction had provided him, Bush set to work that afternoon on the desired memorandum. For him, of course, this was not the plowing of new ground since he had pondered the primary questions of atomic control for years. He worked throughout the weekend and late Sunday asked Conant to review the memorandum he produced. On Monday morning, November 5, it was delivered by special messenger to Byrnes. Bush's memorandum was a levelheaded piece of work without the doomsday forebodings so popular at the time but with a keen appreciation of the seriousness of the problem and of the overriding need for the United States to act quickly. It was divided into two sections: the first covered desired changes in the Quebec Agreement of 1943 which still regulated the atomic relationships of Britain, Canada, and the United States; the second advocated a method of approach to Russia as the first step toward establishing an international system of atomic control. Before touching either of these substantive questions, Bush appealed to Byrnes to establish a new atomic policy planning group to supplant the Interim Committee which had never been active in the field of international control and had finished its work relating to domestic control. Bush also

suggested that this new group should include members of the
United States Senate which would have to ratify any international
treaty concerning atomic control.

On the substantive questions Bush urged Byrnes to try to convince the English "that the Quebec Agreement was intended for
the war period only" and that the two nations should therefore
select a committee to renegotiate the compact. He envisioned the
new agreement as a simple document, "providing merely for
sharing of materials, leaving political clauses and the dissemination of information to be worked out on a more general international basis."

It was the approach to Russia that was "the great question
before the conference," Bush told Byrnes. The objective was
clear to Bush. A secret atomic armaments race which could end
in the devastation of American cities as well as those of the
enemy must be avoided. The obstacle was also very clear to him:
"Russia is naturally secretive and suspicious and very intent on
its own immediate interests." The solution, Bush suggested, was
"to make the agreements in such manner that it will be in Russia's
interest to keep them." He proposed a system of "partial pay-
ments," a step-by-step plan in which Russian compliance with
the first step would lead to a second step by the United States,
and so on. Above all, the American program must not involve
any premature outlawing of the bomb, because if a future war
could not be avoided, then the United States must have atomic
bombs and "be in a clear position to use them promptly if there
is any chance that our enemy has them." Cautioning Byrnes that
America must "be tolerant of minor irritations or departures,"
Bush declared that the goal was "to open up Russia, and it will
take time."

Bush's plan was the most detailed yet put before an American
official. But in its specificity it eschewed the desires of Bush's

former mentor, Henry L. Stimson. Step one involved not an attempt to work out a comprehensive agreement with the Soviet Union as Stimson had suggested, but merely an invitation to Russia to join with Britain and the United States in proposing the establishment of a scientific agency within the United Nations which would be "charged with the full dissemination of fundamental information on science in all fields including that of atomic fission." As a "prerequisite" to this proposal, it would be understood that every country would allow access to its scientific laboratories by foreign scientists and free travel by its own scientists to the laboratories of other nations. Bush thought that this first step would allow the United States "to find out whether Russia really wants to proceed with us," for, he thought, there "was little incentive for her to join us genuinely on this step unless she does."

The second part of Bush's plan called for the creation of an international inspection force whose jurisdiction would go beyond scientific laboratories into manufacturing establishments. It would also publish reports of atomic development activities throughout the world. Since this would involve the American atomic plants directly, Bush counseled that "we do not wish to open this whole affair up until we are assured that the inspection system is really going to work." The United States "should approach the matter gradually" and be certain that there be "a deliberately restricted scope of the Inspection Commission's function at the outset."

Finally, step three of the Bush plan, which he said should not go into effect until "many years" after the first step, would restrict fissionable materials to commercial use only. For the United States, this apparently would mean the conversion of its atomic bombs for use in power plants. In fact, as Bush admitted in his memo, there was then no knowledge of how to accomplish such conversion, but "presumably we will know this by the time we are ready for this third step." After this stage went into effect, "a period of years" would have to be allowed for the complete conversion of atomic weapons to commercial purposes.

Bush's system could not reasonably be expected to deter Russia from developing atomic weapons of its own, because it offered nothing to Russia in return for atomic abstinence except the very future prospect that the United States would dismantle its own nuclear arsenal and share its nuclear capability. On the other hand, Russia was being asked to open up her laboratories and factories to international inspection and ultimate control, an extremely generous *quid* to expect from so xenophobic a nation in return for the thoroughly insubstantial *quo* that was being offered.[10]

The reason for Vannevar Bush's departure from the spirit of his earlier accord with Stimson is not clear. The most logical explanation is that he was affected by Secretary Byrnes's deep distrust of the Russians and absolutely negative view of the prospects of international control. Bush therefore wrote a plan which could not help but appeal to Byrnes, since it was, in effect, without risk for the United States. The Secretary of State took Bush's memo with him to a meeting with the President on Wednesday, November 7, to discuss the coming three-power conference with the English and the Canadians. Truman and Byrnes found Bush's position very acceptable and the Bush plan therefore quickly became the American plan. On the following morning, November 8, Byrnes summoned Bush and General Groves to his office to ask them the one question which had come to his mind in reviewing Bush's memo with the President: "What do we do with our bombs in the meantime, assuming that a plan similar to the previous memorandum is being carried out?" Bush and Groves said they would put their heads together and prepare a memorandum for Byrnes in response to the question. During his discussion with Byrnes that day, Bush was startled by the way in which the Secretary "had quite completely shifted his position" since their conference on Monday. This time, Bush told Conant afterward, "we were discussing carefully ways and means toward an effective accord rather than merely struggling with the question of whether any accord is possible." [11]

Bush and Groves had an answer for Byrnes by the following morning, November 9. They said that their plan assumed that the United States would continue to manufacture the explosive material for atomic bombs. When the negotiations with Russia reached a "propitious point," however, America could announce that it would no longer assemble this material into atomic bombs but merely store it in bar form. Later, when there was a workable international inspection system in operation (a period of years in Bush's plan) the United States could invite inspection of this material to prove that it was being held in nonweapon form. "The cost of this step to us," Bush and Groves assured Byrnes, "is merely that it would make the material unavailable for atomic bombs without a period of preparation." [12]

Bush and Groves discussed the new American plan with Secretary Patterson on Saturday, November 10, and then briefly with George Harrison and Gordon Arneson for a final review. The resulting policy paper was changed from Arneson's earlier draft so that it "suggested only in general terms the nature of the approach which the three governments might agree the United States should make to Russia." In his minutes of this meeting, Arneson wrote: "The further step of setting up an organ of the UNO to control the field of atomic energy was stated as an ultimate objective, to be achieved, however, only after a considerable period and only after the effective cooperation of Russia had been proven in practice." [13] After a week of extraordinarily casual policy-making, the American government was ready with a plan for the international control of atomic weapons which it could show to its British and Canadian allies.

After a farewell luncheon at the Lord Mayor's Mansion House in London on Friday, November 9, 1945, Clement Attlee went to the city's airport to board a plane for America. Setting aside the larger problems of international atomic energy control, Attlee passed the trip pleasantly talking about cricket with his party. He discussed particularly the similarities between picking a properly balanced cricket team and choosing a Cabinet. With the Prime Minister on this excursion was Sir John Anderson, who, in spite of his Tory background, had been asked to stay on in the Labour government as overseer of Britain's atomic energy program. *Newsweek* magazine reported that week that Attlee was coming to America, "ready to stand up to Harry" on the question of atomic sharing. In fact, Attlee had resolved to make it plain to President Truman that Britain's contribution to the development of atomic energy left no question in his mind that "whatever security measures the United States felt impelled to take ought not to be allowed to stand in the way of the continued exchange of information between the United States, Canada and Britain." Attlee's other major purpose was to satisfy the political pressures on him in England by inducing Truman first to involve the Russians and then to turn the matter of atomic energy control over to the United Nations.[14] The British party landed at Washington airport at 9:32 A.M. on Saturday morning, November 10. The weather, which had been unusually sunny and warm for November, suddenly turned bleak and windy that morning.

The Prime Minister of Canada, Mackenzie King, also arrived in Washington that morning, but he did so by train from New York. Although a junior partner in the atomic association, King was a remarkable figure. Then seventy-one years old, he had dominated Canada's Liberal party and public life for three decades. The grandson of a leader of the Canadian Rebellion of 1837, King was a small, round bachelor with flat features and a thoroughly unimpressive manner. Underneath this deceiving exterior, however, there existed a brilliant mind, an extraordinary talent for manipulating people, and the spirit of a mystic who once claimed communication with various personages long since dead.

King came to America for the conference from England where he had gone on urgent, unexpected business. Igor Gouzenko, a cipher clerk in the Russian embassy in Ottawa had just defected with the startling news that he was part of a Russian spy ring that included several employees of the Canadian government and was involved in large-scale espionage, particularly with reference to the atomic bomb. Distressed by Gouzenko's story, which preliminary investigation had shown to be true, King traveled first to America to tell Truman and then on to London. This news undoubtedly affected the manner in which the conferees in Washington during that week considered their relations with Russia.

The conference began formally with a state dinner at the White House on Saturday night, November 10. This was "not a very impressive affair," Sir John Anderson wrote to his wife, adding that after dinner, which was "an ordinary three course meal," Truman and Attlee "made short and slightly platitudinous speeches." The event was over by ten o'clock that evening.[15]

More substantive discussions began the following morning, which was Armistice Day in America. After laying wreaths at Arlington National Cemetery, the three delegations boarded the Presidential yacht, *Sequoia,* and cruised down the Potomac River and out into the Chesapeake Bay. Accompanying Truman, Attlee, and King were Secretary of State Byrnes, Admiral Leahy,

Lord Halifax, Sir John Anderson, and Lester Pearson, the Canadian ambassador. Also present as unofficial members of the party were Leslie Rowan, Attlee's private secretary, and Clark Clifford, a young Lieutenant Commander in the United States Naval Reserve who served as a personal aide to Truman. During the morning the party simply enjoyed the cruise, sitting and chatting in small groups on the boat's deck. Truman showed Anderson through two very large albums of photographs of his trip to Potsdam. After lunch (lobster salad, turkey soup, and soufflé en surprise), the table was cleared and another smaller one set up, around which the conferees sat for serious discussion of atomic energy. The American position, which was essentially Bush's memorandum, was presented to the group as a basis for discussion. There seemed to be general agreement on the step-by-step progression which Bush had proposed, and on the involvement of the United Nations. When it came to the question of approaching the Soviet Union, Admiral Leahy understood that the meeting had agreed "as to the desirability of waiting for a request or suggestion from Stalin." Attlee made it clear that he favored the issuance of some joint statement on the subject of atomic energy to satisfy English public opinion.[16] At 8:30 that evening the *Sequoia* returned to shore with its passengers apparently in agreement on the preeminent question of the day.

The most critical problem from the British point of view had not yet been raised, however. On that Sunday, as the leaders of the three nations were at sea, the *New York Times* published a cartoon by the famed Englishman David Low, which showed Attlee and Stalin looking quizzically at Truman who was holding an atomic bomb with a sign saying "private" on it under his right arm, a statement of peaceful intentions under his left arm, and the caption "Why can't we work together in mutual trust and confidence?" emanating from Truman's mouth. In spite of this pictorial suggestion, that most nettlesome topic had not been interjected by the Americans or the English aboard the *Sequoia*.

The newspapers of Monday morning carried a surprising story, apparently leaked by Attlee's press secretary, that the British Prime Minister had argued on the previous day for the internationalization of all science and for the sharing of the atomic bomb with all the members of the United Nations so long as the Soviet Union first formally made clear its political and territorial aims, especially in Eastern Europe. According to the news story, Attlee had concluded that it would be impossible to establish a proper inspection system and a simple ban on the bomb was foolhardy.[17]

In fact, the British Prime Minister had made no such proposal aboard the *Sequoia,* as Vannevar Bush soon learned. Byrnes called Bush to his office on Monday morning and startled him with the news that the conference had already come to a complete agreement. What was the nature of it? Bush asked. It was entirely along the lines of Bush's memo, Byrnes said. Bush was now puzzled. Had not the British made a proposal? he asked several times, relying upon the morning's press. Each time Byrnes answered negatively. Bush then inquired about the discussion of the Quebec Agreement and how it might be renegotiated. Once more, he was startled to hear that the subject had not even come up. Warning Byrnes that this question was surely uppermost in the minds of the British delegation and that it would certainly be brought up before the end of the conference, Bush said that he and Harrison and Groves had prepared a lengthy memorandum on the matter, which was now in Patterson's possession. Bush urged Byrnes to acquaint the President with its contents before the British raised the subject.

Then came the final assault of the day on Bush's steady Yankee composure. Byrnes asked him to draft the communiqué for the

conference, although he had not been at any of its formal sessions. Bush protested, asking how he could do this if he did not
know what had transpired. But Byrnes responded that he had
just been told what had happened and besides, it was all very
much along the lines of Bush's own proposal. Bush finally agreed
to try a draft, "somewhat under protest."

His work was finished by Tuesday afternoon, November 13,
when the conferees next came together at the White House with
Bush finally among the invited. Secretary Byrnes brought with
him to that session an alternative draft prepared by Ben Cohen
of the State Department staff. Sir John Anderson had done a
similar paper for the British delegation. Although the discussion
that afternoon revolved around the American and British drafts,
it really amounted to an entirely new conference on the subject
of atomic control. Admiral Leahy sparked the new discussion by
arguing two unpopular positions. He first contended that there
should be no joint statement coming out of the conference, but
instead that the parties should quietly proceed to act along the
desired lines. The joint statement which all of the other conferees advocated would, Leahy thought, "contain an excessive
number of words, will make no positive proposals, and will accomplish little or nothing toward prohibiting the employment of
atom bombs in warfare." When the Admiral lost this argument,
he moved on to his next more radical proposal, that the three nations recommend the outlawing of the atomic bomb as a weapon
of war. In the aftermath of Hiroshima, no less than before, Leahy
believed that the bomb made warfare a vile exercise, more inhumane than it had ever been. Leahy thought that Truman
agreed with him in this but had been persuaded by Byrnes and
Attlee not to pursue a ban on the bomb. Vannevar Bush spoke
out against Leahy, claiming that outlawing the bomb was thoroughly premature at that time. Everyone else at the conference

table assented, and there the discussion ended. No final agreement on the wording of the communiqué could be reached that afternoon, and so the three nations returned to confer again on the following day and night. Finally, after midnight on Wednesday, November 14, all were in concurrence. Bush took the lone corrected draft home with him that night and brought it back to the White House for final typing the following morning.[18]

At eleven o'clock on that Thursday morning, November 15, 1945, Truman was prepared to summon the White House press corps to hear the three-nation declaration. The long efforts of the preceding night had left him and his English and Canadian colleagues red-eyed and hoarse-voiced, factors which the press was quick to note in its retelling of the ceremony. The President began with an extraordinary display of candor, consistent with the nonchalance of the entire conference, by announcing to the assembled newsmen that he would read the three-nation declaration, but that questions would have to be held until some later time when the parties were more familiar with its terms. Senators Connally, Vandenberg, and Brien McMahon of Connecticut, and Congressman Sol Bloom of New York were present, along with English and Canadian diplomats, as Truman rose from his seat between Attlee and King and began to read from two legal-size pages:

> We recognize that the application of recent scientific discoveries to the methods and practice of war has placed at the disposal of mankind means of destruction hitherto unknown, against which there can be no adequate military defence, and in the employment of which no single nation can in fact have a monopoly . . . We are aware that the only complete protection for the civilized world from the destructive use of scientific knowledge lies in the prevention of war. No system of safeguards . . . will of itself provide an effective guarantee against production of atomic weapons by a nation bent on aggression.[19]

What followed was Bush's plan, slightly amended. The first two steps — sharing basic scientific information and exchanging practical industrial applications of atomic energy with safeguards — were straight from his memorandum of the preceding weekend. The exception was a more precautionary preface that this exchange of industrial information could not take place without safeguards because "the military exploitation of atomic energy depends, in large part, upon the same methods and processes as would be required for industrial uses."

The United Nations, Truman continued, must establish a special commission to prepare recommendations for the full organization concerning the international control of atomic energy.

In particular, the commission should make specific proposals:

a) For extending between all nations the exchange of basic scientific information for peaceful ends;
b) For control of atomic energy to the extent necessary to insure its use only for peaceful purposes;
c) For the elimination from national armaments of atomic weapons and of all other major weapons adaptable to mass destruction;
d) For effective safeguards by way of inspection and other means to protect complying States against the hazards of violations and evasions.

The work of the commission should proceed by separate stages, the successful completion of each one of which will develop the necessary confidence of the world before the next stage is undertaken. Specifically, it is considered that the commission might well devote its attention first to the wide exchange of scientists and scientific information, and as a second stage, to the development of full knowledge concerning natural resources of raw materials.

Secretary of State Byrnes later wrote of this communiqué: "History will not disclose action by any government comparable to this generous offer." [20] This exaggerated statement by Byrnes reveals how bleak were the prospects of achieving an international atomic accord with the Soviet Union. For if the communiqué which Truman read on November 15 seemed generous to Byrnes, it certainly could not have seemed so to the men who ruled the Soviet Union. It contained no mention of Russia, no semblance of a hint that that other great wartime ally and world power would be consulted on atomic energy, no foundation for the Russians to believe that the English and Americans had in mind any early sharing of atomic energy development, and no assurance whatsoever that the two Western nations were not secretly preparing for their rule by atomic hegemony of a world divided into two hostile blocs.

In fact, another unpublicized agreement was reached in Washington during that week in November 1945, which perpetuated the exclusive Anglo-American atomic energy club. After the conference session of Tuesday afternoon, November 13, Sir John Anderson walked over to Bush and told him that the two of them had been directed to proceed with renegotiation of the Quebec Agreement of 1943. From whom had these directions come? Bush asked. Truman and Attlee had just agreed upon them, Anderson said. Finding it difficult to believe that so critical a matter would be delegated in this way without any formal discussion by the full conference, Bush immediately approached the President, who confirmed Anderson's statement. This seemed to Bush an improper role for him to play and he told the President so. The matter belonged in the hands of the Secretary of War, Mr. Patterson, who would no doubt want to consult not only Bush, but Groves and Harrison as well. Apparently feeling not at all bound by his previous decision, the President quickly agreed that the method Bush suggested was the proper one. He instructed Bush to inform Patterson accordingly.[21] Once informed, Patterson summoned General Groves and told him that he and Anderson were to get together and draft a written agreement covering the decisions already reached at the White House on the nature of postwar collaboration between America and England. Groves asked what the decisions were. Patterson was startled because he had understood that Groves had been at the White House discussions, even though he himself had not been invited there. Groves explained that he had not been present presumably, as he put it, "because the State Department had not wanted me there." [22] Patterson immediately telephoned Byrnes, who said that he had just learned of this turn of events from Bush and could not be of assistance in describing the agreements because he had left the White House discussion at that point. The dilemma confronting Groves and his resolution of it were later described by the General in these remarkable terms:

> I was thus faced with the difficult problem of writing a memorandum based upon decisions of which I had no knowledge whatever and which had been made by persons whose identity I did not at the time know. It was possible only because I was familiar enough with the subject to know what those decisions should have been, regardless of who arrived at them, or what they actually were.[23]

Over the following three days, Groves, Anderson, and their various assistants met to discuss renegotiation of the Quebec Agreement. The American participants argued that the agreement "could be implemented only by treaty but not in any event by any secret Executive arrangements." The British felt that the form of the renegotiation was a "political question which should not be decided at this time or at this level." [24] The best course, they all agreed, would be to have Truman and Attlee issue a directive to the already existing Combined Policy Committee, which had been established under the Quebec Agreement, to proceed with detailed renegotiation of the Anglo-American relationship. Groves and Anderson might also issue a more detailed memo of intention.

On Friday, November 16, the day after the three-nation declaration, Truman, Attlee, and King signed a brief secret memorandum:

1. We desire that there should be full and effective cooperation in the field of atomic energy between the United States, the United Kingdom and Canada.

2. We agree that the Combined Policy Committee and the Combined Development Trust should be continued in suitable form.

3. We request the Combined Policy Committee to consider and recommend to us appropriate arrangements for this purpose.[25]

The Groves-Anderson memorandum of intention, signed on the same day, sustained the earlier agreements by the three governments not to use the weapons or disclose any atomic information, or enter any negotiations without prior consultation with each other. They also agreed to attempt to obtain possession of all available quantities of uranium and thorium and to share these, "in such quantities as may be needed, in the common interest, for scientific research, military, and humanitarian purposes." Full and effective cooperation was to be continued in the field of basic scientific research. In regard to the design, construction, and operation of atomic plants, cooperation was also recognized as "desirable in principle," although the particular terms of sharing were to be regulated by *ad hoc* arrangements of the Combined Policy Committee.[26]

The terms of these statements went far beyond what men like Stimson and Bush had contemplated over the years of their concern with postwar atomic development. The Anglo-American atomic hegemony which they had fought was emerging nonetheless. It is understandable, therefore, why Attlee left Washington on November 16, "well-content." In fact, agreement had been reached much more easily than he and the rest of the British delegation had anticipated.[27]

When it was all over, Bush decided to report to his former mentor, Henry Stimson. Describing the three-power meeting as "a most extraordinary affair," Bush told Stimson that he "had never participated in anything so completely unorganized or so irregular." This he attributed to the fact that the meeting had been "in the hands of amateurs." His experiences of the preceding week, Bush told Stimson, "would make a chapter in 'Alice in Wonderland.' " Yet somehow, progress had been exactly along the lines that Stimson had suggested at his last Cabinet meeting, Bush declared.[28] This statement was either a vain attempt to please an old man in retirement, or a total failure of insight on Bush's part. For where Stimson had urged direct and immediate discussions with the Russians, the conferees had turned the problem over to the United Nations and not even mentioned the Soviet Union or agreed to consider discussions with the Russian leaders. About all the Russians received from the conference was an advance copy of the resulting communiqué which they accepted in silence. Where Stimson had cautioned against continuing the intimate atomic relationship with Britain, the conference had done just that. In short, Stimson had no cause for satisfaction as he reflected on these matters at his estate overlooking Long Island Sound.

The sloppiness and nonchalance with which the Truman Administration organized and conducted the three-nation conference had one other unfortunate result. It offended some of the ranking members of Congress and left them in a bitter frame of mind. They would return little more than a month later to make life very difficult for Truman and Byrnes. Bush had sensed the problem in the week before Attlee and King arrived during a conference with Senator Brien McMahon of Connecticut, the chairman of the Senate Special Committee on Atomic Energy. McMahon complained that he had not been consulted on the coming conference and did not even know what were the existing relationships on atomic questions between England and America. Bush mentioned McMahon's attitude to Byrnes, suggesting that a number of members of the Senate be placed on a new advisory committee to consider the international control of atomic weapons. But neither Truman nor Byrnes consulted with the Congress before or during the conference.

When McMahon and a few of the other leading members of Congress, including Arthur Vandenberg and Tom Connally, were invited to attend the announcement of the three-nation communiqué on November 15, they were therefore in a most unpleasant mood. Before the formal ceremony began, the chairman of the Senate Foreign Relations Committee cornered Byrnes and complained that "he and the President were treating atomic energy as if it were their private possession" while, in fact, "they had no authority to propose sharing atomic energy information with other nations or to plan its future control without Congressional approval." Vandenberg, the ranking Republican member of the Foreign Relations Committee, bemoaned the peremptory way in which he and the others from Congress had been summoned to the White House after having been allowed no participation in the business of the conference. When Truman had finished reading the declaration, Vandenberg and Connally did not even stay for the customary picture-taking. Vandenberg claimed that he was scheduled to speak on the floor of the Senate. Connally simply left without explanation.[29]

10

Moving Slowly toward Moscow

TWENTY-FOUR HOURS after Senators Connally and Vandenberg stomped out on him, Secretary of State Byrnes found himself on much friendlier ground. As soon as Attlee and King were seen off, Byrnes left Washington for Charleston, South Carolina, where he was feted at "Jimmy Byrnes Homecoming Day." On that Friday evening, November 16, he addressed a Mayor's Dinner in his honor. Striking much of his prepared text on international trade, Byrnes spoke at length of atomic energy and the three-nation declaration of the previous day. His stress was on America's willingness to exchange information and practical experience as soon as there were adequate safeguards. With Russian propaganda undoubtedly in mind, he decried "the suggestion that we are using the atom bomb as a diplomatic or military threat against any nation" as simply "untrue." [1] Even in the homey atmosphere of his native state, however, Byrnes would not talk bluntly about the determinative part Russia played in the entire effort to establish international atomic control. Nor did he give any indication that America planned to approach the Soviet Union on the question in the foreseeable future.

At his regular news conference on the following Monday morning, November 20, President Truman said that the next step toward international atomic energy control would be for the plan announced in the three-power declaration to be placed on the agenda of the first meeting of the United Nations General Assembly which was scheduled for London during January 1946. The President's most generous statement of the morning was that all members of the United Nations should participate in the choice of members of the proposed special commission on atomic energy. In an apparent effort to reassure the more nervous of his constituents, Truman also announced that morning that the United States was going ahead with the manufacture of atomic bombs "for experimental purposes and with a view to learning more regarding the peaceful uses." [2] Byrnes continued this trend of thought a day later at a press conference of his own when he acknowledged that there had been no attempt to involve Russia, or even China and France, as co-sponsors of the United Nations resolution on atomic energy, although the United States, Britain, and Canada might well offer the plan jointly.[3]

Circumstances soon conspired to change this ungenerous and unproductive American view. On November 17, America's ambassador to the Soviet Union, Averell Harriman, cabled Byrnes from Moscow that the Soviet press and propaganda networks were distorting America's atomic energy policy within the Soviet Union and around the world. People were being led to believe that "an Anglo-American bloc, bomb in teeth, intended to array the United Nations against Russia." [4]

Similar concern was emerging closer to home in circles not subject to the Russian propaganda machine. On Capitol Hill, the fledgling Federation of Atomic Scientists was hard at work, educating Congressmen to the need for international control and lobbying for a direct American approach to the Soviet Union. On Thursday, November 23, Congresswoman Helen Gahagan Douglas of California introduced a resolution, drafted by the atomic scientists, which asked that "the President of the United States immediately invite to a conference the Governments of Great Britain and the Soviet Union, in order to discuss the common danger created by atomic weapons, and to plan for the joint approach by these three nations to the other members of the United Nations Organization." [5] A similar resolution was introduced in the Senate by a bipartisan group of Senators including Tobey, Morse, Smith, Taylor, Kilgore, and Fulbright. Moved by the atomic scientists' appeal, they resolved to go one step further. Adding Senator Saltonstall of Massachusetts to their ranks, they requested and received an appointment at the White House. It was scheduled for November 29. There they planned to ask the President about the state of American efforts to encourage participation by the Soviet Union in atomic energy development and control. They were particularly interested to know whether the Soviets had been invited to the three-nation conference of the preceding week, and, if not, why not? [6]

Meanwhile, Byrnes was doing some thinking of his own. With the three-power conference behind him, he turned his attention once more to the subject which was really of first importance to him — the successful negotiation of European peace treaties. That topic had been the primary concern of the ill-fated Foreign Ministers conference in London during September. No progress could be made unless the parties began talking to each other again, and so Byrnes decided to propose to Soviet Foreign Minister V. Molotov that there be another meeting of the Foreign Ministers of the Big Three. His one inspiration in this regard was that the meeting should be in Moscow, on the theory that this act of deference might please the Russians and also make decision-making and agreement more feasible since Stalin would be close at hand. In any case, Moscow was the logical site because the preceding conferences had been held at San Francisco, Berlin, and London. On November 23, Byrnes cabled Harriman and asked him to convey to Molotov the suggestion that the Foreign Ministers meet in Moscow during December in accordance with their understanding at the Crimea Conference that they would hold regular consultations every three or four months.[7]

Harriman personally delivered this message to Molotov at the Kremlin during the late-night hours of November 23. The Russian Foreign Secretary was "obviously much pleased" by the suggestion and asked Harriman what subjects Byrnes wished to discuss. He had received no specific information, Harriman answered, but assumed that "all open questions" between the three nations could be considered, mentioning specifically "Far Eastern questions, civil strife in China, disturbing developments in Iran, Bulgaria, etc." Molotov promised to consult with his government immediately concerning this proposal and added that he personally would always welcome Byrnes in Moscow.[8]

There is no indication that Byrnes had atomic energy in mind when he proposed this meeting in Moscow. On November 25, he informed the British Foreign Secretary, Ernest Bevin, of his cable to Molotov, but omitted mention of atomic energy as a possible topic at the conference.[9] Later that same day Byrnes received Molotov's formal acceptance of his invitation, along with a request that they exchange proposals for the agenda of the meeting. Byrnes agreed and the conference was scheduled for mid-December.[10]

If Byrnes did not yet have atomic energy uppermost on his mind, others close to him did. On November 24, Ben Cohen, Counsellor of the State Department, and Leo Pasvolsky, a State Department staff member whose primary work had been in the affairs of the United Nations, put into memo form their shared concern over the phlegmatic pace of planning on atomic energy and its international ramifications. If the proposed atomic energy commission was to be established at the January session of the United Nations, some preliminary work must be done. It was imperative that Britain and Canada be consulted on details of the proposal and that some attempt then be made to secure Soviet involvement. Working independently, Cohen and Pasvolsky suggested what Byrnes had already arranged — a conference in Moscow during December. The difference was that they wanted atomic energy to be the primary concern of the meeting.[11]

This memorandum clearly had an effect on Byrnes. He even seemed to be coming around now to the belief that there might be a connection between America's approach to Russia on the atomic bomb and Russia's response to other critical diplomatic problems such as the European peace treaties. On November 27, Byrnes had a transatlantic teletype conference with Bevin in which he spent most of the time mollifying the British Foreign Secretary's anger that he had not been consulted before Byrnes proposed the conference in Moscow to Molotov. When Bevin asked what items would be on the agenda, Byrnes answered:

> First of all, I think that you and Mackenzie King and I should agree as to the proposal we are going to make to the Assembly with reference to the atomic bomb. When we agree I believe it wise that we should advise Molotov of our proposals. If we do not we are going to risk the success of the first meeting of the assembly.[12]

A day later Bevin sent Byrnes a message saying that he had thought the matter over and still did not want to go to Moscow, preferring instead to have a Foreign Ministers conference in London during January when the parties would all be attending the first session of the United Nations General Assembly there anyway. Bevin agreed that the United States, Canada, and Britain should have a prior agreement on the tactics they would employ at the United Nations to establish the special atomic energy commission. Once this concurrence was achieved, they might inform the "other permanent members of the Security Council." All this, Bevin thought, could be done "through ordinary diplomatic channels." He added that before their conversation of the previous day he had telegraphed a memo on the subject of atomic energy to Lord Halifax. He expected that Halifax would be delivering this to Byrnes shortly.[13]

The British ambassador visited Byrnes at noon on Thanksgiving Day with a copy of Bevin's memorandum. In it Bevin suggested the desirability of having the Soviet Union "associated with the sponsorship of the tripartite proposals before the United Nations Organization." Based on past experience, he thought it "very doubtful that the Russians would associate themselves with the sponsorship of a proposal in regard to which they had not been previously consulted." He therefore proposed having Harriman inquire in Moscow whether the Russians would be willing to co-sponsor the atomic energy resolution. Byrnes told Halifax that he could not accept this idea but believed instead that at a meeting in Moscow, Molotov "would be more pliable as a host and might consider it important that the other two Secretaries would take the trouble to come to Moscow." [14]

The Canadian ambassador, Lester Pearson, sent a similar message to Byrnes on November 30. Pearson's idea of an approach to the Soviet Union was even less generous than Bevin's. He was worried that if the Russians were consulted they "might also complicate the whole procedure by insisting at this stage that the subject was one which should properly be considered by the Security Council."

Influenced by Cohen and Pasvolsky, Byrnes had made up his mind and was pushing ahead in preparation for his trip to Moscow. He sent Bevin a proposed nine-point agenda for the conference. The first item was: "The proposal for the establishment of a commission under the United Nations Organization to consider the control of atomic energy in the interest of peace." When John Winant, America's ambassador in London, delivered this agenda to Bevin on the last day of November 1945, the British Foreign Secretary complained that the first item related to the creation of an organ of the United Nations and he therefore did not see how discussion of it could be confined to just three nations. When Michael Wright, the British Minister in Washington, conveyed this response to Byrnes, he dismissed it as baseless and explained that all "he hoped to tell Russia [was] what we propose to present to UNO and thereby try to save UNO from the failure that would probably result from the group action being presented without the Russians having been informed." When Wright persisted on Bevin's behalf, Byrnes told him that he would be disappointed if Bevin did not agree to go to Moscow, but that he would go on ahead himself in any case. Bevin believed Byrnes's threat and so on December 6 finally cabled his American colleague that he was prepared to go to Moscow, but only out of deference to Byrnes's strong views.[15]

James Byrnes was now able to announce to the public on December 7, 1945, the fourth anniversary of Pearl Harbor, that a meeting of the Big Three would take place in Moscow, beginning on December 15, to discuss "matters of current concern to the three countries and also for an exchange of views on the subject of the control of atomic energy." [16] Bevin's belated agreement allowed Byrnes to end an embarrassing period of silence in his communications with Molotov about the coming meeting. On that same day, December 7, he wired Molotov a copy of the proposed agenda. The Soviet Foreign Minister's response was quick and affirmative, except for one minor change in the agenda. He mystified the Americans by requesting that the first point on the agenda, namely discussion of atomic energy, be transferred to the bottom.[17]

Byrnes was surprised by this request but could find no reason to refuse it. Meanwhile Cohen and Pasvolsky, acting now at

Byrnes's request, had proceeded with the development of an American position on atomic energy control for the conference in Moscow. They had assembled a committee to work with them which included Herbert Marks, assistant to Dean Acheson; Carroll Wilson, assistant to Vannevar Bush; and Joseph E. Johnson, a professor of history from Williams College who had become chief of the Division of International Security Affairs at the State Department. To add scientific expertise, Cohen and Pasvolsky invited Robert Oppenheimer and Henry Smyth to participate in the committee's deliberations. Oppenheimer was soon gravely disappointed by the work of this committee because it revealed to him that four months after Hiroshima America "didn't have a very well thought through notion of what international control was or what we could say to the Russians." [18]

The Cohen-Pasvolsky committee finished a draft statement of policy on December 7 and presented it in Cohen's office to George Harrison of the War Department, Charles Bohlen, the Russian specialist at State, Admiral William Blandy of the Navy Department, and Vannevar Bush. The focus of discussion that day was on the tactics to be employed with the Russians at Moscow. In the end, a broad agreement was reached and expressed in a final draft statement which was approved by the committee on December 10. Using the Truman-Attlee-King declaration of November 15 as a base, the committee spelled out an approach to Russia in more detailed and realistic terms. The memorandum of December 10 was more realistic because it offered the Russians some assurances of a return for their cooperation. As the committee saw it, the problem consisted of four "separate although related segments." These segments were similar to the stages that Bush had proposed in his work prior to the Washington conference during November. First would be an exchange of scientists and scientific information, techniques and materials; second, the development and exchange of knowledge concerning natural resources; third, the exchange of technological and engineering information; and fourth, safeguards against, and control of, methods of mass destruction. Unlike the earlier proposals, however, this one was not rigid in requiring that Russia prove itself step by step before the United States would offer anything of substance in return. The Cohen-Pasvolsky draft declared:

> It is the belief of this Government that successful international action with respect to any phase of the problem is not necessarily a prerequisite for undertaking affirmative action with respect to other phases. Affirmative action should be taken whenever it is likely to be fruitful.

The first ideas for the structure of the proposed United Nations commission were also delineated by the Cohen-Pasvolsky group. The commission should be composed of a representative from each of the nations represented on the Security Council, plus Canada when that nation was not a member of the Security Council. It should be established by the General Assembly and report back to that body.[19]

The policy recommended by the Cohen-Pasvolsky Committee represented a more rational approach to the Soviet Union for direct collaboration on atomic energy. It would have had more hope of success if it had been issued four months before, but even now in its limited terms, it aroused stormy opposition within the American government. When the Secretary of the Navy, James Forrestal, saw it, he immediately telephoned Byrnes to say that he felt "most strongly that the proposed basis of discussion goes too far." There should be "no discussion of proposals as to the specific kinds and types of information in this field to be made available by this country to other nations," Forrestal said, "until a procedure for the exchange of such information has been worked out that will guarantee genuine reciprocity in such exchange." His suggestion was that the Truman-Attlee-King declaration serve as the basis of America's position at the Moscow conference.[20] General Groves was similarly displeased. He did not want the discussions in Moscow to go beyond an agreement to exchange basic scientific information. Even the exchange of visits by scientists of the two countries seemed excessive to Groves. He wrote to Secretary of War Patterson:

> The visits of foreign scientists to this country would have to be carefully supervised to prevent them from gaining appreciable information applicable to wartime uses of atomic energy. Furthermore, I know of no way to ensure that American scientists traveling in Russia will not disclose vital information.[21]

Byrnes adhered nonetheless to the Cohen-Pasvolsky policy, even in the face of strident Congressional opposition which confronted him on the eve of his departure for Moscow. Remembering the earlier error he had made by not involving members of Congress in his deliberations prior to the three-power conference during November, Byrnes invited a select group of Senators who were members of the Foreign Relations Committee and the Special Committee on Atomic Energy to his office on Wednesday morning, December 12. He began by introducing James Conant, who was going to Moscow with him and then proceeded to read from the Cohen-Pasvolsky statement of December 10.

From the beginning the Senators were not in a friendly mood toward Byrnes. When his appointment as Secretary of State had been announced months before, Vandenberg and Connally, the two most powerful members of the Foreign Relations Committee, were dismayed. Connally felt that "Byrnes was not trained in foreign service and knew little about foreign affairs." He also believed that Byrnes "did not take a broad view of a given situation" and was "devoted to expedience." [22] Vandenberg felt very much the same way. When Byrnes was appointed, the Michigan Republican had written to his wife: "Jimmy Byrnes is a grand guy (for any other job down here). But his whole life has been a career of compromise." [23]

Their views had, if anything, become more harsh during the first months of Byrnes's service. Now, as they listened to the Secretary read from the Cohen-Pasvolsky memo, they simmered over his failure to involve them before a plan had already been adopted. The plan itself was "a great shock" because it sounded to them as if Byrnes was prepared to give away "atomic secrets." Vandenberg expressed their displeasure this way:

> We agree that Russia can work out this science in perhaps two years; but we are unanimously opposed to hastening the day unless and until there is absolute and effective agreement for world-wide inspection and control . . . We are opposed to giving any of the atomic secrets away unless and until the Soviets are prepared to be "policed" by UNO in respect to this prohibition. We consider an "exchange" of scientists and scientific information as sheer appeasement because Russia has nothing to "exchange." [24]

Senator Connally grumbled something about bringing in "college professors," a not very subtle reference to Conant, and then proceeded to tear into the substance of the Cohen-Pasvolsky draft, especially the section which outlined four stages of cooperation. Why was the establishment of adequate safeguards listed last, the Senator wanted to know? Did that not imply that exchange of information could take place before adequate protection was afforded this country's interest? "Don't you have your four points in reverse order?" Connally asked. "Number four should be number one." Byrnes, according to Connally, took this remark as an insult. [25]

When their heated meeting with Byrnes was over, the Senators felt that they had "made little impression on the Secretary." [26] As a result, the entire Senate Special Committee on Atomic Energy met in emergency session later that day and unanimously agreed to seek an immediate meeting with the President in the hope that they might alter Byrnes's plans for the Moscow Conference. And so, as Byrnes's plane moved through the air toward Moscow on Friday morning, December 14, the Senators were filing angrily into Truman's office. When he arrived in the Russian capital, Byrnes would hear more of all this.

In Moscow, the leaders of the Russian nation had begun active preparations for the arrival of James Byrnes and Ernest Bevin. The distinguished visitors' accommodations and activities must be as satisfying as possible. There was also considerable activity and discussion within the Kremlin concerning the various international problems that were on the agenda of the conference. On the question of atomic energy control, however, very little work was being done. The Soviet leaders had already made some decisions on that matter which were based on two factors: the spirit in which their wartime allies, now atomic monopolists, were handling nuclear weapons, and their assessment of the capabilities of Soviet science and industry to match the previous Western effort.

Before the Second World War, the Russian scientific community enjoyed great respect throughout the world, particularly for its work in nuclear physics. During the 1920s two Russians, Dmitri Skobeltsyn and Peter Kapitza, had achieved world renown for their work in atomic energy. In 1923, Skobeltsyn had begun advanced research on the measurement and detection of radioactivity; he was later the first to observe the flight path of cosmic rays. In 1921, an exploration of the Soviet Union's natural resources was initiated at Lenin's direction, under the supervision of Professor Vernadskii, a prominent Russian geologist. It ultimately revealed ample deposits of the precious metal uranium.[27]

During the 1930s, Russian scientists followed and confirmed the exciting breakthroughs in atomic energy which were occurring throughout the world. A public congress dealing exclusively with problems of nuclear physics was held in Moscow in 1939. In that same year, A. I. Brodsky published an article on the separation of uranium isotopes, while Kurschatov and Frenkel offered theoretical explanations of the fission process in the uranium atom at the same time that Bohr and Wheeler in America and Frisch in England did the same. In 1937, the Russians began operating a cyclotron at the Radium Institute in Leningrad. The pace of activity increased in 1940 after the splitting of uranium atoms by Hahn and Strassman. Two Russian physicists, Flerov and Petrzak, soon performed experiments in the shaft of a Moscow subway which confirmed the work of Hahn and Strassman. On April 16 and 17, 1940, an All Union Conference on Isotopes was held in Moscow and heard a paper on industrial production of heavy water, one of the ingredients necessary for atomic development. A short while later, the Presidium of the Soviet Academy of Sciences created a Special Committee for the Problem of Uranium which included some of the leading Russian scientists of the day. The academy also established a State Fund for Uranium Metal during the spring of 1940 to finance a study of "the more important deposits of uranium in Central Asia." In November 1940 another Conference on the Physics of Atomic Nuclei was convened in Moscow. And on the last day of the year, an article appeared in *Izvestia,* entitled "Uranium 235," which predicted that "mankind will acquire a new source of energy surpassing a million times everything that has hitherto been known . . . Human might is entering a new era . . . man will be able to acquire any quantity of energy he pleases and apply it to any ends he chooses." At the end of 1940, the second year of the fission era, Soviet atomic energy development was clearly equal to American work in the field.

By June of 1941, however, with the German Army marching on Russian soil, the Russian scientists, like the rest of Soviet society, turned their energies to the immediate problems of war. *Leningrad Pravda* declared at that time: "Now the scientists of the Motherland must work for the front and only for the front." This call was fully heeded. The head of the Leningrad cyclotron, for example, left his work and was sent to the Black Sea to contend with the problem of protecting Russian ships from German mines. The outbreak of the Second World War therefore had an effect on Soviet atomic development which was entirely opposite to the one it had on American work in the field. Russian physicists, however, were not ignorant of the potential of atomic energy. On October 13, 1941, Peter Kapitza made the following declaration to a meeting of Soviet scientists which had been called to stimulate their efforts aimed at winning the war:

> One of the basic weapons of modern warfare is explosive materials. Science demonstrates in principle that it is possible to increase their destructive force by one and one-half to two times. But recent years have seen the opening up of still newer possibilities — that is, the utilization of internal atomic energy. Theoretical calculations show that, whereas a modern high explosive bomb can destroy an entire city block, an atom bomb, even one of small size, if it can be manufactured, could easily destroy a major capital city with several million inhabitants.[28]

During the first years of the war, the Russians continued to publish articles in scientific journals about atomic energy development. These continued to appear long after the Americans and Germans had prohibited open publication in the interest of security. Not until 1943 when the Soviet atomic energy program was reinvigorated was censorship of nuclear studies imposed. In May and June of 1945, Soviet censors temporarily lifted their ban and allowed publication of a few articles on atomic research which had been done within the Soviet Union during 1943 and

1944. This openness could well have been an attempt by the Soviet leaders to show their wartime allies that they too were interested in atomic energy and were making progress in their work, regardless of whether or not the English and Americans invited them in as atomic partners.

Throughout the spring of 1945, as the Soviet espionage network continued to supply information on the Manhattan Project, America and England took a series of steps which made it clear to the Russian leaders that their Western allies had little intention of sharing atomic development. During May 1945, the Soviet Academy of Science held a conference and celebration in Moscow in honor of its 220th anniversary. A number of British and American scientists were invited to the convocation and quickly accepted. When General Groves learned this on the eve of the scientists' departure for Moscow, he immediately stepped in, fearing a security leak. Scientists working with the Manhattan Project were compelled to wire their regrets to Moscow, while others with peripheral contacts with the American atomic effort were visited by military security guards and asked not to go. This struck some of them, including Irving Langmuir of General Electric, as absurd since they had received passports for Russia and were set to travel in airplanes provided by the State Department. Only when Langmuir proved how little he knew of atomic energy work was he allowed to go. At the insistence of the United States War Department, the same restrictions were imposed in Britain on eight English physicists who had accepted the Russian invitation, received their passports, and were at the airport waiting to depart when they were forced to return to their homes. The English newspapers gave great publicity to the cancellation of these passports and demanded that Churchill explain the matter before the House of Commons. All this, of course, was known in Russia, although it was never mentioned in the American press. It is inconceivable that the Russians could have misunderstood these last minute cancellations and the total absence of any American scientist who had anything remotely to do with atomic energy. This episode was an insult to Soviet scientists who believed in the internationalization of science as much as their American colleagues did. For their part, the Russian diplomats could not have misinterpreted so clear a statement of mistrust by their wartime allies.

Stalin must have had the very same response to Truman's painfully obtuse notification to him at Potsdam of the imminent explosion of a strong new weapon. The Russian Generalissimo had already heard the news with more specificity during June when Klaus Fuchs, the British atomic spy who was working in America on the Manhattan Project, informed his Soviet contacts that the American work had gone so far that the first test of an atomic weapon in the United States was scheduled during July 1945.

The explosion at Hiroshima was greeted by almost total public silence within the Soviet Union — a mixture perhaps of wounded pride and fear of upsetting the masses of Russian people with the knowledge that there was an extraordinary new weapon that had deprived them of their hard-won, short-lived security. One must look to Soviet history and the repeated invasions by land of Russian territory to appreciate the satisfaction which the Russian people must have felt at finally repelling the Nazi onslaught and extending Soviet boundaries west to create a barrier against future attacks. One must also consider the paranoia of the Russian Communist leadership, which had spent most of its days in constant fear of internal subversion and plots. These perceptions of the Soviet character are not simply afterthoughts but were very much available to the Western governments at the time. A few months after Hiroshima, the British ambassador in Moscow, Archibald Clark Kerr, explained all this to his government in London:

Then plump came the Atomic Bomb. At a blow, the balance which had now seemed set and steady was rudely shaken. Russia was balked by the west when everything seemed to be within her grasp. The three hundred divisions were shorn of much of their value. About all this the Kremlin was silent but such was the common talk of the people. But their disappointment was tempered by the belief inspired by such echoes of foreign press as were allowed to reach them that their Western comrades in arms would surely share the bomb with them. That some such expectation as this was shared by the Kremlin became evident in due course. But as time went on and no move come from the West, disappointment turned into irritation and, when the bomb seemed to them to become an instrument of policy, into spleen. It was clear that the West did not trust them. This seemed to justify and it quickened all their old suspicions. It was a humiliation also and the thought of this stirred up memories of the past. We may assume that all these emotions were fully shared by the Kremlin.[29]

Similarly thoughts were forwarded to the American government after Hiroshima by Ambassador Harriman:

Suddenly, the atomic bomb appeared and they recognized that it was an offset to the power of the Red Army. This must have revived their old feeling of insecurity. They could no longer be absolutely sure that they could obtain their objectives without interference . . . The Russian people have been aroused to feel that they must face again an antagonistic world. American imperialism is included as a threat to the Soviet Union.[30]

On the day after Hiroshima, the Russian press printed a brief digest of Truman's prepared statement about the bomb which had been issued from the White House. Ambassador Harriman visited with Stalin and Molotov at the Kremlin on the evening of August 8, 1945. Their discussion was primarily concerned with Russia's entrance into the war against Japan, but Harriman asked Stalin what effect he thought the atomic bomb would have on the Japanese. The Russian leader answered quite directly that he

thought it would cause them to surrender. Seizing the opportunity, Harriman engaged Stalin in a brief discussion of atomic
energy which, in spite of its brevity, was more than the Russians
would hear from the West on this particular subject until the
Moscow Conference in December. It was a good thing, Harriman
remarked, that "their side had invented this weapon and not the
Germans; that no one had dared think it would be a success; and
that the President had learned that it would work successfully
only a few days before he told Stalin about it." Stalin seemed impressed and said that the Soviet scientists had told him that it
was a very difficult problem. Harriman suggested that "if the allies could keep it and apply it for peaceful purposes it would be a
good thing." Stalin agreed, saying "that it would mean the end of
war and aggressors . . . but the secret would have to be well-
kept." He then told Harriman that the Russian troops had uncovered a German atomic laboratory in Berlin, but that the Germans
had not progressed very far. Even England, Stalin continued, "although it had excellent physicists had gotten nowhere with its research in this field." This certainly was a little private joke of
Stalin's since Klaus Fuchs had been feeding the Soviet government information on the joint Anglo-American effort. Harriman
deferred to the statement and routinely explained that the British
had pooled their knowledge with the Americans since 1941, but
that the project had required enormous installations to conduct
the necessary experiments and that the American government
had spent more than two billion dollars on the project.[31]

Stalin's willingness to discuss the atomic bomb and appreciate
its power in private conversation with Harriman was not reflected
in the public policy of the Kremlin. The official posture was silence and minimization of the effect of the bomb. An officer of
the Polish provisional government who was in Moscow at the time
of Hiroshima asked a Soviet diplomat about the significance of

the bomb. "This is the usual American propaganda," he was told. "It has no significant military meaning, and has as its single purpose the rapid forcing of the Soviets into the Japanese war with which the Americans are having difficulty." Molotov gave exactly the same answer to the same question at supper the following evening: "This is American propaganda. From a military point of view it has no important meaning whatsoever." [32]

General Eisenhower arrived in Moscow on August 11 for conversations with Russian leaders about military matters, but the overriding subject of the atomic bomb was not discussed. During this period, the foreign press corps in Russia found that Soviet censors who screened their reports home were striking any implication that the atomic bomb and not the Russian invasion had caused Japan to surrender. Writing in *Izvestia* ten days after the attack on Hiroshima, "The Observer" complained that the American press was overestimating the atomic bomb and underestimating the importance of the Soviet move against Japan. "No miracle but the powerful joint efforts of all the allies brought the war to an end," the anonymous commentator declared.

By the end of August 1945, the "sacred trust" theory of American atomic policy had emerged; the Russians heard no more from their Western allies. On September 1, Modest Rubinstein, a prominent Soviet commentator, wrote the lengthiest Russian statement yet on atomic energy in *New Times,* a Soviet magazine published in several languages and assumed to reflect the views of the Soviet Foreign Office. After hailing the bomb as "one of the greatest inventions of modern science," Rubinstein quickly added that "it is clear to all right-thinking men that the discovery does not solve any political problems internationally or within individual countries." He warned that "those who cherish illusions in this respect will suffer inevitable disappointment." The American "Hearst-McCormick-Patterson press," which had been exhorting the American government to protect the atomic secret with its life, came in for special criticism: "These flagrant imperialists forget history's lessons. They ignore the collapse of Hitlerite plans for world hegemony which were based on intended utilization of temporary superiority in technical developments."

Rubinstein carefully omitted mention of the dreams of a luxuriant new age based on the commercial use of atomic energy which were current in America. Decrying the "illusion that atomic energy can be practically applied to industry immediately," he warned of the "unlimited economic abuses possible by exploitation of atomic energy production under conditions of capitalist monopoly." These would bring "monstrous mass unemployment, permanent elimination of millions of miners and other industrial workers, and intensification of monopoly rule." Rubinstein's climactic declaration was aimed at American statesmen: "Many other countries have scientists who studied the problem of splitting the atom and who will work with redoubled energy to invent weapons as good or better . . . The fundamental principles are well known and henceforth it is simply a question of time before any country will be able to produce atomic bombs." This being so, Rubinstein said he favored "an immediate agreement to establish international control by representatives of the Five Great Powers over the production and employment of atomic bombs." He also endorsed a suggestion of the *Manchester Guardian* that the atomic bomb and the means to produce it be turned over to the United Nations.[33]

The Soviet policy, as Rubinstein articulated it, was clear. The Russians could and would build the bomb unless some international control agreement was reached quickly. This inviting posture faded during September because of America's continuing failure to approach the Soviet Union on the question of atomic energy. Observers close to the Russian delegation at the London conference of Foreign Ministers during September reported that the Soviets were irked over the refusal of the Western powers to offer them an equal share in atomic development. In the aftermath of President Truman's October 3 message to Congress on atomic energy, *New Times* accused the United States of "atomic diplomacy" — a term that would become unhappily familiar in the two-power propaganda dialogue that occurred over the following years. Still adhering to a relatively moderate position, however, the Soviet journal viewed Truman's declaration as a compromise between the opposing camps within America, one of which hoped for international cooperation, while the other urged "atomic diplomacy." The article concluded with a warning: "History convincingly proves that the attempt of any country to attempt world domination with the aid of new weapons is doomed to failure." [34]

Throughout October, America's silence, perpetuated particularly by Secretary of State Byrnes, continued. Then came the announcement of the Anglo-American-Canadian conference on atomic energy in Washington. To the Russians, this was further proof of the exclusive intentions of their wartime allies. On the morning of November 7, as Byrnes discussed America's still unarticulated atomic policy with Truman at the White House, Vyacheslav Molotov's voice was cascading off the walls of the huge hall of St. Andrew in the Kremlin with the first public comment on atomic energy by a member of the Politburo. An overflow crowd had gathered there to celebrate the twenty-eighth anniversay of the Bolshevik Revolution. The Soviet Foreign Minister, a small, solid, balding man with rimless glasses and a slight, gray-black mustache, was indomitable in spirit that day. On the matter of atomic energy his message was clear:

> It is not possible at the present time for a technical secret of any great size to remain the exclusive possession of some one country or some narrow circle of countries. This being so, the discovery

of atomic energy should not encourage either a propensity to exploit the discovery in the play of forces in international policy or an attitude of complacency as regards the future of peaceloving nations.

The enemy interrupted our peaceful creative endeavor but we shall make up properly for all lost time and see to it that our country shall flourish. We will have atomic energy and many other things too.

With this declaration the immense crowd sprang to its feet and released itself so completely in exhilarated applause that a signal bell finally had to be rung to restore order. Molotov continued: "Let us tackle these tasks with all our inexhaustible, Bolshevik energy, with all the boundless energy of the Soviet people. Let us work as Comrade Stalin teaches us to do."

Connecting the bomb with the notion of world domination "as preached by some particularly zealous advocates of capitalism," Molotov finished with a plea: "Only by the joint efforts of the three powers who carried the burden of the war can we secure the victories of the democratic countries over fascism." [35]

One week later, as Truman, Attlee, and King cruised out into the Chesapeake Bay to discuss atomic bombs, *Pravda* wrote of them: "These are people who have not learned anything from the Second World War. It seems to these people that it is possible to return to the old time and to build a European policy on the creation of anti-Soviet blocs." [36] The following issue of *Krokodil,* a Soviet humor magazine, carried on its cover a cartoon depicting two parents, John Bull as the mother and Uncle Sam as the father, pushing a baby carriage on which was draped an American flag with the words "atomic energy" embroidered on it. A bystander asks, "How do you intend to bring up your youngster?" The parents reply: "In a strictly private boarding school." [37]

After the Truman-Attlee-King declaration was issued, officials at the Soviet embassy in Washington refused comment, but the *New York Times* reported that "they were known to be expecting

a more substantial offer than the communiqué conveyed." [38]
Within the Soviet Union there was no comment at all. Radio
Moscow simply reported the three-nation declaration without
comment. During that time, however, a series of Soviet statements
appeared which bore the mark of policy. On November 14, *Izvestia* reported that a Russian research team working under Professor Kapitza at Mount Alagrez near Lake Karagel in the Ar-
menian Socialist Republic had discovered a way to knock pro-
tons out of lead atoms. This, *Izvestia* said, was a discovery "of
outstanding interest . . . and might have a direct bearing on
Soviet investigations of atomic energy." [39] The November 15 issue of *New Times* featured an escalation of the Soviet propaganda
position on atomic energy. It charged: "The atomic bomb served
as a signal to the incorrigible reactionaries all over the world to
launch a lynching campaign against the Soviet Union . . . Can
hypocritical phrases about moral leadership mask the appetite
of the imperialist who dreams of eliminating from the path of imperialist dreams the Soviet Union?" [40] And, on November 16, a
day after the three-nation declaration, a verse by the Russian
poet Kirsanoff was published and widely circulated in Moscow:

> Let no atomic bomb
> Remain a puzzle for us!
> The magic atom of uranium
> We shall refill with creative soul.[41]

The Russian press continued its assault on the atomic policies
of the Western countries right up until the arrival of Byrnes and
Bevin in Moscow on December 15. As befits Russian hospitality,
however, the hostile proclamations suddenly ceased during the
weeks of the Moscow Conference. *Pravda* published its final blast
on December 9, attacking those who, the newspaper said, appealed for alteration of postwar agreements:

When they are asked what has happened in recent postwar months to require such radical changes the revisionists reply to this question in three words — the atom bomb. By making this reply, they give themselves away . . . Atomic diplomacy . . . [is] dragging the world back to its ill-fated pre-war policy, with its League of Nations, its antagonistic blocs, and groupings.[42]

By the time Byrnes and Bevin arrived in Moscow, there was every indication that the Russian leaders had come to the conclusion that the United States had no intention of sharing atomic power and that, therefore, the Soviet Union must push vigorously ahead on its own atomic development program. Molotov's strange request that discussion of atomic energy be taken from the top of the agenda of the Moscow Conference and placed at the bottom was probably the Soviet Union's way of showing how unimportant it thought this tardy American approach was.

The Moscow Conference

A SWIRLING BLIZZARD wrapped itself around the plane carrying Secretary of State James Byrnes as it approached Moscow on Friday, December 14. Losing his way in the snow-filled Russian skies, the pilot of Byrnes's plane was unable to locate any of Moscow's airports. Authorities on the ground recommended that he turn back to Berlin, but Byrnes ordered the plane to proceed. Meanwhile, Ambassador Harriman was informed by the confused Russian aeronautical personnel that Byrnes's plane might be landing at an airport twenty miles south of Moscow and rushed to be there for the arrival. In fact, Byrnes's pilot had finally made contact with the Central Military Airport in Moscow and was preparing to land there. America's Minister to Moscow, George Kennan, had returned to his office from a leisurely lunch to learn of Byrnes's surprise descent and immediately jumped into a small duty car and sped out to meet the Secretary of State. Finding the airport to be one large blur of snow, Kennan was nevertheless assured that Byrnes was about to land. He was taken out to a small building at the edge of the field and soon heard and then saw a plane pass overhead. They rushed out onto the field. Someone had quickly put up two iron posts with the American and Russian flags flying from them. The four-engine American plane slowly emerged from the blur and taxied to a stop in front of the sturdy little welcoming party. Byrnes alighted jauntily, wearing a felt hat, light tan overcoat, and no overshoes, to find himself standing deep in snow. This made for a bizarre contrast with the Russian delegation which wore fur hats, huge wraparound coats, and high winter boots. "We had some trouble getting to Moscow," Byrnes said to the tiny group, "but we are not the only ones who have had trouble getting here" — an allusion, one assumes, to the German Army, if not to Napoleon. His whole purpose in coming to Moscow was to establish "contact and better understanding," Byrnes added. Kennan then put Byrnes, Cohen, and a military aide in the first available car and drove them to Spaso House, the residence of the American ambassador to Russia. There, Harriman's daughter Kathy entertained with hot soup until the ambassador returned from his futile trip to the suburban airport.[1]

As Byrnes was successfully negotiating his way to Moscow on December 14, several angry members of the United States Senate were entering the office of the President of the United States to protest the actions of his Secretary of State. From their conversation with Byrnes, the Senators said that they had gained the impression that the Secretary intended to divulge scientific information to the Russians at Moscow. Conant's presence on the mission apparently confirmed this suspicion. Their more important concern, however, was that the memorandum of policy which Byrnes had read to them indicated that Byrnes was prepared to enter into an agreement at Moscow which would call for the exchange of information and even technique before adequate safeguards were devised. Senator Tom Connally put the argument flatly: "We must have an inspection system before we exchange information about the atomic bomb and atomic energy." "That's what I told Jimmy," Truman declared. "You must be mistaken about the order of the items." But when the President began to read from a paper which he called his "directive" to Byrnes (probably the Cohen-Pasvolsky statement), it contained the stages of agreement in exactly the order which the Senators had feared. Truman quickly assured them that regardless of the order of the points in the memorandum, his Administration had no intention of disclosing any scientific information at Moscow or of making any final commitments for the eventual exchange of information. Byrnes's primary mission in Moscow on the question of atomic energy was to secure Soviet support for the establishment of the proposed United Nations commission. Truman added one final assurance: "Jimmy's already on his way. I'll get in touch with him en route and have him change that order." He instructed Acheson to prepare such a message to Byrnes and approved it for transmission early the next morning.[2]

Byrnes responded to Acheson in a brief cable on Monday, December 17: "You can tell the President that I do not intend presenting any proposal outside the framework of the three power declaration." He also transmitted a copy of a paper entitled "United States Proposals on Atomic Energy," which he planned to distribute to the conference. This paper was a definite step away from the Cohen-Pasvolsky policy which Byrnes had earlier adopted. While expressing the desire of the United States "to collaborate with other nations for the purpose of developing with the greatest practicable speed international measures to prevent the use for destructive purposes of atomic energy," this new American policy statement nevertheless did no more than request that the Soviet Union join in the sponsorship of a United Nations commission "to study the problems raised by the discovery of atomic energy." The brief paper ended with an excerpt from the Truman-Attlee-King declaration concerning the exchange of scientific information which prohibited the disclosure of any information concerning the industrial application of atomic energy before adequate safeguards were devised because "the military exploitation of atomic energy depends, in large part, upon the same methods and processes as would be required for industrial uses." [3]

The protective American Senators obviously had an effect on Byrnes. Some members of the American diplomatic corps in Moscow, particularly George Kennan, also left their mark. While Byrnes was in Moscow, Kennan handed him a memorandum on the way to handle atomic energy with the Russians. He also gave the Secretary an economic review of the Soviet Union for 1945 which was prepared by Thomas P. Whitney, attaché at the United States embassy in Moscow. Whitney had written:

> The U.S.S.R. is out to get the bomb. This has been officially stated. The meager evidence available indicates that great efforts are being made and that super priority will be given to this enterprise.

Kennan's own vision of the problem as contained in the memorandum he gave Byrnes was gloomy and full of mistrust:

> I have no hesitation in saying quite categorically . . . that it would be highly dangerous to our security if the Russians were to develop the use of atomic energy . . . along lines of which we were unaware and against which we might be defenseless if taken by surprise. There is nothing — I repeat, nothing — in the history of the Soviet regime which could justify us in assuming that the men who are now in power in Russia . . . would hesitate for a moment to apply this power against us if by doing so they thought that they might materially improve their own power position in the world. This holds true regardless of the process by which the Soviet government might obtain the knowledge of the use of such forces, i.e., whether by its own scientific and inventive efforts, by espionage, or by such knowledge being imparted to them as a gesture of good will and confidence.

As Kennan saw it, the revelation of any vital atomic knowledge to the Russians without adequate guarantees for the control of its use in the Soviet Union "would constitute a frivolous neglect of the vital interest of our people." [4]

After a round of courtesy calls and a welcoming dinner, the Big Three conference in Moscow began formally at five o'clock on Sunday evening, December 16, in the marble-walled conference room of Spiridonovka Palace, a sumptuous castle built by a nineteenth-century Russian textile king. As the hour for the opening of the conference approached, lines of Buicks, Packards, and Rolls-Royces, flying their respective country's flags, drove up to the palace. The delegates ascended a marble staircase to the conference room where they sat around a large round table, covered in green baize, with a small white vase in the middle holding the flags of the three nations. Two crystal chandeliers lighted the room, and paintings hung on the wall depicting the signing of the Anglo-Russian Agreement of 1941 and the Moscow Conference of 1943.[5]

Although substantive discussion on a number of issues including the European peace treaties began at this first session, atomic energy was considered only in procedural terms when the agenda was adopted. Molotov repeated his earlier desire to have atomic energy taken from the top of the agenda and placed at the bottom. Bevin asked whether the matter should necessarily be discussed last, suggesting that it might be considered at a point later on in the conference whenever it seemed proper. Molotov, knowing of Bevin's reluctance to come to Moscow and of his chagrin over Byrnes's failure to consult him earlier, saw a fine opportunity to further exacerbate Anglo-American relations. Mr. Byrnes had already agreed to his proposal, Molotov said, but if it was necessary to change it, then he would consent. Bevin hastily admitted that he had not known of Byrnes's agreement and therefore would withdraw his objection. Now slightly embarrassed, Byrnes suggested that there should be "no hard and fast agenda," but that the delegates should feel free to bring up any questions which they desired and that the agenda should be kept open at all times. That was fine with Molotov, but he still wanted atomic energy placed at the foot of the formal agenda. Since there was no further objection expressed, that is where the topic went.[6]

Byrnes believed that Molotov had insisted on this procedural change in the agenda because one of the leading Soviet nuclear scientists was in Paris. When the scientist returned to Moscow and did not make an appearance at the conference, the Secretary of State looked for another explanation: "I then came to the conclusion that Molotov's request had been made solely to give us the impression that the Soviet Government did not regard the atomic energy problem as important."[7]

Postponing consideration of atomic energy was something of a setback for James Conant, who had hoped the matter would be discussed early in the conference so that he could return to his presidential duties at Harvard. He was compelled instead to sit through more than a week of meetings. His extended presence, however, provided a revealing experience. At one of the afternoon social gatherings for which Molotov was host to the three delegations, Conant and he fell into a discussion of scientific matters. Molotov suggested to Conant that during his visit to Moscow the president of a great university like Harvard should deliver an address on atomic energy at the University of Moscow. This remark had the earmarks of a humorous poke at America's reluctance to discuss atomic energy matters with the Soviets. But Conant took it as an opportunity to open up the kind of communication for which he and Bush had long hoped. He discussed the prospect with Byrnes that night and the Secretary promised to discuss it with Molotov the next day. When he did, the Russian Foreign Minister seemed taken aback and said that "he had not been serious, that he had no authority to extend an invitation on behalf of the University, and that he had only been trying to be pleasant."

Byrnes circulated the new American policy statement on atomic energy to the conferees at the end of their third formal session on Tuesday afternoon, December 18. Molotov asked whether the document had previously been published and Byrnes said it had not.[8] Bevin responded to the distribution of this American paper with silent dismay. Unhappy about coming to Moscow in the first place, Bevin had declaimed furiously on his arrival when he learned that Byrnes had a position paper on the subject of atomic energy. The Englishman insisted that this paper not be presented to the conference until it had been cleared by His Majesty's government. Byrnes agreed to give Bevin until Wednesday to secure this consent but then proceeded to distribute the document on Tuesday, without prior word to the British. Bevin viewed this as an instance of "direct bad faith" and was furious.[9]

At the fifth formal session of the conference on Thursday, December 20, Byrnes asked that atomic energy be taken up. He also said that he wished to add a paragraph to the earlier American policy paper which he had presented. This paragraph, Byrnes said, "should have originally been included but had been omitted by mistake." It was a very substantive addition, however, and reflected the continued reports to Byrnes from Washington of Congressional anxiety over his activities in Moscow. Earlier that day he had received from Acheson, who was acting at Truman's direction, copies of newspaper articles, particularly one from the *New York Times,* which described the disgruntled Senators' confrontation with Byrnes before his departure and their beliefs that he was distributing atomic secrets in Moscow.[10] The paragraph Byrnes added to the American policy statement was taken from the Truman-Attlee-King declaration and concerned the critical matter of stages of atomic control:

The work of the Commission should proceed by separate stages, the successful completion of each one of which will develop the necessary confidence of the world before the next stage is undertaken.

The Soviet government was still studying the American proposal, Molotov said, and therefore requested that the discussion of atomic energy not be taken up yet. Byrnes agreed.[11]

Acheson sent Byrnes another cable on December 21, conveying Truman's concern that the previous reports from Washington not alarm the Secretary of State or cause him to be too cautious in Moscow. The President, Acheson said, had asked him to make clear "that he was not disturbed by these incidents and that the reports were being sent . . . merely for your information." Truman approved the policy paper which Byrnes had distributed and, apparently feeling that it was somewhat too protective, urged him to take further steps if he thought "it would be helpful in promoting cooperation and useful discussion." The President specifically suggested that Byrnes say to the Russians

that the United States Government does not purport to have the solution to the very troublesome questions involved in the atomic energy problem, but is eager and willing to work with the Soviet Union and other nations toward the establishment as rapidly as possible of mutually acceptable arrangements for full collaboration in respect to the problem and that to this end the United States will be glad to consider such proposals as the Soviet Government may wish to make in respect to any phase of the problem and to discuss them with the Soviet Government both in the United Nations Commission and separately.[12]

Byrnes, however, never followed Truman's suggestion. Molotov circulated a Soviet draft on atomic energy at the sixth formal session at Spiridonovka Palace on Saturday afternoon, December 22. The Russian paper was not a new proposal but merely a response to the earlier American suggestions. Molotov announced that the Soviet government was in agreement with the American proposition that the five permanent members of the Security Council, together with Canada, should sponsor the United Nations resolution creating a special atomic energy commission. The Russians wished to offer one major modification, however. The proposed commission might be created by the General Assembly, but it should be subordinate to the Security Council. From the Russian point of view, this modification made great sense. In the Security Council, the Soviet Union would have the power of veto. In the General Assembly, there was clearly a majority of nations which were favorably disposed to whatever the Western powers, and specifically America, wanted. Molotov, of course, did not argue in these terms at the Moscow conference table. He stressed instead the principal responsibility which the United Nations Charter gave to the Security Council for "the maintenance of international peace and security."

After a half-hour recess, Byrnes expressed his pleasure at Molotov's cooperation in the matter and said that he was very hopeful that the delegations would be able to agree on the problem. He wished to study the Soviet paper overnight and proposed that a meeting be held on the following day to discuss it. The other delegations quickly concurred.[13]

At noon on Sunday, December 23, the representatives of the three nations gathered once more with atomic energy finally at the top of the agenda. Byrnes began by announcing the willingness of the American government to accept Molotov's suggestion that the atomic energy commission report to the Security Council, but the Soviet wording on the issue bothered him. The Russians had put the matter in this way: "The Commission shall be attached to the Security Council and work under its direction." Byrnes preferred the language of the earlier American proposal:

"The Commission should not infringe upon the responsibility of any organ of the United Nations, but should present recommendations for the consideration of those organs in the performance of their tasks under the terms of the United Nations Charter." Molotov, however, persisted, relying heavily on the role of the Security Council under the United Nations Charter in matters of security and arguing that security was "the most important aspect of atomic energy." Bevin disagreed. In addition to the security aspect, he declared, atomic energy affected industrial and economic questions, and these could not be ignored. To make the commission solely responsible to the Security Council, he said, "would create the impression that its work would deal only with the security aspect of atomic energy." But, Molotov insisted, the security aspect was "the one that aroused the most interest and therefore should be dealt with on a clear-cut basis." He pointed out that the Soviet draft provided for the submission of reports of the commission in appropriate cases to the General Assembly or to the Social and Economic Council. Bevin was unconvinced and proposed some compromise language: "The Security Council is authorized in appropriate cases to send special instructions to the Commission on matters affecting security." Byrnes immediately accepted this language, but Molotov was still unhappy. He said he would consider Byrnes's suggestion, but since they had all agreed that the Security Council was primarily concerned with security, and since security was the chief factor in the atomic energy question, then the work of the atomic energy commission should be under the direction of the Security Council. The discussion continued in this manner for some time until the parties agreed that they would set the question of atomic energy aside until a subsequent meeting. Along the way Byrnes had proposed one other addition to the earlier American draft resolution creating the atomic energy commission. He wanted to add the state-

ment which he had already added to the American policy paper
that the commission's work should proceed by stages, the successful completion of each one being a precondition to the initiation
of the next step. Molotov's response was abrupt. It was a new
suggestion, he said, and he would have to have time to consider
it.[14]

The conferees' attention then turned to the very different questions of North China and the Kattegat Straits at the approaches
to the Baltic Sea. When the discussion was over, the delegations
moved to Spaso House where the Americans entertained in honor
of Molotov and Bevin at a stag luncheon. Bevin's casual remarks
during lunch caused considerable amusement among the Americans and equal confusion among the Russians. When someone
proposed a toast to the King, Bevin, who had come to power in
England through the trade union movement, added "and all the
other dockers." At one point, Harriman raised his glass to the
success of the conference. Bevin agreed and added, "And let's
hope we don't all get sacked when we get home." Molotov left
immediately after the luncheon was over, no doubt to prepare
Stalin for a visit later that afternoon from the American delegation.[15]

Secretary of State Byrnes, Ambassador Harriman, and Charles
Bohlen (the State Department Russian specialist and interpreter)
arrived at the Kremlin at five o'clock that afternoon to be greeted
by Stalin, Molotov, and their interpreter, Pavlov. After exchanging the customary amenities, they began a lengthy discussion that
ranged over the problems associated with Iran, Hungary, the
Balkans, North China, and atomic energy. At one point, Stalin
asked Byrnes to discuss certain proposals he and Bevin had made
regarding Hungary and Bulgaria. With the apparent intent of
making a joke, Byrnes said that although England and America
were supposed to have a bloc, he had even neglected to inform

Bevin soon enough about the proposed meeting in Moscow. That, Stalin said, "was obviously only a cloak to hide the reality of the bloc." When it came to atomic energy, Byrnes reported that the two sides were near total agreement and had only to make certain procedural decisions. "The Soviet Government had accepted nine-tenths of the American proposal and had only proposed one-tenth for their side," Stalin declared, asking Byrnes what was wrong with putting the proposed commission under the Security Council. The United States, Byrnes responded, had already accepted the Russian proposal that the commission report to the Security Council instead of the General Assembly but still felt that there were other questions besides security involved in which the General Assembly would have primary interest. After some discussion, Stalin agreed that "there was little difference in substance between our positions" and that Byrnes and Molotov could work out the drafting difficulties.[16]

That busy Sunday, December 23, ended for James Byrnes at a special performance of *Zolushka* (*Cinderella*) given by the Bolshoi Ballet for the visiting Foreign Ministers. The theater was packed and very stuffy that evening as Molotov paced outside awaiting the arrival of his foreign guests. Inside the hall, the members of the audience fanned themselves with their programs. George Kennan, who was seated in a box with one of Byrnes's assistants, began to worry at the absence of the Secretary more than fifteen minutes after the curtain was scheduled to rise. "I suppose the Secretary has forgotten to come," Kennan joked to Byrnes's aide. "Oh, no," the aide replied, "they are only sitting up in his room at the embassy telling stories and having drinks and no one dares to go in and interrupt them." Kennan jumped from his seat and walked quickly to the nearest telephone to call the embassy and urge someone to inform Byrnes of diplomatic protocol. An insightful member of the Russian secret police came

up to him, however, and reported that the Secretary's party had
just left for the theater. Byrnes soon arrived, having kept numerous members of the Soviet government and diplomatic corps
waiting for more than a half-hour.[17]

Atomic energy was discussed for the final time at an informal
meeting of the delegations at 3:15 P.M. the following afternoon.
The linguistic discussion of how to describe the relationship of
the special atomic energy commission to the Security Council
continued. Molotov also added a new obstacle when he took the
position that it was unnecessary to include within the United Nations resolution Byrnes's section on the work of the commission
proceeding by stages. The commission, he said, should be able to
establish its own rules of procedure. Bevin objected, declaring
that it was extremely important to England and Canada to include this paragraph on stages from the three-nation declaration.
But, Molotov quickly responded, it would not be "convenient"
to include a reference to a matter in which the Soviet government had not participated. Bevin said he did not care whether
there was a reference to the declaration itself, so long as the idea
of stages was included. This latest disagreement troubled Byrnes,
because it was at the heart of the anxieties he had been hearing
from Washington. And so he offered to accept the better part of
Molotov's wording on the relationship of the atomic energy commission to the Security Council if Molotov would accept the
principle of stages of control in the draft resolution. Ultimately,
these were exactly the terms to which the parties agreed, referring
the matter of atomic energy finally to a drafting committee for
its attention.[18]

Stalin was host to the three delegations that evening at a
Christmas Eve dinner in the Kremlin. Molotov stood at one point
and proposed a friendly toast to Conant, quipping that he hoped
the American scientist did not have an atomic bomb in his pocket.

Stalin, however, was unprepared for such levity on this subject. He rose and said that it was improper for Molotov to have dismissed Conant's work in such a flippant manner. Conant and his colleagues had done a great service for mankind and Stalin personally wanted to congratulate them.[19]

At eleven o'clock at night on Wednesday, December 26, a customary hour for the Russians to be pursuing diplomatic matters, representatives of the three nations gathered at Spiridonovka Palace to sign the communiqué of the Moscow Conference. It covered the wide range of subjects which the parties had discussed in their several days of conference. On the matter of atomic energy, they agreed to ask China, France, and Canada to join them in sponsoring the resolution to create a special atomic energy commission within the United Nations. The commission would report primarily to the Security Council and only to other organs of the United Nations when it seemed appropriate. In matters affecting international security, the commission would receive directions from the Security Council and be accountable to the council. The paragraph on stages, taken directly from the Truman-Attlee-King declaration, was included without alteration.[20]

The parties therefore had done little more in Moscow than agree to talk again later about atomic energy. There were absolutely no substantive discussions of Russian-American collaboration on atomic development. The procedural arguments which so preoccupied the nations at Moscow amounted, in fact, to no more than maneuvering for position in the propaganda race that would follow while the atomic arms race, which had actually already begun, grew more intense. The United States had continued its production of atomic weapons while bumbling along toward some policy for international atomic control, but never really pursuing a course that held any hope of Russian agreement. For their part, the Russians had apparently made the decision that their own self-interest would be better served by the development of atomic capability than by waiting for the Americans to come up with a control plan that offered them any hope of equality.

Byrnes left Moscow early on the morning of December 27. When Molotov and the entire Russian delegation came out to the airport in the predawn cold to see him off, the Secretary of State seemed "visibly touched." "The important thing," Byrnes said in departing, "is that closer relations have been established, so that the possibility of agreement has been greatly increased." [21]

In reporting the communiqué of the Moscow Conference, the *New York Times* strung a banner headline across its front page, proclaiming BIG THREE RE-ESTABLISH UNITY IN WIDE ACCORD. It was a deceptively pleasant note on which to end the year that had seen the birth of the atomic age. From beneath the amicable headlines, however, there immediately emerged spasms of insecurity and doubt, so that the old year actually ended in the centers of American power on a note far more defensive than the chord of optimism sounded in Moscow. In Washington, reaction to the Moscow communiqué was mixed. The scientists seemed pleased because on first glance the West had finally extended a hand which the Russians had apparently clasped. Now America was moving away from a two-bloc world and toward international cooperation.

Others — though pleased by the friendly spirit of Moscow — were nonetheless troubled by the reference to the Security Council and the resulting emergence of the veto in atomic energy relations because they "had hoped that the Big Three would gradually guide the world toward a rule of law in which all nations were equal before the law and no nation had the right to veto the rule of the majority." [22] At the completely opposite pole were men like Senators Connally and Vandenberg who viewed the veto happily as protection against an unthinking surrender of America's atomic advantage. They and so many of their countrymen had become very strange bedfellows of the Russian Communists on the question of the Security Council and the veto. Each was moved by chauvinistic, self-protective instincts, worried that the world would ask more of them than they were prepared to give, and each was therefore enamored with the veto that would allow them to serve their nationalistic concerns.

Even with the American veto in the Security Council, however, Vandenberg did not feel that America was sufficiently guarded. The Moscow Declaration had listed the four stages in the same order which he had protested. He worried again that the United States would disclose first and receive safeguards last. As soon as the communiqué arrived from Moscow, Vandenberg protested to Acheson, who arranged for the Senator to bring his anxieties once more to the President.

It was of the greatest importance for Truman to pacify Vandenberg because he was a member of the United States delegation to the first United Nations General Assembly meeting in London and would have to be involved in the joint resolution creating an atomic energy commission. His resignation from the delegation, which had already been threatened, would severely damage the American position. Truman told Vandenberg that he agreed with him about the stages and was sure Byrnes did too. But Vandenberg desired more than this. He wanted to make certain that the Soviet Union and Britain understood America's interpretation of the four-stage progression. Back to the State Department Vandenberg went with Acheson to draft a statement which Truman and apparently Byrnes, en route home from Moscow, approved later that day. Declaring first that the President and State Department had ratified what he was about to say, the Senator from Michigan read this statement to the press:

> I would not be able to agree that the problem can be handled by separate and unrelated stages. I particularly share what I believe to be the general Congressional opinion that any disclosures regarding the atom bomb should be part of a complete plan for adequate world-wide inspection and control. For these reasons, I have sought additional official information today regarding the program announced in the Moscow communique. I am advised by the State Department that while the communique listed four separate objectives with inspections and control listed last, it is not intended that the objectives should be taken in the order indicated but that it is intended that the four shall be read together, and that each shall be accompanied by full security requirements — all being finally subject to Congressional approval. This help fully clarifies the situation.[23]

In addition to dramatizing his point for the great world powers, Vandenberg had made it clear to the executive branch of American government that it was the responsibility and privilege of Congress to check and finally approve all parts of the country's atomic energy policy. The exclusion that marked the Truman-Attlee-King conference should never again be repeated. Perhaps that was Vandenberg's major point.

Byrnes returned to Washington on December 29, striding briskly down the airplane ramp, "buoyant and the freshest appearing member of the party," still dressed in the lightweight suit he had worn on his snowy arrival in Moscow. Borrowing a line from Molotov, he turned to Ben Cohen who was carrying a traveling bag and announced to the press, "He has an atom bomb in the suitcase." Four hours later, Byrnes was aboard the *Williamsburg,* cruising the Potomac in Virginia, talking to the President. Perhaps Truman's stories of continued Congressional suspicion dampened some of Byrnes's enthusiasm, for when he reported to the nation by radio the next night on his trip to Moscow, his tone was more defensive than satisfied. While praising the Moscow Declaration as a source of "hope to the war-weary people of the world," Byrnes seemed more concerned with telling the American people, their Congressmen, and their Senators what he, Molotov, and Bevin had not done in Moscow:

> The four objectives set forth in the proposed resolution establishing the commission are not intended to indicate the order in which they are to be considered. In particular, it was intended and is understood that the matter of safeguards will apply to the recommendations of the commission in relation to every phase of the subject and at every stage. Indeed, at the root of the whole matter lies the problem of providing the necessary safeguards . . . At no time did we discuss any technical or scientific matters. Neither we nor any nation would be expected to share our armament secrets until it was certain that effective safeguards had been developed to insure our mutual protection . . . The Security Council can give directives to the commission, and restrain publication of reports detrimental to peace and security, but such action can be taken only with concurrence of all its permanent members.[24]

Despite these assurances Connally and Vandenberg continued the attack during the first week of 1946. They had gone to London where both of them were to serve as members of the United States delegation to the United Nations, and the change of scenery apparently swelled Vandenberg's doubts that the rest of the world really understood how jealous the United States was of its secrets. On Saturday, January 5, representatives of the American delegation wired Byrnes of Vandenberg's unhappiness. When the Secretary arrived at the National Airport in Washington to depart for London on January 7, he had with him another statement of reassurance, this one even more explicit. He said that the proposed United Nations Atomic Energy Commission (UNAEC) would not have "the authority to decide what information the United

States or any Government should place at its disposal." This time, Byrnes's espousal of the veto as an instrument of protection for America became much more complete. Even if there were no veto, he added, "it would still be for the Government of the United States by treaty or by Congressional action" to determine to what extent a recommendation of the United Nations should be acted upon. "The language of the resolution makes clear that even as to the exchange of basic scientific information for peaceful purposes, the commission has authority only to make recommendations," [25] Byrnes said.

When Byrnes's plane landed in London fourteen hours later, headlines in the English papers blared: UNITED STATES READY TO USE ATOM VETO and U.S. TO SAFEGUARD OWN INTERESTS. The Secretary went immediately to Claridges Hotel where he had invited Senators Connally and Vandenberg and their wives to dine with him. Later, in Suite 101, the entire American delegation convened to discuss atomic energy. In somber tones, Vandenberg warned that the United Nations might stand or fall on the fate of the Atomic Energy Commission, but that only an international control plan with adequate safeguards would give America the protection it needed. Mrs. Eleanor Roosevelt, a member of the American delegation, asked if it was not possible to have faith in the Russians on this matter. But Byrnes shook his head and said sadly, "In atomic energy matters we can never afford to have faith in anybody." Before long Vandenberg came out of the meeting and was able to tell newsmen: "I have talked with the Secretary. I am completely assured . . . My interest has been to make a record that avoids any possibility of international misunderstanding at home or abroad." [26] Vandenberg and John Foster Dulles, another member of the American delegation, sat together at the end of the evening over clinking glasses of bourbon and congratulated each other. "Thank heavens, Jimmy Byrnes hates disagreements," Senator Vandenberg said. "I do not know where I'd be if he decided to continue to fight." [27]

On January 21, the important Political and Social Committee unanimously adopted the Moscow resolution, 47–0, after Senator Connally had read into the record the qualifications Byrnes had spelled out in his December 30 statement, and the small nations had loudly protested the extreme deference being given to the veto power. The total absence of substantive discussion on this historic resolution led the Philippine delegate, Tomas Cabil, to complain, "The question is so transcendental that there should be full discussion and I do not think we should railroad this through." Mexico asked for an adjournment to clarify the resolution, but Ernest Bevin silenced the protesters with this caveat: "The people of the world will be rather upset if there is a delay in coming to a conclusion." The full General Assembly passed the resolution on the following day with only the voice of the Philippines in dissent. "The general attitude of the Assembly," James Reston wrote, "was that members could not change it without antagonizing the powers that controlled the atomic secrets, so they did not try." Andrei Vishinsky, the tall, stocky, gray-haired Russian lawyer who represented the Soviet Union in London, applauded the resolution as "the first important act of the joint efforts of the United Nations to ensure peace and security throughout the world," and added: "May this noble act be attended with complete and genuine success." With the resolution passed, Byrnes returned happily to Washington.[28]

It was only on atomic energy, however, that matters ran smoothly in London. Paul Henry Spaak was elected President of the General Assembly only over the vigorous opposition of the Soviet Union and its allies. Elections of the nonpermanent members of the Security Council embroiled the East and West in bitter argument. In the Security Council, Russia filed a complaint against the continued presence of British armed forces in Greece and Indonesia, and the Western powers asked Russia when it would remove its troops from Iran. The harmony of the Moscow Conference was fast fading. Even in their discussions of the atomic energy resolution to which they had agreed already in Moscow, the big powers stressed their own nationalistic concerns more than the merit of international control. Vishinsky emphasized the superiority of the Security Council over the new Atomic Energy Commission, and Connally made it clear that the United States did not feel it had committed itself to giving up anything.

III

The American Plan

12

A Feeling of Acute Revulsion

THE GULF that separated the dancing crowds in Times Square from troubled statesmen like Henry L. Stimson on V-J Day did not diminish in the first months after the war. The public was undoubtedly conscious of the atomic bomb and probably somewhat troubled by it, but the focus of attention was elsewhere. Everyone wanted to forget about war and armaments and enjoy the peace. The most pressing concerns were personal and not global. The existence of the atom bomb and the potential for nuclear warfare seemed very distant from the needs which occupied people — getting a job, earning a decent wage, and finding adequate housing.

"The American people is gradually readjusting itself to the dynamics of peace," an anxious Hanson Baldwin wrote. "But nothing has been done about the atom bomb. The first great psychological surge of mixed fear and hope . . . has passed, and therefore the key moment is gone." [1] The only question of military or international significance that concerned a mass of the people was demobilization. Everyone wanted the sons and husbands returned home from war. On August 9, 1945, Stimson wrote in his diary:

It seems as if everybody in the country was getting impatient to get his or her particular soldier out of the Army . . . The success of the first atom bomb and the news of the Russians' entry into the war which came yesterday has rather doubled this crusade. Every industry wishes to get its particular quota of men back and nearly all citizens join in demanding somebody to dig coal for the coming winter . . .

Stimson himself was bothered by requests for the discharge of soldiers. Cordell Hull asked that his wife's nephew be discharged; Henry Morgenthau requested the release of his son, Henry III, because of his wife's illness; and a relative of Stimson's pleaded for the discharge of another member of the family, Chaplain William Stimson.[2]

This popular demand for the return of American soldiers had a direct effect on the attempts to control atomic weapons. In fact, the desire for demobilization was justified in the minds of many by the very existence of the atomic bomb. Two weeks after Hiroshima an American corporal stationed in Germany said what seemed to be on everyone's lips: "It is downright stupid to keep a whole lot of divisions here now when a few bombers and some atomic bombs would keep the Germans in line."[3] This was the attitude that most unsettled America's military planners, although the cause for their concern was now not the Germans but the Russians. On the day after the Hiroshima attack, the American War Department warned that this strange, new weapon which had been used in Japan would not allow reduction of the Army below the seven million men which had previously been established as the desired total for June 1946.[4] But one week later, President Truman responded to the pressure that had already mounted by announcing that monthly inductions would drop from 80,000 to 50,000, and that in the following twelve to eighteen months almost five and a half million men would be released from service. Chairman May of the House Military Affairs Committee followed this immediately with an appeal to Secretary Stimson that inductions be stopped for a period of three months to try a program of voluntary enlistments. Truman was not prepared to accept such a solution and warned that world conditions demanded the continued drafting of eligible men between the ages of eighteen and twenty-five: "I must emphasize the danger that lies in a too early unqualified termination . . . The situation in the Pacific continues to have many elements of danger." [5] This was surely a not too finely guarded reference to the Soviet Union, whose postwar posture had troubled Truman since Potsdam. Yet, on the very next day, the Army General Staff, under great pressure from Congressmen who were returning to Washington for the new session, reported to the House Armed Services Committee that the size of the United States Army would go from 8,500,-000 to 2,500,000 by July 1, 1946 — a drastic alteration of the announcement made less than a month earlier. Troops in the overseas zones would be reduced to the minimum number required. By the first week in September, when most of the Congressmen and Senators were back in Washington, they found themselves deluged with mail urging the immediate release of servicemen. "If all the requests were met," one Congressman admitted, "there would be no one left to man occupational forces anywhere." [6] The most popular idea on Capitol Hill was the desirability of trying a system of voluntary enlistments. In a message to Congress on the state of the postwar world, on September 6, Truman said that the nation's number one goal was to "demobilize as soon as possible the armed forces no longer needed."

At a Cabinet meeting on September 7, Leo Crowley, the Foreign Economic Administrator, interrupted a discussion of the nation's future military policy with a stark report from the field.[7] He had just returned from the Middle West and "was sure that the country would be violently opposed to the continuation of any universal military training." The popular "assumption was that we had fought a war now to get rid of war, that we had the atomic bomb, and we had the San Francisco Conference and all the various affirmations of faith in the possibilities of an organiza-

tion to create the foundations of world peace." Stimson, so preoccupied at this time with the control of atomic energy, argued
that "the only way we could convince the world we were serious
about preventing another war was to show that we took our responsibility in that direction with great seriousness." Forrestal
strongly supported Stimson's position, but Crowley insisted that
"no matter how much we felt as we did, the country would not
support that point of view." Stimson countered with an expression of righteous dismay, refusing to accept what he called "that
statement of cynicism about the good sense and the willingness of
the nation to accept its serious responsibilities." But, a day later,
the War Department announced that 800,000 men would be released in the following sixty days. For most members of Congress
that was not enough. Senator Thomas of Utah introduced a bill
prohibiting the drafting of eighteen- and nineteen-year-olds. And
Senator Richard Russell of Georgia recommended a one-year
trial of a system of voluntary enlistments.

On the last day of his long career in public service Henry L.
Stimson gave a final public warning. The preservation of America's primary position in the world depended on "acceptance by
our people" of the necessity for maintaining America's military
and naval strength: "We must be particularly alert that no system
is established — however palatable it may seem — which fails
to provide the power we need at this stage of the world's development . . . We must not make early and easy assumptions that
the days of armies and navies are over."

A more pointed warning came from a foreign observer. Field
Marshal Sir Henry Maitland Wilson, Chief of the British Joint
Staff Mission in Washington, told newsmen during September
1945 that when the Soviet Union had the atomic bomb, "as
naturally she will," it would make her the most powerful nation
in the world because of what Wilson called "the incredible demo-

bilization of American conventional military strength." "By with-drawing its occupation forces on a large scale and by limiting drastically the size of its future draft," Wilson said, "the United States is leaving the field alone to Russia." He suggested that an atomic war between great powers was highly unlikely, but that conventional wars still would go on. "I am very worried about the Balkans — with the United States curtailing its military in-fluence in Europe," Sir Henry said, adding, so that no one would mistake his specific concern:

> Her [Russia's] great Army is being maintained. I cannot see why there is all the talk of security by Russia and all the demand for bases unless she is bent upon territorial gain . . . By making itself weak, the United States will not gain the respect of Russia. Stalin will seek to dominate wherever he can.

The British Foreign Office hastily disclaimed Wilson's views, describing them as strictly his own.[8] There was no formal re-sponse from the American government, but the foremost Ameri-can military men clearly shared the outspoken Englishman's fears. On October 9, Chief of Staff George Marshall issued his official report on the final two years of the war, but his concerns went beyond the past. Marshall recommended the immediate establishment of a universal military training system that could activate four million men within a year. His tone was altogether anxious:

> We finish each bloody war with a feeling of acute revulsion . . . and yet on each occasion we confuse military preparedness with the causes of war and then drift almost deliberately into another catastrophe . . . A rich nation which lays down its arms as we have done after every war in our history will court disaster . . . Technology does not eliminate the need for men in war.[9]

With little heed to this warning, the Congress was offered more comfort on October 17, when Brigadier General Robert W.

Berry, a Deputy Assistant Chief of Staff, told the Senate Military Affairs Committee that 1,100,000 men would be able to leave the Army during the month. "General," Senator Edwin Johnson of Colorado exclaimed, "You have given Congress and the country a lot of good information." [10]

Growing very anxious, James Forrestal told Secretary of State Byrnes and Secretary of War Robert Patterson on October 16, 1945, that at the current rate of demobilization "there will necessarily come a point between the present time and the time when the Army and Navy reach their planned postwar strength at which neither the Army nor the Navy will have sufficient trained men to be able to operate efficiently." It was absolutely mandatory, he argued, for the President to explain to the people fully why America had to maintain its military strength and to acquaint them with "the details of our dealings with the Russians and with the attitude which the Russians have manifested throughout." Byrnes, however, was reluctant to accept such a policy. He believed that "it would give the Russians an excuse for claiming that we had furnished provocation which justified their actions." [11] Robert Patterson informed Forrestal and Byrnes three weeks later that the Army was trying a program of voluntary recruiting but that thus far only 51,000 men had signed up and most of these were "old regular Army men." [12]

Although the President expressed his support of the universal training bill that had been introduced in Congress at General Marshall's behest, in no way did he use the powers of his office on behalf of this proposal — not a surprising response on so unpopular an issue from a new President who had not yet stood the test of the voting booth. In his Navy Day Address on October 27, Truman had said only that the talk of scrapping all navies, armies, and air forces because of the atomic bomb was "one hundred percent wrong."

Over the following months, other prominent citizens including Forrestal, Marshall, Bernard Baruch, and the new Chief of Staff Dwight Eisenhower portrayed the foolhardiness of demobilization, but the mind of the public, and therefore of their Congressmen, was closed. Forrestal made his most fervent appeal at a Cabinet meeting on January 11, 1946, after Acheson had reported that the American demobilization was "a matter of great embarrassment and concern to his own department in their conduct of our foreign affairs." Forrestal erupted:

> I said that I thought the President should get the heads of the important news services and the leading newspapers — particularly Mr. Sulzberger of the New York Times, Roy Roberts, Palmer Hoyt, the Cowles brothers, John Knight, plus Roy Howard, and Bob McLean of the AP — and state to them the seriousness of the present situation and the need for making the country aware of its implications abroad. I said these were all reasonable and patriotic men and that I was confident that if the facts were presented we would have their support in the presentation of the case. The President agreed to do so.
>
> I also suggested that the heads of the broadcasting systems be called in and that a canvass be made of the important radio commentators . . .
>
> Secretary Ickes suggested that the State Department arrange a nationwide hook-up to present the impact of the over-rapid demobilization on our foreign policy.[13]

The record reveals no such urgent call to the nation. By the beginning of April 1946, Hanson Baldwin reported that "The Army already has been disabled by too rapid demobilization." [14] At a White House press conference on April 17, 1946, President Truman called attention to the fact that discharges in the Army had reached nearly seven million. He termed this "the most remarkable demobilization in the history of the world, or 'disintegration,' if you want to call it that." [15]

This turn of events would inevitably have a major effect upon America's desire to establish international control of atomic energy. As the nation's conventional military resources grew weaker and weaker at a time when Soviet dynamism made it imperative that the United States be strong, the place of atomic weapons in the overall American military posture would naturally become more critical and worthy of protection.

13

The Acheson-Lilienthal Report

BEFORE BOARDING his plane on January 7, 1946, for the first session of the United Nations General Assembly in London, James Byrnes held a press conference at the Washington airport. He wanted to pacify the nervous members of the United States Senate who seemed in perpetual doubt about Byrnes's common sense, if not his loyalty, when it came to the handling of the atomic bomb. Now Byrnes emphasized the veto power which the United States would hold over the actions of the proposed United Nations commission on atomic energy and restated his own desire never to let the secrets go. He also announced that he had appointed a special five-member committee "to study the subject of controls and safeguards necessary to protect this government" during the inquiry which the United Nations would soon undertake. To serve on this committee, Byrnes appointed Dean Acheson (chairman), Vannevar Bush, James Conant, General Leslie Groves, and John McCloy, the former Assistant Secretary of War who had returned to his Wall Street practice of law. Although Byrnes's charge to the committee in his airport conference that day was entirely defensive and protective, he had told Acheson privately that he expected the committee to come up with a comprehensive policy for America to take into the deliberations of the United Nations Atomic Energy Commission. It was typical of the manner in which Byrnes approached the problem of atomic energy control that he had been stirred to appoint this much-needed committee largely because Senator Brien McMahon, the chairman of the Senate Special Committee on Atomic Energy and a good friend of the atomic scientists' lobby, had planned to begin a series of public hearings on the question of international control. The only way Byrnes could delay this unwanted intrusion into his jurisdiction was to convince the Senator from Connecticut that a high-level study of the problem was about to begin within the State Department.

Acheson was apparently dismayed at the assignment Byrnes had given him because he had little understanding of atomic energy beyond the most general considerations of how it affected the international relations of the United States. His committee, however, consisted of the men in American government who were most seasoned in their thoughts on the international control of atomic energy. Acheson called the group together in Byrnes's office on January 14, 1946.[1] All the members were there except Conant who had a conflicting engagement. Herbert Marks, Acheson's assistant, was also present. The meeting began with a general exposition of points of view. Bush, Groves, and McCloy had worked closely with each other over the years, and so their opinions were well known to one another. Acheson expressed the belief that they could not do their job without the most sturdy factual foundation. The area was so bound up in technology, he said, that policy planning on the diplomatic level alone would not be enough. He hoped the committee would break new ground and offer the kind of innovative conclusions that could not be achieved without comprehensive data. Marks had long urged this idea on Acheson, who had suggested it himself to the President, claiming that going ahead in this area without men who could transfer the facts of atomic energy into public policy would be "as if one called in a very intelligent and well-intentioned South Sea Islander and said, 'There are too many cows being killed on railroad tracks and I want you to do something about it.' But the South Sea Islander, although smart and meaning well and wanting to be helpful, had never seen a cow or a railroad." [2] What the committee needed was a board of consultants, Acheson said, men who were skilled in such matters and could investigate the facts and then formulate plans. He wanted a man with governmental experience as well as technological skill to head this panel. General Groves, however, did not like Acheson's idea. He argued that Conant, Bush, and he "knew more about the broad aspects of the problem . . . than any panel that could be assembled." Besides, Groves continued, he "had access to all the scientific assistance that might be needed on any particular point." [3] But Acheson wanted a fresh look at the subject and the rest of the group agreed with him. Groves consented, suggesting that the board of consultants be limited to five members.

Acheson wasted little time in contacting the man he had in mind all along for chairman of the board of consultants. David Lilienthal, a Harvard Law graduate and, like Acheson, a devoted follower of Justice Brandeis, was behind his director's desk at the Tennessee Valley Authority on January 14, when Acheson called and asked him to come to Washington as soon as possible to discuss an assignment which concerned atomic energy and international relations. For an hour on Wednesday, January 16, Lilienthal listened to Acheson's brilliant sales pitch. The men whose job it was to worry about controlling atomic energy — namely Truman and Byrnes — had neither the facts nor an understanding of the issue. "Commitments on paper and in communiqués have been made and are being made without a knowledge of what the hell it is all about — literally," Acheson declared. Control of atomic energy was centered thoroughly in the War Department and actually under one man, General Groves, who had single-handedly been running foreign policy in this area. "He has entered into contracts involving other countries (Belgium and their Congo deposits of uranium for example) without even the knowledge of the Department of State," Acheson complained. Now, the job was to put the right people in control of the problem and to build a knowledgeable policy on questions of control, safeguards, enforcement, and international competition. Would Lilienthal lead a small advisory panel whose job would be to give the facts to Acheson's committee so that it might pass them on to the President, Secretary of State, and finally to the American delegate to the UNAEC? Yes, was the quick response. For Lilienthal, Acheson's invitation was "one of the most flattering proposals ever made to me, and yet one of the most humbling possible." [4]

Lilienthal's mind began to move excitedly over the subject area which had been entrusted to him. He wrote in his diary after meeting with Acheson:

> Inevitably . . . the assignment would force an examination of the crucial question: What is there that is secret? Are those facts really "secret" in the sense that is assumed by our international policy . . . If my hunch . . . that in the real sense there are no secrets . . . would be supportable by the facts . . . then it would be clear that the basis of present policy-making is without foundation. For present policy and commitments are made on the Army-sponsored thesis that there are secrets. And since it is in the Army's hands (or, literally, Gen. Groves') to deny access to the facts that would prove or disprove this vital thesis, there has been no way to examine the very foundation of our policies in the international field.[5]

Lilienthal also turned his powers of logic on America's handling of the safeguards question which Acheson had told him was of primary importance to their work. What troubled him in the three-nation declaration and the Moscow communiqué was America's unwillingness to offer up any facts until safeguards had been established. If the other countries did not have the facts, Lilienthal wondered, how could they know enough to talk about safeguards? The section on safeguards and stages in the Truman-Attlee-King declaration sounded to him like a Nebraska statute which Dean Pound of Harvard was fond of quoting: "When two trains approach each other at gradings, neither shall pass till the other has gone." [6]

Within a week, Acheson had completed a talent search which resulted in the appointment of four other men to serve with Lilienthal. Each of them was a figure of independent strength: Chester Barnard, the fifty-nine-year-old head of the New Jersey Bell Telephone Company who had led the United Service Organizations during the war and had recently been active in the United Nations Relief and Rehabilitation Administration, was the oldest of them all and had been Lilienthal's own choice; Harry A. Winne, another businessman and elder statesman of the relatively young group, was vice president in charge of engineering for General Electric and an engineer; he had solved some of the toughest industrial production problems of the Manhattan Project and was Groves's choice; Dr. Charles Thomas, vice president of the Monsanto Chemical Company, a chemist who had coordinated work on plutonium chemistry for the Manhattan Project; he was one of the select group at Los Alamos on July 16, 1945; Robert Oppenheimer was Robert Oppenheimer, the pillar of Los Alamos and troubled father of the bomb. Herbert Marks and Carroll Wilson of Vannevar Bush's staff would sit with the group as staff members.

On Wednesday morning, January 23, Acheson presented this five-man board of consultants to his own committee in the Secretary of State's office. In somber tones he outlined the assignment, refusing, however, to draw very clear lines. Lilienthal and his board should be free to move where their investigations took them. It was understood that General Groves would hold nothing back in the way of access or information from the consultants. As Lilienthal saw it, his mission was to find an answer to the fundamental question: "Can a way be found, a feasible, workable way, to safeguard the world against the atomic bomb?" In one sense, however, Lilienthal's understanding was really more narrow than that. "Our work," Lilienthal wrote, "the work of this group for which I have been made chairman, is to develop a position, based on facts not now known by our political officers, that will 'work,' and have a good chance of being accepted, especially by Russia." [7]

That afternoon the consultants held their first meeting in an impressive, oak-paneled room with unimpressive furnishings on the top floor of the American Trucking Association Building — the former headquarters of the Office of Scientific Research and Development (OSRD). [8] The furniture had been moved in hastily to accommodate them and looked like war surplus. Each man had a desk or table and chair. Telephones sat on windowsills and on the floor. Conant was there on behalf of Acheson's committee to get the Lilienthal Board on its way and to offer some of his own advice. Don't become entangled in the problem of sanctions, he told them. Leave that to the Security Council. The consultants' mission, as Conant saw it, was to devise a system of atomic control which promised to warn the world at the instant any nation took the first step toward building atomic weapons. They must also provide an explicit schedule for putting the full program into effect.

When Conant departed, the Lilienthal Board turned to its own future. Guided by Chester Barnard, who was accustomed to thinking "scientifically about organization," the members of the group talked first not about atomic energy but about themselves. They agreed that their mission was too important to be subjected to the "hazards of the push and pull of the committee approach." As one member of the Lilienthal Board recalls:

> It seemed to be fairly well agreed that most committees break down because many members come to their job with fully formed conclusions, having almost property rights in their own ideas, and spend all their time proposing and exhorting rather than listening and considering . . . Our first joint discussion, then, was to liberate all our discussion from idea possessiveness. No point would be argued down; we agreed that we would attack the problem inductively, working from the ground up, assembling all facts pertinent to the problem as a basis for conclusions implied . . .
>
> We agreed, too, that we were not going to issue a watered down report just for the sake of coming out with a report. We were not going to get into the usual type of barter system, trading off one pet idea against another, getting into committee deals just for the sake of carrying off individual honors. We agreed that we would issue five reports if any of us felt that the group report lacked directness and honesty . . .[9]

Having settled on their methodology, the consultants were ready to go to work. Their first step was entirely consistent with Acheson's charge to them. They were going to get the facts. Each of them was a specialist of one kind or another; only Oppenheimer and Thomas had any substantial understanding of atomic energy, and only Oppenheimer knew the full story of the atomic bomb. Their next move was obvious. A blackboard was set up and on the following Monday morning, January 28, 1946, Robert Oppenheimer began a series of lectures on nuclear energy and its application for military and industrial purposes. During the evenings, he gave private tutoring lessons in the same subject to Dean Acheson and John McCloy.

Over the next six weeks, the lectures and discussions continued — in New York, Oak Ridge, Los Alamos, and Washington again, in Pullman cars, aloft in General Groves's Army plane, and back at the old OSRD headquarters in the capital. Whenever a question arose that they felt could only be settled by firsthand observation at one of the atomic installations of the Manhattan Project, they would bundle themselves up and make the trip. Slowly, personal bonds developed among these seven very different men. At the outset, some had expressed a reluctance to proceed before the course of postwar international relations was clear. "I think that at first we were subconsciously inclined to shy away from specific ideas as much as possible," Marks has said. "The problem was too vast. We needed the time to get the feel of it." Whenever such timidity appeared Lilienthal would reach for a newspaper clipping of the three-nation declaration which he carried with him. Waving it in the air, he would admonish: "Gentlemen, maybe if you were President of the United States you might have decided differently, but this man who is President has committed us to international control, so let's quit considering something our government is opposed to."

Slowly, the group considered the alternatives, rejecting some and setting others aside for further attention. One of the first ideas to be discarded was a simple international covenant outlawing atomic weapons. Their education in atomic science had convinced them that, as Lilienthal put it, "there was no security whatever for people everywhere, no prospect of a moment's freedom from fear of an atomic armament race if this is all we had to offer." [10] But, Lilienthal asked at one meeting, what if a prohibition on all atomic development was the only way to save the world from nuclear holocaust? The response was predictable, and Harry Winne of General Electric stated it most emphatically: "If that was the aim of this board of consultants, this was no place for me, because I thought that the development had to go forward. We had to devise, if possible, some means for controlling the development in such a way as to prevent the use of atomic energy for weapons." [11] They were simply too excited by the commercial and humanitarian prospects of atomic development to conclude that the best control system was one that prevented all uses of atomic energy, including the nonmilitary. They were looking for a system of control that would impede military uses of atomic energy and encourage peaceful uses.

A plan of atomic control had to be based on some form of inspection, if it was to be realistic, but the Lilienthal Board soon agreed that a system based solely on inspection was undesirable. In New York, they met with the Technical Committee on Inspection and Control, which General Groves had established for the Army after Hiroshima. It was composed of scientists who had worked on the Manhattan Project. Finally allowed to throw off the compartmentalization that Groves had imposed on them throughout the war, these men turned their attention to the problem of whether atomic energy control could be achieved through the inspection of plants. Their answer was a halting yes, but as they explained why, Lilienthal's board came to the conclusion that inspection was not enough. "The more we listened," Marks later recalled, "the more convinced we became that something might go wrong with the system at least part of the time and that, in the case of atomic weapons, would be too often." Lilienthal himself put it this way: "The inspector must know at least as much about atomic energy as the people he's supposed to watch. And there's the rub. An inspector — a high grade policeman — simply wouldn't know enough to detect a skillful evasion." [12]

Doing the job right would require enormous numbers of inspectors and all of them would have to be exceptionally well trained scientific men. The Army's Technical Committee had estimated that it would take three hundred inspectors just to watch one of the diffusion plants at Oak Ridge. And how could the great numbers of scientists be recruited if all they were offered was the prospect of "becoming a flatfoot."

That was not the only flaw which the consultants saw in an atomic control system based entirely on inspection. They had learned from Oppenheimer that the initial steps leading toward the development of atomic energy for military purposes are exactly the same as those aimed at peaceful applications. A team of international atomic inspectors could wander about the globe, periodically checking sites, but this would allow plenty of time to divert peaceful atomic energy to weaponry; and it would not be impossible to hide such covert development in unrelated industrial facilities.

The political implications of relying on inspection alone were also great. Was any country, including the United States, prepared to welcome thousands of foreign inspectors into its factories and natural resource areas?

Inspection might do part of the job, but it could not be relied on exclusively for the control of atomic energy.

In Washington at the end of January 1946, the Lilienthal Board heard from experts on raw materials. George Bain, an Amherst College professor and geologist on the Manhattan Project, offered a comprehensive view of the world's deposits of uranium and thorium. Captain Joseph Volpe of Groves's staff explained how the raw materials had been converted for use in building the atom bomb. "They droned on and on unemphatically," Marks said of these two. "I wondered if they knew how important the things they were saying were. They told us in their precise way, where the earth's crust happened to be embedded with uranium and thorium — of the deposits in Colorado, in Africa, Czechoslovakia, and the Arctic . . . I got the willies listening to them. So did the others. Here was this stuff lying about in widely scattered regions of the world, exposed to the same pressures and rivalries that have developed over oil . . . I could easily imagine interested powers buying up bush-league parliaments or engineering rebellions in the strategic areas in the name of 'freedom.' "

The sober geologists, however, had the salutary effect of convincing the Lilienthal panel that the problem before them was manageable. There were only two ores from which atomic energy could be produced, and those two ores, although found in heavy concentrations in some areas of the world, do not exist at all in most parts. It would be necessary therefore to provide comprehensive control of those ore-rich areas, but since these were not widely found, that control would be altogether possible. Oppenheimer was now ready to offer a new idea — one that he had probably nurtured for years in the New Mexican desert. His vision was of an international agency whose job would be not only to control atomic energy but to develop it. This dual function would appeal to scientists and might induce them to serve as inspectors, albeit under a different name. Atomic processes, according to Oppenheimer, could be separated into safe and dangerous categories. Certain small atomic installations were incapable of significant military activity and they need not really be watched. They were safe, but all other activities, which could be classified as dangerous, would be completely within the domain of the international agency, as would all the raw materials. The agency would coordinate worldwide development of atomic energy and would therefore have a more positive function than simply prohibiting atomic weapons. Charles Thomas, the man from Monsanto, was the one who liked Oppenheimer's idea most. "Now, I'm just a chemist," he said to them, "and I'm thinking out loud, but if we had an international corporation — I like that word — which would control the mines and not have any individual nation in charge . . . " Herbert Marks later remarked:

Only something as drastic as the atomic bomb could have got Thomas to suggest that the mines be internationalized. Don't forget he's the vice-president of a hundred-and-twenty-million-dollar firm.

As Thomas envisioned it, the nations of the world could be the stockholders in this international corporation. This was a form that people could understand. The Bank of England was one example, and even the Russians had some experience with state-owned industry. Lilienthal, who despised bigness with the passion of his idol, Brandeis, was troubled by the idea because he felt it might create a huge international Frankensteinian bureaucracy which would trample on individual rights. Barnard and Winne, slightly more conventional businessmen than Thomas, shared this uneasiness. But what was the alternative?

Later, on a plane to Los Alamos, Lilienthal had an innovation of his own. He called the group together for a talk in General Groves's airborne conference room. Oppenheimer had once mentioned the possibility of denaturing atomic energy. Now, Lilienthal grasped the implications of such a procedure. If adding an isotope of uranium to U-235 and plutonium — the end products of thorium and uranium — made them useful for purposes of power but very difficult to make into weapons, would this not be an excellent way to allow nations to work on their own nuclear development without the shadow of the proposed international atomic agency always present? Lilienthal was still trying to minimize the comprehensive powers of the agency. His thought was that the agency would control all of the relevant natural resources and the "dangerous" atomic activities, but it could give denatured materials to individual countries to use for peaceful atomic development. It would only be necessary to subject these independent atomic development centers to periodic inspection. Removing the denaturing element would take time, and it would be easy for any inspector to spot. It would be like the watered alcohol that was peddled during Prohibition, Lilienthal said, "A drink of straight alcohol would blow your top off, but, cut, it would just give you a lift." Marks provided an illustrative scenario of how it might work:

> Supposing denatured material had been allocated to a plant which is located in Ruritania, and the Ruritanian Pooh-Bah decides to welsh on the Atomic Development Authority by removing the denaturants. The Authority's representatives, made up of people of many nationalities, try to check on the plant, on the watch for just such a move. So the Pooh-Bah sends soldiers to get the ADA people out of the way and seize the factory. Assuming that the Pooh-Bah has the scientists working for him, it will still take him in the neighborhood of a year to turn out a bomb. While he's at it, the member countries of the Authority, having received no satisfactory answer to what's become of their inspectors, go to war with Ruritania . . . the war would have to be along conventional lines. Naturally, the atomic plant would be the first target for the attacking planes.

When the group returned to Washington to begin the arduous business of drafting, they were in basic agreement. Earlier hesitations about the power of the international authority had faded. For three weeks in February and early March 1946, they labored there in the American Trucking Association Building on Sixteenth Street. The room began to take on the messy appearance that characterizes such working quarters. A cleaning lady insisted that they let her in to do her duty, but they refused, saying their work was very important and there were secret documents in the room. This argument was not compelling for the dutiful woman. "Important?" she exclaimed. "Secret? Why, I cleaned up after Dumbarton Oaks."

By the first week in March their work was done. Lilienthal was pleased that they had found a new way to describe the control they sought — "security through cooperative development." That was their slogan. On March 7, they would rejoin the Acheson Committee to present their plan. During February, while they were isolated and thoroughly preoccupied with their work, distant events added a new sense of urgency to the mission which David Lilienthal and his colleagues pursued. On February 9, Generalissimo Stalin had delivered a major address to the Supreme Soviet in the Bolshoi Theatre on the occasion of the first Russian general election since 1937. His tone was conversational and void of bombast; as he outlined his five-year plan he said, with directness, that Soviet scientists would "not only catch up with but also surpass those abroad." [13] A week earlier, the United States embassy in Moscow reported to Washington that Soviet scientists Konstantin Petrzhak and Georgii Flerov had received second prize in the Stalin Award for "the discovery of the spontaneous disintegration of uranium." A. Kolmogorov, a noted academician, described this discovery as "one of the greatest achievements in Soviet physics in recent years," and said that it had resulted from work done during 1943 and 1944.[14]

From Ottawa there soon came reports which illuminated the scope and duration of Soviet work on atomic energy. The Royal Canadian Mounted Police had detained twenty-two people for questioning about the disclosure of "secret and confidential information," presumably atomic energy information, to the Russian mission in Ottawa. The Russians had no comment on the matter and said they had not heard of it. Prime Minister Mackenzie King, it will be recalled, had told President Truman during their talks in November of the defection of Igor Gouzenko, a member of the Soviet mission in Canada, who had implicated a number of Russians and Canadians in atomic espionage. Investigations over the months since then had led to the arrest on February 14, 1946, of twenty-two people, many of them employees of the National Research Council, Canada's atomic energy agency. King announced that he was immediately appointing a top-level commission to investigate the entire incident and report back to him as quickly as possible.

The reaction in America was predictable. They had taken our secret. Secretary of State Byrnes, however, said he expected no arrests of American citizens and assured the nation that the important technical information of atomic weaponry was still a secret. General Groves's response was more derisive. There had been more leaks in the last few months, he said, than in all the previous years of development, implying that as soon as military control of atomic energy was no longer clear, things went awry. Congressman Rankin of Mississippi said that the incident confirmed his suspicions that a Communist spy ring was operating in Canada and down through the United States.

There was cause for more anxiety when the Soviet Union issued its own response to the charges. Instead of adopting a posture of coyness, the Russians chose to admit their espionage. Moscow Radio accused the Canadians of unfriendliness and of attempting to build world hostility toward the Soviet Union. In a note to the Canadian government, the Russians declared:

> In the last period of the war many persons became interested in and were friendly disposed toward the Soviet representatives and might have had talks with them on some technical matters, on military questions, and also on atomic energy.
>
> The Soviet Embassy attaché in Canada received from acquaintances among Canadian citizens certain information of a secret character which, however, did not present a special interest to Soviet authorities. These matters had already been published . . . in the well-known pamphlets by the American Smyth on atomic energy . . . The data concerned such technical details as were not needed by the Soviet Government in view of the fact that in the U.S.S.R. higher technical achievements are in existence. In

view of this, it would be ridiculous to assert that the communication of such insignificant secret data could create any danger whatsoever for the security of Canada.

The Russians also complained of the "extraordinary fact" that the Canadian government had published its charges instead of first asking for an explanation from the Soviet government. They also denied that their ambassador in Ottawa was in any way involved.[15] The matter came closer to America a short while later when Dr. Alan Nunn May, a thirty-four-year-old British physicist, who had worked with the atomic project in Canada and had visited the Chicago Met Lab, was arrested at his laboratory in King's College, London, and charged with violation of the Official Secrets Act. The Chicago scientists remembered Alan May very well. He had made several visits to Chicago as early as 1942, which were stopped finally when Arthur Compton decided that the information May was seeking was much too detailed for anyone's good. All visits from Canadian scientists were halted after this incident.[16] Senator Bourke Hickenlooper of Iowa soon revealed that General Groves had informed him that Alan May "has a general knowledge of the construction of the atom bomb" and some know-how on how to operate an American atomic bomb.[17] On March 5, Dr. May was arraigned in a small London courtroom jammed with his students; he immediately admitted his guilt and was sentenced to ten years in prison.

The report of the Canadian Prime Minister's commission, which was issued early in March, revealed a network of spies operating in Canada under the leadership of Colonel Nicolai Zabotin, the Russian military attaché, but with control exercised directly from Moscow. The spy story was replete with code names, Zabotin going as "Grant," and instructions coming from "The Director" in Moscow. One of the requests sent from The

Director to Grant in August 1945 was "to take measures to obtain particulars as to the materials of which the atom bomb is composed, its technological process, and drawings." [18] The House Un-American Activities Committee followed with a report that it had been probing the world of atomic energy since August 1945 and was in possession of enough information to send the committee chairman, John Wood of Georgia, on a ten-day secret trip to investigate an alleged spy ring operating between Oak Ridge and New York. No more of substance was heard from Congressman Wood concerning this exercise in counterespionage. [19]

These unsettling events had a profound effect in Washington. Men who had set themselves on keeping the secret grew even more conspiratorial and protective. More drastic was the impact on those who had argued that America must assume the good faith of the Russians until proven wrong in the hope that mutual trust and international cooperation might be achieved. The Federation of Atomic Scientists was dismayed to note that the heavy flow of mail which had been reaching it in support of civilian control of atomic energy abruptly ceased after the news from Canada. With this disturbing episode in the air and on their minds, the Lilienthal Board sat together on March 6, planning its strategy for the next day's meeting with Acheson and his committee. They had not specifically concerned themselves with the particulars of Soviet foreign policy or Soviet psychology. This was alien to the path they set for themselves which was to go from the scientific facts to the best control plan. They were building something reasonable, and although they knew it was crucial that Russia find their work acceptable, they seemed more concerned with making a good proposal than with the certainty of Soviet acceptance. In this sense, the Canadian spy story did not seriously affect their deliberations, although Lilienthal wrote in his diary at that time: "The situation in respect to a rational dealing with the problem has been deteriorating though it is by no means hopeless. I refer to the announcement of Russian spies and what not issuing from Canada." [20]

Lilienthal continued his groundwork for the coming meeting with Acheson's committee in a ninety-minute conference with Acheson himself on the morning of March 6, 1946. Although Lilienthal intended primarily to inform Acheson in outline of the conclusions of the board of consultants, the Undersecretary dominated the conversation with a rambling presentation of two international developments that were closely related to atomic control. Each concerned one of America's wartime allies. Acheson was most troubled this morning by a recent British demand that the United States construct an atomic plant in England. This request was entirely consistent with the secret agreement for atomic cooperation that had been signed by Truman, Attlee, and King during the preceding November, but the American government now had no intention of performing such a generous act. Its change of heart was largely an act of deference to the increasingly chauvinistic attitude of Congress toward atomic energy. In regard to the Soviet Union, Acheson told Lilienthal that he had just received a long and compelling report on the state of the Russian character and the prospects for Russian foreign policy from George Kennan at the American embassy in Moscow. Lilienthal read the thoroughly harsh and pessimistic Kennan statement, as Acheson had requested, in conjunction with his work on atomic control. This was the document which later appeared in *Foreign Affairs* under the pseudonym "X," and provided the rationale for American foreign policy during the first period of the cold war. Its appearance before Lilienthal at this stage of his deliberations on atomic control was neither encouraging nor productive. Finally, Lilienthal moved the conversation to a description of his committee's work. Pleased with what he heard, Acheson agreed that their report should eventually be published as a basis for informed public discussion, but cautioned that this could not be done before the President and Secretary of State had approved. It was most important, Acheson declared, for America's atomic control policy to enjoy wide public support or they would find themselves again in the position of Woodrow Wilson who asked the people to support the League of Nations only after he had already committed himself.[21]

Dean Acheson opened the joint meeting of his committee and Lilienthal's board the next morning in the great conference room at Dumbarton Oaks in the Georgetown section of Washington. Magnificent tapestries hung on the walls; the ceiling, three stories high, was done in carved and painted beams; a Byzantine cat of ebony was encased in glass; and a painting by El Greco, "The Visitation," hung in a bracket at an angle so that it attracted the sunlight coming through one of the great french doors that opened out into a garden. Gathered there were a remarkable group of men who were altogether equal to these surroundings: Acheson, McCloy, Bush, Conant, Groves, Lilienthal, Oppenheimer, Winne, Thomas, and Barnard. Acheson immediately turned the meeting over to Lilienthal who said, by way of introduction, that their labors had confirmed their original belief in the value of looking to the science and technology of atomic energy before reaching policy conclusions. His board of consultants had done so and was now agreed on an approach to the problem. If such a varied assemblage of individuals could come from different sources to the same conclusion after studying the facts, was it not possible that the same could occur for the country as a whole? The consultants, Lilienthal continued, did not see their report as the last word. Many questions had not been considered and still others would have to await international negotiation. What they offered was "a place to begin, a foundation on which to build." [22]

Now the reading of the report began, with each of the five members taking part in the presentation. Barnard first presented the arguments against relying on inspection alone. Oppenheimer, Winne, and Thomas read the second section, which described the dependence of atomic energy development on uranium and thorium and the concentrated existence of these metals in the earth's surface. They talked also of desirable safeguards, not in terms of protection at each stage of exchange, for their plan was integral and void of stages, but more in response to the need for a rapid warning when the control plan was violated. Winne continued with the third section, in which the consultants suggested the desirability of combining positive atomic development with negative atomic control by establishing an international atomic authority. If this was done, the best men could be attracted to service, "not the type that had staffed the Prohibition squads." Winne also read the fourth section, which was the heart of their proposal. The only way to overcome the intense rivalries now rampant in matters of atomic energy was to restrict individual nations and their citizens from any atomic activities deemed "dangerous." An international authority must be constituted with control of the full atomic procedure from the ore deposits to the final plants. The authority would license individual nations and persons to embark upon safe uses of nuclear energy. Thomas read the second part of this fourth section, explaining how the line might be drawn between safe and dangerous atomic activities. Dangerous activities included securing the raw materials, producing U-235, plutonium, or U-233 of the proper quality, and building these fissionable materials into a bomb. The possibility of denaturing the materials to make them safe was considered at some length. Winne expanded on the functions of the international authority; it would own the ores, mine them, build the production facilities, operate them, and sponsor atomic research. There would still be a need for inspection, especially of the safe activities. Lilienthal read the final chapter, which covered the fundamental policies and organization of international control. Many questions could not be answered until the nations of the world, particularly the big powers, sat and talked them over. How would the staffing of the authority, which surely must be international, be worked out? How would the countries assure their control of the powerful new agency? Might it be done by the United Nations General Assembly or Security Council? The categories of safe and dangerous would have to be defined. An equitable geographical distribution of atomic facilities was an obvious need. How would the availability of atomic power from internationally controlled facilities be coordinated with utilities in the individual countries?

Lilienthal finished his reading. He put the report down on the table in front of him, and said, "This, gentlemen, is our recommendation of a plan for security in a world of atomic energy." At the other end of the long table, Acheson put his own copy down, removed his glasses, and spoke: "This is a brilliant and profound document."

The reading had taken all morning. Now the two groups recessed for lunch. During the afternoon, the Acheson Committee began its response. General Groves was worried that the plan could be circumvented if some nation found a way to utilize lower grade ore deposits. Lilienthal and Oppenheimer said that this made a comprehensive authority more advisable than a simple inspection system. Vannevar Bush had a far more crucial comment. Acknowledging the great Soviet superiority in conventional military forces over the demobilized American Army, he was worried that a one-step conversion to this international control system would deprive America of its atomic monopoly and thereby leave the Russians a much stronger people. Would it not be proper to think of the Lilienthal plan as a worthy objective and arrange for a step-by-step transformation to international control so that the United States could be protected? Lilienthal did not think so. The plan, as presented, was self-consciously complete and adequately protected the interests of the United States, he said. Oppenheimer, Thomas, and Winne pointed out that there were some stages built into their proposal. For instance, a worldwide survey of raw materials would be carried out. But Bush persisted. The other nations of the world would surely want to have the clearest possible idea of the schedule of control and development for the proposed international authority, he declared. There could be no fuzzing over in the report, or the Russians would not accept it.

Changing the subject, Acheson wondered whether there would be any danger in the fact that some Russians would surely have to hold important positions in the atomic authority. Lilienthal conceded that there was, because a Russian might believe his highest loyalty to be national, not international, but it would take more than a leak or two for a nation to embark on a prohibited atomic military development.

In spite of these questions, the general tone of response that emerged throughout the afternoon was favorable. Bush, who had tried his own hand at the questions of atomic control on many occasions before, described the Lilienthal report as "the best proposal that has ever been put forward." But still the Acheson Committee wanted more said about stages and about what would happen if the plan broke down. Conant also suggested that there be less vehement opposition to inspection in the report. They should talk about the possibility of inspectors going everywhere and seeing everything. Lilienthal said this could be done. The Acheson Committee's primary concern was clearly the matter of safeguards, and Acheson asked the consultants to put themselves to work on that. With little enthusiasm, Lilienthal and his committee agreed.

That night at the Carlton Hotel and over the following week at their Sixteenth Street headquarters, far from the somber elegance of Dumbarton Oaks, the Lilienthal Board struggled with the question of safeguards. They did not want to spell it out, because the report, as it stood, assumed the good faith of the Soviet Union. To write in stages of transition, they thought, was to express a lack of American trust in the other nations of the world and especially in Russia. But they concluded, why jeopardize all their work on this one point? The substance of the report still stood intact. Their disagreement was only over tactics. The chiefs had spoken and they would obey. The fourth section was rewritten to include a statement about stages of transition.

The two groups returned to Dumbarton Oaks on the following Saturday, March 16.[23] Winne read the revised fourth section outlining a system of stages, and Lilienthal said they had gone about as far as they could go. In their turn, Acheson, Conant, and Bush each said that the report, already good, had been greatly improved. But Bush still felt uneasy about the inability of the board of consultants to suggest a more specific schedule of transition which would guide America's representative to the UNAEC. General Groves added that he wanted the stages spelled out more explicitly so that it would show "where the American people would come out if someone suddenly double-crossed them." Conant joined with Groves in saying that what the report should do is announce explicitly that the United States would continue making bombs until the new system was fully secured. Lilienthal resisted these entreaties, asking Groves, Bush, and

Conant how they could know what protection the American people wanted until the American people had a chance to see the plan and react.

Acheson's committee went into session alone on Saturday night. When they rejoined the Lilienthal Board on Sunday morning they again expressed their concern over the amount of information that would have to be disclosed at the earliest stages of the proposed plan. Bush stated his own position, which was the strongest of the Acheson group: "The board's plan was unquestionably attractive. The only danger was disclosing a great amount of data at the outset." Bush did not want this on his conscience if the whole effort broke down at the end of the year. He suggested dividing the important information into categories and specifying what would have to be accomplished before a category of information was revealed. As the day progressed, the disagreements seemed to fade away. Finally Bush, in response to a question from Acheson, said that he would be happy to give his endorsement to the report so long as it stated that an explicit schedule was feasible. This was done, and in fact stages of information exchange were specified.

In its letter of transmittal to the Secretary of State, the Acheson Committee emphasized that the disclosure of information and transfer of authority from national to international control would definitely proceed by stages. At the first level, it would be necessary for the United States to make enough information available to the other members of the United Nations so that they would understand the American proposal. On the question of continued production of bombs, the report took no definite position, implying therefore that atomic weapons would continue to be built. Bomb-making would have to stop sometime, but that was a question for the President to determine, consistent with constitutional processes and in light of the world situation.

This letter of transmittal was pure Acheson, an elegantly phrased piece that espoused the innovative, somewhat radical, internationalist approach of the Lilienthal Board while deferring also to the concerns of Acheson's group that American interests were fully protected.

14

The Baron of Hobcaw

DURING THE EARLY MONTHS of 1946, a vigorous Congressional duel to determine who would control atomic energy within the United States occupied the public's attention. Concern over international control lagged behind. The original plan for domestic control of atomic energy had emerged during the preceding autumn from the old Interim Committee, with the apparent blessings of the scientific members of that body. Known as the May-Johnson bill, after its Congressional sponsors, it offended most scientists because of the predominant role it gave to the American military in controlling atomic energy. With the assistance of the scientific lobby and others of like mind, Senator Brien McMahon, the freshman Democrat from Connecticut, introduced an alternate proposal which ultimately received the endorsement of President Truman. It provided for civilian control of atomic energy. The British were infuriated by the McMahon proposal because it also seemed to them to limit their rights under the renegotiated Quebec Agreement. But the Congress did not know about the unpublicized covenants made at the Anglo-American-Canadian conference during November 1945 and Truman, moved by the fundamental self-protectiveness with which most Americans approached the atomic bomb, had decided not to inform the Congressmen of them.

While the British were angry over the selfishness of the McMahon bill, the Truman Administration was worried that

Congress might impose additional terms which would further restrict the latitude of the Administration in entering into international agreements for the control or development of atomic energy. As the Acheson and Lilienthal Committees concluded their work in March 1946, Secretary of State Byrnes turned his mind to this thoroughly political problem. He and the President agreed that they must quickly appoint an American representative to the United Nations Atomic Energy Commission who would be so trusted by the members of Congress that they would not feel the need to tie his hands or Truman's in the domestic control legislation which they were about to enact. Truman and Byrnes soon settled on the one man in America whose presence in the international negotiations for atomic energy control would most soothe the Congress and the public. Whether he was the man best suited to see the international negotiations through to a successful conclusion is, however, a more doubtful proposition.[1]

Bernard Mannes Baruch, the baron of Hobcaw, had by his seventy-fifth year become a symbol of America to his fellow Americans as well as to people all over the world. An immensely successful financier who had built a fortune in the lusty days of business boom, a public servant and sought-after counselor to Presidents of both political parties, Baruch was one of the most trusted men in all of America. The fact that he was Jewish seemed to assure his place in the public mind because it gave his life that quality of equal opportunity realized, of Horatio Alger, that is so important to America's self-image. Through the years of his prominence in business and public service, Baruch had proven himself to be, in the words of his friend James Byrnes, "a true American." In the spring of 1946, Byrnes wrote that Baruch had behind him "a career of that universal quality rarely achieved since the days of the great figures of the American Revolutionary era."[2]

Baruch's family, on his mother's side, had been in America since pre-Revolutionary days. His father, however, had come from Posen, East Prussia, during the mid-nineteenth century to assume the role of the kindly, devoted doctor of Columbia, South Carolina, and had served with the Confederate Army during the American Civil War. Bernard Baruch had gone from South Carolina to New York for his education and moneymaking but then returned to Hobcaw, 17,000 acres of beautiful South Carolina plantation land that was his estate, to enjoy the baronial life, to hunt, to ride, to follow the birds, and to listen to the sound of the four rivers against the shore.

There at Hobcaw, during the first days of March 1946, his fellow South Carolinian, James Byrnes, spoke with him about atomic energy. Baruch had suggested Byrnes to President Roosevelt for the powerful position of Director of Economic Stabilization during the war. Now Byrnes had a job for Baruch. Would he come to the aid of his country once more and accept appointment as the United States representative to the United Nations Atomic Energy Commission? Baruch was not sure. He asked Byrnes to send him a copy of the United Nations resolution creating the commission. On March 13, having examined the resolution and done some thinking of his own, Baruch wrote to Byrnes. His mood was pessimistic:

> I do not see how we can proceed at present. If Russia will not permit entry of newsmen or any others, can we believe they will permit any inspection? That would immediately stop the discussions regarding atomic energy . . .

Baruch's other concerns were far more personal:

> Another thing, I can only work between the hours of ten and twelve in the morning and from 2:30 to 4:30 in the afternoon. I cannot go to any night sessions . . . I understand that this will not stop me from expressing my views on any other question . . .

This is a very important matter and I do not want to say no, but I should like to have an alternate or assistant . . . besides the scientific advisers . . . In view of all this, if you still want me, I'll accept.[3]

Byrnes's immediate response was affirmative, even with all the conditions and pessimism. Now Baruch hesitated again, as he had before in his long career. His enormous ego was gratified by this invitation to assume another position of public trust, but still he felt uncertainty. Could he do the job? Did they really want Baruch to participate in the formulation of American policy or did they just want to use his good name? In truth, they wanted more of the name than the man, although of course the two came together at some points. Baruch must have resolved the question otherwise or decided that regardless of the motives of Byrnes and Truman this was an enviable opportunity to affect the movement of human events. After a few days of "torsions" ("I was bitterly unhappy . . . my conscience smote me," he said later), Baruch summoned his chauffeur and rode to nearby Georgetown, South Carolina, where, from a humid hotel telephone booth, the tall, white-haired southern gentleman told the Secretary of State that he would accept.[4]

The White House announced the appointment of Bernard Baruch immediately on March 18. He had decided, Baruch told reporters, just the day before at Byrnes's insistence to accept the post. "I felt it my duty to accept." He assured them that he approached "the subject with an open mind" and would "do the best I can." Truman had told him he could choose whatever assistants he wanted. "You know I never do any work myself," he joked, with the familiar self-effacing humor that neither he nor anyone else believed. As assistants, Baruch soon selected a very personal team: John Hancock, a partner in the Lehman Corporation, had worked under Baruch on the War Industries Board during World War I and on the rubber survey during

World War II; Herbert Bayard Swope, a journalist friend of Hancock's who was loyal to Baruch since his service at the War Industries Board and had headed the New York State Racing Commission in recent years; Ferdinand Eberstadt, a lawyer and New York investment banker, who had been chairman of the *Daily Princetonian* when James Forrestal tried out for it and served with distinction on the War Production Board during World War II; and Fred Searls, a mining engineer and successful businessman who had worked under Byrnes at the Office of War Mobilization. "I asked these four to serve with me," Baruch announced. "One will be with me at every meeting of the commission and if I am unable to attend I will name one of them to serve for me." [5] Baruch also told the press that he planned to rely on scientific men like Conant, Arthur Compton, and Bush for technical advice.

The response to Baruch's appointment was predictable. Editorial writers and members of Congress were delighted, and so presumably was the public, that the principled old gentleman had agreed to do battle for them once more. In Georgia, the *Macon Telegram* expressed the popular sentiment when it wrote: "We will sleep more comfortably in our beds knowing that clear-eyed Barney Baruch is on guard." The *Paterson* (New Jersey) *Evening News* called Truman's choice of Baruch "an inspirational appointment." [6] On Capitol Hill there was not an unhappy soul among the members of the Special Atomic Energy Committee. As for the Foreign Relations Committee, Senator Vandenberg wired Baruch that he need not even come before the committee for a hearing if he would just put into writing his assurance that there would be no treaty and disclosures without safeguards, and that no agreements of any kind would be entered without the consent of Congress. It was no labor for Baruch to give these assurances. Vandenberg wired back that the committee would meet for automatic approval of Baruch's nomination on March 27, 1946.[7]

Elsewhere there was less joy. When David Lilienthal read the news of Baruch's appointment, he "was quite sick." He believed that the United States needed a man who was "young, vigorous, not vain, and whom the Russians would feel isn't out simply to put them in a hole, not really caring about international cooperation. Baruch has none of these qualifications." As for Baruch's four top assistants, Lilienthal could only say, "It is the old crowd . . . God! Isn't this something!" [8] The atomic scientists were troubled less by Baruch than by the quality and experience of his chosen advisers. They were Wall Streeters and could not be counted on to give Baruch any technologically intelligent advice. The Association of New York Scientists passed a resolution urging Baruch to appoint as personal advisers two of the men who had worked on the Manhattan Project.[9]

Dean Acheson was similarly nonplused by Baruch's appointment. On the day on which it was announced, Acheson formally transmitted the report of his atomic control committee to Byrnes. Now he and Lilienthal were worried that Baruch might reject or ignore their work. They did not know any more than Byrnes or Truman what were Baruch's ideas about atomic energy control, but their suspicions led them to conclude that the baron would not be of like mind with them on the subject.

Lilienthal and then Acheson had argued during the latter stages of their committee's work for the early publication of their report as a basis for informed public discussion of the issues it covered. John McCloy and Vannevar Bush had overruled them with the argument that the report was "for the benefit of the United States delegate [to the UNAEC], that it should be shown first to him and that he should not be prejudiced by its prior publication." [10] Byrnes, however, wrote to Lilienthal on March 23 saying that he hoped it would "shortly be possible to make the document public for I believe that it provides the most suitable basis for the informed public discussion which is one of the essential factors in the development of sound policy." [11]

On Monday, March 25, Acheson appeared before a closed meeting of Senator McMahon's Special Committee on Atomic Energy, which had deferred its own inquiry into the problem of international atomic control as a result of the work of Acheson, Lilienthal, and their colleagues. Now Acheson felt obliged to report to them on the committee's work. On the day after his appearance, the newspapers carried extensive coverage of this supposedly closed hearing. All the important features of the Acheson-Lilienthal Report were well reported.[12]

For Baruch, this news leak came as an assault not only on his jurisdiction but also on his ego. They were using him, taking him for granted, not caring what he thought about atomic control. Byrnes had sent Baruch a copy of the Acheson-Lilienthal Report on Thursday, March 21. To Baruch, it looked less like a report than a definitive statement of American policy. On Sunday, March 24, he had called David Lilienthal at his home in Norris, Tennessee, and asked whether he was not correct in believing that if the President and Secretary of State approved the report, "then the policy of the country was fixed." Was there anything for him to do but be a messenger boy? Lilienthal said he did not know that the President and Secretary of State had approved his report, and if they had, then there was still an immense job of advocacy to be done to convince the ten other members of the United Nations Atomic Energy Commission to agree to the American plan. Baruch said he thought that Lilienthal and his team knew the report best and probably could do a better selling job than he. But then he added quickly that he could also do it himself and would have the best technical advisers to help him.

Lilienthal suggested that there was no substitute for the men who had worked on the Manhattan Project, especially Oppenheimer. Conant had told Baruch the same thing. One more point Lilienthal added from his own experience with the board of consultants. Baruch would have to go through the arduous business of learning all the technical material himself before he could appreciate what it was all about. That was all well and good, Baruch said, but he "wasn't much on technical scientific stuff." He would have to "smell his way through it" as he had always done successfully in the past.[13]

Baruch's sensitivities therefore were already offended before the "leaked" news reports of Acheson's Senatorial testimony. When he saw Tuesday morning's newspapers with their premature publication of most of the Acheson-Lilienthal Report, his anxieties deepened. He immediately composed a letter to the President and directed his driver to take him to Washington where he delivered it personally to the President late that afternoon. Expressing his gratitude to Truman for the appointment to the UNAEC, Baruch declared that there were now "certain elements of it which are causing me concern." Baruch's primary problem was that he could "see nowhere any duty or responsibility on me to participate in the formulation of policy." This situation was made more difficult by the press announcements that morning of the report of Mr. Acheson's committee, which seemed to Baruch to bring that report "pretty close to the category of the United States Government policy." Reaching climactically for the source of his strength, Baruch declared: "I have no doubt that the public feels that I am going to have an important relation to the determination of our atomic energy policy." As far as Baruch could see, however, there was no basis for this view. He would need more time to consider whether he could proceed with this mission. "I think that embarrassment all around would be avoided," Baruch con-

cluded, "if you would ask Chairman Connally of the Foreign
Relations Committee to postpone any action on confirmation of
my appointment until I have had a little more time to think things
over." [14]

In spite of Baruch's threat to resign, which was a devastating
prospect, Truman remained visibly unruffled. He explained first
that the Acheson-Lilienthal Report was "very plainly marked as
a working paper and not as an approved policy document." Besides, the President continued, whatever policy Baruch would be
asked to present would have to be approved by the President
himself. Under the law, all representatives of the United States
in these matters were accountable to the Secretary of State, although Truman was sure that Byrnes would probably request
Baruch's aid in the preparation of a policy proposal for the
President's view. Privately, Truman concluded that Baruch's
major concern "was really whether he would receive public recognition" for America's atomic energy policy. Baruch later recalled
that when he asked the President who was going to draft the
American proposals, Truman answered, "Hell, you are." [15]

As Baruch left the White House that afternoon, a group of
newsmen clustered around him and asked whether he had read
the Acheson-Lilienthal Report. "Frankly, I did," Baruch answered. What did he think of it, they wanted to know. Putting
his finger to his hearing aid, Baruch laughed, said "I can't hear
you," and walked away.[16] This performance endeared Baruch
even less to the scientific lobby which had bubbled over with
delight at the tone and substance of the Acheson-Lilienthal document. If Baruch did not like it, Baruch was suspect.[17]

The members of the Senate Foreign Relations Committee, who
gathered the next day to approve Baruch's nomination, were surprised when Senator Connally revealed that the nominee had asked
that their automatic confirmation be postponed until he could

consult further with the Secretary of State. The Senators' astonishment soon spread throughout Washington and no doubt induced Byrnes and Truman to try to nullify Baruch's unhappiness. On March 28, however, at Acheson's prodding, Byrnes released the full text of the Acheson-Lilienthal Report on the theory that since most of it had already been leaked, it would be wise to present the document itself. In issuing the report, Byrnes gave public assurance that "the document is being made public not as a statement of policy, but as a basis for discussion." This action further aggravated Baruch and led him to mount a counteroffensive in a letter to Byrnes on March 31, 1946:

> If I accept the responsibility of representing the United States on the Atomic Energy Commission . . . it is clear that my duty will be to support the policy of the United States as laid down by the President and transmitted to me by yourself . . . It might, however, be assumed and I venture to say that it has been assumed by some fairly large part of those American citizens who have interested themselves in the subject that I would have some voice in framing and deciding upon the policies that I am to advocate before the Commission.
>
> However, release of the [Acheson-Lilienthal] report simultaneously with its delivery to me seems to reduce seriously any influence I might otherwise have been able to bring to bear on the formation of policies it will be my duty to support . . .
>
> The report appeared to carry the endorsement of the State Department and, being now on sale by the Superintendent of Documents at the price of twenty cents per copy, will probably rival "Atomic Energy for Military Purposes" [The Smyth Report] as a best-seller in the world's capitals . . .

Nevertheless, Baruch, who had discussed the Acheson-Lilienthal Report with Fred Searls, now had some questions to ask about the contents of the document. If the power of the proposed Atomic Development Authority is derived from the Security

Council, "is not any act of the Authority subject to the veto of any one of five members of the Security Council?" Would it be possible to recruit the enormous manpower needed to protect the raw materials of atomic development from misuse? Who would negotiate collective bargaining agreements at the atomic plants which, for example, might be located in the Soviet Union? "What do the other members of the Atomic Energy Commission do for the common good? Is there to be no consideration?" Baruch's conclusion was clear:

> I trust that you will excuse me thus laying before you these immature queries on a few points that seem to me to have received insufficient consideration by your committee. There are others . . . Nor do I feel that the thoroughness with which your committee has covered the ground has entirely obviated the desirability of considering alternative plans. To suggest any such will require more study and deliberation than I have so far been able to give to the subject. What I seek now is assurance that I am not committed to the support of a program or of policies which seem to me to require extensive amendment. Such assurance could be obtained by convincing me of the fallacy of the anxieties herein suggested, or by making it clear that the report of your committee will be subject to study and discussion by me before it becomes the settled policy of the United States Government.[18]

Moved by the continuing Congressional concern over Baruch's reluctance, Byrnes gave the baron all the assurances he desired. Baruch had made his point. On April 3, Senator Connally brought the Foreign Relations Committee together once more. This time, the nominee was reported to be willing and the Senators acted with their expected dispatch. The full Senate did the same two days later.[19]

Meanwhile, publication of the Acheson-Lilienthal Report had produced a flood of reaction, and most of it was favorable. The criticism came primarily from more conservative newspapers, like the *Chicago Tribune,* which viewed the report as no more than a scheme for giving the atomic bomb to the Russian Communists. The more common response was expressed in the *New York Times,* which called the document a worthy starting point. Others were less restrained. The renowned newscaster Raymond Gram Swing saw the Acheson-Lilienthal plan as "one of the most significant pointers ever erected on the long road to world peace." Edward Teller, the nuclear physicist, hailed it as "the first ray of hope that the problem of international control can actually be solved." And another scientific member of the Manhattan Project, Harold Urey, said that it was "the most statesmanlike pronouncement that has been made on the subject since the atomic bomb fell on Hiroshima." [20]

This public response to the Acheson-Lilienthal Committee's report obviously did not go unnoticed by Baruch. On April 3, he asked his staff to consider the advisability of continuing the Acheson and Lilienthal groups in an advisory capacity. "There will have to be something like this," Baruch said. "Why not keep them? It will take months for anybody else to get the information and feel of the subject which these committees already have. They would only advise and sift. If they study their own recommendations further, they may see to what they lead and how they may have to change them." [21] When his advisers agreed that this was a good idea, Baruch asked Byrnes to make the formal request of Acheson, Lilienthal, and their colleagues. Acheson, McCloy, and Groves responded quickly and affirmatively, but Bush and Conant were reluctant, as were all the members of the Lilienthal Board. Partially because they were preoccupied with other matters and partially because they had little respect for Baruch and his team and wanted to be free to criticize its work, Bush, Conant, and the members of the Lilienthal Board suggested to Byrnes that it would be better for Baruch to have a full-time working staff of advisers. They, however, would be available periodically and on an individual basis for consultation.[22]

Vannevar Bush was much more explicit about the matter in a meeting with Baruch later in April. Apparently wounded by the fact that neither he nor Conant had been asked to assume a formal position in the United States delegation to the UNAEC, Bush told Baruch that he was accustomed to working at higher governmental echelons than as a consultant to the Baruch group, some of whom he characterized as "Wall Streeters." As for Baruch himself, the blunt Yankee scientist said that in many ways he was the "worst qualified man in the country for this job." The baron, though startled by the remark, did not respond in kind. "Doc," he said, "you couldn't be righter. What shall I do, resign?" In spite of his personal attitude, Bush knew well what effect a Baruch resignation would have: "Oh hell, stay in; it would all blow up if you got out." [23]

It was not Bush but Robert Oppenheimer whom Baruch wanted as his full-time scientific adviser at the United Nations. Baruch invited Oppenheimer to meet with him and his associates in New York on April 5, 1946. After rendering his personal view of several of the atomic scientists in whom the Baruch team expressed an interest, Oppenheimer discussed the job Baruch had to do at the United Nations. He agreed, when pressed, that the Acheson-Lilienthal plan was essentially incompatible with the present Russian system, but he thought that the procedure "should be to make an honorable proposal and thus find out whether they have the will to cooperate." [24] Oppenheimer left this meeting depressed by the failure of Baruch and his men to grasp the fundamentals of atomic energy development and control. He was troubled also that they seemed to have no hope of reaching an agreement and spoke in terms of "preparing the American people for a refusal by Russia." Most worrisome, however, was their desire to digress from the Acheson-Lilienthal Report at several critical points. Baruch and his assistants were indeed moving in new directions in their beliefs: that the United States should not limit itself to atomic energy control but move on to a broad appeal for disarmament; that the United Nations should maintain a stockpile of atomic weapons as a deterrent; that the Atomic Development Authority should not work the uranium mines but only own the concentrates "because the Government couldn't operate anything successfully" as Hancock put it; and, finally, that there must be absolutely no veto power over atomic energy control. To Oppenheimer, these new ideas seemed far astray. He asked for more time to consider Baruch's request that he join the American delegation to the United Nations commission. They met again later in April with even less success at Baruch's offices in the Empire State Building in New York. When the meeting was over, Baruch showed Oppenheimer to the elevator and offered some private reassurance: "Don't let these associates of mine worry you. Hancock is pretty 'Right' but [with a wink] I'll watch him. Searls is smart as a whip, but he sees Reds under every bed." But, of course, Baruch's associates did worry Oppenheimer, so much so that he decided finally that he could not accept the invitation to join the American delegation. He offered only to remain available for consultation.[25]

The continuing rebuffs from the most prominent atomic scientists and administrators soured Baruch and increased his paranoia over the making of America's atomic control policy. In this state, he had an unhappy chance meeting with Sir Alexander Cadogan, the representative from Great Britain to the United Nations. Cadogan remarked casually that he understood that the Acheson-Lilienthal Report was to be the basis of the American proposal to the United Nations Atomic Energy Commission. Baruch became indignant at hearing this altogether logical and widespread conclusion. Where, he demanded, had Cadogan heard this? "From Acheson" was the Englishman's answer.[26]

Once more the baron and his men marched on Washington for reassurance. On Thursday morning, April 19, Baruch, Hancock, and Searls met with Byrnes, and again the Secretary of State pacified his fellow South Carolinian. Baruch told Byrnes of his encounter with Cadogan and said that at seventy-six he was too old to be a Western Union messenger boy. If that was what they wanted they had better find someone else. Byrnes began his response where he always did. It was the President who had the final word, he said, although Truman would surely want Byrnes's views in determining policy and Byrnes would, in turn, definitely consult Baruch. "That is why I had asked you to be good enough to fully explore the subject," Byrnes declared. He had been "favorably impressed" by the Acheson Committee's report but did not consider it the last word on the subject. On the contrary, Byrnes said he would give careful consideration to any views that might be presented by Baruch to him after Baruch had considered the problem. Once an American atomic policy was established, Byrnes said, he believed that not the President but Baruch should announce it to the world. This pleased Baruch, although he told Byrnes that his worries could not finally be allayed until he knew where Acheson stood.

Hancock's record of this meeting with Byrnes reveals a startling piece of misinformation which the Secretary of State conveyed to these men who were now his emissaries on atomic energy matters: "Mr. Byrnes briefly reviewed his impression that the Russians don't know much about atomic energy or its use in bombs. Dr. Conant got no facts regarding it while he was in Russia and the assumption is that they know nothing." [27]

Hancock followed this conference with a visit to Acheson later in April. He was pleased to learn that the Undersecretary of State did not have a large staff at work on atomic energy, and that Herbert Marks who "did not impress [Hancock] as a man of clear ideas on the questions under discussion," seemed to be about the only one in the State Department who was formally concerned with the problem. Acheson told Hancock that he expected the Baruch team in New York to draft all the necessary papers including a charter for the proposed Atomic Development Authority and a report from the Atomic Energy Commission to the Security Council.[28] Above all, Acheson said, the public clamor for convening the United Nations Atomic Energy Commission could not be resisted much longer. Baruch and his men must get right to work. This was just the assurance Baruch had sought. With his psyche now temporarily soothed, the baron set his staff moving with some energy as the month of May 1946 began.[29] He was also finally able to enlist a full-time scientific adviser for the delegation in the person of Professor Richard Tolman of the Manhattan Project and the California Institute of Technology. Tolman had been recommended by Conant and convinced to join by General Groves.[30]

Through the muddle of conflicting personalities and emotions, the Baruch group had managed somehow to formulate and hold those few ideas of their own on the international control of atomic energy. Each new thought was less a matter of independent initiative than a response to the particular contents of the Acheson-Lilienthal Report.

From the beginning, Fred Searls, a mining engineer and corporate executive in private life, had portrayed for Baruch the difficulty of policing all the potential sources of raw material for atomic production. Then, on April 4, General Groves brought

Edgar Sengier of Union Minère to Baruch's apartment in New York for a meeting with the baron and his staff. Sengier and his company operated the largest uranium mine in the Belgian Congo and had supplied the Manhattan Project during the war, which made Groves forever grateful to him. After describing the major world sources of uranium ore for the Baruch team, Sengier launched an assault on the Acheson-Lilienthal Report. He had minimal respect for the document since there were no mining men among its authors. It was foolish, Sengier declared, for an international authority to own the mines. The mines should be operated by their owners under reasonable regulations established by the proposed Atomic Development Authority. The authority might, however, control the product of the mines and the stockpiles. Sengier feared that the Atomic Development Authority would "upset wages, dissatisfy people and have tremendous difficulties of operation on account of the different nationals involved." [31] One month later, on May 8, Baruch and Searls met with two executives of the Union Carbide company who, as one might expect, were "violently opposed to the Acheson Report in its emphasis on the ownership of raw material in the ground." They made a plea instead for a survey of all resources in the field as a first step. Their alternative to international ownership was a system of rigorous inspection and accounting procedures for the separation operations at mining locations throughout the world.[32] These arguments of the mining industry had an effect. The Baruch team, under the continuing influence of the mining tycoon Searls, concluded that international ownership of the raw materials for atomic development was a bad idea and should be replaced by some less restrictive relationship.

Searls made another argument to Baruch which eventually gained great favor. If the Atomic Development Authority derived its authority from the Security Council and was accountable to that body, as appeared in the Acheson-Lilienthal Report, then the actions of the authority would be subject to the veto power. Searls and Baruch viewed international atomic control as a process whereby the United States gave up information and technique and received nothing in return. They therefore did not want the American gifts to be misused with no recourse in the authority to punish the wrongdoer. Searls's thoughts appealed to Baruch because they had the effect of putting teeth into the Acheson-Lilienthal Report. Byrnes had been argued into accepting the veto over atomic energy by Molotov at Moscow and then presented the veto to the doubting United States Senators as excellent self-protection for the United States. Bernard Baruch now felt that he would best uphold the trust which the Senators had placed in him by removing the veto and therefore making the international control system as foolproof as possible for America. He had in mind a deterrent theory based on the certainty that rapid punishment would be imposed on a violator of the international control treaty.

Baruch's other major departure from the Acheson-Lilienthal Report was very different; it amounted in fact to an expression of his idealism and expansive self-image. In the weeks after his appointment, Baruch became possessed by a dream of the golden road down which his latest, and perhaps last, public effort might take mankind. Perhaps this is why he became so jealous of his jurisdiction. Touched by some of the apocalyptic writings of the day, Baruch began to see himself approaching one of the most significant acts in the long history of man on the planet. Sitting with Ferdinand Eberstadt on his famed park bench, Baruch enjoyed the spring sunshine, while Eberstadt nurtured a dream: "You are on the threshold of your greatest accomplishment. You are offering the world one of the most elevated programs ever given mankind — one which, if followed, not only can solve the atom, but the entire problem of war." Although he would probably have cringed at the description, Baruch became a "one worlder," who believed that the atomic weapons were so startling in their dimensions that they could lead the world's nations to serve their own interests by disarming. Once atomic weapons were controlled, so too might all other weapons be. Baruch was at least part romanticist, a practical dreamer whose optimism was born, with good cause, in an incredible series of personal triumphs that had taken him to the top of the American economy and society. Why not world disarmament too? [33]

As Baruch and his staff privately departed at these significant turns from the Acheson-Lilienthal Report, that document continued nonetheless to gain wide publicity and acceptance as the American plan. The reluctance of the Acheson-Lilienthal team to come to his side gnawed at Baruch. On May 9, he traveled again with Hancock to Washington to confront Dean Acheson. Baruch made clear to the Undersecretary of State that he was "embarrassed by the declination of the two committees to go forward with their work" under him. Acheson wanted Baruch and Hancock to know that the President, who was the final arbiter, was committed to no policy at that point. Truman had seen the Acheson-Lilienthal Report "and thought well of it," but "there had been no pressure upon him to accept it." That was all well and good, Hancock responded, but unless Baruch and his staff went rather far in listing their reservations to the Acheson-Lilienthal plan, they "might be condemned by our silence into a position of accepting the report as a statement of policy." Acheson then asked for some indication of the points at which they had differed from the report, and Hancock and Baruch quickly mentioned the veto and international ownership of the raw materials. A short discussion of these matters convinced Acheson that the breach was serious and potentially destructive. He therefore suggested a joint meeting of the Baruch team with the Acheson and Lilienthal groups and quickly scheduled it in Washington during the following week.

Vannevar Bush was informed of the meeting a short while after he had conferred with Baruch. He wrote Carroll Wilson that the entire situation was "decidedly disturbing" and expressed his concern that "the meetings will have to be handled with a good deal of care or they might result in a blow-up." [34]

The eminent members of the Baruch, Acheson, and Lilienthal teams assembled at the historic Blair-Lee House on Pennsylvania Avenue in Washington at two o'clock on Friday afternoon, May 17, 1946.[35] Dean Acheson, looking typically meticulous and elegant, opened the conference with a short statement. His committee and the Lilienthal Board were there to help Mr. Baruch in any way they could. Baruch thanked Acheson and said that he would like to have John Hancock act as chairman of the meeting. The baron was going to sit back and listen. As Hancock understood and stated it, the major purpose of the meeting was to discuss the Acheson-Lilienthal Report, its authors' thoughts on it, and the ideas of the Baruch team. However, Hancock wanted first to mention an idea which, he said, their staff had conceived for a preliminary worldwide survey of raw materials. Searls expanded on the thought. It would probably take a year or two for the United Nations commission to agree on an international control treaty. In the meantime, a raw materials survey might set the foundation for later atomic control and also test the good faith of the various nations. The Acheson and Lilienthal groups immediately attacked this plan with remarkable unity. Lilienthal worried that it would compel America to disclose some of the secrets of the Manhattan Project. Oppenheimer viewed the raw materials question as "trivial" when compared with the more difficult problems of controlling atomic manufacturing plants.

Harry Winne suggested that Soviet leaders might take the position "that if it were ascertained that Russia did not have enough uranium to make her dangerous in the atomic field, then the other nations might not go ahead with the whole atomic [control] program." To Bush, Acheson, and most of the others, the idea of testing Russia with this preliminary raw materials survey was foolish. If that was the purpose of the survey, Acheson said, he was against it. He believed "that any good faith point should be tested so that no one could doubt it and that reluctance to approve or carry out a general survey proposal based on an informal agreement or resolution of the members of the AEC would not be a clear showing of good or bad faith." Hancock was now on the defensive and managed a temporary retreat. There was no thought of following a "bull in a china shop" method and "pursuing prematurely such a proposal." He hoped, however, that consideration would be given to it sometime early in the negotiations.

Now Hancock wanted to move on to the Acheson-Lilienthal Report. Did its authors have any changes they would make in hindsight? Lilienthal, somewhat taken aback by the form of Hancock's inquiry, said that he had none. Barnard, however, thought that Section IV of the report, which dealt with stages of transition to international control and had been forced on the Lilienthal Board by the Acheson Committee, "emphasized too much the idea of the United States holding back information until we saw the good faith of countries." Oppenheimer agreed, adding that Section IV seemed to be saying quite one-sidely: "This is what the United States wants to do." He also felt that the question of whether raw materials would be "owned" or "controlled" should have been stated more clearly. Baruch now spoke up for the first time and said that his group was moving away from the notion of international ownership of the raw materials toward some form of international licensing of private mining operations. He said he liked Acheson's obfuscating term *dominion* as a description of the relationship between the international authority and raw materials.

The discussion meandered along this linguistic trail until Hancock asked once more whether the members of the Lilienthal Board had any other additions or modifications to suggest. This time Oppenheimer answered: "If we are to have lively talk, I submit that someone else, rather than the authors of the report, suggest changes or amplifications." But the Baruch team refused the invitation and continued, under Hancock's leadership, to elicit more discussion on a host of subsidiary issues. Finally, Hancock picked up an earlier remark of Swope's and put it to the other two groups. Why did the Acheson-Lilienthal Report omit penalties? Had any thought been given to the idea that punishment of violators might be carried out with an internationally controlled stockpile of atomic bombs? Herbert Marks was the first to answer. Hancock had been warned about Marks by General Groves who described Acheson's assistant as "an internationalist . . . a mental gymnast who needs continuous watching." [36] Hancock in turn had reported this in a memo to the rest of the Baruch team. Now Marks said that there was nothing in the report one way or the other about stockpiles of atomic bombs, but that "the theory of the board's plan was inconsistent with such an idea." The whole purpose of their report "was to protect nations against surprise use of atomic weapons." If the plan was put into effect, it would take approximately a year for a nation violating the treaty to have atomic bombs ready for use in warfare. The existence of an atomic stockpile would raise the possibility of seizure and immediate use by an aggressive nation in international atomic warfare. Fred Searls was not interested in the strategic intricacies Marks had presented. Some consideration must be given, he said, to writing a charter which would provide for immediate and certain penalties for violation. Herbert Swope, the most bombastic member of the Baruch team, now joined the battle. The Acheson-Lilienthal Report purported to provide "controls and safeguards," but what inducement would there be for any nation to join unless there were sanctions provided for misbehavior and evasion?

Acheson now responded in his most judicial tones. This was a most interesting problem. He had spent weeks pondering it with Mr. Hull prior to the adoption of the United Nations treaty. They had decided finally that "if a major power violated a treaty, or wanted a trial of strength, then no matter what words or provisions were set forth in the treaty, it was obvious that the international organization had broken down and any kind of words or provisions to cover the situation would be of little value." That was exactly the theory of the Acheson-Lilienthal Report. Charles Thomas added that the Lilienthal Board had decided that there was no hope for absolute security, but that the best they could do was to eliminate the possibility of surprise attacks and to build cooperation among nations through their joint operation of the Atomic Development Authority.

This, Swope said, his voice rising, was not enough. The United States representative had "to set his sights high and to provide . . . for an automatic and certain penalty in the event of evasion or violation."

Baruch then spoke for the second time in the long afternoon's discussion. He admitted that Swope's question was his own and asked the Acheson-Lilienthal group what they would propose to do if there was a violation of the international control treaty? There was no such condition as complete security, John McCloy answered. The question of penalties was "a matter of high state policy," and it "might be considered presumptuous" for the Acheson and Lilienthal committees to suggest such penalty provisions. It would not, Swope retorted, be presumptuous for the United States representative to make suggestions along these lines.

Eberstadt was ready with the coup de grâce. The public had been led to believe that the Acheson-Lilienthal plan eliminated the atomic bomb from warfare, but now it was clear that all the report offered was a warning of violations of the control system. He subscribed to Swope's idea regarding penalties. If there were no penalties, then the public should be told this clearly for right now they had been lulled into a "false sense of security."

Swope demanded to know what would be done if another nation began to build atomic bombs? Acheson answered that there were two additions that could be made to their report which might cover this situation. One would be to provide within the treaty that any violation would produce an automatic declaration of war. The other would be to have a world government which would supersede national sovereignties and have an international police system. Neither of these solutions, Acheson exclaimed, was worth a "damned thing."

Harry Winne tried to calm the discussion, but to no avail. It ended at ten minutes to six with Swope's final declaration that "a law without a penalty was useless."

They returned to Blair-Lee House on the following morning, Saturday May 18, each apparently with a personal resolve to avoid the acrimony of the previous day. Hancock began with a measured exposition of his opposition to international ownership of mines. Lilienthal and Barnard discussed their work on stages of transition and received the general approval of the Baruch group. Opposition to the veto power was still on Acheson's mind, however; he pointed out that the international authority would be created by a separate treaty so that, although it would have ties to the Security Council, there would be no veto over its day-to-day operations. Eberstadt asked Acheson whether violation of the treaty would not amount to an act of aggression and therefore come before the Security Council and be subject to the veto? Yes, Acheson conceded, in that instance, the veto would control.

Finally, as the discussion waned, Baruch spoke up once more. After thanking everyone for his aid at these two discussions, the baron said that what he most needed now was a brief statement of what the authors of the Acheson-Lilienthal Report thought it contained. The matter had not yet settled in his mind and he needed a piece of paper in front of him which contained the essentials of their idea. It was up to the Lilienthal Board to help him know what he was talking about. Give him a chart, Baruch said, and he could steer his way.[37]

This request depressed the Lilienthal group, coming as it did after two days of discussion of their report. There was nothing, however, that they could do but agree to give Baruch the condensation he wanted. By Sunday evening, after a weekend's work, their summary was ready to be forwarded to Baruch. They had reduced their labors to twelve essential points, including: the need for an international agreement, the importance of creating an international authority with managerial control of all dangerous atomic activities, the desirability of licensing nondangerous atomic activities, the folly of relying solely on inspection, and the need to establish categories of danger signals. Their plan was primarily a warning device, they said, and not a system for abolishing atomic warfare because there could be no such system.[38]

The members of the Lilienthal Board were dismayed by this confrontation with Baruch and his men. Preparing to depart for the University of California campus where he would teach once more, Oppenheimer wrote to Lilienthal that he was "still very heavy of heart." [39] Lilienthal tried to be more optimistic and encouraging a few days later in his response to Oppenheimer: "While we must speak out against proposals we deem to be wrong, the 'clue to action' for everyone is to try to be helpful to Mr. Baruch for he is the man who, from the earliest days of our conferring (long before we knew who 'Joe Doakes' would turn out to be), we realized would have one of the toughest responsibilities that has ever fallen to a human being." [40]

For his part, Baruch was happy about the meetings at Blair-Lee House. He wrote to Lilienthal, thanking him for his help and expressing his regrets that they had been unable to get together before the report was released. However, Baruch also indicated that the Blair-Lee conference had not diminished his interest in making the "punishment fit the crime" and going beyond atomic energy in his work to discuss "all other weapons adaptable to mass destruction." [41]

The baron wrote a similar thank-you note to Herbert Marks with a word of South Carolina philosophy at the end:

> It is unfortunate that we did not get together from the very beginning — even before the report was released. But, the mill never grinds with the water that is past. Let us see that it grinds well from now on. [42]

15

"The Last, Best Hope on Earth"

BACK IN NEW YORK during the last week in May, Baruch directed Hancock to begin a draft of their position. The heart of it was taken from the Acheson-Lilienthal plan, but there were three major alterations: removal of the veto and delineation of particular crimes and punishment; provision for the international authority to exercise "dominion" over the raw materials instead of ownership; and a requirement for a preliminary raw materials survey.[1] This first articulation of the Baruch Plan was very timely since the opening session of the United Nations Atomic Energy Commission had now been scheduled for June 14, 1946, less than a month away.

While Hancock prepared his initial draft of policy, Eberstadt had an idea. On May 23, he sent a memorandum to Baruch asserting "the necessity of having our proposal in line with our military policy and the needs of our national security."[2] The logic of this suggestion struck Baruch immediately, and on the very next day he wrote to each of the members of the Joint Chiefs of Staff describing his goals at the UNAEC and asking their advice on the relation of his mission to the national security.[3] It is remarkable that the counsel of the generals was not sought until the eleventh hour and then at the casual suggestion of one of Baruch's staff aides. Since the departure of Henry L. Stimson from the War Department and the seizure by the State Department of influence over international atomic control, the American military establishment had been detached from the making of decisions in this area. Now, in response to Baruch's request, the generals poured forth their views with unanimity and zeal. Their responses to Baruch revealed great anxiety over his work at the United Nations, which was based largely on their unhappiness with the demobilization of America's conventional military might.

Fleet Admiral Chester W. Nimitz, the chief of naval operations, wrote to Baruch:

> The United States is now in a position of advantage with respect to the atom bomb. We should exploit that advantage to assist in the early establishment of a satisfactory peace and should relinquish it no more rapidly than is justified by the proven development of agreed controls. It will be desirable for international agreements concerning the atom bomb to follow European peace treaties and definitely to precede the time when other countries could have atomic bombs.[4]

General Carl Spaatz, the leader of America's Army Air Forces, was more specific:

> We are faced with a critical period in World politics. There are conflicts of thought, purpose, and ideology. In our efforts through diplomacy to solve these vexing problems and to bring about a condition of relative stability, military power is a considerable factor. Possible causes of war appear on every hand and no effective control has yet been devised. The conventional military strength of the United States has been reduced drastically by the hysterical pace of demobilization. The atomic bomb because of its decisive nature is now an essential part of our military strength. Our monopoly of the bomb, even though it is transitory, may well prove to be a critical factor in our efforts to achieve first a stabilized condition and eventually a lasting peace. Any step in the near future to prohibit atomic explosives would have a grave and adverse military effect on the United States since the result is reduction in our advantage without a proportionate reduction in the

strength of other powers. Such action in my opinion would threaten the security of the United States and the peace and security of the entire world . . . Because of our dependence on the atomic bomb for military strength, any agreements which diminish our capacity of producing and employing the weapon must follow, and not precede, assured methods of enforcing the agreements for control of raw materials and production of atomic energy on a worldwide basis . . .

Few nations emerged from World War II as pre-eminent military powers. The possession of the atomic bomb by the United States materially affects the distribution of this power. There has been little indication to date of good faith on the part of all nations to carry out the provisions of control necessary to render effective any treaty. Until there are such assurances, no steps should be taken which would enhance another nation's military strength through the reduction of our own.[5]

The Chief of Staff, Dwight David Eisenhower, wrote to Baruch in similarly anxious terms:

If we enter too hurriedly into an international agreement to abolish all atomic weapons, we may find ourselves in the position of having no restraining means in the world capable of effective action if a great power violates the agreement. Such a power might, in fact, deliberately avoid the use of atomic weapons and embark on aggression with other equally decisive weapons. If, on the other hand, we enter into agreements providing for the maintenance of atomic weapons under international control, we face extraordinary difficulties. First, in providing adequate control and inspection systems and second, the possibility that the national leaders of a totalitarian state, possessing a supply of the weapons, might choose to strike first rather than to compromise. This dilemma, unless other approaches to a solution come to hand, must be solved before we should proceed to any treaty, abolishing atomic weapons . . .

To summarize:

a. The existence of the atomic bomb in our hands is a deterrent, in fact, to aggression in the world. We cannot at this time limit our capability to produce or use this weapon . . .

c. Atomic weapons are only a part of the problem. There will be other equally terrible weapons of mass destruction. The whole problem must be solved concurrently with the problem of controlling atomic energy. To control atomic weapons, in which field we are pre-eminent, without provision for equally adequate control of other weapons of mass destruction can seriously endanger our national security.[6]

The message from America's foremost generals to Baruch was clear. Unless he could achieve the thoroughly impossible goal of total world disarmament (particularly of the conventional military ground might of the Soviet Union), international control of atomic weapons would not be in the national interest of the United States. The military establishment was suggesting that Baruch's mission at the United Nations was primarily one of propaganda value, for the perimeters they set for him were far short of what would be necessary to induce Soviet cooperation.

When Hancock completed his draft of policy, Baruch and he traveled to Washington to meet with Byrnes and Acheson at the State Department. It was Memorial Day, 1946. With the opening session of the UNAEC now only two weeks away, it was time to make some final decisions. At their first session that morning, Baruch did not bring out Hancock's statement. He began instead by asking the Secretary of State what his policies were in this field, for, in fact, Byrnes had not yet declared himself. "Oh hell," he now told Baruch, "I have none. What are your views?" As the discussion proceeded, however, it became quite clear that Byrnes was either being facetious or misleading. The Secretary of State initially turned his attention to tactics, stressing the importance "of laying on the table a working document on the day before it was up for discussion in the general meeting or a subcommittee." Language was of great importance in these negotiations, Byrnes said. He hoped that Baruch would avail himself of the expert treaty draftsmen at the State Department. Moving to more substantive matters, Byrnes asked the same unproductive question that had perplexed him since the days before Hiroshima. What would Baruch say if the Russians asked America to stop making atomic bombs? Under his approach, Hancock answered, there would have to be some agreement covering both the further making of bombs and the disposal of the bombs then in existence, but he did not want to use any words in the opening round of negotiations that would imply an "approved plan as to the manner of disposal or transfer to anyone else." A solution would have to be worked out within the Security Council and would need the approval of the United States at every step of the way.

Baruch was now ready to reveal his dream. The communiqué of the Moscow Conference had referred to controlling not only atomic weapons but all other weapons of mass destruction as well. He hoped therefore to use atomic energy control as a lever to world disarmament. But Byrnes would have none of this vision. It would be "a serious mistake," he said, to attempt to cover these other weapons as part of Baruch's present assignment. Baruch was equally strong in response: "The problem of atomic energy is a problem of the hearts of men — No plan so far proposed gives any guarantee of assurance." Only total disarmament offered such a guarantee. Byrnes was unmoved. Acheson was silent. And the discussion moved on to the question of penalties. Hancock predicted that both Acheson and Byrnes would eventually accept the idea of sanctions, although they said that they thought it was useless since a violation of the treaty would automatically be met by the ultimate sanction — war. Their attention moved, in turn, to the makeup of the proposed international authority, its power over atomic development plants, and proposals for a raw materials survey. On this last point, Byrnes was as adamant as the Acheson and Lilienthal committees had been. An early call for a survey of the world's raw materials would be "worthless because the Russians would disagree." Some such survey should certainly be part of the eventual treaty, but "proposing it as part of our national platform would invite an early breakdown without a clear and adequate basis for such a breakdown." Byrnes now rose to leave. He had to attend a funeral. As Byrnes walked toward the door, Baruch made one final declaration about penalties, directing his remarks to Acheson while Byrnes was still in hearing distance. He had "to be in the position of advocating something in which he believed," Baruch said.

The four of them met again that evening in Byrnes's apartment at the Shoreham Hotel. Acheson took the initiative with a proposal to Byrnes that there be some group established within the State Department to coordinate the government's policy on atomic energy matters and to be available to Mr. Baruch as he desired. He even broached the idea of having the Baruch team move its base of operations to Washington. Up to this point, Baruch and Hancock were mildly interested, but then Acheson proposed reconstituting the Lilienthal Committee within the State Department as an advisory body. To this notion, Hancock objected; he believed it "could only complicate our problem" because, in the end, Baruch would have to make his determination of policy with his own staff. Hancock continued: "These problems are not often purely scientific problems. They blend very quickly into political problems . . . The scientists tend to be unbending and calculating in the field of science — which is natural — but they carry over their inelasticity into arguments in the field of international affairs, politics in the proper sense, and negotiation." Baruch and Acheson agreed to discuss this matter further between themselves.

The relation of their work to military questions and national security had been clarified, Hancock announced, with the appointment, by the Joint Chiefs, of General Groves to serve as an interpreter of military policy for the American delegation at the

United Nations. But, Acheson said flatly, Groves would be speaking without the support of the military authorities. Hancock retorted: "I have seen nothing in General Groves' conduct to lead me to support that belief." Acheson was pleasant but firm in restating his reluctance about Groves, which Hancock took to be "a relic of the fight of false issue about military versus civilian control and also it may be a by-product of the feeling of the scientists toward General Groves."

Hancock was now ready to distribute his ten-point policy statement. Two of the points were discussed at length: automatic sanctions and ownership of raw materials. On the question of sanctions, the discussion covered old ground with Baruch firm in his insistence that there must be penalties or "otherwise we had to tell the world that this plan gave us a warning of between three months and a year, which was zero in our form of Government." Acheson again doubted the wisdom of the suggestion, but he was not adamant. Byrnes seemed to think that penalties would provide some deterrent to violation and said he would discuss the issue with the President.

The argument over whether the international authority should own the uranium ore in the ground was more heated. To Acheson, licensing and inspection were simply not enough. Hancock, on the other hand, could see no reason "to give Government the power to seize the property of one citizen, with the object of converting it to purely commercial uses." Cleverly changing his tactic, Acheson argued that Russia would never accept the notion of roaming inspectors, but Hancock rebutted that Russia would be much less likely to accede to international ownership of their land. "Unless we own," Acheson declared, "we cannot stop diversion in Russia." [7]

On the following morning, May 31, Baruch and Hancock met with General Groves from whom they received a much warmer reception. He approved of their ten-point program, suggesting only that the proposed penalties be described as "immediate and certain" instead of "prompt and certain" as Hancock had written.[8]

Baruch and Hancock visited Byrnes again that evening. This time Acheson was not present. Byrnes informed them that he had spoken with President Truman during the day about their discussions. The President had approved the idea of penalties in the treaty. As for the other points of disagreement, Byrnes had told the President that they were minor and "could be worked out in the ordinary course." The Secretary of State then handed Hancock a memorandum of policy which he said Dean Acheson had dictated in about a half-hour. The reason for this, according to Byrnes, was that he wanted their policy "put in the usual form of a State Department paper, in order to make it more in keeping with the practice of informing the President about contemplated national positions to be taken during the course of the negotiations." As Hancock read through Acheson's memorandum, it seemed to him that this was not a rewrite of his own proposal but "nothing but a review of the Acheson plan." When Hancock pointed this out to Byrnes, the Secretary assured him that the statement had been written "for form rather than content, although it was partly to inform the President." Angered by what appeared to be an attempt at subterfuge, Hancock insisted that Acheson's memorandum was significantly different from his own. The best thing for him to do, he continued, would be to revise his own statement of policies in the same form so that its points of divergence from Acheson's memorandum would be clear. Byrnes agreed.

The other major topic of the evening was the continuing disagreement over whether the international atomic authority should own the raw materials in the ground or exercise some lesser form of control over them. Hancock wanted licensing and inspection, and Acheson wanted ownership. "I cannot conceive of Russia agreeing to turn over to an international sovereignty her own State property," Hancock declared. He was also obviously having some difficulty conceiving of such a "turnover" in other, closer countries of the world: "This plan [of ownership] would seem to all men in the capitalistic economy as the first start to an international socialized State." Byrnes remained noncommittal.[9]

Secretary of State Byrnes must have been somewhat perplexed by this discussion because he phoned Hancock on the following morning to make sure that he was going to write the memorandum they had discussed in the form of a comparison between the Acheson plan and his own. The Secretary of State intended to give this memorandum to Truman "so that the President would be informed and would not make any slip or possibly be misled through Byrnes' emphasis upon the minor points of difference, which could be reconciled." The Secretary also had one final piece of reassurance for Hancock. He would oppose Acheson's plan for reestablishing the Lilienthal Committee within the State Department.[10]

Hancock canceled a 12:30 appointment with Acheson to work on the memorandum Byrnes had requested and left it for the Secretary before the day was over. In it, he outlined four areas of difference between his approach and Acheson's. As Hancock saw it, the Undersecretary still favored ownership of the raw materials, omitted any penalty provision, overemphasized the possibilities of denaturing atomic material, and excluded an early survey of the world's raw materials.[11]

Hancock spent the next few days trying to write a statement of America's atomic policy which showed some deference to the concerns that Acheson and Byrnes had expressed. It was ready by June 4. When Byrnes received the document he did not even look at it but sent it over to Acheson who gave it to Herbert

Marks with instructions not to be timid in editing. Marks quickly deleted a section in which Hancock had specified crimes, and another which provided for licensing of raw materials. On the question of safeguards, Marks struck Hancock's call for "immediate and certain penalties for certain defined crimes" and replaced it with a passage recognizing the need for "a clear statement of the consequences of violations of the system of controls, including definitions of the acts which would constitute such violations and the procedures and concerted action which would follow." Marks also rewrote the section on the powers of the international authority so that it skipped over the question of whether raw materials should be owned or licensed by allowing for both possibilities and others including dominion, lease, inspection, operation, and control. By June 6, Acheson and Marks had polished their draft and presented it to Byrnes.[12]

On that same day, Bernard Baruch's ego and psyche went out of control once more. If not that, then the old gentleman was cleverly managing to stage a confrontation from which he would emerge victorious. Word had reached him that Acheson and Marks were doing a total redraft of Hancock's policy paper. Then, Fred Searls, who had been in Washington, returned to say that Byrnes had told him that the President viewed the Acheson-Lilienthal Report as the basis of America's atomic policy. This infuriated Baruch, who had been frustrated by his isolation from Truman in the preceding weeks. He reached for the phone and called Byrnes. Recounting Searls's story and citing the countless other people and groups who viewed the Acheson plan as the American plan, Baruch exclaimed:

> Thus, the minds of all seem to be made up in that direction. In view of the difficulties involved, this may be the solution. Then Acheson or Lilienthal or Barnard or Winne could present the report and have negotiations come up after that. All of them have

the utmost confidence in the Report. They believe in it without limitation, deductions, or additions and can advocate it more wholeheartedly than I can. Even what I had to suggest, I would have to admit had a lot of loopholes which I would have to tell to the Congress or the American people, or anybody who wanted explanations or asked me questions. I have lost confidence in my being able to work this out with the President and you satisfactorily. Only friction will result and that will be bad for the goal we all want to reach . . . I have waited patiently for word from you and the President regarding the policy . . . There are so many limitations that without many additions which we should advocate I am sure it would not do anything except hold out false hopes. That is what I have been trying to tell you and would have told the President and will tell the Senate Committee if I am asked.[13]

Byrnes's long life in politics prepared him for moments such as this. Knowing full well what Baruch's open opposition could do to Truman's atomic policy, Byrnes asked the baron to come to Washington as soon as possible. Together, they would go to see the President and settle these matters once and for all.

Baruch arrived at Byrnes's office in the State Department at 2:45 on the next afternoon, Friday, June 7.[14] He brought a statement of policy with him to guide the conversation. Byrnes had the Acheson-Marks redraft which he told Baruch did not really make any substantial changes in the Hancock paper. Together they proceeded to the White House to put the matter before Truman. Byrnes handed the President the Acheson-Marks paper and the statement Baruch had brought with him. Truman reached for both documents and went over them paragraph by paragraph as the baron explained his position. Each paragraph received the President's initials, indicating approval. The document adopted the essentials of the Acheson-Lilienthal plan, with a few of the additions Baruch desired. There was a section on penalties which was similar to the one Acheson and Marks had written; a call for the prohibition of stockpiles of bombs once the full control plan was in effect; a proposal to extend the talks to biological warfare though not to total disarmament; the allowance for various forms of control by the authority over raw materials, but not necessarily ownership; a proposal for "continuous surveys" of the world's raw materials; and a section on carefully defined stages of transition to international control which Truman marked "most important." When it came to the veto, Baruch wanted to be sure the President understood his position. "Of what use is a treaty if there is not a way of enforcing it?" Baruch asked. Truman answered simply: "I quite agree with you." In fact, the President added his belief that the whole notion of the veto power was a mistake and should never have been put into the United Nations Charter. The situation reminded Truman of the Manchurian Crisis of the early 1930s when Henry L. Stimson, if he had some power behind him, probably could have avoided World War II.

There was one other point which Baruch wanted to clarify. How did the President wish him to handle Britain and Canada, America's atomic allies? Truman had just received a telegram from Attlee and King, asking for atomic cooperation particularly at the United Nations. The President said "that he wasn't going to do anything, although he thought that cooperation meant that they should have the know-how that we have." This pronouncement elicited a very strong response from Baruch which would have surprised and pleased some of his most acerbic, scientist-critics. If the British and Canadians "got any knowledge or know-how that we did not give the other nations," Baruch declared, "it would torpedo the Atomic Energy Commission and . . . no shred of respectability would be left to the American representative because he did not know, which was silly, or if he did know it, he was engaged in fooling his colleagues on the Atomic Energy Commission." Truman said that he agreed.

When they reached the end of the statement of policy, the

President wrote: "Above general principles approved June 7, 1946. Harry S. Truman." To buttress Baruch's ego even more, Truman dictated a letter to go along with the policy guidelines. In it, he said:

> The statement is general in character because I want you to have authority to exercise your judgment as to the method by which the stated objectives can be accomplished . . . I want you to know that I am relying upon you to exercise your own discretion in those negotiations, subject only to the general statement of policy attached . . .[15]

This was what Baruch wanted. It had been a tortuous struggle, but finally the baron had the feeling that he had won and that was most important. In truth, he had adopted almost all of the Acheson-Lilienthal Report. Only the removal of the veto and the insertion of the threat of swift and certain punishment for a wrongdoer could be credited to him.

All that remained to be done was final drafting of Baruch's opening speech and clearance of the American plan by the proper parties within the American and British governments. On June 12, Baruch sailed smoothly past the last obstacle — the Senate Special Committee on Atomic Energy. Here, the baron was at home. The Senators received his report warmly and were particularly pleased with Baruch's abolition of the veto on atomic energy matters — a dramatic change of attitude from the espousal of the veto six months earlier by Vandenberg and Byrnes as the major method of self-protection for the United States and its secrets. For better or worse, Baruch had done it. One note of acrimony crept into Baruch's dialogue with the Senators that day. He had modified his dreams of total disarmament to a statement, probably based on his correspondence with the Joint Chiefs, that the secret of the atomic weapon should not be disclosed until all other nations reduced their armies to the proportions of a constabulary. Senator Connally was angered when he heard this and told Baruch that disarmament was not within his jurisdiction.[16]

Baruch was now ready for the United Nations. Swope had put the final flourishing touches on the statement. Shortly before eleven o'clock on the morning of June 14, Baruch and his assistants arrived at the three-story, one-million-dollar gymnasium of Hunter College in the Bronx, New York, that had been transformed into an international meeting hall for the first session of the United Nations Atomic Energy Commission. Where iron girders had shown on the ceiling a short while before there were now sound-absorbent tiles. The eleven delegates sat in green upholstered chairs around a large mahogany horseshoe table with seats behind them for their staffs. To the rear, mahogany plywood covered the gymnasium brick wall. Rose-brown drapes covered each of the other walls. Thick dun-colored carpets went from wall to wall. To the right of the delegates was a translation booth where remarks would be turned into English and French after each speech. Arthur Compton, Harold Urey, Oppenheimer, and Charles Thomas were there at Baruch's invitation. Lilienthal was at home in Norris, Tennessee, pulling weeds from his onion garden when his wife yelled to him that Baruch was on the radio. Secretary-General Trygve Lie opened the session and asked Baruch, as the representative of the host country, to assume the chair. The baron rose, a magnificently erect and ruddy figure for his seventy-five years, six feet four in height, dressed in a diplomat's special double-breasted dark suit. His tempo was slow, his tone measured. He radiated both seriousness and hope. "We are here to make a choice between the quick and the dead. That is our business." What followed was the Acheson-Lilienthal plan with the amendments which Truman had approved. Calling for the abolition of the veto in atomic energy control, Baruch declared: "If I read the signs right, the peoples want a program not composed merely of pious thoughts but of enforceable sanctions — an international law with teeth in it." That apparently was to be his contribution — putting the teeth into it. Baruch even got in an appeal for general disarmament although it was not lucidly worded:

> But before a country is ready to relinquish any winning weapons it must have more than words to reassure it. It must have a guarantee of safety, not only against the offenders in the atomic area but against the illegal users of other weapons . . . why not? against war itself.

It was approaching twelve-thirty, as Baruch closed:

> And now I end. I have submitted an outline for present discussion. All of us are consecrated to making an end of gloom and hopelessness. It will not be an easy job. The way is long and thorny, but supremely worth traveling. All of us want to stand erect, with our faces to the sun, instead of being forced to burrow into the earth, like rats . . .
>   We say we are for Peace. The world will not forget that we say this . . . We shall nobly save, or meanly lose, the last, best hope on earth. The way is plain, peaceful, generous, just — a way which, if followed, the world will forever applaud.[17]

IV

Failure at the United Nations

16

The Russian Response

When Bernard Baruch delivered his solemn apocalyptic oration at the Hunter College gymnasium on June 14, 1946, he was careful to address it not only to his fellow members of the United Nations Atomic Energy Commission but also to his "fellow citizens of the world." That this latter constituency was listening became apparent over the next few days from the favorable responses issued around the world. There was one man, however, whose initial response had been determined long before Baruch finished his remarks. Andrei Gromyko, the thirty-six-year-old dark-haired, stone-faced Russian representative to the UNAEC sat expressionless, leaning forward intently when Baruch reached his statements about the veto power. Leaving the hall at the end of the meeting, Gromyko would only tell reporters that "so far matters are going smoothly." [1] A fuller exposition of his attitude would have to await a later day.

Others were not as noncommittal as Gromyko. The *New York Times* applauded Baruch, "surely no fuzzy-minded dreamer, a patriot who has served his country devotedly," for having the courage to present a plan which would intrude upon the national sovereignty of the United States. "We believe," the *Times* said, "the mass of the American people . . . will agree with what Mr. Baruch has so movingly and solemnly said . . . Better foreign inspectors at Oak Ridge than foreign bombs over our cities." [2] The *Toledo Blade* was effusive with praise: "There is not type in any newspaper office anywhere big enough to emphasize the importance of the American proposal today." [3] Brazil's representative to the UNAEC exclaimed that the Baruch Plan "heralds the dawn of a new era to humanity." [4]

There were also a few predictable voices of dissent. The Hearst newspapers called the proposal an "imbecilic New Deal" plan to surrender to "foreign masters" the American secret of the atomic bomb. When Senator McKellar was told about the Baruch Plan, he blurted out sanctimoniously, "Then I pray God that we will never have the agreement." [5] There was some disappointment, among liberals, on the other hand, that the United States had not gone far enough. The Baruch Plan itself was a fairly generous proposal, some said, but it was unclear in its stages and therefore unfair to the Soviet Union. Worst of all, it allowed the continued manufacture of atomic weapons by the American government. Walter Lippmann felt Baruch had erred strategically by emphasizing abolition of the veto, because abolition of the veto was a mere legalism that the Soviets could effectively protest but which would offer little protection to countries that obeyed the treaty. Among the thousands of congratulatory telegrams Baruch received in the days after June 14, however, was a joint one from Justice William O. Douglas, Ely Culbertson, and John Foster Dulles that applauded his refusal to allow the veto to protect treaty violators. And Senator Vandenberg, whose voice was weightier in Washington than McKellar's, said that Baruch's report was "more important to the peace of the world than anything" else that had happened in recent times. James Reston described the plan as "a combination of Truman's Missouri philosophy, Baruch's statesmanship, and the patient planning of the Acheson-Lilienthal committee." In Washington, Reston reported, the executive branch liked the Baruch Plan because it passed the ball to Congress, and Congress liked it because it left the next, tough moves to the Kremlin. [6]

Most of the atomic scientists, although troubled by Baruch's veto position, joined the chorus of praise. Their colleagues overseas in France, Holland, England, and Belgium, were reported to be reacting with "a sense of relief and gratitude." James Forrestal cabled Baruch a one-word message, "Bull's-eye," and several prominent national organizations, including the League of Women Voters, the American Veterans Committee, the Church Peace Union, and the United Council of Church Women, announced that they stood behind Bernard Baruch.

The baron of Hobcaw himself was exhilarated by the entire experience. In the days that followed Baruch's pronouncement, the other members of the Atomic Energy Commission offered their own proposals which were essentially reactions to the Baruch Plan. Most of them were favorable. Canada, Mexico, England, Brazil, China, Egypt, France, and Australia all supported the American idea. Canada felt that Baruch was worrying too much about the veto, and the Netherlands was not yet ready to state a preference. But the most important response, the one which would make all the others ultimately insignificant, would come from Andrei Gromyko on June 19. On the eighteenth, perhaps as a last innocent salute to hope and amity, Baruch invited the other members of the UNAEC to be his guests for dinner at the Stork Club. Afterward, he took them to Madison Square Garden for the Joe Louis–Billy Conn fight. There, Baruch and Gromyko, their arms entwined, stood and posed for pictures that appeared in the next day's newspapers with the caption: "Baruch and Gromyko in accord on Louis." If they had reached an agreement on the Brown Bomber, it was their last such accord on any matter.[7]

No official comments on the international control of atomic energy had made their way out of the Kremlin during the first six months of 1946, but there were enough unofficial Soviet press statements to let the world know that darkness was falling over East-West relations in general and over atomic relations in particular. In his "election" eve speech during February, Stalin had spoken of the irreconcilability of the communist and capitalist systems and foreseen a lengthy period of strain. After Churchill's famous cold war speech at Fulton, Missouri, on March 5, 1946, Stalin attacked the former English Prime Minister as the "warmonger of the Third World War." In Paris, during the spring, another Foreign Ministers conference became tangled in dissension. Molotov attacked the English and the Americans for uniting in a "desire to impose their will upon the Soviet Union." In the United Nations Security Council, Russian participation was characterized by frequent use of the veto power. At one point, when the council refused to act on a Soviet resolution on Iran, Gromyko simply walked out for two weeks.

The long report which George Kennan had cabled from the American embassy in Moscow during February 1946 made its way around the highest levels of American government, proclaiming to all who read it that the "Kremlin's neurotic view of world affairs" stemmed from the "traditional and instinctive Russian sense of insecurity."

> . . . Russian rulers have invariably sensed that their rule was relatively archaic in form, fragile and artificial in its psychological foundation, unable to stand comparison or contact with political systems of Western countries. For this reason, they have always feared foreign penetration, feared direct contact between the Western world and their own, feared what would happen if the Russians learned the truth about the world without or if foreigners learned the truth about the world within. And they have learned to seek security only in patient but deadly struggle for the total destruction of rival power, never in compacts and compromises with it.

Kennan maintained that the Soviet Union was "committed fanatically to the belief that with the United States there can be no permanent *modus vivendi,* that it is desirable and necessary that the internal harmony of our society be disrupted . . . the international authority of our state be broken, if Soviet power is to be secure." [8] For many men in Washington, Kennan's long cable offered intellectual confirmation of suspicions of the Soviet Union which they had long nurtured.

In its references to atomic energy, the Soviet press gave little cause to dispute Kennan's gloomy observations. During March 1946, *Pravda* and *Izvestia* wrote often of the importance of atomic energy to the postwar recovery of the Russian economy, echoing thereby a similar expression by Stalin in his February speech.[9] Putting such statements alongside Kennan's portrayal of Russian anxiety over foreign penetration of Soviet soil gave American diplomats little reason to believe that the Russians would ever accept the prerequisites of the Baruch Plan. On March 16, the Soviet commentator Modest Rubinstein came forth with a lengthy statement on the international control of atomic energy which was printed in *New Times* and read over Moscow Radio. He accused "American imperialist circles" of undermining world peace by monopolizing atomic energy for purposes of war and of trying to "utilize the discovery of atomic energy for gambling in foreign affairs." Rubinstein added a new touch to these now-familiar accusations. "United States military circles are already hindering the use of atomic energy for peaceful purposes," he charged, by promoting a policy that "sharply restricts scientific information and treats with supercilious scorn the scientists who discovered atomic energy and created the atomic bomb." [10]

The first months of 1946 also saw the beginning of a Soviet propaganda campaign to claim credit for the discovery of everything from baseball to airplanes. Atomic energy was not overlooked in this chauvinistic enterprise, aimed at sustaining the pride of the Soviet people in the nuclear age. Late in March,

Alexander Kazantzey, writing in the magazine *Round the World,* reported that on June 30, 1918, a great explosion had occurred in a forest area of eastern Siberia, and was heard 600 miles away, erupting into a column of fire 250 miles high. Previously known as the "fall Siberian meteorite," this event was now realized to be the first atomic explosion, a spontaneous affair caused by the sudden disintegration of uranium.[11]

After the Acheson-Lilienthal Report was made public late in March, the Soviet Union enjoyed a couple of months to develop a plan of its own based on a general knowledge of what the American approach would be. The speed with which Gromyko responded to Baruch at the U.N. and the fact that his response contained no specific references to Baruch's statement made it seem likely that he had come to America with a comprehensive statement of Russia's position on international atomic energy control. The speech which Gromyko presented on June 19 contained the minimum Russian conditions for atomic control. They were thoroughly irreconcilable with Baruch's plan.

The last unofficial Soviet statement before Gromyko's speech foreshadowed what was to come. In *New Times* on June 15, Rubinstein charged that modern capitalism could never oversee the peaceful development of new productive forces such as nuclear energy because of its innate contradictions. Rubinstein was most unhappy with the notion that the United Nations could be made into a world state "whose mission it will be to save the world from atomic war." Such "florid talk about a 'world State' " was "actually a frank plea for American imperialism."

When Baruch had finished his revelation of the American plan, there was no immediate response from the Russian press. The American *Daily Worker,* however, pointed out that in an international authority without a veto, the United States and

Britain "with their satellites would be able any time they desired to carry the day against the USSR." Bernard Baruch, the Communist newspaper continued, "was not releasing the dove of peace; he was demonstrating a new predatory flight of the American eagle."

The exact ornithological species which Gromyko himself let loose on June 19 at the Hunter College gym was difficult to determine, but it was certainly no dove. His proposal boasted great simplicity but had little else to recommend it to the United States. In the realm of general principles, Baruch could agree with Gromyko's statements that peace was impossible "if the discovery of atomic energy is not placed in the service of humanity," and that international agreements must be reached "forbidding the production and use of weapons based upon the use of atomic energy for mass destruction." [12] But then Gromyko went on and constructed an impenetrable wall between the Americans and himself. The first step toward atomic control must be an international convention to prohibit the production and use of atomic weapons, followed within six months by passage in each signatory country of legislation providing penalties for those who violated the international agreement. The second step of Gromyko's plan was the creation of two United Nations committees, one to plan for the exchange of scientific information, and the other to work on a control system of safeguards against violation of the treaty. The Soviet Union wanted to ban the bombs first and provide safeguards second.

Gromyko also offered a draft of his proposed international agreement. It called for all atomic weapons to be destroyed three months after ratification. Ratification would occur when one half of the nations who signed the treaty endorsed it and the Security Council approved it.

At the end of his speech, Gromyko stated briefly but in a tone of unmistakable finality that the Soviet Union viewed the veto power as untouchable. When he left the hall, Gromyko had but one additional comment for the press: "The veto must be retained under any circumstances." Baruch sat impassively during the Russian's speech and then cupped his hand to his ear as the English translation began. When reporters asked him afterward what he thought, Baruch, fully appreciative of the gap which Gromyko had revealed, said that he would have to wait until he had seen the text. "You know, I talk very deliberately and to the point."

Although Gromyko did not distribute advance copies of his speech, Baruch had gleaned from him some idea of what was coming during a final round of drinks at his apartment after the Louis-Conn fight on the night before. Baruch met with the French, Canadian, and Australian delegations to the United Nations Atomic Energy Commission on the following morning to discuss Gromyko's speech and how they might respond to it. A suggestion that Gromyko be subjected to immediate and comprehensive cross-examination was rejected by Baruch. The Russian must never be allowed to feel or say that there was a "gang up" against him, the baron contended. And so, later that day, John Hancock held a placid press conference at which he reassured newsmen that he was not downhearted over the Russian proposals because he viewed them as "an argument rather than a final Soviet position." [13]

It was also possible at that early date for the *New York Times* to explain optimistically that the two plans were not necessarily irreconcilable because the international convention which Gromyko had proposed could enact the Baruch Plan. The French delegate, Alexandre Parodi, had a more marvelously phrased piece of reassurance regarding the divergent Russian and American plans: "It would seem that they are nevertheless not entirely irreconcilable on the points where they are not in perfect harmony." [14]

Baruch spent most of the day after Gromyko's speech in strategy conferences with his staff. Anxious to avoid open conflict with the Russians so early in the negotiations, they decided to leak a story to the *New York Times* which reported, from anonymous but reliable sources, that the United States delegation had concluded that it was impossible to accept the Russian plan as it stood because it involved surrender of America's superior atomic position without any of the safeguards Baruch had requested. When President Truman was asked what he thought of the Russian plan at a news conference that same day, he would say only that he fully supported the Baruch proposals. A day later, the members of the American delegation released another anonymous story to the newspapers, this time revealing their willingness to establish the proposed Atomic Development Authority outside of the United Nations to avoid diminishing the United Nations veto system. The Soviets continued the negotiations by answering the offer in the same public medium. On the twenty-third of June, the press reported that "Soviet circles" had decided to insist on the veto in matters of atomic energy and therefore could not accept an international atomic agency outside of the United Nations. "You Americans invented the bomb and now you are afraid of it," was the disconcerting addendum offered by an anonymous Soviet spokesman.

Within the Soviet Union, *Pravda* gave klieg light treatment to Gromyko's proposals, mentioning incidentally that Bernard Baruch had presented some new ideas for the United States a few days earlier. A week later, on June 24, *Pravda* offered the first direct Russian response to the American proposal calling it "a product of atomic diplomacy." The Baruch Plan, *Pravda* declared, "reflects an obvious tendency toward world domination." These are "ambitions that cannot succeed in our time," the Russian newspaper warned. The lack of clarity in the stages of transition to international control seemed to bother *Pravda* more than the plan to abolish the veto:

> During this period, the United States intends to produce and store atom bombs, conditioned by the development of the activity of the international control organ . . . Later the United States government plans gradually to share information on the production of atomic energy . . . In doing so, the United States government apparently is planning to determine according to its own estimates, the periods wherein it will permit the international organ, in gradual stages, to peep into the secrets of its atomic kitchen. Why does the United States government want to continue production and storage of atomic weapons if this weapon is being forbidden? . . . Why are all other countries obliged to display blind confidence in the United States' intentions while the United States obviously distrusts not only its partners but also the international control organ? [15]

When all the members of the United Nations Atomic Energy Commission had delivered their opening statements, the alignment and the dilemma were clear. Nine nations had endorsed the Baruch Plan in one form or another; two nations, Russia and Poland, were behind the Gromyko proposals; and one nation, the Netherlands, was still without a clear position. How then should the UNAEC proceed? Herbert Evatt, the fiery Australian politician, historian, and jurist who was the first chairman of the Atomic Energy Commission, suggested breaking into a Working Committee of the whole to draft a plan for an international authority which would be based on all the ideas that had been put before the commission. Lacking any other suggestions, the members of the commission agreed to Evatt's plan.

At the first meeting of this Working Committee, on June 28, Baruch, who had gloried since his days of service to Woodrow

Wilson in being called "Dr. Facts," offered a chart, listing the
twenty key points of the United States plan and showing that
all the nations agreed on all the points, except the Netherlands,
which abstained, and Poland and the Soviet Union, which were
unhappy about the veto and inspection.[16] This attempt to
reveal a vast expanse of common ground also exposed the breach
that would divide the member nations everlastingly. Gromyko
described Baruch's chart as a helpful document but suggested
they get down to the substance of the problem and consider
the Soviet proposal. Baruch hastened to agree that the Soviet
call for an international convention was a consideration of "primary" importance but added that other equally critical matters
must now be considered in detail. *Primary* was not the proper
adjective, as Gromyko saw it. His proposition entailed the
"primordial subject." Evatt would have none of this. It was
foolish for the Working Committee to go off in study of but one
of the matters before it. A smaller drafting committee was needed
to consider all the major options in the field and formulate specific
questions for the full committee to consider. The title "Drafting
Committee," bothered Gromyko. "We are not at the stage of
drafting a text," he declared. The meetings of the Working Committee should continue. Evatt agreed that they were not yet ready
to draft but argued that he wanted to "put before us the possibilities of what a plan could cover." Gromyko's response was
abrupt: "The name you suggest for it does not correspond to
the task attributed to it." Now, the Australian's temper was up:
"Mr. Gromyko probably knows that the question of a name may
not be important, but I am quite agreeable to calling it Sub-
Committee Number One . . . or Alpha, if you like, Beta, or
Gamma." Gromyko said that he liked the name Subcommittee
One, and that is what it became. France, Mexico, the United
Kingdom, the United States, and the Soviet Union were chosen

as members of the new committee, along with Evatt from Australia as chairman. They were to gather for a first meeting on July 1.

During the last week in June 1946, Baruch telephoned Dean Acheson to discuss the strategy which the United States should now follow at the UNAEC. First, however, they considered a long telegram from Bedell Smith, the American ambassador in Moscow, expressing alarm that Gromyko, through his simple proposal for an international convention outlawing atomic bombs, had seized moral leadership for the Soviet Union on the atomic questions and obscured the basic issue which Smith took to be inspection and the Russians' opposition to it. He suggested that America "boldly recapture the moral ascendancy" by proposing to discuss control not only of atomic weapons but all other weapons of war as well, with the provision that there be universal inspection. Ambassador Smith thought his proposal would put the Soviet Union on the spot:

> If USSR accepts, well and good, we shall have attained the millennium. If USSR equivocates or refuses, the Soviet pretensions will have been exposed for what they are worth.[17]

Baruch's initial response to Smith's telegram was to ask Acheson whether the Baruch Plan was being distributed in the foreign capitals of the world. Acheson promised to check on this and let Baruch know immediately. After giving his personal view of what had happened in the first round of statements, Baruch asked Acheson to consult with the President so that he might be guided as to how firm he should be on questions such as the veto and the powers of the Atomic Development Authority which seemed to arouse most opposition. After hanging up the phone, Baruch reflected further on Ambassador Smith's telegram which had taken him back to his earlier preoccupation with world disarmament. He then wrote to Acheson:

While he [Gromyko] is telling us to get rid of the atomic bomb because of its inhuman qualities of destruction, at the same time everyone in Russia is talking about increasing and holding up the great Russian army. Without the atomic weapons just as many people can be killed but not so quickly. All wars are inhuman . . . Is no one going to say this? [18]

One week later, Acheson wrote back to Baruch, reporting that he had discussed Baruch's thoughts and Ambassador Smith's telegram with the President. The President's desire, and Acheson said he had "expressed it very clearly," was "that the efforts of the Atomic Energy Commission not be diverted by the Soviets or by anyone from the task of devising practical and specific measures for the international control of atomic energy." Truman felt that "for the United States to raise the question of general disarmament would be to distract attention from the task at hand and to confuse the public mind about the nature of our proposals." Taking issue with Smith's contention that the Soviet Union had seized the initiative, Truman told Acheson that he believed Baruch was "off to a fine start" and that through his efforts "the United States has the initiative and should keep it." [19]

This flattery from the top did not stop Baruch from sending a somewhat defensive response to Acheson:

You misunderstood my reference to disarmament. It wasn't that I wanted to raise the point, but to say that a wide opening had been left if there was anybody considering that matter. Everyone discussing atomic energy or other weapons of mass destruction says that elimination and outlawing of war are the only answers. But as the President and you say, that is not my task.[20]

Acheson's conference with Truman about the state of affairs at the United Nations must have included a word about Baruch's psyche, for at the end of June the baron received a telegram from the President:

As the Atomic Energy Commission on which you have so ably been representing our country begins its more detailed discussions, I want to assure you again of my full support and of my confidence that our participation in this great task so vital to the peace of the world and the welfare of mankind is in good hands.[21]

17

The Breach Grows Wider

THERE WAS CALM at the United Nations at six o'clock on Sunday evening, June 30. The first exposition of approaches to atomic control had revealed serious differences but calcification had not yet set in. More detailed consideration and presumably more genuine negotiations were to begin the next day, July 1, at the initial meeting of Subcommittee One. At the lagoon of Bikini Atoll in the Marshall Islands in the Pacific, it was already July 1. There, things were only momentarily calm. At thirty-four seconds after nine, the world's fourth atomic bomb, with a picture of Rita Hayworth pasted proudly on its side, exploded in the midst of a fleet of seventy-three ships, floating like clay ducks on a huge atomic firing range. This was no anxious, covert test like the one at Los Alamos nine months before. A large crowd of newsmen, Congressmen, and representatives of foreign governments, including the USSR, stood on the skydeck of an observation ship and watched the big bomb boil the water into a great cloud of fire and foam.

The Bikini tests had been announced more than a half year earlier during December of 1945 and zealously debated since. The Navy had requested these tests originally and argued most strenuously for their relevance as the chorus of public criticism rose.[1] Naval planners had been just as jolted by Hiroshima as the rest of the world. Theirs, however, was a more professional concern. How, they wondered, did the atom bomb affect the role of navies in wartime? Such questions assumed the failure of the negotiations at the United Nations. Most of the military expected such an end. But their request for atomic tests at sea was made quite apart from the realm of international diplomacy. They were specialists with narrow vision, operating in an area where the personal and national risks of unpreparedness were unnerving.

Many civilians, including high government officers like the Secretary of Commerce, Henry Wallace, however, were displeased that the United States would first pledge itself to abolition of atomic weapons and then proceed with tests that prepared for atomic war. At a Cabinet meeting on March 22, 1946, Wallace argued that the Bikini tests, which were scheduled for sometime that spring, should be postponed until the Christmas holidays when the Congressmen who were to observe the explosion would be free to travel to the Pacific and when the negotiations at the United Nations would have enjoyed the opportunity to proceed without any implication of atomic intimidation by America. He also wondered why it was necessary to do any more than deep underwater testing. Forrestal came quickly to the defense. Only "months of continuous effort" could give the Navy the kind of information it needed; it was mandatory to have some shallow water tests because "ships were in port a large part of the time, even in war, and it was desired to find out what would happen to a group of ships under those conditions." Vice Admiral Blandy, the Bikini task force commander, added that he would lose his scientists by September when many of them planned to return to university teaching. The tests must occur earlier. Secretary of the Interior Krug was of the same mind as Wallace. He suggested that the scientists would come back at Christmastime if they were offered adequate salaries. Secretary of State Byrnes, whose duty it was to trouble over negotiations at the United Nations and not just military prepared-ness, asked Blandy how crucial the scheduled tests were. "Very," was the Admiral's answer. The Navy was not the only branch of the armed services that felt that way, he added. The Air Force, for one, was particularly interested in testing the prospects of employing atomic weapons from the air on enemy ships. In the end, of course, the decision was President Truman's. He made it without hesitation and also apparently without much considera-tion of the tests' probable impact on international negotiations. The tests should occur as soon as possible, which Truman judged to be July 1, since Congress would probably be able to free its members for observation by then. No further objections were made at that Cabinet meeting, and Blandy turned his oper-ation toward the target date which Truman had established.

Senator James Huffman, a freshman Democrat from Ohio, rose in Congress on the next day, March 23, to introduce a resolution prohibiting all atomic tests, because the world did not "need any more evidence of the weapons' effectiveness." Huffman and those who sided with him, like Senator Scott Lucas, worried that the tests would inevitably diminish the trust which other nations, especially the Soviet Union, felt toward America in atomic matters and would thereby lessen the possibility of international accord. The coincidence of the Bikini tests with the deliberations at the United Nations, Senator Huffman said, would make it look as if the United States was brandishing its nuclear sword to frighten the Russians into a treaty.

There is little reason to believe that this was, in fact, the American motivation. The stimulus appears to have been com-pletely military and not at all diplomatic, and therein lies the tragedy. The most predictable result of the testing at Bikini was not that it would terrify the Russians, but that it would accelerate their already active drive to achieve nuclear capability. The tests would also give the Soviet propaganda machine a fine source of commentary and criticism of American motives.

New Times began the campaign in March, when Modest Rubinstein portrayed the coming Bikini tests as the best example of "jingling with atomic arms." The American press, he reported, had urged that foreign observers be invited to Bikini "to instill fright of the atom bomb." British newspapers were also generally unhappy, condemning the tests at Bikini as "playing with fire." In a magnificent demonstration of the British capacity for paternalism more than 150 years after the American colonies had declared their independence, the *Manchester Guardian* wrote of Bikini: "There is something a trifle irresponsible which may be due to a certain boyishness in the American character in the United States Navy's unconcealed enjoyment of the business." [2]

The Bikini tests turned out to be something of a military disappointment as well as a diplomatic disaster. Only five of the seventy-three ships went down, although there were fires burning on many of the other vessels. Later reports gave more detailed evidence of the destruction and sustained respect for the weapon. The second test, on July 25, took place beneath the surface and was more visually impressive. But the fact that the explosions did not bring extraordinary destruction to the Pacific seemed to make the weapon a more ordinary source of fear in the minds of many and lessened anxiety over the atomic future. The year's time that had passed since Hiroshima had also helped to lessen popular fear of the bomb.

Pravda had a different view of the results, charging that the failure of the Bikini tests to cause as much destruction as expected had disappointed "the warmongering, blood-thirsty American public." After Bikini, *Pravda* continued, Russians could no longer believe in the good intentions of the United States. There was no doubt in the minds of the Russian commentators that the tests were meant to coincide with negotiations at the United Nations and showed that the United States was aiming not at restriction of the atomic bomb but at its perfection.[3]

One of the Soviet observers at Bikini, Professor Simon Peter Alexandrov of the Moscow Institute of Non-Ferrous Metals and Gold, explained to reporters in San Francisco that he had been sent to watch the Pacific explosion because "the Soviet government is planning sometime to have a demonstration of the atom bomb. I was sent to Bikini to see how it was carried out." When would the test occur? "In the measurable future," was Alexandrov's response. "I do not know whether we have an atom bomb right now," he added. "Perhaps we have. Perhaps we have not. But I believe that very soon we will have everything that you have in the United States. We have worked for many years on atomic energy and I guess that we shall soon have atomic energy . . . Russia has the raw materials and the personnel." [4]

Vice Admiral Blandy came back from the Pacific in a different mood. The tests had apparently convinced him of the need to abolish both war and atomic weapons. Until that was done, however, he favored periodic nuclear tests. "We're not going to accept a Kellogg-Briand Treaty, where nations agree they won't use it. I mean a practical plan such as the United States is demanding." And, Secretary Forrestal, who was at Blandy's side, added firmly, "An enforceable one." [5]

More than a month later, during the first week in September, President Truman announced that the third Bikini test, scheduled for March 1947, was going to be postponed for reasons of "economy, secrecy, and the international negotiations going on at the United Nations," a rather belated recognition of the unfortunate diplomatic consequences of these military exercises.

*

Although the atomic explosions at Bikini probably helped confirm Soviet distrust of the United States, it is doubtful that those ill-timed tests seriously affected either Russia's urgent quest for atomic capability or her strategy at the United Nations Atomic Energy Commission. On those two issues, the Bikini tests merely offered confirmation of decisions which had already been made within the Kremlin. One wonders, however, whether the tests contributed to the distemper which Andrei Gromyko exhibited at the first meeting of Subcommittee One in the Grand Ballroom of the Henry Hudson Hotel in New York on the afternoon of July 1, 1946.[6] Unlike Baruch, Gromyko made it a practice to sit personally on every committee and subcommittee of the United Nations Atomic Energy Commission. Baruch was represented that day by his assistant, Ferdinand Eberstadt, the investment banker who was once described by a friend as "a man whose manner is pleasantly abrasive, like a rough towel after a cold shower." The chairman, Herbert Evatt of Australia, opened the meeting by offering a series of topics for discussion. In sum, these looked very much like the Baruch Plan. Atomic war must be prohibited, Evatt declared, but only if there were adequate safeguards.

That was not the agenda Gromyko had in mind. Interrupting Evatt's presentation, the Russian representative argued that the commission could not move toward an international agency and safeguards until the nations of the world had first joined in a treaty prohibiting atomic weapons. He added that he could never accept the American plan because it contradicted the United Nations Charter by sidestepping the Security Council and abolishing the veto. With an eye on the morning's reports from Bikini, Gromyko demanded that Eberstadt explain why the United States was still manufacturing atomic bombs. "The United States," Eberstadt said calmly "was as anxious as any other Government to dispose of these bombs but differed on the effective measures to be taken."

Over the next two weeks, Eberstadt and the other American representatives consistently refused to match the fire of Gromyko's oratory or allow themselves to seem flustered by the increasingly obvious breach with the Soviet Union. Instead, the Americans placed three memorandums before Subcommittee One, each expanding on a central theme of the Baruch Plan. Baruch hoped in this way to elicit a response from the Soviet Union which was more delineated than Gromyko's simple continuing call for an international convention to outlaw atomic weapons.

Eberstadt introduced the first of these memorandums at the second meeting of Subcommittee One on July 2, 1946. Bowing slightly to Gromyko's concerns, this memorandum discussed the kind of international treaty which the United States would support. It went far beyond Gromyko's conception, however, and included transitional stages, inspection, a definition of violations, and international control of uranium and thorium as well as atomic production facilities. Eberstadt also emphasized the importance of granting the international agency "unhindered access to, and power to control, license and inspect all other facilities which possess, utilize, or produce materials which are a source of atomic energy." [7] Also listed for coverage in the proposed treaty was the "legal capacity and privileges and immunities of the Authority in the territory of each signatory State . . . [and the] measures to insure adequate protection and strategic location of the premises and property of the Authority."

The second memo, presented on Friday morning, July 5, explained the functions of the proposed Atomic Development Authority. In its specifics, this document borrowed liberally from the detailed work of the Acheson-Lilienthal committee, including the reliance on uranium and thorium, the distinction between safe and dangerous activities, and the subordination of national controls to international development. On this occasion, Gromyko had a number of questions to ask. Would the atomic authority's installations be distributed evenly throughout the world? Would it be necessary to have many inspectors? Why did the United States not find it possible to accept an international convention outlawing atomic weapons? Eberstadt's answers were measured and revealed a considerable desire to please. Atomic facilities would definitely have to be fairly distributed throughout the world and the treaty must establish some standards for doing this. The American plan would minimize the number of roving inspectors necessary. The United States was not willing to go ahead and speedily abolish atomic weapons because the Kellogg-Briand Pact had demonstrated the foolishness of such a course. Evatt added his opinion that such one-sided atomic disarmament would never be accepted by the American public or its Senators in Washington.[8]

The third memo was presented on July 12 and concerned the relationship between the proposed Atomic Development Authority and the other organs of the United Nations. It sought to make clear that Baruch's call for an end to the veto in atomic energy affairs would have no bearing on the other activities of the United Nations. By specifying three different classifications of violations, the American delegation hoped to build some bridge between its ideas and the Soviet position. The first type of offense was described as "administrative" and could be acted upon by the Atomic Development Authority itself. The second class of violation was more serious but still not of sufficient gravity to threaten the peace of the world. Deciding whether there had been a violation would be the authority's responsibility, subject to review either by an independent board or by the International Court of Justice. Enforcement decisions in this second category of violations would be made by the Security Council in a majority vote. The third type of offense would cover the most serious breaches and threats to the peace. These would be acted upon by the Security Council in a majority vote. According to the American memorandum, the United Nations veto was "an instrument for the protection of nations, not a shield behind which deception and criminal acts can be performed with impunity." The Baruch Plan "in no way impairs the doctrine of unanimity," Eberstadt declared. "No state need be an unwilling party to the treaty . . . Such undertakings would become illusory if the guarantee against their breach resided solely in the conscience of the one who commits the breach . . . This in no manner impairs or diminishes the power or the *modus operandi* of the Security Council in any other situation." [9]

In the five meetings of Subcommittee One which were held during the first two weeks in July, Eberstadt and Evatt fared badly in their attempts to force Gromyko to describe what he viewed as an adequate or reasonable system of safeguards. When Evatt asked Gromyko the direct question of whether he was for an international atomic agency, the Russian said that "it was not of the first importance to decide this question." First, the international convention outlawing atomic weapons must be enacted. Eberstadt then asked whether Gromyko thought the international authority would be a sensible second step. "This question should be considered later," was the Russian's answer. Now Eberstadt was prepared to be blunt. The United States could never accept the simple prohibition of atomic weapons before, or without, safeguards and control, he said flatly.

If the work of Subcommittee One did not make clear exactly what the Russians would accept, it had aired the American plan and demonstrated that it was unacceptable to the Soviet Union. While this activity was proceeding in Subcommittee One, the

Russians caused a series of minor disturbances over procedural questions in the full Atomic Energy Commission which had continued to meet. Evatt had proposed that the commission act by majority vote. Gromyko objected, asking for a two-thirds vote. An angry debate followed, even though any action taken by the commission would have to go before the Security Council before it was finally accepted and there, of course, the Soviet Union still enjoyed the veto. Finally, Gromyko acceded to the majority vote principle. It is a measure of the gloominess which had slowly pervaded the process that even this small Soviet concession was applauded by the *New York Times* as "the most hopeful omen thus far."

With progress nonexistent and his own term as rotating chairman coming to an end, Evatt proposed to the full commission on July 12 that it temporarily leave the political obstacles behind and form committees to pursue technical questions which might reveal some grounds of agreement. Looking back at the weeks of discussion, Evatt said that, although a majority of Subcommittee One had expressed agreement with the American plan, Mr. Gromyko objected to the international agency and the abolition of the veto. Therefore, Evatt concluded, a drafting committee such as Subcommittee One was premature. He suggested three new committees of the whole: a Scientific and Technical Committee, a Legal Committee, and a Committee on Controls. Only the first of the three was voted upon favorably by the Soviet Union. Gromyko objected to the proposal for a Legal Committee on the ground that it was unnecessary. Since the main questions were still political and technical, there was no need for legal assistance, he said. It seemed too close to the drafting stage for the Russian representative. Poland joined the Soviet Union in abstaining from the vote to create this committee. The Committee on Controls, proposed by Evatt, displeased Gromyko even more. He insisted that the jurisdiction of this committee be described in such a way as to embrace the Russian suggestion of an international convention. Evatt tried to rephrase his proposal to include this possibility and even changed the name of this body to Committee Two to avoid any mention of controls but Russia and Poland still voted no. Each of the other nine member nations voted yes. Throughout the meeting Gromyko and Evatt hurled unhappy charges and innuendoes at one another. At the end, Baruch praised the fiery Australian for the job he had done as chairman and said that he was "happy to find that his report conforms basically to the United States proposals which I had the honor to submit to the primary meeting on June 14." [10]

As the Soviet-American breach grew ever wider, some of the other members of the United Nations Atomic Energy Commission began to talk with the American delegation about the possibility of compromise on some parts of the Baruch Plan. One diplomat privately proposed a system of national atomic controls in which international inspection was limited to the records and reports of the national control bodies. To this and more reasonable suggestions, the Americans offered absolute resistance. "I fear," John Hancock said, "that if we once start even an orderly retreat on minor points, we may well be facing a rout later on." [11] Word of these pressures toward compromise reached President Truman and he quickly wrote to Baruch that "we should stand pat on our program." Expressing confidence that Baruch and he "understood each other on this subject," Truman said that he believed "that we should not under any circumstances throw away our gun until we are sure the rest of the world can't arm against us." [12]

Evatt's hope of avoiding some of the problems of Subcommittee One by breaking into new specialized committees was never realized. In their earliest efforts these new committees did nothing but draw out more disagreement.

The amorphously titled Committee Two was the first to begin deliberating. As John Hancock said privately to Fred Searls at that time, little could be expected in the way of substantive agreement from a committee that had expended so much bitter energy in deciding what its name should be.[13] Committee Two moved immediately, as if guided by some death wish, to the same discussions that had crippled Subcommittee One. Evatt's hope that they would move on to detail was forgotten in a Niagara of political charges and countercharges.

On July 24, at the second meeting of Committee Two, even the most optimistic observers lost hope. Gromyko chose that day to offer his government's first specific response to the Baruch Plan, which had been presented almost six weeks before. Like so many other expressions of Soviet policy, this one was foreshadowed during the preceding week by an article in a Soviet journal, "Soviet Russia Today." It stated that neither France nor the Soviet Union would need more than a few years to develop atomic energy and predicted, therefore, that neither of them would approve the United States proposals for a timetable "of gradual surrender of atomic information." The Soviet Union and France desired atomic energy as a power resource and for industrial modernization — a fact which could not be understood by "American industrialists such as Mr. Baruch and his principal advisers," the magazine said. The Soviet position was stated bluntly:

> No country which desires atomic energy and is independently capable of getting it by 1949 will consider an Atomic Development Authority, which, through its process of stages, would postpone the event for many years, as the Baruch proposal would require.[14]

Gromyko's unsettling speech at the United Nations on July 24 coincided with the second atomic test of the Bikini series, therefore giving the headline writers of the *New York Times* the opportunity to string a banner three columns long across their front page, the first two proclaiming the world's fifth atomic explosion, and the third announcing, "Soviet Flatly Rejects Baruch Control Plan." That, in fact, is just what the Russian representative did. "The United States proposals in their present form cannot be accepted in any way by the Soviet Union either as a whole or in separate parts," Gromyko declared. Technically, he confined himself to discussion of the third memorandum which the United States had submitted on July 12, but his words left no room for doubt that he was rejecting the entire Baruch Plan. The veto question received special consideration: "I should like to make clear again the position of the Soviet Union that we cannot accept any proposals that would undermine in any degree the principle of the unanimity of the permanent members of the Security Council in the maintenance of peace and security . . . It would be dangerous and maybe fatal to undermine this principle . . . The great powers . . . will provide the main means against aggression." The Soviet Union believed that the existing organs of the United Nations were capable of dealing with atomic energy. There was no need for any new autonomous authorities. "The Authority which the United States proposes," Gromyko said, "cannot be reconciled with the Charter of the United Nations."

He saved equal fire for the broader American notion of international control and inspection. The argument he propounded was new and came as "a surprise and a shock" to the members of the committee. To propose as the Americans had done that "matters related to atomic energy should be considered as matters of international and not of national importance" would be, according to Gromyko, a violation of Article 2, Paragraph 7 of the United Nations Charter which protected member states against interference in their internal matters. He declared:

When the Charter of the United Nations was prepared by the conference at San Francisco, the question of sovereignty was one of the most important questions considered. This principle of sovereignty is one of the cornerstones on which the United Nations structure is built; if this were touched the whole existence and future of the United Nations would be threatened.

When Gromyko finished, Captain Alvara Alberto, the representative from Brazil who was serving as chairman, could only say that he hoped all nations would consider the atomic problem "in the interests of humanity." He then quickly adjourned the meeting. Baruch was away at one of his vacation retreats that day; John Hancock had sat, without comment, in his place at the meeting. Only Herbert Swope eschewed silence. Gromyko's statement, Swope said afterward to the press, "expresses the view of only one and possibly two of the twelve members of the Security Council, and it will be interesting to see how many of the fifty-one countries composing the United Nations take the American view and how many the Soviet view." The *New York Times* had a one-word description for the Russian statement: "amazing." [15] John Hancock deemed it proper to report personally to Secretary of State Byrnes later that day on this most comprehensive articulation of Russia's atomic control policy. Not wanting to alarm Byrnes, Hancock said that "there wasn't anything unexpected in the speech and there wasn't any new problem presented by it." [16] Nevertheless, on the following afternoon he summoned representatives of the British, French, Canadian, and Australian delegations to a strategy conference. They agreed to continue their plan of questioning Gromyko to establish a record. The Canadian representative, General A. L. McNaughton, urged that their questions "be carefully phrased with the thought in mind that the record would be sent to Moscow and that it might influence the people who call the plays there." [17]

Two days later, Gromyko spoke out loudly again in Committee Two presenting what he described as a new Russian plan. It was, however, no more than a restatement of his original call for an international convention. It punctured the optimism of those who had viewed his statement on July 24 as a temporary tactical maneuver from which the Russians would recede. His words of attack were, if anything, less restrained: "The Soviet proposal has, compared to those of other countries which may on the surface appear to be radical but cannot carry us to our goal, the merit of being a practical one, providing for immediate and practical steps towards control over atomic energy." He also criticized the United States for its continued production of atomic weapons, describing this as inconsistent with the "task of using atomic energy for peaceful purposes only and with the spirit and principles of the United Nations."

John Hancock was nevertheless still willing to be cordial and hopeful. He agreed with Gromyko that a treaty was important but how would the Russian go from that to a workable, effective program? Dr. Eelco N. VonKleffens, the representative of the Netherlands, chose this same day to end the neutrality of his country on the atomic question. Mere prohibition was simply not enough, he said, there had to be some safeguards and a control system. To prove his point, and thereby the insufficiency of the Soviet proposal, VonKleffens went back to 1868 and cited a series of international conventions which had failed because they had no provisions to guarantee their observance and no sanctions to punish those who were not faithful. The Soviet proposal was quite sound in principle, VonKleffens said, but it "needs considerable elaboration if it is to have a practical effect." [18]

Evatt of Australia and General McNaughton of Canada pursued Gromyko at the next meeting of Committee Two on July

31, trying to induce him to articulate some more detailed and acceptable scheme of Soviet control. McNaughton said he believed that the Soviet proposal assumed the eventual establishment of inspection or some other form of safeguards, adding his hope that Gromyko would elaborate on this point. But Gromyko was not in the mood for conciliation: "The idea of inspection of atomic energy is greatly exaggerated in importance. It is a too superficial understanding of the problem of control . . . No inspection as such can guarantee peace and security . . . The guarantee . . . lies only in the genuine desire of the members of the United Nations to cooperate to that end."

Each time the delegates asked a question of Gromyko, he disappointed them with an even more divisive statement of the Russian position. Now the Mexican delegate, Luis Padilla Nervo, had an idea. It was crucial to have safeguards, but what kind of safeguards and when? That was a technical question, so why not have the Scientific and Technical Committee consider it and report back to the full group? Alexandre Parodi of France, relieved to see some path that would take them away from the troubled ground of political controversy, immediately endorsed Nervo's proposal. It was even possible that the Scientific Committee could come back with technical answers that would hurdle some of the most difficult stumbling blocks, including national sovereignty, Parodi said. John Hancock, however, was not pleased with the idea; he worried that a scientific investigation would derail the Atomic Energy Commission for months. It seemed to him like simple avoidance, without cause or hope, of the most difficult issues that would have to be faced if there was ever to be an agreement. But Hancock found it difficult in these circumstances to raise public objections to the idea; Gromyko went along too, not at all unhappy with the possible delay.[19]

As if to ratify this change in direction, the members of Committee Two spent August 6, the first anniversary of Hiroshima, in so bitter and fruitless a debate on the same old issues that finally R. L. Harry, representing Australia, suggested that the meetings of the group be suspended until the Scientific and Technical Committee reported back. There was no objection, and so Committee Two went to a temporary and unpeaceful rest.[20]

18

Henry Wallace and the American Consensus

AT THE BEGINNING of August 1946, the members of the Scientific and Technical Committee were the only people associated with the United Nations Atomic Energy Commission who were actively at work. Everyone else enjoyed time to reflect on the first month and a half of the commission's existence. Bernard Baruch retreated to Camp Uncas, a spacious and luxurious lodge at Raquette Lake, New York, in the Adirondacks, built originally by J. P. Morgan, Sr. The baron was alone there, except, that is, for his valet, cook, nurse, and chauffeur. In time, Baruch felt the need to discuss his atomic mission with someone and so he wired David Lilienthal, asking him to come to Camp Uncas "to talk over atomic control for which you have done so much." Lilienthal responded in kind, accepting the invitation, as he put it, "in the hope that I can be of help to you, however slight, in your great task." [1] In the pastoral isolation of that setting, the previous coolness between these two eminent men ended.

Baruch and Lilienthal spent July 29 and 30 sitting on the hard ground, looking out at the lake, discussing many things but particularly the problems of atomic energy control. Baruch was not discouraged by the Russian posture, which Lilienthal had publicly attacked as "dewey-eyed, naive, and ignorant of the realities of human nature." Perhaps Baruch had long since lost any genuine optimism in the possibility of agreement with the Russians. In any case, he now told Lilienthal that he was convinced that "Gromyko understands the veto" and that "his real objection isn't the veto but rather the whole idea of permitting their country to be subjected to inspection from without." If this was so, the chances were indeed slim, for what could happen to change the Russian mind on that fundamental question? Baruch made it clear to Lilienthal that he appreciated the tragedy of failing to reach agreement, and that he had no illusions whatsoever about a final 10–2 vote being a major personal triumph. It would be the best he could do under the circumstances — a dramatization, Baruch believed, of the fact that Russia stood as an intransigent minority, thwarting the will of the majority of the world's nations.[2]

John Hancock was also involved in reflection during this summer respite from negotiation. His thoughts eventually went into a rambling memorandum for the American staff, which reveals all the mixed pessimism, optimism, self-protectiveness, idealism, and chauvinism that characterized America's entire atomic control policy:

> Russia was a good ally during the war . . . She is now treating us as an enemy and is asking us to give up our arms without proposing to give up any of her own . . . This is unilateral disarmament. Gromyko asks why the United States produces bombs if we have good intentions. We believe we are firm in our good intentions. Most of the world is satisfied we are . . . I don't think there is undue self-righteousness in asserting that our promises regarding atomic weapons will be kept . . .
> [Gromyko's plan is like] a poker game where the money is paid over on a mere statement by each player as to what hand he held.

Pierre Auger of France had spoken with Hancock of America's continued manufacture of atomic bombs, claiming that the world would feel much better if the United States ceased such production. Of this proposal, Hancock wrote:

I query as to why it would feel better and how much better it would feel. It probably wouldn't take our word in either event. He [Auger] doesn't know how many bombs we have or how fast we are making them. We would face an impossible problem if we promised to quit for a time and then had to resume. The main fact is that he is afraid of the bomb and I see no reason for him to have added fears because of our continuing to make the bomb.

Of Gromyko's anxiety over a loss of sovereignty to the Atomic Development Authority, Hancock thought:

Sovereignty is the right of a nation to exercise its own free will. It seems impossible for anyone to argue that any infringement of sovereignty is dangerous.

Hancock also had some ideas about strategy:

Our objective now is to work out an agreement with the Russians and to get as a result of it a workable plan. We are not to discuss nor give any thought to alternate plans which might come into effect should we fail on this first effort . . . I think we are in the position of fighting through on our present line without waivering.[3]

In New York during early August, Ferdinand Eberstadt had finished his reflections and decided to put his pessimistic conclusions to a test. Along with Swope, Eberstadt would have to be considered least likely on Baruch's staff to believe that the Russians would ever agree to what the United States required as minimum conditions. Now, he went to Andrei Gromyko's quarters, where he was received courteously. No time was wasted before Eberstadt got to the point: "If you are prepared to accept a plan, the details are not really important. If not, our only problem is when to quit." This time, Gromyko avoided circumspection, finishing Eberstadt's sentence with two devastating words: "And how." [4]

Eberstadt found Baruch quickly and told him the story. "Boss," he said heatedly, "this thing is a short sale. I want to get out." Baruch disagreed. Perhaps, the baron mused, the Russians did not yet understand the American plan. Eberstadt was convinced that they did, however, "a damn sight better than either the French or the English." Baruch had other reasons for not wanting to draw the struggle to an abrupt halt. "We can't do that," he told Eberstadt. "We must go on until the people generally come to the opinion we have." The baron was not going to quit until he felt it was clear to the world that the Russians, and not the Americans, were responsible for mankind's failure to control atomic energy.[5]

The labors of the Atomic Energy Commission proceeded privately throughout August. Prohibited from political considerations, the Scientific and Technical Committee moved easily through the exercise of examining scientific facts and arriving at scientific conclusions. In the absence of open dialogue there was no controversy, and therefore the delegates were able to be optimistic. Dr. VonKleffens of the Netherlands told an American radio audience that "the scientists are able to steer clear of political problems. They deal only with what is possible and technically feasible. When they finish their job, then it will be up to us to translate their plan into political reality." [6] In Washington, the impasse had drawn another response. Secretary of War Robert Patterson opened a series of lectures for key Army personnel on atomic energy, explaining coincidentally that he was squarely in favor of the Baruch Plan, but that "those responsible for the defense of the nation must make their plans on the basis that there is and will be no adequate control on the international level . . . this until the time when we may be directed by the Congress to plan on another basis." [7]

At the United Nations, during the early weeks of August 1946, pressure was building within Baruch's staff to force an early break with the Soviet Union. Men like Herbert Swope had seen

enough to arrive at some conclusions about where it was all going to end. They worried that the longer the United States waited
the less advantageous would be its ultimate position. In response
to a memo from Swope which made this argument, John Hancock still counseled patience:

> I agree with you that the time has passed for arguments about
> committees and their tasks . . . I think we have to allow Gromyko
> time to carry the developments here back to the Soviet and then we
> have to wait until an altered position comes from their head-
> quarters . . .
> I think we would make a fatal mistake if we were to think of
> American opinion as the first objective . . .
> We can break off any day but if we were to start drawing lines
> at this moment, I think we would lose every bit of American
> support which I think we now enjoy.[8]

To Swope and anyone else urging a confrontation at that
time, Hancock recalled a story from Uncle Remus, analogizing
the United States to Brer Rabbit who was chased by a bunch
of hounds inside a fenced-in area and finally saved himself by
climbing a tree. A boy listening to Uncle Remus tell this tale
asked, "Yes, but a little rabbit can't climb a tree." To which,
Uncle Remus responded: "That's right sonny, but this rabbit
was just 'bliged to climb that tree." And so, Hancock would say,
was the American delegation just obliged to achieve international
control according to the Baruch Plan.[9]

Sensing the crosscurrents of opinion within the American
delegation, Bernard Baruch called together his full staff for a
review and planning session on Friday, August 23, 1946.[10]
Baruch began the discussion. He had called the meeting to discuss their future course and the relation of their work to the
world situation. Hancock then reported on several recent conversations, including one with Senator McMahon, who had

warned that no final vote should occur on the question of international atomic control until at least a year had passed; otherwise Baruch and his team would lose public support. The French delegate, Alexandre Parodi, had told Hancock at lunch a few days before that the commission should recess so that all the representatives could return home to consult with their governments. The British, Hancock continued, felt the same way. These admonitions drew a predictable response. As far as Fred Searls was concerned, "it would soon be time to bring into sharper relief the basic political problems." He advocated the early submission of a draft charter for the Atomic Development Authority as well as a progress report on the work of the UNAEC. Ferdinand Eberstadt could see in the history of the negotiations thus far "no prospect of a unanimous report" and argued that "interminable dragging out of procedures would reflect only discredit on the Atomic Energy Commission." Baruch's scientific adviser, Richard Tolman, who had been the busiest member of the American delegation in the preceding weeks because of his work on the Scientific and Technical Committee, now interrupted with a word of optimism. His committee was moving smoothly toward a report. The first two chapters of it, Tolman said, would be "a diluted version of the Smyth Report," and the last two chapters would be "a diluted version of the Lilienthal Report"; but, nevertheless, when it was done it would be an official Atomic Energy Commission document. The Russian members of the committee had been generally independent and cooperative, Tolman continued, to the point of even disagreeing with one another.

General Groves spoke next, urging some final vote on the issues before Poland became chairman of the commission, early in 1947. Herbert Swope took Groves's statement as a cue for an oratorical explosion. Delay and toleration amounted to appeasement, he declared. "By prolonging negotiations, we play into the hands of the Russians." Timing was a more important virtue in this case than unanimity. The American delegation should be moving right then toward a showdown, Swope concluded. Only Albin Johnson, a junior member of the staff, responded to Swope. He urged that Baruch go slowly. The focus of the world attention was on the reconvened Foreign Ministers conference in Paris. Johnson advised Baruch to wait and see how events in Paris developed before taking any drastic steps at the United Nations.

Johnson's position was the one Baruch chose. The tempo must not be hurried, he concluded. Therefore, the preoccupation of the Scientific and Technical Committee was not an undesirable circumstance. Gromyko must not be made to feel that the rest of the countries were pushing him into a corner, and, of course, world opinion could not be allowed to view the work of the Atomic Energy Commission in that way. Baruch himself would not be at ease unless he felt that he had made the strongest effort (consistent, of course, with his own view of the national security) to secure an atomic control treaty. He also believed that public opinion was moving away from the Soviets and toward the United States. Time was on his side. "The great thing Bernie did," Eberstadt later said, "was to prevent us from being victimized." [11]

Early in September, the Scientific and Technical Committee realized everyone's highest hopes and announced that after sixteen informal private sessions, it had reached an agreement. Using the factual data found in the Smyth and Acheson-Lilienthal Reports, the committee had considered several possible forms of atomic control. To the specific question of "whether effective control of atomic energy is possible," which had been asked by Committee Two, the Scientific and Technical Committee gave a guarded but positive answer:

We do not find any basis in the available scientific facts for concluding that effective control is not technologically feasible. Whether or not it is politically feasible is not discussed or implied in this report, nor is there any recommendation of the particular system or systems by which effective control can be achieved.[12]

At each stage of the committee's deliberations, all of the members, including the Russian representative, Professor Skobeltsyn, had expressed their agreement. When the Soviet Union cast its formal vote for the report, it would have admitted to the feasibility, if not the desirability, of an international atomic control system. But not even that limited progress was to be achieved without considerable struggle and suspense.

The final meeting of the Scientific and Technical Committee was scheduled for Friday, September 6. That day, the committee was to give formal approval to its completed report. Then, on September 3, the Soviet delegation announced that their scientific representative, Professor Skobeltsyn, had been called home to Russia, purportedly as part of a routine change in personnel. He was to be replaced by Professor Alexandrov, the man who had witnessed the explosions at Bikini and then announced the imminence of a Soviet nuclear weapon. But, when Friday, September 6, came, Alexandrov asked for a postponement, explaining that he needed more time. Gromyko had been too busy in the Security Council to read the Scientific and Technical Committee's report, Alexandrov explained, and therefore could not give his permission for an affirmative vote. The meeting was rescheduled for the following Monday, September 9, but instead of assembling and announcing their agreement, on that day a brief statement was issued by the United Nations Secretariat, revealing that the session had been postponed because "not all members of the committee have been authorized as yet to cast their votes." The scientific report had apparently gone further than Gromyko desired. The political impasse had intruded itself upon the supposedly nonpolitical scientific exploration.

This turn of events bothered Baruch. He wondered now whether the policy of patience which he had chosen was best. On Tuesday morning, September 10, he called his full staff together once more.[13] He had decided it was necessary to go to the President with the facts and ask for instructions. To Baruch, it had become "obvious that the Atomic Energy Commission negotiations are now only a sideshow in the international picture." The side show must be tied in with the main rings of the circus, he said. Perhaps the Baruch team should merely become advisory to the State Department, because if the United States was to adopt a "temporizing procedure, this might better be carried out by the bureaucrats." Searls agreed, but he wanted Baruch to do more than merely set the problem before the President. He asked Baruch to recommend quite explicitly that there be a showdown vote within the Atomic Energy Commission at the earliest possible date.

Hancock, Searls, and finally Baruch also agreed that the letter to Truman must contain a strong plea that the United States prepare itself militarily for the now inevitable day when the atomic control negotiations would break down. One of the advantages to an early Russian-American atomic breach, Eberstadt argued, was "that the public would be aroused to the danger that confronts us and the world and it would result in widespread popular support for military preparedness."

Now Baruch worried that some of America's closest allies might not go along with the American strategy of a confrontation. Eberstadt agreed that the British, French, and Canadians had all "indicated pretty clearly that they do not want the issue forced." If it was, however, he was confident that they could be pressured into going along. By the end of the meeting, Baruch and his assistants had agreed that they should put the two alternatives before the President and argue for a showdown before January 1 unless there was some dramatic change in the Russian posture.

On September 13, Eberstadt offered Baruch a small additional incentive to reaffirm this decision when he told the baron that one good reason for "moving to a climax" was that otherwise the people following the deliberations of the Atomic Energy Commission were likely "to express the opinion that no progress is being made and to vent their spleen on the Commission generally and possibly on individual members." [14] By September 17, Swope had put the finishing touches on Baruch's letter to Truman. It would be hand-delivered by the baron himself on the following day. The letter described the depth of the deadlock at the United Nations, as Baruch saw it, and included an admission by him that the dreams of world disarmament which he had entertained such a short time before were without foundation. He now saw no chance of securing an agreement with the Soviet Union on the most basic questions of atomic energy control. Therefore, there were two paths the United States could follow. One would be to bring the American proposal to a vote as soon as practical. The result would undoubtedly be 10–2 in favor, of the Baruch Plan. This would bring the world no closer to atomic energy control but might put the Soviet Union on the defensive. The other option was to avoid a break by recessing the Atomic Energy Commission and reconvening it only when and if the course of international diplomacy made such a step hopeful. Baruch's own recommendation was to continue the policy of patience and technical exploration but only for a month or two. If the President thought that the matter should then be forced to a vote, that should be done before January 1, 1947, because on that day, according to the rotating system of commission membership, three nations — Egypt, Mexico, and the Netherlands — would go off the commission. All three had stood firmly with Baruch behind the American plan. Whether the same could be said for the probable replacements, Belgium, Columbia, and Syria, was not clear. In any case, the new members, with Gromyko's certain support, would reasonably ask for an extended period of time to familiarize themselves with the commission's work before being able to vote. Baruch added one other note to Truman, which derived logically from his gloomy report. The United States must continue to build atomic bombs and strengthen its nuclear arsenal so that it would be fully prepared when the final break in negotiations came.[15]

If Baruch's decision to wait awhile and then bring his plan to a vote within the United Nations was to be a success, he would have to have unified support not only from the ten non-Communist members of the Atomic Energy Commission but also from the American public. No attempt to paint the Soviet Union as a solitary obstructionist would succeed if there was not agreement among the ten desired nations and the people of America that the Baruch Plan was desirable. At the middle of September 1946, when Baruch signed his letter to the President, such a favorable consensus seemed to exist.

Although the scientists were slightly troubled by Mr. Baruch's tactics and still suspicious of his advisers, they provided no vocal opposition to the Baruch Plan and even gave it halting support. The lay public was less restrained. One poll taken during September showed that 76 percent of the American people favored the Baruch Plan — a remarkable amount of support for a plan which required the presence of foreign inspectors in American factories and seemed to give away the cherished secret of the bomb. Some small voices of dissent had been heard periodically on

Capitol Hill, but these never endangered the prevailing consensus.

On September 12, this harmonious foundation began to crumble at Madison Square Garden in New York.[16] Before a standing-room-only rally sponsored jointly by the National Citizens Political Action Committee and the Independent Citizens Committee of the Arts, Sciences, and Professions, Secretary of Commerce Henry A. Wallace launched a broad-scale attack on the foreign policy of the Administration he served. The "get tough" posture of Secretary of State Byrnes was Wallace's major target. "The tougher we get, the tougher the Russians will get," he said. Calling this no way to handle the most important forces at work in the world, Wallace advocated a policy of recognized spheres of influence, with the Soviet sphere extending beyond what most Americans seemed to think was proper. But his audience that night accepted it all excitedly and even hissed Wallace when he appealed for Soviet understanding of American aims. The speech became more than a small rupture when the former Vice President assured the crowd that President Truman had read his remarks and approved them. Truman had, in fact, seen the speech, but whether he had read it is another question. He later denied having done so. In either case, his support was apparently motivated by a political conclusion that the tone of Wallace's remarks would serve his Administration well in the liberal Democratic circles of New York State. At an informal White House press conference on the afternoon of Wallace's speech, a reporter asked the President whether he approved of his Cabinet member's comments, a copy of which some of the reporters already had received. Truman said he did and quickly went on to the next question. He later explained that what he really meant, and should have said, was that he agreed only that Wallace had the right to make the speech. The State Department had not received a copy until late that afternoon. Their subsequent frantic efforts after six o'clock to have the White House demand that Wallace at least remove the sentence about the President's approval were futile.

Newspapers throughout America, and the rest of the world, gave the Wallace speech front page coverage the next morning. Secretary of State Byrnes, once more in Paris working on the peace treaties, was furious. He felt that Wallace's harangue and Truman's apparent approval had undercut his position. "I tried to avoid delegates to the conference or other foreign ministers," he has said, "because I wanted to avoid answering questions about whether the policy of our government had changed."

Truman tried to douse the fires on September 14 by qualifying and explaining his approval of the Wallace speech and saying that there was no change at all in American foreign policy. He himself fully supported Secretary of State Byrnes. Still the dispute festered. Finally, Truman asked Wallace to the White House for a conference on September 18, but by the time Wallace got there the gap between him and the rest of the Truman Administration had grown much wider.

On the evening of September 17, the Department of Commerce had released copies of a letter Wallace had written to the President on July 23, almost two months before. In it, the Secretary of Commerce had declared his displeasure at the course of American foreign policy. The conduct of the negotiations at the United Nations Atomic Energy Commission came in for special criticism. A spokesman at the Commerce Department explained that the letter was being released because columnist Drew Pearson had somehow obtained a copy of it and was about to begin printing it in his syndicated column. White House Press Secretary Charles Ross had apparently approved the Commerce Department's release of the letter. Truman became irate at the publication of this private, internal correspondence and demanded that

Ross take responsibility for its publication without the approval of the President. But the damage had already been done. Wallace's letter was a more potent and particularized attack on the Baruch Plan than Gromyko had yet managed. It was a twelve-page statement, for whose length Wallace apologized ("Personally, I hate to write long letters and I hate to receive them"). Nevertheless, he proceeded:

> I am even more troubled by the apparently growing feeling among the American people that another war is coming and the only way we can head it off is to arm ourselves to the teeth . . . The months just ahead may well be the crucial period which will decide whether the civilized world will go down in destruction after the five or ten years needed for several nations to arm themselves with atomic bombs.

Wallace predicted that the spread of nuclear weapons would "inevitably result in a neurotic, fear-ridden, itching-trigger psychology in all the peoples of the world." Talk of "preventive war" with atomic weapons, which Wallace claimed he had heard, was "not only immoral but stupid." As he saw it, "The only solution . . . consists of mutual trust and confidence among nations, atomic disarmament, and an effective system of enforcing that disarmament." In spite of what he acknowledged as the "apparent inconsistencies of Russian representatives" in international negotiations, Wallace was convinced that the real obstacle to agreement was a "defect" in the Moscow Declaration, the Acheson-Lilienthal plan, and the Baruch Plan:

> That defect is the scheme . . . of arriving at international agreements by "many stages" . . . We are telling the Russians that if they are "good boys" we may eventually turn over our knowledge to them and to the other nations. But there is no objective standard of what will qualify them as being "good" nor any specified time for sharing our knowledge . . .
>
> Would we have been enthusiastic if the Russians had a monopoly

of atomic energy and offered to share the information with us at
some indefinite time in the future at their discretion if we agreed
now not to try to make a bomb and give them information on
our secret resources of uranium and thorium? I think we would
react as the Russians appear to have done . . . We would put up
counterproposals for the record, but our real efforts would go into
trying to make a bomb so that our bargaining position would be
equalized. That is the essence of the Russian position.

To Wallace, a step-by-step plan "in any such one-sided form
is not workable." The "entire agreement" would have to be
"worked out and wrapped up in a single package." He agreed
that this "may involve certain steps or stages, but the timing of
such steps must be agreed to in the initial master treaty."

Baruch's call for the abolition of the veto in atomic energy
affairs was the other major cause of Wallace's disillusionment:

> The veto issue is completely irrelevant because the proposal to
> abolish the veto . . . has no meaning with respect to a treaty
> on atomic energy . . . Once the treaty is ratified . . . the ques-
> tion of veto becomes meaningless. If any nation violates the treaty
> provision, say of permitting inspection of suspected illegal bomb-
> making activities, what action is there that can be vetoed? As in the
> case of any other treaty violations, the remaining signatory nations
> are free to take what action they feel is necessary including the
> ultimate step of declaring war.

He closed with a sympathetic listing of factors which explained
Russian distrust of the United States, including its history of foreign invasion, and the fact that it was the sole Communist country in a world that was hostile to Communism.

Baruch was in Washington with Hancock on September 18
to give the President his letter on alternative courses of action
in the United Nations. When he awoke to find Wallace's harsh
statement splashed across the newspapers, he became obstreper-
ous. Although he knew that there were those who did not ap-

preciate either his manner or his tactical emphasis on the veto, the baron was unaccustomed to having his good faith challenged as Wallace seemed to have done. He felt that the Commerce Secretary's charge about the stages of transition was inaccurate, because he believed that he had agreed to spell out the stages to transition in a charter written by all the participating nations. The potential damage resulting from Wallace's attack in the midst of the negotiations could only be estimated by Baruch, but his estimates were none too pleasing.

Baruch and Hancock were in a minor state of rage when they called on the Acting Secretary of State, William L. Clayton. He was sympathetic and accompanied them to the White House later that morning. They found the President "very pleasant but grim." Baruch first handed Truman his own letter on the course of negotiations at the United Nations but said that Henry Wallace's letter of July 23 was a more pressing topic of conversation. Andrei Gromyko had told him over a month before, Baruch said, that "we were not aware of the differences in American public opinion, the principle implication of that statement being that it was the Russian plan to propagandize and undermine our position." The President should demand that Wallace reveal the source of his information, Baruch declared, "because it quite obviously came to him from somebody who was trying to preach Red doctrine." In Baruch's view, there were three courses open to the Truman Administration: "a full retraction by Wallace . . . an utter repudiation of his statements by others . . . or that we [Baruch and his staff] resign as our usefulness was ended."

Truman, however, was confident that he could work the problem out short of such drastic alternatives. Asking them not to be in a hurry about resigning, the President said that he was going to see Wallace that afternoon and thought that the action he planned to take would be satisfactory to them. If it was not, then they could put out any statement they wanted. As their allotted time with the President ended, Baruch assured Truman that their position on this matter "was in no ways an ultimatum" but that they "still saw only three courses open." Outside the White House, Baruch and Hancock were asked by reporters for a comment on the Wallace letter. "The President will do all the talking — whatever there is," Baruch told them.[17]

At three-thirty that afternoon, Henry Wallace — full-faced, gray-haired, handsome, and hatless — arrived at the White House. He was alone and grinning. "This is the best show I've seen in a long time," the Secretary said on his way in. Truman had received much advice that day about how to handle his errant Secretary of Commerce. Democratic National Chairman Robert Hannegan had counseled the President to go easy on Wallace or risk offending his considerable legions little more than a month before the Congressional elections.[18] Truman ultimately followed Hannegan's advice. Henry Wallace spent two and a half hours with the President that day, explaining his view of the atomic negotiations with great sincerity and conviction but, as Truman saw it, with little judgment. At the end, the President asked him to limit his criticism to private expressions within the Administration. Wallace was unmoved until Truman documented for him the complications his speech and letter had caused Byrnes in Paris. Finally, Wallace agreed to remain quiet until Byrnes had done his job. Would the Secretary campaign for Democratic candidates in the coming elections? the President asked. No, Wallace said, his silence would be comprehensive. Shortly before six o'clock, Henry Wallace faced reporters outside the White House and happily read a penciled statement to them: "The President and the Secretary of Commerce had a most detailed and friendly discussion after which the Secretary reached the conclusion he would make no public statements or speeches

until the Foreign Ministers' conference in Paris is concluded."
Asked if everything was patched up, Wallace bubbled, "Everything's lovely." Why had he agreed to keep quiet? "Because I am
an honest man." [19]

If this solution pleased Wallace, he was probably the only one
so gladdened. The more typical response was expressed by the
New York Times when it called the Truman-Wallace agreement
"inconclusive and unsatisfactory." From New York, Hancock
talked by phone with Acting Secretary of State Clayton and told
him that no one at the United Nations was satisfied with the
agreement.[20] After an all-day conference with his staff, Baruch
issued a short statement to the press which simply affirmed the
fact that Wallace's blasts had not changed America's approach
to international atomic energy control, as outlined by Baruch on
June 14. Sources within the American delegation let it be known
that Baruch was convinced that no one had ever accurately explained the American plan to Henry Wallace. That morning
Baruch called Wallace and urged him, "in the interest of the
country and of their relationship," to come up to New York
promptly to discuss their disagreement. Baruch said he was as
concerned as Wallace "about the increasing difficulty of seeing
eye to eye with the Russians." When he urged Wallace to consider correcting certain errors of fact in his July 23 letter, the
Secretary replied that "since he had been muzzled by the President he was in no position to make any public statement whatever on this matter." The decision was up to Wallace, Baruch
declared, but if he felt he could not make the corrections himself
then Baruch and his staff would make them publicly for him. In
the end, Wallace agreed to see Baruch in New York on the
coming Sunday, September 22.[21]

From Byrnes in Paris, the response to the Truman-Wallace
détente was more severe. Byrnes believed that Wallace's pledge

not to talk until after Paris did nothing to diminish the doubts among other nations about America's foreign policy. The Secretary of State immediately cabled the President: "If it is not completely clear in your mind that Mr. Wallace should be asked to refrain from criticizing the foreign policy of the United States while he is a member of your cabinet, I must ask you to accept my resignation immediately." Truman tried to reach Byrnes by telephone the next day, but a faulty connection forced them to communicate via teletype. Again, Byrnes stated his position bluntly:

> I respectfully submit that if Mr. Molotov believed that on October 23 there would be a re-examination of the question of permitting Wallace to again attack your policy he would derive great comfort . . . You and I spent 15 months building a bipartisan policy. We did a fine job convincing the world that it was a permanent policy upon which the world could rely. Wallace destroyed that in a day.[22]

Truman considered the problem overnight and then acted decisively. Shortly after ten o'clock, on Friday morning, September 20, the President called his Secretary of Commerce and asked him to resign. If that was Truman's wish, Wallace said, he would naturally comply. It was all very quick and friendly. At 10:50 A.M. Truman read a mimeographed statement to the White House press corps:

> I have today asked Mr. Wallace to resign from the Cabinet. It had become clear that between his views on foreign policy and those of the Administration — the latter being shared, I am confident, by the great body of our citizens — there was a fundamental conflict.

After adding that he thought Wallace would be happier expressing his views as a private citizen, Truman offered a quick "Thank you, gentlemen" and left. It was a complete victory for

Byrnes. That night, Wallace spoke on nationwide radio, insisting that "winning the peace is more important than high public office." [23]

For Baruch, the victory was less than complete because, although Wallace had been removed, no one had yet offered a rebuttal to his claims about atomic energy control. Nor had Wallace altered those allegations in the slightest. Baruch telegraphed the former Secretary, restating his desire to talk with him on Sunday, but Wallace said that now he could not come. Baruch would not accept the answer and finally forced Wallace to agree to a meeting in New York on Friday, September 27. [24]

In the meantime, Baruch put his staff to work on a long memorandum which methodically answered each of Wallace's accusations. It was sent to the President on Tuesday, September 24. On the matter of stages of transition to international control, the memo argued that not only the United States but the Soviet Union had been committed to this concept in the Moscow Declaration. Baruch then quoted statements from his June 14 speech and from two of the subsequent memos which he had presented to the commission, making clear the American belief that the stages should be spelled out in the charter as agreed to by all the signatories. This was what Wallace had asked. There had been no specific American proposal on the stages of transition as yet, Baruch said, because

> the delegation has felt it futile to make detailed proposals on this point until there is some reasonable prospect of basic agreement on the broad principles of the plan.

On the matter of one-sidedness of the stages, Baruch wrote: "We have not asked others to disclose their own material resources and would not do so unless we were prepared to disclose our own."

To Wallace's claim that the veto was "irrelevant," Baruch argued:

> The United States proposal is designed to extend as far as possible the domain of effective international law in support of peace by defining the various classes of crimes provided for carrying out appropriate punishment. This proposal is in sharp contrast with the assumption that the only possible sanction against international crimes is resort to the ultimate political measure of war — an assumption seemingly made by Mr. Wallace. Even if resort to war should prove necessary as a punishment, this action should not be a mere series of unilateral steps by the nations who "are free to take what actions they feel necessary," as Mr. Wallace says, but should rather be united action pursuant to a recognized international agreement.[25]

In the two weeks following Wallace's outburst and resignation, the Soviet Union took steps which seemed too coincidental to be anything but the logical, Russian tactical response to the freshly revealed division in American ranks. At the United Nations, Soviet delegates began asking the other nations whether they thought Baruch really represented the American people. Then, on September 24, from behind the great red sandstone walls of the Kremlin came answers Generalissimo Stalin had given to a series of written questions left by Alexander Werth of the *Sunday Times* of London. Werth was one of many correspondents who periodically deposited such queries at the Kremlin Gate, opposite the Old Imperial Stables, hoping to be graced — as one or two were every year — by answers from the man behind the walls. Stalin's message for the world on September 24 was calm and confident. "Do you believe that the monopoly possession of the atom bomb by the United States of America is one of the principal threats to peace?" Werth asked Stalin, who answered:

> I do not believe the atom bomb to be as serious a force as certain politicians are inclined to regard it. Atom bombs are intended for

intimidating weak nerves but they cannot decide the outcome of war, since atom bombs are by no means sufficient for this purpose. Certainly, monopoly possession of the secret of the atom bomb does create a threat, but at least two remedies exist against it: a) Monopoly possession of the atom bomb cannot last long; b) Use of the atom bomb will be prohibited.

Henry Wallace hailed the statement as a vindication of his faith in the Russians. In New York, the Soviet delegation quickly asked for a meeting of the Scientific and Technical Committee. They were apparently ready to cast the vote that had been delayed for almost a month. The meeting was scheduled for September 26. Professor Alexandrov, the Soviet delegate, was twenty minutes late that day — tardiness which was read by the nervous delegates as a bad sign. Dr. H. A. Kramers of the Netherlands, the chairman of the committee, paced anxiously back and forth while the other members waited in their seats. Alexandrov finally arrived and went quickly and formally to his place, with no indication of what decision he carried. The preliminaries were accomplished and then the roll was read. When the Soviet Union was called, Alexandrov answered with a flat Russian *da* ("yes"). The other nations were delighted, but after the vote the Soviet representative moderated their happiness. He asked for the floor and said:

> In voting for the report . . . I regard it as necessary to make the following statement: The committee had at its disposal, as is recognized in the report, limited and incomplete information. The majority of the conclusions in the committee's report are therefore hypothetical and conditional. With this reservation, I vote for adoption of the report.

On Friday morning, September 27, Henry Wallace reluctantly kept his appointment with Bernard Baruch at the latter's offices in the Empire State Building. Wallace brought Philip Hauser, an assistant from the Commerce Department, along with him. It began as an amicable discussion and continued that way for most of the morning. Baruch first assured Wallace that their conceptions of what was necessary with regard to the stages of transition were exactly the same. On the veto, Wallace apparently agreed with Baruch's position as it was expressed in the memo to the President of September 24. Returning to his central theme, Wallace then tried to elicit from Baruch and his staff some definite plan to overcome Soviet distrust. He suggested an immediate declaration by the United States that it was voluntarily stopping its manufacture of atomic bombs. The Security Council might then be invited to inspect American installations to prove that production had stopped, Wallace suggested. Eberstadt asked Wallace to consider what such a generous move would do to America if the negotiations broke down, and Wallace apparently agreed that the time was not yet right for the cessation of atomic production. "It is obvious that I was not fully posted," Wallace declared at one point in the discussions. At other moments, the conversation was more heated. When Wallace protested, "I have a right to write to the President," Swope answered, "You have no right to write these things when with five minutes on the phone with either Baruch or me you could have been set right. You should have checked with our group on the facts." Wallace left Hauser to work with Baruch's staff on a statement that he might issue. But the final statement, in which Hauser admitted Wallace's lack of correct information and committed him to the Baruch Plan, as he thought Wallace had done in the discussions, was refused by the former Secretary. There followed exasperating days of negotiation marked by Baruch's inability to contact Wallace, who had gone into hiding. Baruch and his people became irate again when a two-day conference of Wallace's political allies, meeting in Chicago on September 28 and September 29, passed a resolution which repeated the substance of Wallace's earlier charges against the Baruch Plan.[26]

By Tuesday evening, October 2, Baruch was through trying. He called what he described as "one of his rare press conferences" at his Empire State offices. Wearing one of the checkered suits in which he spent his leisure time at the Long Island estate where he was staying, Baruch revealed the history of his relations with Henry Wallace, adding unhappily that "this is the first difficulty I've ever had with a public official. I refuse to deal in emotional or political activities as you know," he said. "I deal in facts." Baruch then distributed copies of his September 24 memo to the President, of Hauser's earliest draft statement which Wallace had rejected, and of a telegram which Baruch had sent Wallace that day. The baron also let it be known that his suspicions of Wallace's ignorance had been confirmed when the former Secretary told him that his information about the Baruch Plan and atomic energy policy had come "from a man from UNRRA who is now abroad." Wallace's letter "didn't do us any good" with the other members of the United Nations Atomic Energy Commission, Baruch declared, although he added: "I think we will be able to correct it. Every man has a right to his opinions, but no man has a right to circulate errors." In his telegram to Wallace, Baruch was anything but the unemotional Dr. Facts: "I assured my colleagues of my conviction that you would carry out what was regarded as a fair expression of your attitude as stated to me on Friday morning. I now find I was quite wrong." Baruch continued in a most personal tone:

> You have disappointed me sorely . . . You have no monopoly of the desire for peace. I have given thirty years of my life to the search for peace and there are many others whose aims have been the same.

James Byrnes read Baruch's response in Paris and happily cabled his old friend: "Your letter to Wallace unanswerable." [27]

Wallace brought a halt to the episode the next day in a lengthy statement, accusing Baruch of trying to "intimidate" him into giving a "full blank-check endorsement" to Baruch's own "stern and inflexible" position. As far as Wallace was concerned, his discussions with the baron had not moved him from the views he had expressed in his July 23 letter. If there was anything productive that did come from this Wallace-Baruch interchange, it was the clearly articulated American position that Baruch had put down in his memo to the President. This responded in the most comprehensive manner yet to the major arguments of the domestic and foreign critics of the Baruch Plan.

Of all the issues Wallace had raised, the one that became his battle cry over the next few months was the call for the United States to stop making bombs. The *Washington Post* said this was the one good point Wallace had made. He and his supporters, tending to make it their only point, argued that America's continued manufacture of atomic bombs was the major cause of Russian suspicion and covertness.[28]

19

A Hollow Victory

AFTER THEIR UNHAPPY ENCOUNTER with Henry Wallace was over, the members of the American delegation to the United Nations Atomic Energy Commission were able to enjoy the illusory sense of satisfaction that had prevailed among the other delegations as a result of the unanimous adoption of the report of the Scientific and Technical Committee. That report, after all, represented a minor victory for Baruch because it contained statements which were favorable to the American position, including:

> It is clear that the major assurance against clandestine activities would lie in the existence of effective safeguards applied to peaceful activities . . . Unless appropriate safeguards are taken at each of these stages, it will be difficult to insure that no diversion of material or installations will take place.[1]

And so even Baruch, who had grown thoroughly pessimistic about his mission, was able to say that the adoption of the report of the Scientific and Technical Committee "represents a forward motion in our deliberations." On October 2, the report was brought before Committee Two, which had been reassembled for the occasion. After formally accepting the work of the Scientific and Technical Committee, Committee Two decided to pursue the next step itself by investigating the safeguards which would be necessary at every stage of the atomic control process.

Throughout October, the members of Committee Two met calmly at Lake Success, New York, the new United Nations headquarters, to hear testimony from experts on the raw materials and chemical processes.

The peaceful gestures of the Soviet Union at the end of September 1946, did not, as it turned out, herald a sustained period of harmony. On October 1, nine days after Stalin's reassuring statement to Alexander Werth, Modest Rubinstein returned to the pages of *New Times* with another critical Soviet commentary on atomic energy. He charged that the United States was arming for an atomic war and obviously had no desire to convert atomic energy to peaceful purposes. The Russian people, Rubinstein said, were not frightened because they were confident of their own "moral and material strength." As he saw it, the world could take comfort from the knowledge that the United States monopoly "cannot continue for long." [2]

Secretary of State Byrnes alluded to the changeable Russian mood on October 3 in a speech before the American Club of Paris, where he was still toiling. Agreeing with Stalin's earlier statement that there was no immediate danger of war, Byrnes urged the Russian leader "to put an end to the unwarranted charges that the United States is seeking to use its possession of the atom bomb as a threat against the Soviet Union." The best test of Stalin's words, Byrnes argued, would be his willingness to modify Soviet propaganda.[3]

At the United Nations, the American delegation, which still had not received further instructions from the President, began to stir once more. On October 5, Swope and Eberstadt agreed with each other that it was now absolutely imperative to bring the Baruch Plan to a final vote by the end of December. With this same thought in mind, Franklin Lindsay, an administrative officer within the Baruch staff, started a quiet canvass of the other delegations. He found representatives of the Netherlands "increasingly aware that the end of the year was growing near" and they would then go off the commission. They hoped that "some sort of decision on basic principles" could be made before then.[4] General McNaughton of Canada was not of like mind. He told Lindsay that it was impossible for the commission "to take any sort of position even on the basic principles before the first of the year."[5] The French delegation agreed and represented the other major source of opposition to the emerging American strategy of a showdown.[6] The British delegate, Sir Alexander Cadogan, however, told Eberstadt that he thought it imperative for the commission to come to some decision before long, and certainly before the end of the year. He believed that the commission was "bound, as we know, sooner or later to run into serious political difficulties" and suggested facing those difficulties soon before the General Assembly convened so that they might be referred to the higher government officials who would be in New York for the assembly session "rather than gloss them over, or avoid them, until we shall not have the advantage of being able to refer them immediately for solution at a higher level."[7]

By the third week in October, the American men who plotted a showdown with the Soviet Union in the Atomic Energy Commission could point to other events as confirmation of their strategy. The Paris Peace Conference had ended acrimoniously with Molotov charging that collusion by a group of nations led by the United States had caused the conference to produce "unsatisfactory and unjust" results. A few days later, Professor Alexandrov was reported, in a routine United Nations press release describing a meeting of Committee Two, to have agreed that control of atomic energy must begin at the earliest level, with unmixed mineral resources and to have called for a worldwide survey of uranium deposits. This was hardly a radical suggestion, since the United States had set it down as one of the minimum conditions of the Baruch Plan. It did, however, constitute a breakthrough in Russia's own position because it accepted the principle of an international control agency and the idea of a world geological survey which would apparently have access to Soviet soil. When the press made much of Alexandrov's statement, as it rightly should have, Gromyko issued a remarkably heavy-handed retraction, denouncing what he termed the deliberate distortion of the American newspapers and adding:

Actually, Professor S. P. Alexandrov said: The question of the raw materials could not be left without attention. Information on this subject was insufficient. This has been recorded in the Scientific and Technical Committee's report. Therefore, while approving the program of our work, it will be necessary to leave the question of studying the raw materials on the agenda. The Soviet delegation considered the national control to be sufficient and therefore it might be possible to extend discussions on the safeguards in the line of national controls.

"All other statements published in the press, in connection with Professor S. P. Alexandrov's remarks," Gromyko concluded, "do not correspond to the realities."

On October 19, the American delegation was further educated in the gap existing between it and the Soviet Union in a private conversation with a Soviet citizen. The New York newspaper *PM* had earlier carried a column by F. Kuh describing the deadlock within the Atomic Energy Commission and contending that the real reason for Soviet opposition was the Russian belief "that United Nations supervision and management of nuclear energy is designed as the entering wedge by which capitalist America and other conservative powers would undermine the socialist economy of the Soviet Union." The inevitable control by the

Western powers of a majority of the members of the proposed international authority was cited by Kuh as the reason for Russia's anxious adherence to the veto power.[8] This newspaper column quickly came to the attention of the American delegation, which contacted Kuh and discovered that his secret source of information was Antonin Sobolev, a Russian diplomat who served as Assistant Secretary General of the United Nations. Kuh described Sobolev as "one of the few Russians abroad who knew what was going on in Moscow and would talk freely with foreigners he trusted." When Kuh had asked Sobolev if he thought there would be a greater chance of reaching an atomic agreement after Russia attained nuclear capability, Sobolev had replied "quite definitely that he thought after they had developed the bomb themselves, there would be far less agreement than there is now." [9]

With Baruch's consent, Eberstadt and Franklin Lindsay arranged a private meeting with Sobolev "with the purpose of establishing a point of contact with the Russian Government in addition to the official contact established through Gromyko." Through the mediation of Pendleton Herring, an American member of the United Nations Secretariat, this meeting occurred at dinner on Saturday evening, October 19. Sobolev, Herring, Eberstadt, and Lindsay were there. The Russian diplomat began the discussion by asking why the United States persisted in its production of atomic bombs? This, he argued, was "an unstabilizing force in the world." What purpose could America possibly have for more bombs at this time, Sobolev asked? Eberstadt did not answer this pointed question but launched an offensive of his own. Six weeks ago, he said, he had come to the conclusion that the Soviet government "did not wish to reach an agreement for the international control of atomic energy." In all the Soviet statements on atomic control, Eberstadt could find "no insurmountable obstacles with the exception of our provision for international inspection and control" which "seemed to be completely unacceptable to the Soviet Government." Sobolev described the American plan as a plan for world government, adding that the world was not yet ready for it. Turning to the Kuh article in *PM,* Eberstadt began a rebuttal of its major contentions. The purpose of the international authority was not to capitalize the Soviet economy. Russia would have a role in the activities of the authority, whose intervention would occur equally within the United States and Russia. Sobolev replied that "the Soviet Union was not seeking equality, but, rather, freedom to pursue its own policies in complete freedom and without any interference or control from the outside." Again, Sobolev raised the question of continued production of bombs by the United States. This time Eberstadt answered that America was perfectly willing to stop such production as a stage in the transition to international control. In fact, Eberstadt continued, he was prepared to argue within his own government that cessation of bomb production should be "the very first step in the transition stage." This could only be done with a system of adequate controls, for otherwise the American people would not accept such a move. The discussion ranged then over many subjects, including Sobolev's unhappiness with what he described as the anti-Soviet attitude of the American press and public. When it was over, Lindsay and Eberstadt had drawn some conclusions: (1) The Russians were most anxious to have America stop its bomb production but such a step would in no way induce them to accept any form of international inspection and control which was "the real obstacle to agreement"; (2) Sobolev's statement that "the Soviet Union does not desire equality, but requires unlimited freedom to pursue its own policies," was proof "that no general understanding based on mutual trust and cooperation is possible between the two systems of government." [10]

Franklin Lindsay's memorandum to Baruch and others on the staff regarding the conversation with Sobolev convinced everyone of the need to force the issue within the Atomic Energy Commission. Baruch, however, had still not received a response to his letter to the President of September 17. It must have been lost in the simultaneous uproar over Henry Wallace. Growing more anxious when word reached him that the Soviet Union was planning an atomic counterproposal of some kind, Baruch called the White House on October 28 and asked the President for guidance. Baruch told Truman that he and Byrnes would have to decide "pretty soon . . . whether the Atomic Energy Commission is to proceed now or stall." Baruch continued:

> We don't have to decide it in the next couple of days. But the time is running out against us. Now we have ten votes to two. Three fellows we are sure of are going to leave us. We will lose three sure votes . . .

Should he hold still in the hope that relations with Russia would improve or should he press forward to a vote, Baruch asked. Truman said he would talk to Byrnes but he felt that Baruch should move toward the vote, as he apparently wanted to do.[11]

Twenty-four hours later the tactical wisdom of this decision became clear and the penalty of not making it earlier was paid. Soviet Foreign Minister Vyacheslav Molotov, who was in New York for another meeting of the Big Four, stunned the United Nations General Assembly with a categorical rejection of the Baruch Plan and a bitter personal attack on Baruch himself. Molotov's speech ended with a surprise call for the Security Council to begin taking the necessary steps to enact a system of world disarmament, which would include conventional weapons. The speech was all the more shocking because, on his arrival in America a week earlier Molotov's tone had been consummately conciliatory. "Any difficulties can be overcome," he assured reporters who met him at the airport, "given good-will and the real desire to achieve mutual understanding." In his speech on October 29, Molotov was so absolutely severe and disparaging that an agreement between the United States and the Soviet Union on anything of substance seemed like a very distant dream.

The American plan, Molotov said, "unfortunately is afflicted by a certain degree of selfishness." Its intent was simply and solely to secure for the United States its "monopolistic possession of the atom bomb." His tone was threatening:

> Science and scientists cannot be put in a box and kept under lock and key . . . It should not be forgotten that atom bombs used by one side may be opposed by atom bombs and something else from the other side, and then the collapse of present day calculations of certain conceited but short-witted people will become all too apparent.

This unclear reference to Baruch was not left in doubt for long. In Molotov's view, Baruch was the leader of a school of American imperialism with "an irresistable trend toward expansion and unchallenged domination of the world." The "common people" of the Soviet Union and of the West did not agree with "the grim philosophy" expressed by Mr. Baruch and "public men belonging to his class."

A conference on disarmament would increase confidence among the world's people that the United Nations "was really permeated by a desire for lasting peace," Molotov declared. It would also strike a "deserved blow" at the "expansionist strivings" of those "who have not yet sufficiently learned the lessons of the ignominious collapse of aggressors in the recent war."

When Molotov finished his speech which he had delivered in Russian, and the French and English translations of his harangue began, a funereal atmosphere overcame the hall. It was "the most deeply disturbing speech ever delivered to the United Nations," one of the delegates said. The *New York Times* reported that Molotov's call for a general reduction of armaments was not received by the delegates with much more seriousness than the Russian proposal at Geneva in 1927 that all armies and navies be abolished. The American public responded not so much with cynicism as with anger. Not only had Molotov once more impinged on the hopes for peace, but he had struck at the most sacred ground by berating Baruch as if he were some common scoundrel. The *Philadelphia Bulletin* said that Molotov's "distortion of the motives of Bernard M. Baruch was shameless . . . the worst form of political mud-slinging." [12]

Warren Austin, the former Republican Senator from Vermont who had become America's delegate to the United Nations, answered Molotov's charges the next day in the General Assembly. Refusing to "participate in any exchange of recriminations," Austin said that he was troubled that Molotov's speech had shown such "distrust and misunderstanding" of the United States. "Can't we fight for peace side by side without recriminations?" he asked. The Senator described the Russian proposal for a general disarmament conference as one that deserved to be placed on the agenda and seriously considered, so long as it involved provisions for adequate inspection. He traced the long-term concern of the United States with the question of disarmament and added that it was particularly appropriate for the Soviet Union to take the initiative on the matter "because of its mighty armies." [13]

Bernard Baruch, however, was one man who did not think it was proper for the Soviet Union to raise the general disarmament question. That the Russians had done so infuriated him because they had thereby achieved a propaganda victory which he felt should have been America's. One of his earliest responses to Byrnes's call to serve at the United Nations was a dream of attaining world disarmament — a dream which Byrnes quickly deflated. After Gromyko's first articulation of Soviet policy in the Atomic Energy Commission, Baruch had written to Dean Acheson asking if someone in the American government would not say something about world disarmament. Acheson and Truman turned back this suggestion on the theory that it would confuse the public and remove attention from the crucial issue of atomic energy control. A few days after Molotov's bellicose speech, Baruch wrote to Acheson again. Complaining that he had not yet received an answer to the request contained in his letter to Truman of September 17, Baruch said:

> The Soviets have taken advantage of our indecision, have moved in, and now apparently have become the advocates of disarmament. As you recall, I strongly advocated that we should do it first . . .
>
> It is disheartening, to say the least, to see the moves that can and so apparently must be made, only to find that somebody else makes them and we are fighting rearguard actions. We cannot deal with this matter with dignity only. We are dealing with police court lawyers to whom the truth is of no importance and the only goal is their particular selfish ends without reference to the rest of the world.[14]

Two days later, on November 4, Baruch wrote to Byrnes, who was in New York for the General Assembly session and Big Four Conference, setting out the same two alternatives he had outlined in his letter of September 17 and asking for guidance.[15] Byrnes gave it within a day. Although he had not had an opportunity to discuss the question with the President, the Secretary of State advised Baruch to set his staff working in preparation for a showdown before the end of the year. Meanwhile, Byrnes promised to send a letter to the President recommending that he approve such a course.[16]

Baruch also had something to say about Molotov's attack on his own person. In the dark-wood, paneled hall at Lake Success on October 30, the baron told newsmen: "The gentleman's slander of my personal motives is of little importance, but it is of great importance what his country does about peace . . . As to his attempts to insult me, that's been tried before. The last who did were Hitler and Mussolini." [17]

John Hancock and Franklin Lindsay met with Dean Acheson in Washington on Friday, November 8. Acheson reported that he had seen the President that morning for a discussion of atomic energy control. Truman had agreed with Byrnes's suggestion and was drafting a letter to Baruch confirming his recommendation of an attempt to force the issue within the Atomic Energy Commission before the end of the year.[18]

Now finally blessed with direction from Washington, Baruch and his staff began to move the United Nations Atomic Energy Commission toward a final vote. On Wednesday, November 13, the members of the commission gathered for their first plenary meeting in four months. Colonel Mohammed Bay Khalifa, the Egyptian delegate, was chairman. He proposed immediately that the body report its findings and recommendations to the Security Council by December 31, 1946. The speed with which the United States endorsed this motion made clear the source of the Egyptian's action. Professor Alexandrov, representing the Soviet Union, requested time to study the proposal, but the members of the commission had been well prepared for the moment and would not wait. The vote was ten in favor and two, Russia and Poland, abstaining. A deadline had been set.

The direction of American strategy was now obvious and caused the Soviet Union to initiate a series of quick maneuvers whose major purpose appeared to be the strengthening of those within the West who urged patience and counseled against a showdown. First, Molotov went before the Political and Security Committee of the United Nations and offered a resolution requiring a worldwide count of soldiers and military supplies by January 1, 1947, apparently as a first step toward general disarmament. The resolution was worded to include only troops on foreign soil, thus leaving out the larger part of the Soviet armies. Although it contained no provision for international verification, the resolution required disclosure of all national armaments including apparently the atomic bomb. In a stormy meeting of the Political and Security Committee on November 27, Molotov's proposal was voted down. The Soviet Foreign Minister was not in a particularly amicable mood that day. After one of his most exasperating procedural maneuvers, the Philippine representative, Senator Mariana J. Cuena, protested that the Russian's proposal was contrary to "the most elementary rules of parliamentary procedure." Molotov replied acerbically that he was indebted to the gentleman for the lesson and hoped "the procedure would be available when the Philippines have a Parliament." [19] The next day, Molotov returned to the same committee, a model of friendliness and respect. He unsettled the delegates by proposing the establishment of two new commissions on disarmament, apparently with powers of inspection, whose jurisdiction would extend to atomic weapons. "In so far as a decision will be taken on a prohibition of use of atomic energy for purposes of war, effective control over the implementation of this decision is necessary," Molotov assured them. But this apparent Soviet acceptance of the concept of inspection also involved a breakaway from the United Nations Atomic Energy Commission and, in fact, the dissolution of that group. This was a fine piece of strategy at a time when Baruch was driving toward a climax in the Atomic Energy Commission.

Two days later, Molotov's deputy, Andrei Vishinsky, dissipated most of the emergent optimism when he declared that disarmament must begin with atomic weapons, and that the Soviet Union expected to maintain its full veto powers over the two proposed control commissions. The British delegate, Sir Hartley Shawcross, denounced the Soviet proposals as unacceptable to the United Kingdom. "Do not let us foist this humbug on the world," he proclaimed. Senator Connally made clear that the United States felt the same way about any proposals which preserved the veto and banned the bomb first with no assurance that anything would follow. Vishinsky then charged that the United States was "holding on with both hands to the queen of horrors, the atom bomb." [20]

Connally was now ready with an American offensive. He introduced a plan for general disarmament which gave priority to atomic weapons and emphasized that effective disarmament depended on inspection. The resolution left no doubt that the United States viewed the existing Atomic Energy Commission as the place for action, and quickly. To everyone's surprise, Molotov soon announced that the Soviet Union could accept the substance of the United States proposals, with a few amendments. Most startling of all was his implication that Russia would not necessarily wish to have a veto over the inspection powers of a disarmament control agency, once it had been fully established by the Security Council. He said nothing regarding sanctions and the veto power over them. Molotov also wanted to water down the priority given the Atomic Energy Commission by the American proposal. The General Assembly eventually adopted this American resolution unanimously and left it to the Security Council to provide for detailed consideration of the principles enunciated in the resolution.

Baruch was undeterred by this spurt of good spirit. In fact, he viewed it with dismay because he feared once more that the

Soviet Union had successfully taken the initiative and moved the focus of concern and activity away from atomic energy. Baruch foresaw the work of the proposed new disarmament study group dragging on for years while the people of the world remained ignorant of the fact which was now clear to him — that the Soviet Union was unprepared to accept the minimum conditions necessary to achieve international atomic control. Toward such an illustration, he devoted his vigorous efforts during the month of December 1946.

First, it was again necessary for Baruch to put down doubts and opposition within his own American camp. Henry Wallace, his followers, and some of the syndicated columnists had persisted in their appeals for an end to the American production of atomic weapons. This, they argued, was the best way to induce Soviet cooperation. Harold Ickes, a former Secretary of the Interior, wrote Baruch asking him why the United States was still manufacturing the dread weapons. Until a final treaty was agreed upon, Baruch told Ickes, the United States had an obligation to "retain its winning weapon as a means of maintaining security." Baruch placed special emphasis on America's obligation to the smaller nations of the world who feared the Russians and "look to our bombs as a protection to their people and their own national security and well-being." Some diplomats had argued that a cessation of bomb production would be taken as a sign of goodwill by the rest of the nations and particularly by Russia, Baruch wrote to Ickes, but he was convinced that such a move would be interpreted by the Russians as "a definite sign of bourgeois weakness." Baruch's conclusion was strong:

> If we were to accept every official Russian statement made before the Atomic Energy Commission and before the Paris Peace Conference as representing the final Russian position and if we were to accept the actions of Russia in every other part of the world at

face value the only sensible course would be to make bombs as fast as possible and be ready to use them whenever a real need arises. The United States has gone so far in its demobilization of the Army and Navy that if we were to stop making bombs we would be almost defenseless and would certainly have only a modicum of military power with which to stand up to the U.S.S.R.[21]

Ickes thanked Baruch for this explanation and admitted that he found it very persuasive.[22] At the end of November, Hancock informed his staff that he wanted to marshal all the arguments against the suggestion that America stop making bombs and to prepare a memorandum on the subject which could be distributed privately to people who might affect public opinion. The resulting memorandum was very much along the lines of Baruch's letter to Ickes, stressing America's obligation to protect its own national security and the one-sidedness of a bomb halt if Russia maintained its substantial armies.[23]

The other major internal opposition to the Baruch Plan, as Baruch headed for his showdown with the Russians, was based on its abolition of the veto. Many of the scientists and columnists argued that in his stress on ending the veto Baruch was fighting for something that meant nothing and also thereby giving the Russians an opportunity to base their opposition on a more appealing ground. At the end of November 1946, Dean Acheson told Herbert Swope that privately he too felt that Baruch was putting too much emphasis on the veto. When Swope reported this to the baron, he fumed. In a letter and then in a phone conversation, Baruch demanded that Acheson explain exactly what was his private viewpoint on the veto question. The transcript of Baruch's end of his conversation with Acheson shows the baron in a wounded and haughty mood:

> I understood from him [Swope] that your private opinion was that we should not play up the veto at all, and not even discuss it now,

and I was disturbed to think you would have any private view as opposed to the public view and that is what I wanted to clear up . . .

I got the impression from Herbert that you didn't even want us to mention the subject of the veto — which has been enlarged by the One-Worlders to mean something different than the language I put in and what I have reiterated all along . . .

I had seen Alsop's story that we were going to let down on the discussions of the veto and Lippmann and especially the left-wing crowd talking of us dragging in the veto and it wasn't necessary . . .

I was just wondering that when you talked to the "private viewpoint" as it was expressed, that if you had talked to somebody else, it would upset the whole course of inspection because they might agree to inspect and yet they might turn right around and veto the whole act of inspection. Do I make myself clear? . . .

I wouldn't want to think that an important man such as you would express one opinion privately and another publicly. I didn't think so and I wanted to clear it with you . . .

I think you're a good public servant and an honorable man and I think the best way to clear a thing is to call up the man himself . . .

I got from Herbert's remarks that perhaps you thought we ought to drop it [the veto], now I get from you, you don't . . .[24]

Having taken these steps to smother opposition within his own ranks, Baruch went before the other nations of the Atomic Energy Commission at a formal meeting on Thursday evening, December 5, and asked them to adopt the Baruch Plan as their recommendation to the Security Council.[25] "Let us delay no longer," Baruch declared. "To delay may be to die." The months of debate and wrangling had not induced Baruch to alter his original proposals in the slightest degree. "We seek especially the participation of the Soviet Union," Baruch said. "We welcome the recent authoritative statements of its highest representatives. From these, we are justified in concluding that it no longer regards the original American proposals as unacceptable as a whole or in their separate parts, as its member of this body stated at an earlier meeting."

The draft resolution which Baruch placed before the commission began with a section titled "Findings," in which the feasibility of inspection systems was described and the necessity of establishing them argued. In a section on "Recommendations," Baruch set forth a treaty which established an international atomic control authority and gave it wide powers of inspection and dominion over the processes of atomic development from the ore in the ground to the final weapon. With an eye to Henry Wallace and his supporters, Baruch placed special emphasis on a requirement that explicit stages of transition, as agreed to by all of the member nations, be spelled out in the proposed treaty. Finally, there would be no veto over any aspect of the international authority's work.

The old rhetorical flourish, largely Swope's doing, tied Baruch's package together. Time had already accustomed the people of the world to the frightening new weapons, Baruch declared, so that "the keen edge of danger is blunted, and we are no longer able to see the dark chasm on the brink of which we stand." His dream was still of a world where "men can walk erect again, no longer bent over by the . . . fear the atom strikes into their hearts." Baruch's personal concern and stake were not forgotten: "For myself, as I look upon a long past and too short a future, I believe the finest epitaph would be: 'He helped to bring lasting peace to the world!' " This was a rather brave statement for a man who had concluded that his dreams of disarmament and world peace were goodhearted nonsense.

Andrei Gromyko sat expressionless throughout Baruch's presentation. At the end, he objected not to its substance but to its timing. Baruch had orginally asked the commission to finish its work by December 20. Gromyko now complained, "I think that we will need further time to study these proposals." Baruch assured Gromyko that he was not asking for a vote that day. Alexandre Parodi of France, the current chairman of the commission, agreed that since Baruch's proposals were in the nature of a final report, it would be proper to await the conclusions of Committee Two which had continued to consider the scientific and technical aspects of safeguards. Without objection, the commission adjourned. No date was set for its next meeting.[26]

When the General Assembly, with surprising Soviet concurrence, agreed to the American disarmament proposal on December 14, Baruch felt that he had been given the foundation for his next move and Byrnes again urged him to accelerate his drive for a vote. At Baruch's request, the new chairman of the Atomic Energy Commission, Dr. Manuel Sandoval-Vallarta of Mexico, called a meeting for Monday, December 17. Baruch knew that at that time he could count on the support of Britain, China, Australia, Mexico, Brazil, and Egypt. With the United States, that would make seven votes, enough to send the proposal to the Security Council. But, of course, he also wanted the support of Canada, France, and the Netherlands. They had become uneasy about going for all the particulars of the Baruch Plan and believed that more time might bring the Russians around. The baron was confident that in the end he could win them over.

Baruch's message to the members of the Atomic Energy Commission who gathered on Tuesday morning, December 17, at Lake Success was full of urgency:

> Our course is not wholly in the field of free choice. We are under compulsion placed upon us by the General Assembly . . . A new spirit has come into being. It is our privilege to give flesh to that spirit. The injunction has been laid upon the Atomic Energy Commission to proceed expeditiously to the development of a formula of action.[27]

"The time has come to match our words with action. We have debated long enough," Baruch concluded. Andrei Gromyko was unmoved by this rhetoric. The treaty was a complex matter, he said, which left many questions unanswered. Why, he asked, did it say nothing about the existing American atomic bombs? He would need more time to study the proposal. In any case, he had made an appointment for three o'clock that afternoon and therefore would be unable to participate in a lengthy debate and vote that day. "Why is it so necessary to rush along and try to reach hasty decisions?" he demanded. If they had no interest in a unanimous report then haste did not matter, but if they desired unanimity then it could not be achieved in a hurry, Gromyko declared, adding, "I imagine that we want to reach a unanimous agreement here."

Baruch said that he had intended to ask for a vote at that meeting and that the comments of the members of the commission had convinced him that their views were clear "but the representative of the Soviet Union has asked for time." Time was valuable, Baruch continued, but "in the hope that by granting his request we may finally achieve unanimity, I am agreeable to a short postponement of our vote." When Baruch asked that the vote be set for not later than the coming Friday, December 20, Gromyko argued that it would be better to postpone until the following week. Baruch turned around to confer with his staff and then declared:

> I prefer Friday, next week are the holidays and then there may be delays and delays and time goes by and years go by and then nothing is done. So I would prefer Friday.

Knowing that Baruch's preference would receive the support of the majority and therefore that he would not receive the delay he desired, Gromyko turned to the substance of the American representative's urgent call to action. The Baruch proposals were

inconsistent with the disarmament resolution recently passed by
the General Assembly, Gromyko claimed.

> The resolution of the General Assembly does not touch on the
> veto question in any way and this is quite reasonable and under-
> standable because if it did . . . there would have been no possi-
> bility of unanimity in the General Assembly . . . I must admit I
> was surprised to find such a proposal in the United States docu-
> ment two days after the decision of the General Assembly.

The commission then recessed until Friday, and Baruch and
his staff immediately went to work on their reluctant friends,
Canada, France, and the Netherlands. The latter two would be
compelled to come along, but Canada was more determined in
its opposition. Eberstadt went to the Canadian headquarters at
the Hotel Biltmore at eight o'clock on Thursday evening. He
stayed there until three o'clock Friday morning when General
McNaughton finally agreed to go part of the way. He would
amend Baruch's proposal so that a vote on it would simply constitute acceptance of its principles and not a formal recommendation to the Security Council. It would then be up to the Working
Committee — which was the full commission under another
name — to write a report to the Security Council. This tactic
allowed a vote, which Baruch had demanded, but also did not call
the nations to a final commitment.[28]

Baruch's mood during this period is revealed in a letter which
he sent on Thursday, December 19, to David Lilienthal, who had
recently been appointed the first chairman of the United States
Atomic Energy Commission. Baruch told Lilienthal that "immediate steps ought to be taken to cover the raw materials involved, if that hasn't already been done . . . and also, a careful
watch should be placed over the manufacture of instruments and
machinery that go into the building of plants and the making of
bombs." The baron was preparing his beloved nation for the
worst.[29]

Dr. Vallarta of Mexico opened the commission meeting at eleven o'clock on Friday morning, December 20, and immediately proceeded to state his "warm agreement" with the proposals of the United States.[30] Gromyko still felt otherwise. He called for a postponement of action "for six or seven days" so that he might better understand the relationship between the work of the commission and the disarmament resolution of the General Assembly. "I very much regret," the Russian representative added, "that it may rather disturb tranquility during the Christmas holidays." General McNaughton agreed with Gromyko that there was a need for time, but said that he was prepared to offer a resolution in which the members of the commission would be asked to accept only the principles upon which the Baruch proposal was based. This would give them several days before a final vote on the Baruch Plan would be taken. Gromyko was still dissatisfied. "Why if a vote on the Baruch proposals today would have only a preliminary character should the Commission take any such action?" he asked McNaughton. He would insist that his motion for a week's postponement be brought to a vote. It was, and the results were two in favor and ten against. Oscar Lange of Poland next moved that the Baruch proposal be referred to the Political and Social Committee. This was overcome by a nine to two vote, with Canada abstaining. Then, Gromyko quietly announced: "I am not taking part in this discussion." He remained passive and silent, as did the other Soviet spokesmen on other committees of the Atomic Energy Commission, until the final decisive day of the commission's work in 1946. McNaughton now submitted his resolution. It was supported by ten nations. Poland abstained and the Soviet Union refused to have its vote recorded in any way.

General McNaughton immediately returned to Ottawa to consult with his government, which was reportedly at work on a series of critical amendments to the Baruch Plan. The Canadians were still unhappy with Baruch's insistence on removing the veto, and felt, as everyone could see Baruch did not, that there was yet hope of bringing the Soviet government along. On Thursday, December 26, Committee Two responded to the quickened tempo, and passed a report on safeguards which accepted the American idea of an international authority but placed less emphasis on international ownership and more on inspection, especially in the earliest stages of control. The vote again was ten nations in favor, Poland abstaining, and the Soviet Union taking no part. This report was forwarded to the Working Committee for inclusion in its report to the Security Council. On that same day Eberstadt went into another marathon session with General Mc-Naughton, who had returned from Ottawa. When it was over, Eberstadt had accepted a number of changes in wording and emphasis which did no damage to the essence of the Baruch Plan. Only on the veto question were the Canadians and Americans unable to agree.

The Working Committee convened at Lake Success on Friday morning, December 27, and ground on for eight hours in a paragraph-by-paragraph consideration of the Baruch proposal.[31] General McNaughton began the meeting on a harmonious note by moving acceptance of the United States plan. Almost all of the Canadian comments were now "obsolete," he explained. The American and Canadian delegations had reached a full agreement on the entire plan with the exception of the paragraph concerning violations and the veto power. In the detailed consideration of the proposal, a number of minor amendments passed with American concurrence including one offered by the representative from Brazil, whose country was rich with atomic ore, stating that ownership by the international control agency of mines and of ores still in the ground was not regarded as mandatory. This change was thoroughly consistent with the private views that Baruch and Hancock had promoted all along.

With the Soviet Union sustaining its silence, the committee

moved slowly through the entire document until the only area of disagreement remaining was the veto. Baruch's resolution had stated quite specifically that "there shall be no legal right, by veto or otherwise, whereby a willful violator of the terms of the treaty or convention shall be protected from the consequences of violations of its terms." Now, Alexandre Parodi of France spoke up. The "emotionalism" surrounding the veto question made it difficult to reach "an objective and rational decision." A statement of general character should be sufficient, he continued, such as the statement that no violator should be able to protect himself by legal methods. Therefore, France would oppose inclusion of the words "by veto or otherwise" because nothing was gained thereby and much was lost.

Speaking for Great Britain, Sir Alexander Cadogan said that there was no principle to which His Majesty's government "attached more importance than that a violator of the convention should not be protected, legally or illegally, from the consequences of his wrong-doing." However, he continued, this principle would remain "completely and clearly stated" even if the four words which Parodi had cited were omitted. "If their omission would aid in the unanimous acceptance of the principles, nothing would be lost by omitting them," Cadogan concluded with his eyes on the Russian delegation. But the Soviet representative, Professor Alexandrov, refused to break his country's silence. The Australian representative, Paul Hasluck, was not so laconic. Agreeing with Baruch's wording because it said what he believed, Hasluck compared the behavior of the committee to "that of children in a song where, at a certain word, they nod their head and keep silent rather than pronounce the word." Ferdinand Eberstadt was equally dismayed with Parodi's proposal. The United States would not shy from using words which stated the principles clearly, he said. "When the United States said there should be 'no legal right' it meant there should be 'no legal right' by veto or otherwise." Eberstadt would say no more. In view of the great importance of this question, he was going to turn his chair over to Mr. Baruch.

The baron, who had been sitting by quietly, now reached into his briefcase and removed a prepared statement which he proceeded to read in an air of high drama. Much had been made of the contention that the American plan was inconsistent with the United Nations Charter which ordained the veto power, Baruch said. But the American proposal "is at variance only with an extreme and attenuated and, I am sure, unintended use of the veto." Baruch agreed "that if any great nation decides to violate a treaty, no agreements however solemn will prevent such violation." All this Baruch understood and agreed with, but he also believed "that a clear realization of this would be the greatest step toward peace that had ever been taken in history." If the United Nations was not a place where agreements were observed and collective punishment meted out to violators, then the American people wanted no part of it because it would be "no more than a debating society and a place to exchange pious-sounding documents." All that he was asking them to do, Baruch said, was "to vote in favor of the proposition that it should not lie within the power of the criminal to determine by his own veto whether or not he is guilty and shall be punished." Baruch closed with an ultimatum:

> I cannot recommend to the people of the United States. I cannot advocate before the Senate of the United States that this country surrender this potent weapon and dedicate to mankind its tremendous knowledge in the field of the production of atomic energy . . . under any system which is open to nullification of punishment by what can be called subterfuge . . .
>
> Gentlemen, it is either — or. Either you agree that a criminal should have this right by voting against our position — or you vote for this sound and basic principle of enduring justice and plain common sense.

Baruch's oration did not elicit the flood of support he anticipated. McNaughton and Cadogan, however, modified their previous positions by saying that they would vote with the majority on the question although they were still willing to side with Parodi in his deletion if it would secure unanimity. Brazil, Mexico, China, and Egypt spoke strongly in favor of Baruch's stand. But, still there was no consensus. Dr. Vallarta of Mexico had a suggestion. The task of this Working Committee was to draft a report which would be acceptable to the full Atomic Energy Commission. He, therefore, proposed that the final decision on the disputed phraseology be left to the commission and that the report of the Working Committee be submitted to the commission with Baruch's language on the veto, but also with a covering letter stating the dispute on that question. This was something of a charade since the commission consisted of the very same people, but it had the effect of moving the process along and leaving a few more days for private negotiations. The delegate accepted Dr. Vallarta's suggestion. Suddenly, Professor Alexandrov raised his hand. Everyone sat up anxiously, expecting a stunning Soviet surprise, but Alexandrov asked only that the covering letter to the Atomic Energy Commission note that the Soviet Union had taken no part in the discussions of the Working Committee for the reasons stated by Mr. Gromyko at the meeting of the Atomic Energy Commission on December 20, 1946.[32]

With the final meeting of the Atomic Energy Commission scheduled for Monday morning, December 30, the Soviet Union made one final attempt to stop the Baruch juggernaut. On Saturday night, December 28, Gromyko wrote to Secretary General Trygve Lie asking that the Security Council appoint a commission to work out detailed plans for world disarmament and report back within three months. Baruch dismissed this as no more than a last, vain Russian attempt to prevent final action by the commission. Baruch also arranged for some news of his own over that weekend.

Sunday morning's newspapers carried the strongest possible confirmation of his opposition to the veto. On Saturday Senator Arthur Vandenberg had released the text of a wire he had sent to Baruch:

> In my personal opinion, the Senate would not ratify any atomic control treaty which leaves any possible chance for subsequent international bad faith to circumvent total and summary enforcement or for any subsequent disagreements regarding enforcements to paralyze even temporarily the application of effective sanctions.[33]

Andrei Gromyko ended the ten days of Russian silence at the beginning of the plenary session of the Atomic Energy Commission on Monday morning, December 30. Speaking in English instead of his usual Russian, Gromyko repeated all the familiar arguments against the veto and for an international convention to outlaw atomic weapons. He also made it clear that no mere change in wording would win him over: "The retreat from the principle of unanimity of the Great Powers in the Security Council cannot be covered up merely by statements . . . It is insufficient to make only some modifications in the wording . . . leaving the basic sense unchanged." Gromyko closed with a ritualistic proposal that the commission proceed with a paragraph-by-paragraph consideration of the United States plan in order to make the proper changes which would allow the earliest possible convocation of the convention Russia espoused.

Now, Baruch raised his hand and, with no reference at all to Gromyko's final oration, said quietly:

> Mr. Chairman, I move that the draft of the report, Atomic Energy Commission/18, as forwarded to this Commission by the Working Committee be adopted as the report of this Commission to be submitted to the Security Council on December 31.

In their turn, each of the nations explained and cast its vote. Australia and Brazil voted yes. From Canada, Lester Pearson, the Undersecretary for External Affairs and former Canadian ambassador to Washington, had come the night before to ease tensions between the United States and its northern neighbor. Now, McNaughton announced that Canada would vote yes since "the present text is the one that commands the greatest measure of agreement." China voted aye, so did France, because, Parodi said, his government had finally concluded that Baruch was correct in believing that his plan would not involve revision of the United Nations Charter. Egypt and Mexico voted yes. Poland was the one nation to speak in opposition, although its final vote was an abstention. The Polish delegate, Oscar Lange, derided Baruch's threat that the United States would withdraw from the United Nations if the veto remained in atomic affairs. The United Kingdom gave Baruch more cause for worry than he had expected. Prior to the meeting that morning, Sir Alexander Cadogan told Baruch that Whitehall felt it could not vote for the American proposal. Cadogan made some reference to breaking the plan into separate sections for voting and even gave a hint that the English might prefer national and not international control of the atomic factories. Baruch erupted into a tactically wise outburst of anger. When Cadogan's turn came, he said, "My government approves the report that has been submitted to us by the Working Committee." With the favorable vote of the United States, and the expected abstention of the Soviet Union, the final count was ten votes for, none against, and two abstentions.

Although he was privately unburdened by illusions about what he had accomplished, Baruch nevertheless told the press that he viewed the vote as a "complete victory." [34]

By the end of the week, Baruch had given a private "victory" dinner for his international colleagues in New York and then gone to Washington on Saturday, January 4, to leave with the President his letter of resignation. It had been understood by all concerned that once the Atomic Energy Commission reported to the Security Council, Baruch and his staff would resign. In his letter, Baruch explained to the President that

> the first phase of the work of the UNAEC has been completed. The basic principles have been clearly stated . . . and exposed to the study of the world . . . The active undertaking of the problem of general disarmament by the Security Council . . . has created a new situation in which our hand would be strengthened by an identic representation on the Security Council and the Atomic Energy Commission.

America's representative on the Security Council, Senator Warren Austin, was, in Baruch's view, "thoroughly equipped to handle this business as it develops from now on." The *New York Times* added that Austin was "an old hand in the field of politics and since it is into that realm that the atomic question now goes, whereas it has been principally discussed on a scientific and technical basis, Mr. Baruch's surrender of authority will probably not hamper discussions at this stage."

Although Baruch told the President that the agreement of four of the great powers and six other nations "lessened . . . the difficulty of gaining unanimity" on atomic energy control, he also ended his letter with a "final thought," that there was "no reason why this country should not continue the making of bombs, at least until the ratification of the treaty."

Unable to find Truman at the White House, Baruch left his letter of resignation with his press secretary, Charles Ross. Having completed another public tour of duty, the baron returned eagerly to the warmth and tranquility of Hobcaw.[35]

20

The Parallel Monologue

BERNARD BARUCH'S RESIGNATION was greeted with a predictable public chorus of appreciation. The *Birmingham Post* exclaimed, "If the planet survives to have a history, Mr. Baruch's stubborn fight may be written in the history as the secret of survival." [1] David Lilienthal wrote to Baruch in longhand, "not as an Atomic Commissioner but as a citizen, as the father of two children, as one of millions concerned about the future under the shadow of the atom bomb's potentialities" to say "Thank you for your services in the interest of humankind, services rendered at great cost of your own comfort and with inspiring dedication to the cause of peace." [2] A letter from the Historian-General of the United Daughters of the Confederacy was equally effusive: "I feel somewhat let down because you are no longer taking part in the plans, but we shall just have to hope that God will take care of America." [3] Presumably, Baruch's presence had saved the Almighty from such responsibility up until that time. The *St. Louis Post-Dispatch* said that Baruch's "hard-headed counsel should prevail over the fuzzy thinking of those who would give away our atomic advantage without value received." Mr. Baruch, the *Post-Dispatch* concluded, "speaks for the nation." [4]

The St. Louis newspaper was right. Baruch did speak for the nation, and that is one of the reasons why his resignation represents more than the departure of this one remarkable man from the international negotiations for the control of atomic energy. It symbolizes also the great chasm that had been revealed during his tenure between American and Russian ideas and ambitions in the field of atomic energy. At the United Nations, Baruch's resignation marked the beginning of what one diplomat wisely called a "parallel monologue." [5] Effective negotiations ceased, if they had ever really begun. Genuine consideration of one another's national concerns was nonexistent, if it had ever really existed. The process became pure propaganda — an exercise in which success was measured more by the impact of one's maneuvers on public opinion than by the acceptance of one's proposals by the others sitting at the negotiating table. Baruch's resignation stands therefore as a monument, marking the failure of mankind to achieve international control of atomic energy.

Andrei Gromyko spent the first six weeks of 1947 in the Security Council trying to smother the report of the Atomic Energy Commission. He criticized its priorities and vigorously advocated the establishment of a new commission of armaments. When this Commission for Conventional Armaments was created during February, the United States was able to forbid it, as its title implies, from discussing atomic energy. With this accomplished, the Security Council's consideration of the Atomic Energy Commission's report, the Baruch Plan, began in earnest. In seven meetings between February 14 and March 10, Gromyko blew hot and cold, first offering concessions or hints of concession, then implying acceptance of even the idea of punishments, but finally frustrating the hopeful by declaring immovable opposition to the establishment of a control system before atomic weapons were outlawed. On March 5, in a speech to the Security Council which lasted an hour and a half, Gromyko put an end to all optimism. The majority report of the Atomic Energy Commission had defined the management of the Atomic Development Authority as "the direct power and authority to take day-by-day decisions governing operations as well as responsibility for planning." Gromyko described this principle as "thoroughly vicious and unacceptable":

> One cannot imagine a situation in which a control organ would possess establishments in different countries, decide whether or not to allow the creation of such establishments on the territories of these or other countries . . .

This vision of an international authority, Gromyko argued, was "incompatible with sovereignty." His argument was surprisingly explicit:

> Unlimited control would mean an unlimited interference in the economic life of the countries on whose territories the control would be carried out . . . The Soviet Union is aware that there will be a majority in the control organ which may make one-sided decisions, a majority on whose benevolent attitude the Soviet Union, the Soviet people cannot count. Therefore, the Soviet Union and probably not only the Soviet Union cannot allow that the fate of its national economy go over to this organ.[6]

Granting such power to an international authority really meant granting a world monopoly of atomic energy to the United States, Gromyko contended, since America would no doubt control the authority or, at least, a majority of its members. Instead of subordinating national interests to international interests, as it claimed it did, the Baruch Plan really subordinated all other nations' interests to the interests of the United States, Gromyko concluded.

The Security Council sent the problem of atomic energy back to the Atomic Energy Commission on March 10, 1947. There, the familiar topics were trotted out once more. Only the terms used in the dialogues occasionally changed. Slowly, even the most zealous advocates of international control among the scientists, politicians, and public came to see that there was no hope. The atomic scientist Hans Bethe recalls several sad conversations with Robert Oppenheimer at the Berkeley campus of the University of California during this time. Admitting to Bethe that he "had given up all hope that the Russians would agree to a plan which would give security," Oppenheimer said that he was distressed by the degree to which "the Russian plan was designed to serve the Russian interests and no other interests, namely to deprive us immediately of the one weapon which would stop the Russians from going into Western Europe . . ." [7] Oppenheimer's reasoning was typical of the many advocates of international control who changed their minds during this period as a result of the growing political antagonism between the Soviet Union and the United States.

Albert Einstein was similarly despondent at the beginning of 1947 over the failure of the scientific community to penetrate the public's growing indifference to atomic war. "The public, having been warned of the horrible nature of atomic warfare, has done nothing about it and to a large extent has dismissed the warning from its consciousness," Einstein complained. Walking through the Princeton campus with his assistant Ernest Strauss, a young mathematician, Einstein spoke of the importance of political participation and then, perhaps to ease his guilt, said: "Yes, we now have to divide up our time like that, between politics and our equations. But to me our equations are far more important, for politics are only a matter of present concern. A mathematical equation stands forever." [8]

In March 1947, Robert Oppenheimer became so distressed that he flew to New York to talk with Frederick Osborn, the diplomat who had just been chosen to replace Baruch at the UNAEC. [9] Oppenheimer's goal was no less than the withdrawal of the United States from the atomic energy negotiations. The Russians would never consent to a reasonable plan, he told Osborn. He was worried that the United States would someday make the mistake of compromising where it could not afford to compromise. Osborn said he would consider Oppenheimer's suggestion and take it up with others. A short while later, Osborn raised the question in Washington at a meeting of President Truman's Executive Committee on the Regulation of Armaments, whose influential membership included Secretary of War Patterson, Secretary of the Navy Forrestal, Secretary of State Acheson, Lilienthal, and Warren Austin.

Osborn reported that he had talked with the British, French, and Canadian representatives at the United Nations about the possibility of pulling out of the atomic energy talks and found them definitely opposed to such a course. "They said they would be in an impossible position in their own countries if they agreed to calling off the negotiations," Osborn explained. Forrestal said he thought the negotiations in New York had become "a lot of bunk" and felt that the United States should get out. Patterson agreed, as did Acheson and Lilienthal with slightly less vehemence. Now Osborn said that his own position, based somewhat on his conversations with America's allies, was that "it would be very injurious to our international position to take a lone position, refusing to negotiate." He thought that "if we were properly on guard we need not make any bad mistakes or endanger the situation. What do you think, Bob?" Patterson also appreciated the dimensions of the new game. "I think we should go ahead if this is the reason and if we do it with our eyes open," he said. Acheson and Lilienthal similarly consented to those terms.

And so the negotiations continued at the United Nations only because world opinion would not let them stop. That would constitute a formal admission of failure. On June 11, Andrei Gromyko tried again to regain the initiative by introducing what was portrayed as a new Soviet proposal, but it was really not very new at all. It relied on national control, a foundation which the United States had dismissed as thoroughly unacceptable months before. Gromyko's new plan also contained provisions for periodic inspection, but only of the variety that the Lilienthal Board had rejected a year and a half before. The commission decided to break down again into working groups which would develop more of the technical specifics of an international control scheme. On September 11, the findings of these groups were incorporated into the second report of the Atomic Energy Commission which was again endorsed by ten of the member nations. Poland abstained, and the Soviet Union voted no. In this second report, the commission completed its technical exploration of the feasibility of international atomic control. But still the immense, political breach between the East and West which, of course, was widening during 1947 and 1948 prohibited any agreement, regardless of the technical feasibilities.

There was really very little left to do. Meetings of the commission occurred most infrequently. The organs of the group atrophied, and a form of diplomatic senility oppressed debate whenever it occurred. On May 17, 1948, the commission approved its third report which began lugubriously with a tardy understatement: "The Atomic Energy Commission reports that it has reached an impasse." Gromyko voted against the report's conclusion that the commission's proceedings should be suspended and atomic control left to the Security Council. Regardless of which organ of the United Nations became the forum for atomic energy debate, Gromyko argued, the positions of the respective governments would remain the same. In three fruitless sessions during June 1948, the Security Council proved that on this point Gromyko was right. International relations had continued to deteriorate. The Russians had moved decisively into Eastern Europe. In Rumania, the monarchy was overthrown. In Poland and Hungary, opposition leaders were arrested and carried away. In Prague, a Communist putsch overwhelmed the established government. By August 1948, the Berlin Blockade had begun. War seemed increasingly imminent. So, no one was surprised during the summer of 1948 when the Soviet Union vetoed a Security Council resolution approving the reports of the Atomic Energy Commission.

The question of atomic energy control was placed on the agenda of the third General Assembly meeting in Paris in the fall of 1948, but again the only purpose for its inclusion was propaganda. On November 4, 1948, the West won a hollow victory passing the Baruch Plan through the General Assembly by a vote of forty in favor, six opposed, and four abstentions. This amounted to no more than a demonstration of popular support and had no tangible effect at all. In February 1949, the assembly summoned the Atomic Energy Commission back into session and gave it a limited agenda, but the meetings of the commission immediately degenerated into petty haggling and propaganda harangues. On July 29, 1949, the commission willingly agreed (with the traditional two exceptions of Russia and Poland) on an American resolution reporting "that these differences are irreconcilable at the Commission level, and that further discussion in the Atomic Energy Commission would tend to harden these differences and would serve no practical or useful purpose." Over Soviet objections, the Security Council approved this report and sent it on to the General Assembly, where it was passed in November.

During the third week in September 1949, American seismographers detected a large explosion in the Soviet Union. By September 19, scientists were sure that it had been an atomic explosion. Four days later, President Truman told the world the news:

> I believe the American people are entitled to be informed of all developments in the field of atomic energy. That is my reason for making public the following information. We have evidence that within recent weeks an atomic explosion occurred within the U.S.S.R.[10]

The Soviet news agency Tass soon confirmed Truman's announcement and reported that the atomic bomb was built by Russia because of the large-scale, postwar construction program then in progress within the Soviet Union — "The building of hydroelectric stations, mines, canals, roads, which evoke the necessity of large scale blasting work with the use of the latest technical means." Making light of Truman's dramatic announcement, Tass pointed out that "in so far as this blasting work has taken place and is taking place pretty frequently in various parts of the country, it is possible this might draw attention beyond the confines of the Soviet Union." The Soviet press wanted no one to be misled into believing that the Soviet Union had just attained nuclear capability. As early as November 7, 1947, Tass recalled, Foreign Minister Molotov had announced that for Russia the secret of the atom bomb "had been non-existent long ago." That statement had been taken "for a bluff" within American scientific circles which believed that Russia could not possess an atomic weapon earlier than 1952, the Soviet newspaper proudly reported. The fact that the Soviet Union enjoyed atomic capability would have no effect on its advocacy of an absolute prohibition of atomic weapons, Tass concluded.

In his announcement, Truman had said reassuringly that

> ever since atomic energy was first realized by man the eventual development of this new force by other nations was to be expected. This probability has always been taken into account by us.

At the State Department, Dean Acheson took pains to point out that the Soviet atomic explosion was no news to anyone and "makes no change in our policy." General Groves advised the American people not to lose any sleep over the Russian bomb because the United States was "certainly in the lead" in any atomic race. Many men, however, were not quite so confident. "Today," Leo Szilard wrote, "I am as frightened as I was in the years immediately before World War II." Others experienced the same sense of anxiety and urgency they had felt in the immediate aftermath of Hiroshima. They called for an emergency meeting of the United Nations Atomic Energy Commission, feeling sure that now that the Soviet Union had the bomb, it would be more willing to negotiate. But within the Soviet Union another conclusion had been reached. There was still much to be done. The United States already had a large atomic stockpile. Could the Russians afford not to catch up?

In America, similar sentiments were heard. When the nuclear physicist I. I. Rabi learned of the first Russian atomic explosion he anxiously concluded "that somehow or other some answer must be made in some form to this to regain the lead which we had." [11] He immediately began discussions with Ernest O. Lawrence and Oppenheimer regarding the construction of a hydrogen bomb. Rabi later recalled this period:

It seemed to me that we were in the position of two runners in the race, where it was quite clear that your opponent was running and running quite fast. It was probable you were ahead of him in actual distance. It was not obvious that he was not running faster than you were. Our own objectives at that time had to be as far as we could make them to be sure we were running as fast as he was. [12]

On November 1, 1949, Senator Edwin C. Johnson, a member of the Joint Committee on Atomic Energy, revealed in a television interview that American scientists were already building a superbomb, a hydrogen bomb, one thousand times more powerful than the bomb dropped on Nagasaki. In February of 1950, to stem the raging American fears, President Truman confirmed this announcement. America was indeed building a hydrogen bomb.[13]

The American atomic monopoly was over. The nuclear arms race had officially begun.

V

Conclusions

21

Sharing the Guilt

NATIONS, LIKE PEOPLE, are the products of their past. Their present actions cannot be understood out of context. Their future behavior cannot be predicted according to standards of rational conduct for some model nation. No nation is a model nation. The way any nation acts is a function of its particular history and the present state of its national psyche.

Mankind failed to achieve international control of atomic energy after the Second World War because the principal nations involved in the effort were unable to disenthrall themselves from either the drive of their national self-interest, as history had shaped it, or the passion of their ideology as they perceived it. They were unable to isolate the problem of atomic energy from their traditional international relations and view it as the unique and extraordinary development which it was. And so they failed to control atomic energy during this time when the state of the art was so rudimentary and the existence of atomic capability so limited that control — that is, prohibition of dangerous uses and regulation of safe uses — would have been a manageable task, as it is not today. In the guilt and responsibility for this epic failure, the United States shares equally with the Soviet Union.

This is primarily a study of the futile effort to control atomic energy and prohibit nuclear weapons, but if one is to understand this failure it is necessary to consider the histories of the two principal participants in the effort, Russia and America, and to reflect on the state of their relations as the Second World War came to a close.

The first and, in many ways, most critical dimension is space. America was blessed with natural barriers. To its east and its west, two great oceans have provided security from attack. Russia, on the other hand, is exposed. Sitting on a vast plain, there is nothing of military consequence separating Russia from Asia to the east and Europe to the west. Russian history from its beginnings to our own time is characterized by continuous foreign military assaults, particularly from the west. The Huns, the Bulgars, the Avars, the Khazars, the Magyars, the Pechenegs, the Tartars, the Polish, the Swedish, the Turks, the French, and finally the Germans — each of these nations came in their turn to threaten, attack, and often conquer Russia. In generation after generation, thousands and finally millions of Russians died defending their nation from foreign assault. The great Russian cities were burned and pillaged over and over again, their people slaughtered with devastating regularity. Each time, the Russian nation rose up and used its other principal dimension — mass, the force of numbers — to repel the foreign armies. Each time, Russia sought to expand its space, by extending its boundaries, to prevent another intrusion from without. This is not a history likely to breed a nation of internationalists, a people who greeted foreigners with openness and were free of suspicion. This is a history that created a people haunted by fear, who lived without confidence, and viewed the world outside with a sense of mistrust and inferiority.

The history of America, of course, is quantitatively shorter, but the more critical factors distinguishing it from Russia are qualitative. America is a nation populated by continuous waves of immigrants who left their homes to find something better. Protected by the oceans, their principal challenge was to claim and develop the rich, natural wilderness which expanded before them. They accomplished this through the individual labors of millions of men. Justifiably proud of their nation-building deeds, the Americans viewed the world outside their boundaries with confidence and a feeling of superiority. If their spirit was isolationist, that was not because they feared foreign nations but rather because they felt that they did not need foreign nations in order to flourish.

These radically different historical factors naturally produced different political traditions. Compelled by foreign invaders to mass together under strong leadership, the Russians accustomed themselves to rule by a powerful, centralized autocracy. The Americans, on the other hand, came to believe in and preach a political ethic that stressed the independence and power of individual citizens, even if they did not always practice it. America's democratic ideology grew naturally out of America's history. In a somewhat different sense, the communist ideology fit neatly within the contours of Russian history. The communist vision of perpetual conflict with the capitalist world, the communist fear of a hostile capitalist encirclement, the communist principle of an internal dictatorship of the proletariat, the communist theory of national sovereignty which portrayed foreign contact and international involvement as violations — all these tenets found ready parallels in the history of Russia. Several historians have argued convincingly that Russian conduct in world affairs during the twentieth century would have been the same if Karl Marx had never lived and the czars had remained in control of their land.

One of the primary causes of the failure to achieve international atomic control and the concurrent failure to prevent the cold war was the inability of America's statesmen and people to see through the avalanche of Communist rhetoric and deal with Soviet foreign policy as something shaped by Russia's unique history and guided by the Russians' conception of their national interest. In this more accurate light, Russia's goals are seen to be more limited and less in conflict with America's. Similarly, the Russians were unable to emancipate themselves from their own propaganda and to appreciate America's foreign policy after the Second World War as anything other than confirmation of the communist theory of the fatalistic inevitability of conflict with the capitalist countries.

The Soviet Union paid a vast human price for victory in the Second World War. More than 5 percent of the Russian population, literally millions of their people, had died in the conflict. When the war finally ended, however, the Russians experienced one of the proudest, most confident moments in their history. They had repelled Hitler's massive onslaught and, in doing so, had extended themselves westward to occupy the greater part of Eastern Europe. Thus, they had realized the historic Russian ambition of building a buffer between Russian soil and the invading nations of the West. Bulgaria, Hungary, Rumania, and Poland were occupied by Russian troops. In Germany they were at the Elbe River, one hundred miles west of Berlin, and in Austria, at the Danube. Although they did not occupy Yugoslavia, their presence there was clear by virtue of alliance. First at Yalta early in 1945 and then at all the other conferences that followed, the Russians fought to secure the human barrier which their military might had erected. Their plea was for recognition of Eastern Europe as a Soviet sphere of influence. This desire, however, ran counter to America's apparent conception of the postwar world which was to be void of power blocs and dominated by the United Nations. It also unsettled American diplomats because it placed Soviet troops within easy striking distance of America's allies in Western Europe who had emerged from the war in a weak condition. The debate over Eastern Europe affected the attempt to control atomic weapons because of the conclusion it induced among the Russians that the possibilities for cooperation with the United States were severely limited.

Consistency was not one of the characteristics that marked America's side of the argument over the fate of Eastern Europe. While protesting the creation of a Soviet sphere of influence in Eastern Europe on the theory that it would constitute a return to the evil days of international power politics that had caused two world wars, the United States nevertheless zealously protected its own sphere of influence in the Western Hemisphere. From the earliest enunciation of the Monroe Doctrine right down to the twentieth century, America has proved itself willing to resort to arms to keep anti-American governments out of power in Latin America. While employing the rhetoric of American democratic ideology to oppose Soviet desires in Eastern Europe by appealing for free and democratic governments there, the United States nevertheless has moved with ease into intimate and generous alliances with military dictatorships in Latin America — many of which have been able to remain in power solely because of American support.

These inconsistencies soured Russian leaders and confirmed their ideological theories of capitalist desires for world domination, in the same way that their Communist rhetoric confirmed the views of American statesmen who interpreted the Russian occupation of Eastern Europe as proof of a Communist desire for world domination.

In the end, Stalin held the determinative cards in Eastern Europe because his troops were there. Regardless of American objections, he would be able to offer the Russian people the western buffer zone which they had so long desired.

At this moment of supreme satisfaction and confidence for the Russian nation, the atom bomb appeared, and all the historic calculations were thrown off. Against this devastating new weapon, the barrier to the west was impotent. Now, foreign invaders might strike from the air with a weapon against which the Russians could offer no defense. One can appreciate the anxiety which the atom bomb must have caused among the Russian people and their leaders — particularly in the context of the growing breach with their wartime allies who possessed the bomb. The bomb was an assault not only on their security but also on their pride.

The xenophobia which is so weighty a factor in Russian history makes it questionable whether the Soviet Union would ever have consented to the presence of a foreign-dominated, international authority on Russian soil. This presence was a minimum condition of any reasonable plan for the international control of atomic energy and nuclear weapons. When one considers the fear which the atom bomb must have caused within Russia, however, it is reasonable to conclude that there were steps which the United States could have taken in the postwar world which might have induced the Soviet Union to feel that measure of trust necessary to depart from their traditional suspicions and accept a necessary foreign presence. Once such step would have been open American recognition of a Soviet sphere of influence in Eastern Europe, a recognition which would have amounted to the acknowledgment of reality and which was a fact of American foreign policy in the years to follow even if it was never articulated as such. The passivity of the United States in both the Hungarian uprising of 1956 and the Czechoslovakian tremors of 1968 makes it clear that American diplomats have accepted the fact that Eastern Europe is a Soviet sphere of influence. In hindsight, there are several other actions which the United States could have undertaken in relation to the atomic bomb which might have cut through the web of Soviet mistrust.

The first and perhaps most important weakness in America's policy for the international control of atomic energy is that it was tardy. For a drastically long time there was no American policy. Voices pleading for action were heard, but the men with power did not act until it was extremely late. The single-minded drive of the Manhattan Project to build an atomic bomb seemed during the war to take on a life of its own, devoid of diplomatic considerations. Roosevelt and Stimson were too busy and too tired in the closing year of the war to force the necessary diplomatic considerations into the atomic equation. Various scientists urged the American government to consider the question of whether and how to use the bomb in the light of the effect that use would have on postwar efforts for international control of atomic energy. These men argued that the United States must emerge from the war with the moral leadership that would be necessary for a peaceful postwar world and control of atomic weapons. If the world's people viewed the United States as an inhumane power which could not be trusted, the scientists and others argued, then naturally there would be less desire on the part of other nations to enter into a system of atomic control rather than plunge furiously into the pursuit of atomic capability. Russia, of course, was the nation upon whom these factors would play most intimately. The scientists who made these suggestions were turned back politely as General Groves's atomic machine moved heedlessly toward its ordained conclusion. Niels Bohr, Vannevar Bush, and James Conant appealed for an effort to bring Russia into the atomic picture before the bomb was used but were rebuffed by men like James Byrnes, who viewed Russia as an alien nation which could not be trusted. Byrnes never saw how America's handling of the atomic bomb might have made Russia more trustworthy. President Truman's ascendancy to power at the inception of the nuclear age found him unknowing and unprepared to exert the massive and courageous authority that would have been necessary to stop the atomic bomb from thoughtless use. The failure even to inform Russia, let alone to invite her in as an atomic partner, before the end of the war, seems particularly foolish when one considers that American leaders knew that Communist spies had already learned the outlines of the work of the Manhattan Project and that Russian science was capable of achieving nuclear capability in short order on its own.

But the inaction of the American government which had more devastating effects occurred after the war was over. No official contact concerning atomic energy was made with the Soviet government until the end of November 1945, when Byrnes proposed that the subject be placed on the agenda of the Moscow Conference scheduled for mid-December. Three crucial months therefore passed in silence between these two principal nations of the postwar world on the most extraordinary new factor in that world. America's silence in relation to Russia was not equalled elsewhere. During those three months, the United States announced that it was continuing to build atomic bombs, publicly tightened its domination of atomic materials and processes, and formally declared that it was holding the bomb in a sacred trust until the rest of the world proved itself ready for atomic involvement. After the departure of Henry L. Stimson, there was no one within the highest level of American public leadership who was willing to advocate another course. Truman was preoccupied with the maze of domestic crises associated with the postwar readjustment. Byrnes, whose experience in diplomatic affairs was limited, believed from the start that the Russians would never participate in an effective atomic control system and therefore concluded that it was not even worth a try. To Byrnes the bomb was the one strong stick he held to beat the Russians out of Eastern Europe and to secure European peace treaties. That was the attitude he carried with him to the Foreign Ministers conference in London during September 1945 and, no doubt, explains the stormy failures of that meeting.

Only the anxious cries of Clement Attlee, who was under heavy political pressure at home to say something about atomic control, shook the American government out of its atomic policy stupor. The Truman-Attlee-King conference during November 1945 was the manifestation of this new activism, but it did little more than confirm a belief among the Russians that their wartime capitalistic allies were plotting against them. The substantive contributions of the conference were not along constructive lines. Vannevar Bush was exclusively responsible for the communiqué of the conference, whose major contribution was the postulating of stages of transition to an international system of control for atomic energy. Bush, however, departed drastically from the plea of his mentor, Henry L. Stimson, by advocating a commission within the United Nations to work for international atomic control rather than the direct, private approach to the Russians which Stimson had advocated. This course was ultimately as devoid of success as Stimson said it would be. In this formulation of American policy there had been no effort to build a policy which might be acceptable to the Russians, and the Russians were entirely aware of this. When Molotov announced at the time of the Truman-Attlee-King conference that the Soviet Union would "soon have atomic energy and many other things too," he was declaring the logical Soviet response to America's atomic policy. In the face of silence, lacking any indication that the capitalistic West intended to make any sincere attempt to achieve international atomic cooperation, and concerned over what he viewed as the hostile Western designs on Eastern Europe, Molotov was saying that the Soviet Union had decided to build the atomic bomb itself since the Americans were certainly not prepared to offer it to them at a reasonable price.

This Russian conclusion was confirmed in the atomic negotiations with America that followed. From the point of view of the Soviet Union, America never offered a plan which it could afford to accept.

The long charade of atomic diplomacy began at the Moscow Conference in December 1945. There Byrnes asked only that the Russians join the United States in co-sponsoring a resolution in the United Nations to create a special atomic energy commission. Molotov agreed but insisted on a procedural change. He wanted the Atomic Energy Commission to be accountable to the Security Council, where Russia enjoyed the veto power, rather than to the General Assembly, where the West held a clear majority of the votes. For his part, Byrnes insisted on inclusion of a paragraph from the Truman-Attlee-King declaration which made it clear that the international atomic control system would not go into effect in one comprehensive gesture, but that there would be stages of transition. This was a domestically inspired political maneuver by Byrnes, who was anxious to mollify the nervous members of the United States Senate who felt he was going to give away the secret of the atomic bomb without anything in return. The concept of stages of transition gave these chauvinists the guarantee that nothing would be risked by the United States until it was absolutely sure that no other nation had, or could have, atomic capability. Byrnes and Molotov settled this procedural conflict with a horse trade. As the communiqué of the Moscow Conference revealed, Molotov was given the concept of accountability to the Security Council and the veto power, and Byrnes received his paragraph on stages. Never at Moscow was the substance of an atomic control scheme discussed. Never did Byrnes give the Russians any reason to believe that the United States was genuinely interested in prohibiting nuclear weapons and controlling atomic energy. Never did he lead the Russians to hope that America had altered its policy of holding atomic weapons in a "sacred trust."

With the prospect of negotiations at the United Nations on the horizon and Senator Brien McMahon threatening to begin a series of public hearings on the question of international atomic control, Byrnes finally felt compelled to appoint a policy planning group on the subject within the State Department. Five months had then passed since Hiroshima. Dean Acheson was asked to lead this five-man committee, and he, in turn, tapped David Lilienthal to lead another five-man board of consultants.

The Lilienthal Board moved intelligently and idealistically through a comprehensive factual investigation of the new world of atomic energy and came up with a plan for an international control authority which would be guaranteed partially by a system of inspection but largely by actual international ownership of mines, laboratories, and factories. This was a thoughtful and foresighted proposal. In some ways, it was even generous since it required that the United States, as atomic monopolist, ultimately relinquish its monopoly. From the start of its work, however, the Lilienthal Board agreed to be concerned solely with science and technology and not with politics. They never considered the preeminent problem of writing a proposal that could gain Soviet acceptance. In fact, the members of the Lilienthal Board were convinced that adoption of their plan by the Soviet Union would cause no less than another revolution in Russian society — a revolution which was to be accomplished apparently in return for Russian involvement in atomic development. This could not have seemed a very desirable *quid pro quo* to the Russians, who knew that they were capable of building atomic weapons themselves in three or four years.

The members of the Acheson Committee were even less concerned than the Lilienthal Board with the prospects for Soviet

acceptance. Their major additions to the Lilienthal plan were
aimed at minimizing the risks America assumed in proposing it.
They were concerned that the postwar demobilization of the
American Army and Navy had made the atomic bomb the major
factor in America's military arsenal and the primary guarantee
of its national security. The very remote prospect that the Soviet
Union might accept the Lilienthal plan therefore did not please
the Acheson Committee. Its members insisted that the proposal
include a declaration that the control system would take effect in
stages so that at each step the security of the United States would
be absolutely guaranteed. The Acheson Committee also inserted
a requirement that the United States continue to produce atomic
weapons until the final stages of transition to international control. This would be a matter of years, years in which the Soviet
Union would probably be able to develop nuclear capability on
its own, free of the distasteful requirements which the international control scheme demanded. Each of these additions of the
Acheson Committee had the natural effect of making Soviet assent
much less likely.

In selecting Bernard Baruch to take the Acheson-Lilienthal
Plan before the United Nations, Truman and Byrnes gave no
thought to increasing the likelihood of an agreement with the
Soviet Union. The job demanded a less ideological, more flexible
and experienced diplomat. Truman and Byrnes chose Baruch for
one reason only, and that was because his prestige would assure
the anxious members of Congress that the Truman Administration would not be duped into an international control plan that
wantonly distributed atomic secrets to the Russians. With this
comforting knowledge, Truman and Byrnes assumed, the Congress would be willing to enact the domestic atomic control plan
which they had put before it. They were right, of course, but this
did nothing for the cause of international atomic control.

The sincerity of Baruch's entire mission at the United Nations is seriously cast in doubt by the anxious warnings he received during the spring of 1946 from the Joint Chiefs of Staff that international control of atomic weapons would take from America the foundation of its national security, which was the atomic bomb in the aftermath of the demobilization of America's conventional military forces. If the Soviet Union had accepted the Baruch Plan in these circumstances, it is improbable that the United States would have proceeded with its total implementation. That is undoubtedly why the plan involved lengthy stages of transition before the United States would finally be compelled to let go of its nuclear weapons.

Baruch's insistence on eliminating the veto in atomic energy affairs was widely criticized at the time as a tactical blunder which allowed the Russians to assault the entire Baruch Plan on a very insubstantial ground. If this really was a tactical blunder, it was only so in terms of its effect on public opinion. It was hardly consequential in causing the Russian rejection of the Baruch Plan. More determinative in this regard was the continued production of atomic weapons by the United States, the extended stages of transition, and the requirement of an international presence on Soviet soil.

The failure to achieve international control of atomic weapons was therefore a result of the broad and selfish misunderstandings and conflict between the Soviet Union and the United States after the Second World War which came to be called the cold war. At the same time, the failure was also a cause of that conflict because of the anxiety which American possession of the atomic bomb aroused in Russia and the mistrust which America's tight-fisted atomic policy nurtured in the Soviet leaders.

There is a temptation, which will be acceded to here only briefly, to compare the period covered by this study to the attempts at nuclear control which are proceeding during the current time. The problem, of course, has become much less manageable because of the enormous multiplication and dissemination of nuclear weapons which has occurred during the twenty-five years since Hiroshima. In that time, Russia and America have come to understand each other's national interests somewhat better, but only somewhat better. It is still difficult to imagine the Soviet Union accepting international ownership, control, or inspection of atomic facilities on Russian soil. If such acceptance were miraculously forthcoming, would the isolated Chinese participate in such a system? And if the Chinese did not, could the Russians and Americans afford to? Perhaps the only additional cause for optimism that has been provided in the past twenty-five years is technological. The prospect of international inspection of atomic installations by aerial satellites makes the *quid pro quo* of international atomic control slightly less demanding.

In his solemn oration to the United Nations on June 14, 1946, Bernard Baruch warned that the nations of the world were faced with "a choice between the quick and the dead." Clearly, they did not choose the quick. Whether they chose death, only the passage of years will tell.

Notes

Notes

Abbreviations:

BAS — *The Bulletin of Atomic Scientists*
BMB — The Papers of Bernard M. Baruch at the Princeton Library
FROUS — *Foreign Relations of the United States,* Diplomatic Papers
   published by the State Department
HLS — The Papers of Henry L. Stimson at the Yale University Library
ITMJRO — *In the Matter of J. Robert Oppenheimer,* United States
   Atomic Energy Commission
UNAEC — Records of the United Nations Atomic Energy Commission
AEC — United States Atomic Energy Commission

Preface

1. *New York Times,* August 17, 1945.
2. Louis Halle, *The Cold War as History* (New York: Harper & Row,
   1967), p. xiii.

1. A Quiet Beginning

1. Arthur H. Compton, *Atomic Quest* (New York: Oxford University
   Press, 1956), p. 143; *BAS,* December 1962, 18:19.
2. *BAS,* October 1964, 20:16.
3. Lewis Strauss, *Men and Decisions* (Garden City, N.Y.: Doubleday
   & Co., Inc., 1962), p. 171.
4. Compton, p. 31.
5. Richard G. Hewlett and Oscar A. Anderson, Jr., *New World* (University Park, Pa.: The Pennsylvania State University Press, 1962),
   p. 17.
6. Margaret M. Gowing, *Britain and Atomic Energy, 1939–1945* (New
   York: St. Martin's Press, Inc., 1964), p. 46.
7. Gowing, p. 86.

8. Stephane Groueff, *Manhattan Project* (Boston: Little, Brown & Co., 1967), p. 13.
9. Robert E. Sherwood, *Roosevelt and Hopkins* (New York: Harper and Bros., 1948), p. 153.
10. Compton, p. 13.
11. *ITMJRO,* p. 13.
12. *London Daily Telegraph,* October 13, 1941.
13. John Finney, ed., *Hiroshima Plus 20* (New York: Delacorte Press, 1965), p. 22.
14. Alice Kimball Smith, *A Peril and a Hope* (Chicago: University of Chicago Press, 1965), p. 16.

2. The Futile, But Visionary, Efforts of Niels Bohr

1. Gowing, p. 349.
2. *BAS,* September 1963, 19:8.
3. John Wheeler-Bennett, *John Anderson, Viscount Waverly* (New York: St. Martin's Press, Inc., 1962), p. 296.
4. S. Z. Rosenthal, ed., *Niels Bohr* (New York: John Wiley, 1967), pp. 193–94; Gowing, p. 246.
5. Ibid.
6. Wheeler-Bennett, p. vii.
7. Hewlett and Anderson, pp. 264–65.
8. Ibid., p. 268.
9. *ITMJRO,* p. 173.
10. Gowing, p. 139.
11. Hewlett and Anderson, p. 271.
12. Gowing, p. 159.
13. Sherwood, p. 703.
14. Hewlett and Anderson, p. 271.
15. The Earl of Birkenhead, *Halifax* (Boston: Houghton Mifflin Co., 1966), p. 10.
16. Hewlett and Anderson, p. 273.
17. Sir Winston S. Churchill, *The Hinge of Fate* (London: Cassell & Co. Ltd., 1951), p. 703.
18. Hewlett and Anderson, p. 274.
19. Leslie Groves, *Now It Can Be Told* (New York: Harper & Row, 1962), p. 131; Hewlett and Anderson, pp. 274–75.
20. Groves, p. 131.
21. Hewlett and Anderson, p. 275.
22. Groves, p. 132.
23. Gowing, p. 167.
24. Ibid., pp. 346–47.
25. Ibid., p. 437.

26. Letter from Frankfurter to Oppenheimer, November 23, 1962, in The Frankfurter Papers, Library of Congress.
27. Gowing, p. 349; Rosenthal, p. 202.
28. Gowing, p. 352.
29. Ibid., pp. 355–56.
30. Bohr's notes on letter from Kapitza in The Papers of J. Robert Oppenheimer, Library of Congress.
31. Rosenthal, p. 342.
32. Gowing, pp. 356–57. (Based on the author's interview with Bohr. President Roosevelt left no record of the conference.)
33. Sir Winston S. Churchill, *Triumph and Tragedy* (London: Cassell & Co. Ltd., 1951), p. 133.
34. *Hyde Park Memoir* printed in full in appendix to Gowing.
35. Gowing, p. 358.
36. Ibid., p. 359.

3. Bush, Conant, and Stimson Begin to Lobby for Atomic Control

1. Bush to Conant, April 17, 1944. AEC. Historical Doc. 180.
2. Smith, p. 20 and appendix, p. 551.
3. Bush and Conant to Stimson, September 19, 1944. AEC. Historical Doc. 279.
4. Bush Memorandum of Conference, September 22, 1944. AEC. Historical Doc. 185; Bush to Conant, September 23, 1944. AEC. Historical Doc. 186.
5. Gowing, p. 341.
6. Bush Memorandum of Conference with Stimson, September 25, 1944. AEC. Historical Doc. 280.
7. Bush to Conant, October 24, 1944. AEC. Historical Doc. 188.
8. Alexander Sachs, in Transcript of Hearings before the Special Committee on Atomic Energy of the United States Congress, November 27, 1945, p. 561.
9. Bush to Conant, December 13, 1944. AEC. Historical Doc. 284.
10. Stimson Diary, December 30, 1944, in HLS.
11. Stimson Diary, December 31, 1944.
12. Edward L. Stettinius, *Roosevelt and the Russians* (Garden City, N.Y.: Doubleday & Co., Inc., 1949), p. 33.
13. Ibid., p. 117.
14. Ibid., p. 118.
15. Bush to Bundy, February 1, 1945. AEC. Historical Doc. 196.
16. Bush to Conant, February 15, 1945. AEC. Historical Doc. 200; Stimson Diary, February 15, 1945.
17. Stimson Diary, March 5, 1945.
18. Stimson Diary, March 15, 1945.

4. Scientific Agitation

1. Aaron Novick, "A Plea for Atomic Freedom," *New Republic.* March 25, 1946, pp. 399–400.
2. *BAS,* December 1947, pp. 351–53.
3. Otto Nathan, *Einstein on Peace* (New York: Simon & Schuster, Inc., 1960), pp. 304–5.
4. Bohr's Open Letter in Rosenthal, p. 345.
5. Gowing, p. 362.
6. Harry S. Truman, *Memoirs* (Garden City, N.Y.: Doubleday & Co., Inc., 1955, 1956), 1:5.
7. *BAS,* October 1964, 20:16.
8. Franck Memorandum. AEC. Historical Doc. 204.
9. Truman, 1:87.
10. Ibid.
11. Hewlett and Anderson, p. 343.
12. Stimson Diary, April 25, 1945.
13. Bush to Bundy, April 25, 1945. AEC. Historical Doc. 285.
14. Stimson Diary, May 1, 1945.
15. Stimson Diary, May 2, 1945.
16. Stimson to Conant, May 4, 1945. AEC. Historical Doc. 286.
17. Conant to Stimson, May 5, 1945. AEC. Historical Doc. 287.
18. Hewlett and Anderson, p. 354.
19. Stimson Diary, April 2 and April 3, 1945.
20. Stimson Diary, May 10, 1945.
21. Stimson Diary, May 14, 1945.
22. Conant to Bush, May 14, 1945. AEC. Historical Doc. 209.
23. James Byrnes, *All in One Lifetime* (New York: Harper and Bros., 1958), p. 284; Smith, p. 29; *U.S. News & World Report.* August 15, 1960, p. 68.

5. The Interim Committee's Perfunctory Response

1. Groves, p. 265.
2. Fletcher Knebel and Charles W. Bailey, *No High Ground* (New York: Harper and Bros., 1960), p. 244.
3. Sir Winston S. Churchill, *Triumph and Tragedy,* p. 546.
4. Stimson Diary, May 31, 1945; Smith, pp. 34–40; Hewlett and Anderson, pp. 356–60; Compton, pp. 238–39.
5. Elting E. Morison, *Turmoil and Tradition* (Boston: Houghton Mifflin Co., 1960), p. 630; Herbert Feis, *Japan Subdued* (Princeton, N.J.: Princeton University Press, 1961), p. 73.
6. Stimson Diary, June 6, 1945.
7. *BAS,* May 1946.

8. Compton, p. 241.
9. Groves, p. 266.
10. Compton to Stimson, June 12, 1945. Manhattan District Files, cited in Hewlett and Anderson, p. 367.
11. Compton, pp. 240–41.
12. H. L. Stimson, "The Decision to Drop the Atomic Bomb," *Harper's.* February 1947, pp. 99–100.
13. Notes on Interim Committee Meeting, June 21, 1945. Manhattan District Files, cited in Hewlett and Anderson, p. 370.
14. Bard to Stimson, Manhattan District Files, cited in Hewlett and Anderson, p. 370. *U.S. News & World Report.* August 15, 1960, pp. 73–74.
15. Stimson Diary, June 20–24, 1945.
16. Stimson Diary, July 3, 1945.
17. *FROUS,* 1945, 2:12–13.
18. Groves, p. 271.
19. William D. Leahy, *I Was There* (New York: Whittlesey House, McGraw-Hill Book Co., 1950), p. 441.
20. Groves, pp. 271, 273.

6. Potsdam and the Attack

1. Stimson Diary, July 15, 1945.
2. *New York Times,* September 26 and 27, 1945; Hewlett and Anderson, p. 379.
3. Stimson Diary, July 16, 1945.
4. Stimson Diary, July 17, 1945.
5. Truman, 1:340.
6. Churchill, *Triumph and Tragedy,* pp. 640–41.
7. Stimson Diary, July 19, 1945.
8. Stimson Memorandum in HLS, titled "Reflections on the Basic Problems Which Confront Us." Stimson Diary, July 27, 1945.
9. Stimson Diary, July 20, 1945.
10. Stimson Diary, July 21, 1945.
11. Leahy Diary, July 16, 1945, in The Papers of Admiral Leahy, Library of Congress.
12. Truman, 1:412.
13. Stimson Diary, July 22, 1945.
14. Stimson Diary, July 24, 1945.
15. Truman, 1:416.
16. Hewlett and Anderson, p. 399.
17. Compton, pp. 242–43.
18. Farrington Daniels and Arthur Compton, "A Poll of Scientists at Chicago," *BAS,* February 1948, p. 44.

19. Robert Jungk, *Brighter Than a Thousand Suns* (New York: Harcourt, Brace and Co., 1958), p. 171.
20. William L. Laurence, *Dawn over Zero* (New York: Alfred A. Knopf Co., 1946), p. 251. Department of War, United States Strategic Bombing Survey, "The Effect of Atom Bombs on Hiroshima and Nagasaki."

7. The Force from Which the Sun Draws Its Power

1. Michihiko Hachiya, *Hiroshima Diary,* trans. Werner Wells (Chapel Hill: N.C.: University of North Carolina, 1955), August 6, 1945.
2. Groueff, p. 344.
3. Truman, 1:421. *New York Times,* August 7, 1945.
4. Stimson Diary, July 30, 1945.
5. *New York Times,* August 7, 1945.
6. *Hiroshima Diary,* August 7, 1945.
7. *Hiroshima Diary,* August 8, 1945.
8. Stimson Diary, August 1, 2, and 8, 1945.
9. Stimson Diary, August 9, 1945.
10. Gowing, pp. 364–65.
11. *Newsweek,* November 19, 1945, p. 34.
12. Attlee to Truman, August 8, 1945. *FROUS,* 1945, 2:36.
13. *New York Times,* August 10, 1945.
14. *Hiroshima Diary,* August 9, 1945.
15. Attlee to Truman, August 11, 1945. *FROUS,* 1945, 2:40.
16. *Hiroshima Diary,* August 11 and 15, 1945.
17. *Hiroshima Diary,* August 13, 1945.
18. *New York Times,* August 10, 1945.
19. *New York Times,* August 12, 1945.
20. Ibid.
21. *New York Times,* August 16, 1945.
22. *BAS,* January 1951.
23. *New York Times,* August 8, 1945.
24. *New York Times,* August 10, 1945.
25. Ibid.
26. *New York Times,* August 7, 1945.
27. Ibid.
28. *New York Times,* September 5, 1945.
29. *New York Times,* September 16, 1945.
30. *New York Times,* November 11, 1945.
31. *New York Times,* November 29, 1945.
32. *New York Times,* September 6, 1945.
33. *New York Times,* October 2, 1945.
34. Department of State, *The International Control of Atomic Energy:*

Growth of a Policy (Washington, D.C.: Government Printing Office, 1948), p. 13.
35. *New York Times,* August 26, 1945.
36. *New York Times,* August 12, 1945.
37. Ibid.
38. *New York Times,* September 2, 1945.
39. Stimson Diary, July 25, 1945.
40. Stimson Diary, undated memorandum regarding visit to St. Hubert's, titled "August 12 to September 3, 1945."

8. Stimson Departs and Is Forgotten

1. Stimson Diary, September 4, 1945.
2. Hewlett and Anderson, p. 417.
3. Stimson Diary, September 5, 1945.
4. *Hiroshima Diary,* September 11, 1945.
5. *FROUS,* 1945, 2:40.
6. Ibid., 2:41.
7. Stimson Diary, September 12, 1945.
8. Stimson Diary, September 13, 1945.
9. Stimson Diary, September 17, 1945.
10. Stimson Diary, September 18, 1945.
11. Stimson Diary, September 21, 1945; Walter Millis, ed., *The Forrestal Diaries* (New York: Viking Press, Inc., 1951), pp. 94–96; Truman, 1:525–26; Hewlett and Anderson, pp. 420–21; Henry Wallace, "Whose Atomic Secret?" *New Republic.* February 17, 1947, p. 26; *BAS,* February 1952.
12. *New York Times,* September 22, 1945.
13. *FROUS,* 1945, 2:48, 54.
14. Hewlett and Anderson, pp. 426–27.
15. *New York Times,* October 4, 1945.
16. *New York Times,* October 9, 1945.
17. Ibid.
18. *New York Times,* September 25, 1945.
19. *New York Times,* December 15, 1945.
20. *New York Times,* October 8, 1945.
21. *FROUS,* 1945, 2:55.
22. Ibid., 2:61.

9. The Scientists and the British Force America to Act

1. Leo Szilard, "We Turned the Switch," *The Nation.* December 22, 1945, pp. 718–19.

2. Smith, pp. 88–89.
3. Jungk, p. 228.
4. Truman, 1:535.
5. Attlee to Truman, *FROUS*, 1945, 2:58.
6. *New York Times*, October 28, 1945.
7. *FROUS*, 1945, 2:63.
8. Ibid.
9. Bush to Conant, November 7, 1945, in The Papers of Vannevar Bush, Library of Congress.
10. Bush to Byrnes, November 5, 1945. AEC. Historical Doc. 218.
11. Bush to Conant, November 8, 1945, in The Bush Papers.
12. Bush and Groves to Byrnes, November 9, 1945. AEC. Historical Doc. 218.
13. R. Gordon Arneson minutes of November 10, 1945. *FROUS*, 1945, 2:64.
14. Francis Williams with Clement Attlee, *A Prime Minister Remembers* (London: William Heinemann Ltd., 1961), p. 103; *Newsweek*. November 12, 1945, p. 44.
15. Wheeler-Bennett, p. 283.
16. Diary of Admiral Leahy, November 11, 1945, in The Leahy Papers.
17. *New York Times*, November 12, 1945.
18. Bush's memorandum for the file, November 14, 1945. AEC. Historical Document. 160.
19. *New York Times*, November 16, 1945.
20. James Byrnes, *Speaking Frankly* (New York: Harper and Bros., 1947), p. 265.
21. Bush Memorandums. AEC. Historical Docs. 160 and 161.
22. Groves, p. 403.
23. Ibid.
24. *FROUS*, 1945, 2:67.
25. Ibid., 2:75.
26. Ibid., 2:75–76.
27. F. Williams, p. 103.
28. Bush to Stimson, in HLS, November 13, 1945.
29. Bush to Conant, November 10, 1945 in The Bush Papers; Memorandum of Conference, November 15, 1945, AEC. Historical Doc. 162; Arthur Vandenberg, *The Private Papers of Senator Vandenberg* (Boston: Houghton Mifflin Co., 1952), p. 226.

10. Moving Slowly toward Moscow

1. *New York Times*, November 17, 1945.
2. *New York Times*, November 21, 1945.
3. Hewlett and Anderson, p. 470.
4. Ibid.

5. *New York Times*, November 24, 1945.
6. Hewlett and Anderson, p. 470.
7. *FROUS*, 1945, 2:578.
8. Ibid., 2:579.
9. Ibid., 2:580.
10. Ibid., 2:580–81.
11. Hewlett and Anderson, p. 470.
12. *FROUS*, 1945, 2:582–83.
13. Ibid., 2:586.
14. Ibid., 2:77, 591.
15. Ibid., 2:78, 591, 594, 597.
16. *New York Times*, December 8, 1945.
17. *FROUS*, 1945, 2:599, 600, 606.
18. *ITMJRO*, p. 36.
19. *FROUS*, 1945, 2:92.
20. Ibid., 2:96.
21. Ibid., 2:97.
22. Tom Connally, *My Name Is Tom Connally* (New York: Crowell, Collier & Macmillan, Inc., 1954), p. 287.
23. Vandenberg, pp. 224–25.
24. Ibid., p. 227.
25. Connally, p. 287.
26. Vandenberg, p. 227.
27. *BAS*, February 1946; Jungk, p. 260.
28. Arnold Kramish, *Atomic Energy in the Soviet Union* (Stanford, Cal.: Stanford University Press, 1959), pp. 84–85.
29. *FROUS*, 1945, 2:85.
30. Ibid., 5:922.
31. Feis, *Japan Subdued*, p. 115.
32. Kramish, p. 87.
33. Modest Rubinstein, "The Foreign Press and the Atom Bomb," *New Times*. September 1, 1945.
34. M. Tolchenov, "The Atomic Bomb Discussion in the Foreign Press," *New Times*. November 1, 1945.
35. *New York Times*, November 7, 1945.
36. *New York Times*, November 12, 1945.
37. Kramish, p. 90.
38. *New York Times*, November 16, 1945.
39. *New York Times*, November 15, 1945.
40. A. Sokoloff, "International Cooperation and Its Foes," *New Times*. November 15, 1945.
41. *New York Times*, November 17, 1945.
42. *New York Times*, December 11, 1945.

11. The Moscow Conference

1. George Kennan, *Memoirs, 1925–1950* (Boston: Little, Brown & Co., 1967), p. 285; *New York Times,* December 15, 1945.
2. Vandenberg, pp. 227–30; Truman, 1:546–48; *FROUS,* 1945, 1:609.
3. *FROUS,* 1945, 2:663.
4. Whitney and Kennan Memorandums, *FROUS,* 1945, 5:884, 933.
5. *New York Times,* December 18, 1945.
6. *FROUS,* 1945, 2:608.
7. Byrnes, *Speaking Frankly,* pp. 266–67.
8. *FROUS,* 1945, 2:660.
9. Kennan, *Memoirs,* pp. 286–87.
10. *FROUS,* 1945, 2:709.
11. Ibid., 2:664.
12. Ibid., 2:692.
13. Ibid., 2:709–10.
14. Ibid., 2:736, 740.
15. Ibid., 2:744.
16. Kennan, *Memoirs,* p. 289.
17. *FROUS,* 1945, 2:750.
18. Kennan, *Memoirs,* p. 289.
19. *FROUS,* 1945, 2:761–69.
20. Byrnes, *Speaking Frankly,* p. 268.
21. *FROUS,* 1945, 2:822–44.
22. *New York Times,* December 28, 1945.
23. Ibid.
24. *New York Times,* December 24, 1945.
25. *New York Times,* December 31, 1945.
26. *New York Times,* January 8, 1946.
27. *New York Times,* January 9, 1946.
28. *Newsweek,* January 21, 1946, p. 38.
29. *New York Times,* January 21, 1946.

12. A Feeling of Acute Revulsion

1. *New York Times,* September 12, 1945.
2. Stimson Diary, August 9, 1945, September 4 and 14, 1945.
3. *New York Times,* August 15, 1945.
4. *New York Times,* August 8, 1945.
5. *New York Times,* August 28, 1945.
6. *New York Times,* September 6, 1945.
7. Millis, p. 93.
8. *New York Times,* September 23, 1945.
9. *New York Times,* October 10, 1945.

10. *New York Times,* October 18, 1945.
11. Millis, p. 102.
12. Ibid., p. 107.
13. Ibid., pp. 128–29.
14. *New York Times,* April 7, 1946.
15. Truman, 1:509.

13. The Acheson-Lilienthal Report

1. Hewlett and Anderson, p. 533.
2. David E. Lilienthal, *Journals of David Lilienthal: The Atomic Energy Years* (New York: Harper & Row, 1964), pp. 12–13.
3. Groves, p. 411.
4. Lilienthal, p. 11.
5. Ibid., pp. 11–12.
6. Ibid., p. 12.
7. Ibid., p. 14.
8. Hewlett and Anderson, pp. 533–40; Smith, pp. 453–61; Daniel Lang, *Early Tales of the Atomic Age* (New York: Simon & Schuster, Inc., 1948), pp. 92–111.
9. *BAS,* July 1, 1946, p. 11.
10. Ibid.
11. *ITMJRO,* p. 544.
12. *BAS,* October 7, 1946, p. 14.
13. *New York Times,* February 10, 1946.
14. *New York Times,* February 12, 1946.
15. *New York Times,* February 21, 1946.
16. Compton, p. 117.
17. *New York Times,* March 20, 1946.
18. *New York Times,* March 5, 1946.
19. *New York Times,* March 8, 1946.
20. Lilienthal, p. 25.
21. Ibid., pp. 25–26; Hewlett and Anderson, pp. 539–40.
22. Hewlett and Anderson, p. 540–41.
23. Ibid., pp. 551–54; Lilienthal, pp. 24–30; Margaret Coit, *Mr. Baruch* (Boston: Houghton Mifflin Co., 1957), pp. 551–64.

14. The Baron of Hobcaw

1. Truman, 2:7.
2. Harry Irving Shumway, *Bernard M. Baruch* (Boston: L. C. Page, Inc., 1946), in the Introduction by Byrnes.
3. Baruch to Byrnes, March 13, 1946, in BMB.
4. *New York Times,* March 18, 1946.
5. Hewlett and Anderson, pp. 554–56.

6. Coit, p. 564; *Paterson* (New Jersey) *Evening News,* March 21, 1946.
7. Lilienthal, p. 30.
8. Vandenberg to Baruch, April 19, 1946, in BMB.
9. Smith, p. 469.
10. Eberstadt to Baruch, March 28, 1946, in BMB.
11. Byrnes to Lilienthal, March 23, 1946, in The Papers of David E. Lilienthal at the Princeton University Library.
12. *New York Times,* March 26, 1946.
13. Lilienthal, pp. 31–32.
14. Baruch to Truman, March 26, 1946, in BMB.
15. Bernard Baruch, *The Public Years* (New York: Holt, Rinehart, & Winston, Inc., 1957–60), p. 363; Coit, p. 565; *New York Times,* March 28, 1946.
16. *New York Times,* March 27, 1946.
17. Smith, p. 464.
18. Searls to Baruch, March 31, 1946; Baruch to Byrnes, March 31, 1946, in BMB.
19. Hewlett and Anderson, p. 558.
20. *BAS,* April 1, 1946.
21. Baruch to Searls, April 3, 1946, in BMB.
22. Lilienthal Board to Byrnes, April 23, 1946; Acheson to Byrnes, April 19, 1946, in BMB.
23. Hancock notes on April 17, 1946, meeting with Baruch, Searls, and Byrnes in BMB; Coit, pp. 573–74.
24. Hancock notes of meeting with Oppenheimer, April 5, 1946, in BMB.
25. Lilienthal, pp. 42–43.
26. Coit, pp. 575–76.
27. Hewlett and Anderson, p. 560.
28. Hancock memo, May 1, 1946, in BMB.
29. Baruch to Byrnes, May 6, 1946, in BMB.
30. Hewlett and Anderson, p. 562.
31. Hancock notes on April 4, 1946, meeting in BMB.
32. Hancock notes on May 8, 1946, conference in BMB.
33. Coit, p. 578.
34. Bush to Carroll Wilson, May 10, 1946, in The Bush Papers.
35. Notes of J. P. Davis on May 17, 1946, meeting in BMB.
36. Hancock memo re Washington conferences, May 1, 1946, in BMB.
37. Hewlett and Anderson, p. 566.
38. Lilienthal Board to Baruch, May 19, 1946, in The Lilienthal Papers.
39. Oppenheimer to Lilienthal, May 24, 1946, in The Lilienthal Papers.
40. Lilienthal to Oppenheimer, May 28, 1946, in The Lilienthal Papers.
41. Baruch to Lilienthal, May 27, 1946, in BMB.
42. Baruch to Herbert Marks, undated, in BMB.

15. The Last, Best Hope on Earth

1. Hewlett and Anderson, p. 567.
2. Eberstadt to Baruch, May 23, 1946, in BMB.
3. Baruch to the Joint Chiefs of Staff, May 23, 1946, in BMB.
4. Nimitz to Baruch, June 11, 1946, in BMB.
5. Spaatz to Baruch, undated, in BMB.
6. Eisenhower to Baruch, June 14, 1946, in BMB.
7. Hancock notes on meeting of Baruch and Byrnes, May 30, 1946, in BMB.
8. Hancock notes on meeting of Baruch and Groves, May 31, 1946, in BMB.
9. Hancock notes on evening meeting of Baruch and Byrnes, May 31, 1946, in BMB.
10. Hancock notes on phone conversation with Byrnes, June 1, 1946, in BMB.
11. Hancock to Byrnes, June 1, 1946, in BMB.
12. Hewlett and Anderson, p. 572.
13. Transcript of phone conversation between Baruch and Byrnes, June 6, 1946, in BMB.
14. Baruch memo on meetings with Byrnes and Truman, June 7, 1946, in BMB.
15. Truman to Baruch, June 7, 1946, in BMB.
16. *New York Times,* June 13, 1946.
17. *New York Times,* June 15, 1946.

16. The Russian Response

1. *New York Times,* June 15, 1946.
2. Ibid.
3. *Toledo Blade,* June 15, 1946.
4. *New York Times,* June 15, 1946.
5. Coit, p. 587.
6. *New York Times,* June 16, 1946.
7. Coit, p. 587.
8. George Kennan [X], "The Sources of Soviet Conduct," *Foreign Affairs.* 25:566–82.
9. *New York Times,* March 24, 1946, citing *Pravda,* March 14, 1946, and *Izvestia,* March 24, 1946.
10. *New Times,* March 15, 1946.
11. *New York Times,* April 1, 1946.
12. UNAEC Verbatim Record, second meeting, June 19, 1946; *New York Times,* June 19, 1946.
13. Coit, p. 591.

14. UNAEC Verbatim Record, third meeting, June 25, 1946.
15. *New York Times,* June 25, 1946.
16. *New York Times,* June 29, 1946. UNAEC Verbatim Record, first meeting of Working Committee, June 29, 1946.
17. Bedell Smith to State Department, June 26, 1946, in BMB.
18. Baruch to Acheson, June 23, 1946, in BMB.
19. Acheson to Baruch, July 1, 1946, in BMB.
20. Baruch to Acheson, July 9, 1946, in BMB.
21. Truman to Baruch, June 27, 1946, in BMB.

17. The Breach Grows Wider

1. Millis, p. 149; Coit, pp. 592–93.
2. *New York Times,* June 30, 1946.
3. *New York Times,* July 4, 1946.
4. *New York Times,* August 13, 1946.
5. *New York Times,* August 23, 1946.
6. UNAEC Summary Record of first meeting of Subcommittee One, July 1, 1946.
7. Department of State, *Growth of a Policy,* Memorandum One of the United States delegation to the UNAEC, pp. 148–51.
8. Department of State, *Growth of a Policy,* pp. 152–59.
9. Ibid., pp. 160–65.
10. *New York Times,* July 13, 1946; UNAEC Verbatim Record of second meeting of Working Committee, July 12, 1946.
11. Hancock to Searls, July 18, 1946, in BMB.
12. Truman to Baruch, July 10, 1946, in BMB.
13. Hancock to Searls, July 18, 1946, in BMB.
14. *New York Times,* July 19, 1946.
15. *New York Times,* July 25, 1946; UNAEC Verbatim Record of meeting of Committee Two, July 24, 1946.
16. Hancock to Byrnes, July 24, 1946, in BMB.
17. Notes on informal meeting of American, French, Canadian, and Australian delegations to the UNAEC, July 24, 1946, in BMB.
18. UNAEC Summary Record of meeting of Subcommittee Two, July 2, 1946.
19. UNAEC Summary Record of fourth meeting of Subcommittee Two, July 31, 1946.
20. UNAEC Summary Record of fifth meeting of Subcommittee Two, August 6, 1946.

18. Henry Wallace and the American Consensus

1. Baruch to Lilienthal, July 27, 1946, and Lilienthal to Baruch, July 27, 1946, in BMB.
2. *New York Times,* June 23, 1946; Lilienthal, pp. 74–77.

3. Hancock memo, July 29, 1946, in BMB.
4. Coit, p. 595.
5. Ibid.; Notes of Lincoln Gordon on United States delegation staff meeting, August 1, 1946, in BMB.
6. *New York Times*, August 25, 1946.
7. *New York Times*, August 28, 1946.
8. Hancock to Swope, August 8, 1946, in BMB.
9. Hancock memo, August 2, 1946, in BMB.
10. R. Gordon Arneson's notes on United States delegation staff meeting, August 23, 1946, in BMB.
11. Hewlett and Anderson, pp. 594–95; Coit, p. 596.
12. UNAEC Official Records, Report of the Scientific and Technical Committee.
13. R. Gordon Arneson's notes on United States delegation staff meeting, September 10, 1946, in BMB.
14. Eberstadt to Baruch, September 13, 1946, in BMB.
15. Hewlett and Anderson, pp. 596–97.
16. Coit, p. 597; *New York Times*, September 13–15, 1946; Truman, 1:555–58; Millis, pp. 207–9; Byrnes, *Speaking Frankly*, pp. 239–42.
17. Hancock memo on White House conference, September 8, 1946, in BMB.
18. Arthur Krock, *New York Times*, September 20, 1946.
19. *New York Times*, September 19, 1946; *Washington Daily News*, September 19, 1946.
20. Hancock to Clayton, telephone conference, September 19, 1946, in BMB.
21. R. Gordon Arneson's notes of Baruch-Wallace phone conversation, September 19, 1946, in BMB.
22. Byrnes, *Speaking Frankly*, pp. 239–42.
23. Truman, 1:555.
24. Coit, p. 598; Baruch to Wallace, telegram, September 20, 1946, in BMB.
25. *New York Times*, October 3, 1946.
26. *New York Times*, September 27, 1946; R. Gordon Arneson's notes on conference of Baruch, Wallace, *et al.*, September 27, 1946, in BMB.
27. Byrnes to Baruch, October 7, 1946, in BMB.
28. Coit, pp. 599–600; *New York Times*, October 3, 1946; Hewlett and Anderson, pp. 602–6.

19. A Hollow Victory

1. *New York Times*, September 29, 1946.
2. *New York Times*, October 2, 1946.
3. *New York Times*, October 4, 1946.

4. Franklin Lindsay to Baruch, September 25, 1946, in BMB.
5. Lindsay to Baruch, September 30, 1946, in BMB.
6. Lindsay memo to Baruch, September 25, 1946, in BMB.
7. Cadogan to Baruch, October 8, 1946, Eberstadt to Baruch, October 22, 1946, in BMB.
8. F. Kuh column from *PM*, September 26, 1946, in BMB.
9. Lindsay to Baruch, September 30, 1946, in BMB.
10. Lindsay to Baruch, October 21, 1946, in BMB.
11. Coit, p. 562; Baruch-Truman telephone conference, October 28, 1946, in BMB.
12. *New York Times,* October 30, 1946; Coit, p. 602.
13. *New York Times,* October 31, 1946.
14. Baruch to Acheson, November 2, 1946, in BMB.
15. Baruch to Byrnes, November 4, 1946, in BMB.
16. Byrnes to Baruch, November 5, 1946, in BMB.
17. Coit, p. 602.
18. Lindsay memo on meeting with Acheson, November 12, 1946, in BMB.
19. *New York Times,* November 28, 1946.
20. *New York Times,* December 3, 1946.
21. Hancock draft of Baruch to Ickes, August 29, 1946, in BMB.
22. Ickes to Baruch, September 16, 1946, in BMB.
23. Hancock to United States delegation staff, November 21 and 25, 1946, in BMB.
24. Baruch-Acheson telephone conversation transcript, November 26, 1946, in BMB.
25. UNAEC Verbatim Record of meeting, December 5, 1946, in BMB.
26. *New York Times,* December 6, 1946.
27. UNAEC Verbatim Record of meeting of Working Committee, December 17, 1946, in BMB.
28. Hewlett and Anderson, p. 613.
29. Baruch to Lilienthal, December 19, 1946, in BMB.
30. UNAEC Summary Record of meeting of Working Committee, December 20, 1946, in BMB.
31. UNAEC Summary Record of meeting of Working Committee, December 27, 1946, in BMB.
32. *New York Times,* December 28, 1946.
33. *New York Times,* December 29, 1946.
34. *New York Times,* December 31, 1946.
35. *New York Times,* January 5, 1947; Coit, pp. 607–8.

20. The Parallel Monologue

1. *Birmingham Post,* January 7, 1947.
2. Lilienthal to Baruch, undated, in BMB.

3. Historian General to Baruch, January 1947, in BMB.
4. *St. Louis Post Dispatch,* June 6, 1947.
5. Richard J. Barnet, *Who Wants Disarmament?* (Boston: Beacon Press, Inc., 1960), p. 22.
6. *New York Times,* March 6, 1947.
7. *ITMJRO,* p. 327.
8. Jungk, pp. 248–49.
9. *ITMJRO,* pp. 344.
10. *BAS,* vol. 5, October 1949.
11. *ITMJRO,* pp. 452–53.
12. *ITMJRO,* p. 489.
13. *BAS,* vol. 6, March 1950.

Bibliography

Bibliography

GATHERING THE DATA for this book was a most interesting enterprise because of the growing availability of primary materials covering the postwar period. Memoirs of some of the most important participants in the effort to control atomic weapons have appeared in recent years. Other key figures have opened their personal papers for use by researchers. Slowly, the United States government is declassifying the documentary history of the time.

The most important primary sources for this study have been:

The Papers of Henry L. Stimson at the Yale University Library

The Papers of Bernard M. Baruch and David E. Lilienthal at the Princeton University Library

The Papers of Vannevar Bush, Admiral William Leahy, and Robert Oppenheimer at the Library of Congress

Several invaluable government documents were available through the Office of the Chief Historian, United States Atomic Energy Commission. The United States government has also published important primary materials in several volumes, including the following:

U.S., Department of State. *Documents on Disarmament, 1945–1959.* Washington, D.C.: Government Printing Office, 1960.

————. *Foreign Relations of the United States.* Diplomatic Papers, 1945 General: Political and Economic Matters. Washington, D.C.: Government Printing Office, 1967.

————. *Foreign Relations of the United States.* Diplomatic Papers, 1945, Europe. Washington D.C.: Government Printing Office, 1967.

————. *Foreign Relations of the United States.* Diplomatic Papers, 1945, The Conference of Berlin. Washington, D.C.: Government Printing Office, 1961.

————. *The International Control of Atomic Energy: Growth of a Policy.* Washington, D.C.: Government Printing Office, 1946.

————. *The International Control of Atomic Energy: Policy at the Cross-roads.* Washington, D.C.: Government Printing Office, 1948.

Smyth, Henry. *Atomic Energy For Military Purposes.* Princeton, New Jersey: Princeton University Press, 1945.

United States Atomic Energy Commission. *In the Matter of J. Robert Oppenheimer.* Washington, D.C.: Government Printing Office, 1954.

Piecing together the story of the postwar atomic policy of the Soviet Union is a more difficult exercise. Here, I relied on English translations and reports of the more important Soviet journals including *Pravda, Izvestia,* and *New Times.*

The official records of the United Nations Atomic Energy Commission were available at the Yale University Library and in the Baruch Papers at the Princeton University Library.

Probably the most helpful periodical was the *New York Times,* which I read for every day during that period. I have also relied on the *Bulletin of Atomic Scientists* for primary materials as well as more general analyses.

Although the published works concerning the postwar period and particularly Russian-American relations during that time are ample and increasing, the literature on the specific topic of postwar efforts for atomic control is small. By far the best is *New World* by Richard G. Hewlett and Oscar A. Anderson, Jr. (University Park, Pennsylvania: Pennsylvania State University Press, 1962). This is the official history of the United States Atomic Energy Commission from 1939–1946. The authors had access to the files of the Atomic Energy Commission, Department of State, Manhattan District, and the Office of Scientific Research and Development, many of which have not yet been opened to other researchers. Margaret M. Gowing has prepared a similar, excellent volume for the United Kingdom Atomic Energy Authority which is titled *Britain and Atomic Energy, 1939–1945* (New York: St. Martin's Press, Inc., 1965, c. 1964).

Other sources include:

Amrine, Michael. *The Great Decision: The Secret History of the Atomic Bomb.* New York: G. P. Putnam's Sons, 1959.

Aronowitz, Dennis S. *Legal Aspects of Arms Control Verification in the United States.* Dobbs Ferry, N.Y.: Oceana Publications, 1965.

Attlee, Clement. *As It Happened.* London: William Heinemann Ltd., 1954.

Barnet, Richard J. *Who Wants Disarmament?* Boston: Beacon Press, Inc., 1960.

Baruch, Bernard. *The Public Years.* New York: Holt, Rinehart, & Winston, Inc., 1957–60.

————. *My Own Story.* New York: Holt, Rinehart, & Winston, 1957.

Bertin, Leonard. *Atom Harvest: A British View of Atomic Energy.* London: Secker & Warburg, 1955.

Birkenhead, The Earl of. *Halifax.* Boston: Houghton Mifflin Co., 1966.

Blackett, P. M. S. *Fear, War, and the Bomb.* New York: Whittlesey House, McGraw-Hill Book Co., 1949.

Bradley, David. *No Place to Hide.* Boston: Little, Brown & Co., 1948.

Brodie, Bernard, ed. *The Absolute Weapon.* New York: Harcourt, Brace & World, Inc.

Bush, Vannevar. *Modern Arms and Free Men.* New York: Simon & Schuster, Inc., 1949.

Butow, Robert J. *Japan's Decision to Surrender.* Stanford, Cal.: Stanford University Press, 1965.

Byrnes, James. *Speaking Frankly.* New York: Harper and Bros., 1947.

———. *All in One Lifetime.* New York: Harper and Bros., 1958.

Churchill, Sir Winston S. *The Hinge of Fate.* London: Cassell & Co. Ltd., 1951.

———. *Triumph and Tragedy.* London: Cassell & Co. Ltd., 1951.

Coit, Margaret. *Mr. Baruch.* Boston: Houghton Mifflin Co., 1957.

Compton, Arthur H. *Atomic Quest.* New York: Oxford University Press, 1956.

Connally, Tom. *My Name Is Tom Connally.* New York: Crowell, Collier & Macmillan, Inc., 1954.

Cottrell, Leonard, and Eberhardt, Sylvia. *American Opinion on World Affairs in the Atomic Age.* Princeton, N.J.: Princeton University Press, 1948.

Davis, Nuell Pharr. *Lawrence and Oppenheimer.* New York: Simon & Schuster, Inc., 1968.

Dennett, R., and Johnson, J. *Negotiating with the Russians.* Boston: World Peace Foundation, 1951.

Dinerstein, Herbert. *War and the Soviet Union.* New York: Frederick A. Praeger, Inc., 1959.

Feis, Herbert. *Churchill, Roosevelt, and Stalin.* Princeton, N.J.: Princeton University Press, 1957.

———. *Japan Subdued: The Atomic Bomb and the End of the War in the Pacific.* Princeton, N.J.: Princeton University Press, 1961.

Fermi, Laura. *Atoms in the Family.* Chicago: Chicago University Press, 1954.

Finney, John, ed. *Hiroshima Plus 20.* Prepared by the *New York Times.* New York: Delacorte Press, 1965.

Fleming, D. F. *The Cold War and Its Origins.* Garden City, N.Y.: Doubleday & Co., Inc., 1961.

Gard, Robert. *Arms Control Policy Formulation and Negotiation, 1945–1946.* An unpublished thesis presented to the Harvard University Faculty in June 1961.

Gilpin, Robert. *American Scientists and Nuclear Weapons Policy.* Princeton, N.J.: Princeton University Press, 1962.

Goldwin, Robert A., ed. *The Case of the Impenetrable Cloud.* Chicago: American Foundation for Political Education, 1957.

Goodrich, L., and Simons, A. *The United Nations and the Maintenance of International Peace and Security.* Washington, D.C.: Brookings Institute, 1955.

Groueff, Stephane. *Manhattan Project: The Untold Story of the Making of the Atom Bomb.* Boston: Little, Brown & Co., 1967.

Groves, Leslie. *Now It Can Be Told.* New York: Harper & Row, 1962.

Hachiya, Michihiko. *Hiroshima Diary.* Translated by Werner Wells. Chapel Hill, N.C.: University of North Carolina, 1955.

Halle, Louis. *The Cold War As History.* New York: Harper & Row, 1967.

Harrod, R. F. *The Prof.: A Memoir of Lord Cherwell.* London: Macmillan Ltd., 1959.

Hersey, John. *Hiroshima.* New York: Alfred A. Knopf Co., 1946.

Horowitz, David. *The Free World Colossus.* New York: Hill & Wang, Inc., 1965.

Hutchins, Robert Maynard. *The Atomic Bomb versus Civilization.* Washington and Chicago: Human Events, Inc. 1945.

Jaspers, Karl. *The Future of Mankind.* Chicago: University of Chicago Press, 1961.

Jungk, Robert. *Brighter Than a Thousand Suns.* New York: Harcourt, Brace and Co., 1958.

Kennan, George. *Russia, the Atom and the West.* New York: Harper and Bros., 1958.

——. *American Diplomacy, 1900–1950.* Chicago: University of Chicago Press, 1967.

——. *Memoirs, 1925–1950.* Boston: Little, Brown & Co., 1967.

King, Ernest J., with Walter Whitehill. *Fleet Admiral King.* New York: W. W. Norton, 1952.

Knebel, Fletcher, and Bailey, Charles W. *No High Ground.* New York: Harper and Bros., 1960.

Kramish, Arnold. *Atomic Energy in the Soviet Union.* Stanford, Cal.: Stanford University Press, 1959.

Lang, Daniel. *Early Tales of the Atomic Age.* New York: Simon & Schuster, Inc., 1948.

Lapp, Ralph. *Atoms and People.* New York: Harper and Bros., 1956.

Laurence, William L. *Dawn over Zero.* New York: Alfred A. Knopf Co., 1946.

Leahy, William D. *I Was There.* New York: Whittlesey House, McGraw-Hill Book Co., 1950.

Lilienthal, David E. *Journals of David Lilienthal: The Atomic Energy Years.* New York: Harper & Row, 1964.

Masters, Dexter, ed. *One World or None.* New York: Whittlesey House, McGraw-Hill Book Co., 1946.

Millis, Walter, ed. *The Forrestal Diaries*. New York: Viking Press, Inc., 1951.

Morison, Elting E. *Turmoil and Tradition: A Study of the Life and Times of Henry L. Stimson*. Boston: Houghton Mifflin Co., 1960.

Nathan, Otto. *Einstein on Peace*. New York: Simon & Schuster, Inc., 1960.

Newman, Bernard. *The Red Spider Web: The Story of Russian Spying*. London: Latimer House, 1947.

Newman, James, and Miller, Byron. *The Control of Atomic Energy*. New York: Whittlesey House, McGraw-Hill Book Co., 1948.

Nogee, Joseph L. *Soviet Policy Towards International Control of Atomic Energy*. Notre Dame, Ind.: University of Notre Dame Press, 1961.

Nutting, Anthony. *Disarmament*. London & New York: Oxford University Press, 1959.

Pickersgill, J. W. *The Mackenzie King Record, Volume I 1939–1944*. Toronto: University of Toronto Press, 1960.

Rauch, G. *History of Soviet Russia*. Translated by P. and A. Jacobsohn, New York: Frederick A. Praeger, Inc., 1962.

Reitzel, W., ed. *United States Foreign Policy, 1945–1955*. Washington, D.C.: Brookings Institute, 1956.

Rosenbloom, Morris V. *Peace Through Strength*. New York: Straus and Young, 1953.

Rosenthal, S. Z., ed. *Niels Bohr: His Life and Work As Seen by His Friends and Colleagues*. New York: John Wiley, 1967.

Scheinman, Lawrence. *Atomic Energy Policy in France Under the Fourth Republic*. Princeton, N.J.: Princeton University Press, 1965.

Sherwood, Robert E. *Roosevelt and Hopkins*. New York: Harper and Bros., 1948.

Shumway, Harry Irving. *Bernard M. Baruch*. Boston: L. C. Page, Inc., 1946.

Smith, Alice Kimball. *A Peril and a Hope*. Chicago: University of Chicago Press, 1965.

Spanier, J. W., and Nogee, J. L. *The Politics of Disarmament*. New York: Frederick A. Praeger, Inc., 1962.

Stettinius, Edward L. *Roosevelt and the Russians; the Yalta Conference*. Edited by Walter Johnson. Garden City, N.Y.: Doubleday & Co., Inc., 1949.

Stimson, Henry L., and Bundy, McGeorge. *On Active Service in Peace and War*. New York: Harper and Bros., 1948.

Strauss, Lewis. *Men and Decisions*. Garden City, N.Y.: Doubleday & Co., Inc., 1962.

Truman, Harry S. *Years of Decisions. Memoirs, vol. 1*. Garden City, N.Y.: Doubleday & Co., Inc., 1955.

————. *Years of Trial and Hope. Memoirs, vol. 2. Garden City,* N.Y.: Doubleday & Co., Inc., 1956.

Vandenberg, Arthur. *The Private Papers of Senator Vandenberg.* Boston: Houghton Mifflin Co., 1952.

Wheeler-Bennett, John. *John Anderson, Viscount Waverly.* New York: St. Martin's Press, 1962.

White, William L. *Bernard Baruch, Portrait of a Citizen.* New York: Harcourt, Brace, 1950.

Williams, Francis, with Clement Attlee. *A Prime Minister Remembers.* London: William Heinemann Ltd., 1961.

Williams, William A. *The Tragedy of American Diplomacy.* Cleveland: World Publishing Company, 1959.

Index

Index